DIRECTIONS FOR USE

The index is arranged alphabetically by subject. The entries under each subject are alphabetical by symbols standing for the books indexed. The following is a typical entry:

CunE   p 105-30   10 pl (1 col) (f)

CunE is the symbol used for *English Women's Clothing in the Nineteenth Century* by Cecil Willett Cunnington. See "List of Books indexed"

p 105-30 indicates that text is to be found on these inclusive pages

10 pl indicates full page illustrations on these pages

(1 col) indicates that one plate is colored, the others are not

(f) indicates that the plates show feminine costume only

List of Abbreviations

app—appendix
col—colored (Used where all plates are colored; otherwise the number of colored ones is specified)
f—feminine (If neither *f* nor *m* is given, illustration contains both)
fig—figure (Used where an illustration is numbered)
il—illustration or illustrations

m—masculine (If neither *m* nor *f* is given, illustration contains both)
off—officer
p—page or pages
pl—plate or full page illustration
pref—preface
pte—private
s—seaman
v—volume or volumes

COSTUME INDEX

SUPPLEMENT

COSTUME INDEX

SUPPLEMENT

A SUBJECT INDEX TO PLATES
AND TO ILLUSTRATED TEXT

EDITED BY
ISABEL STEVENSON MONRO
AND
KATE M. MONRO

NEW YORK
THE H. W. WILSON COMPANY
1957

Published 1957

Printed in the United States of America

Library of Congress Catalog Card No. (37-7142)

PREFACE

This SUPPLEMENT to the COSTUME INDEX of 1937 is an index to illustrations and text in 347 books. The SUPPLEMENT was undertaken at the suggestion of the Committee on New Reference Tools of the Reference Librarians Section of the Association of College and Research Libraries. As in the main volume, the books indexed include those on a tentative list sent to libraries, many added suggestions, and some that have been published since the list was sent out in 1953. The majority of books indexed have appeared since the original work was finished in 1936, but a few earlier titles have been added at the suggestions of librarians.

In general, this SUPPLEMENT follows the scope and plan of the earlier volume. However, since some of the more recent books emphasize details of costume not found in earlier ones, a few changes and additions in subject headings, such as "Biblical costume," "Fancy dress and stage costume," "Shakespearean costume," have been made, and some more specific articles of attire have been brought out, especially when these were accompanied by patterns. In the earlier volume, the compilers thought it unnecessary to index books on dolls because many of the costumes were merely reproductions of those under countries and periods in the main entries; but because of widespread interest and requests for such information, this class of books has been indexed, though for character dolls only. The subject "Fancy dress" has been expanded with the heading "Fancy dress and stage costume." These entries and those on Biblical costume are intended to show costume for amateur theatricals or masquerades. A few geographical entries have been changed in accordance with political changes.

In the 1937 volume few illustrations unaccompanied by text were brought out under subjects; but because some users of the original index requested such listing and because the illustrations often show figures not found on larger plates, many more have been indexed. Indexing of the *National Geographic Magazine* has been extended from January 1936 to December 1954.

As in the original volume, costumes of the 19th and 20th centuries have been indexed under the centuries, not under separate countries, since it is assumed that style was much the same in all countries during those periods. However, some entries have been made under the United States for the 19th century, because in the earlier part of the century at least, Americans did not always follow European fashions and because some books devote sections to distinctively American costume.

Annotations have been added to the List of Books Indexed to try to assess the usefulness of such books in length of text, type of illustrations, and period covered.

The list of those who have assisted in the preparation of this INDEX by checking lists and giving advice and suggestions is a long one. Special acknowledgment is made to Miss Priscilla MacFadden, Chief of the Fine Arts Department, Boston Public Library; to Miss Olive Sprong, Principal Librarian, Art and Music Department, Los Angeles Public Library; and for information on the names of Catholic orders to the Reverend Oliver L. Kapsner, Catholic University of America.

The compilers appreciate the many courtesies extended by the following libraries: University of Arizona; University of North Carolina; University of Tennessee; Hamilton College, Clinton, N.Y.; Rollins College, Winter Park, Florida; Albertson Public Library, Orlando, Florida; Public Library, Hartford, Connecticut; Public Library, Utica, N.Y.; Public Library, Winter Park, Florida.

The names of the collaborators who checked the tentative list and made additional suggestions appear on the following page. To them especial thanks are due.

ISABEL STEVENSON MONRO

KATE M. MONRO

COLLABORATORS

The editors acknowledge the helpful cooperation from the librarian and the staff of the following libraries:

Baltimore, Md.
 Enoch Pratt Free Library
Boston, Mass.
 Public Library
Brooklyn, N.Y.
 Pratt Institute Free Library
California, Pa.
 State Teachers College
Chicago, Ill.
 Public Library
Cincinnati, Ohio
 Art Museum Library
Cleveland, Ohio
 Public Library
Denver, Colo.
 Public Library
Des Moines, Iowa
 Public Library
Detroit, Mich.
 Public Library
Indianapolis, Ind.
 Public Library
Los Angeles, Calif.
 Public Library
Louisville, Ky.
 Public Library

Minneapolis, Minn.
 Free Public Library
Montclair, N.J.
 Free Public Library
Mount Vernon, N.Y.
 Public Library
New York City
 Public Library
Newark, N.J.
 Public Library
Philadelphia, Pa.
 Drexel Institute
Pittsburgh, Pa.
 Carnegie Library
Portland, Ore.
 Library Association of Portland
Rochester, N.Y.
 Public Library
St Louis, Mo.
 Public Library
St Paul, Minn.
 Public Library
Seattle, Wash.
 Public Library
Springfield, Mass.
 City Library Association
Wilmington, Del.
 Institute Free Library

COSTUME INDEX

SUPPLEMENT

DIRECTIONS FOR USE

The index is arranged alphabetically by subject. The entries under each subject are alphabetical by symbols standing for the books indexed. The following is a typical entry:

CunE   p 105-30   10 pl (1 col) (f)

CunE is the symbol used for *English Women's Clothing in the Nineteenth Century* by Cecil Willett Cunnington. See "List of Books indexed"

p 105-30 indicates that text is to be found on these inclusive pages

10 pl indicates full page illustrations on these pages

(1 col) indicates that one plate is colored, the others are not

(f) indicates that the plates show feminine costume only

List of Abbreviations

app—appendix
col—colored (Used where all plates are colored; otherwise the number of colored ones is specified)
f—feminine (If neither *f* nor *m* is given, illustration contains both)
fig—figure (Used where an illustration is numbered)
il—illustration or illustrations

m—masculine (If neither *m* nor *f* is given, illustration contains both)
off—officer
p—page or pages
pl—plate or full page illustration
pref—preface
pte—private
s—seaman
v—volume or volumes

COSTUME INDEX
SUPPLEMENT

For explanation of symbols, see "List of Books Indexed," pages 191-210

AAL. See Norway—Aal

AALBORG. See Denmark—Jutland

AARGAU. See Switzerland—Aargau

AARHUS. See Denmark—Jutland

ABBÉS
This term is used for illustrations of the dress of the tutors or companions to families of the nobility in France in the 17th and 18th centuries
Bruh pl 51 (col)
Dav v2 fig 1394
Lel v 11 p 19-20 fig 14 (incl pat)
Leld p 1 il
WilF pl p96

ABBESSES
Dav v 1 p368 il
Doy pl 132 (col)
HousM p 152-53 fig 266
NorC pl p 14

ABBOTS
11th century
Dav v 1 p 115 il
13th-16th centuries
HousM p 151 il
NorC pl p47
Norr v3 bk 1 p 159 fig 213

ABOLLA. See Capes and cloaks—Rome

ABORS. See India—Assam

ABRAHAM (BIBLICAL CHARACTER). See Biblical costume—Abraham

ABRAXAS. See Amulets and talismans

ABRUZZI E MOLISE. See Italy—Abruzzi e Molise

ABYSSINIA. See Ethiopia

ACADEMIC COSTUME
See also Processions, Academic
13th century
WaS il p 1
16th century
Wa p 141 fig 144A
England
14th-16th centuries
Hat p279 fig 131
HousM p 153-57 il

May pl p42
Norr v3 bk 1 p74-76, 321 il; bk 2 p692-93 il
Trev v 1 fig 120 il
17th century
AirT il p56
Dav v2 p594-96 fig 1560-78
WaS il p4
19th century
WaS p4-5 il

France
16th century
WilF pl p62-63

Germany
16th century
BruK pl 69 fig 1, 10

Italy
15th century
BruK pl 55 fig 3 (col)
16th century
WilH pl p85
18th century
Mora pl 18

Korea
Keit p58 pl p50, 56, 64K

Netherlands
17th century
BruK pl 93 fig 4

Scotland
Nat v69 Ap '36 il p563; v89 My '46 pl p597

Spain
16th century
LavR pl p246
Rea p24 pl 52
17th century—date
Dav v2 fig 1759
OrT pl 194

Sweden
18th century
Berg fig 29

United States
WaS p6-9 2 pl (1 col)

ACADEMIC COSTUME (SECONDARY SCHOOLS)

United States

WaS p 10-12 il

ACADÉMIE FRANÇAISE. See Academicians—France

ACADEMICIANS

France

LelD p225 il; pl p347 fig 8

ACCESSORIES AND ORNAMENTS

See also Bags, purses, etc.; Canes, walking sticks, etc.; Chatelaines; Fans; Gloves; Hair ornaments; Jewelry; Perfume containers

African tribes

Leb pl 17-18, 20-21, 23, 33, 45-46 (col)

Assyria and Babylonia

Wa p25 fig 41
WilC pl p 10

Egypt, Ancient

Wa p 15 fig pl p7

Europe

15th century

CunM p 118-19 pl

16th century

CunS p50-52, 66-68, 85-86, 182-89 pl 16, 70
Lint p265-77 pl
Wa p 150-51, 156-57, 163-64 fig 154

17th century

LelD il p 122
Lint p265-77 pl
Wa p 179, 184, 190-92, 195-96, 199, 201, 235-37 fig 165, 181

19th century
1800-1850

CunE p38-44, 110-21 pl p28, 128
Wa p249, 254, 259, 266-67, 271 fig 201-02, 204, 207, 214-15, 218, 220

1850-1900

Wa p278-79, 281, 285-86, 290-92, 299, 304-06, 310, 314-15, 319, 326-27 fig 226, 232, 235, 237, 241, 244, 247-48, 251, 254

20th century

CunPr p214, 221, 225, 232, 236-38, 242, 257, 262-63 il (f)
Kle p 127-28 il
Wa p324-43, 350 fig 259, 264-68

Greece, Ancient

Wa p39, 45-46 fig 55

Finland

Prim pl p96

Indians of North America

MasB p68-73, 87-89 il

Persia, Ancient

Wa p28 fig 39A, 41A

ACOLYTES

Nat v77 F '40 pl p227 (col)
NorC p31 pl p30

ACROBATS

18th century

Dav v2 p715 il (f)

19th century

QuV fig 114-16

ACTORS

Japan

Haa pl 83-84, 87-90
Int v2 pl 88-89

ADMIRALS

England

17th century

Dav v2 p571-72 il

18th century

AirH il p92

France

16th century

BluL p22 pl 40
BruK pl 76 fig 13
LavR pl p96, 107

Germany

16th century

Dav v2 p603 il

Spain

14th century

BruK pl 62 fig 18

United States

1917—date

Nat v82 Jl '42 il p 13

AEGEAN ISLANDS. See Chios

AFGHANISTAN

See also Military costume—Afghanistan

BruK pl 176 fig 1-5 (col)
Nat v69 Ja '36 pl p26-27 (col) (m); v90 O '46 il p537
TiK pl 81-82 (col)

AFRICA

EvnR p30-31 pl 6 (incl pat) (f)
See also African tribes; Algeria; Bedouins; Berbers; Cameroons, French; Egypt; French Equatorial Africa; Liberia; Libya, Ancient; Mauritania; Natal; Nigeria; Senegal; Sudan; Tunisia; Uganda

AFRICAN TRIBES

BruK pl 189-90 (col)
Gen v 1 fig 31-32 (f)
MusE pl 1 (col)
Nat v76 O '39 p512-13, 524-25, 544-45, 548-49 2 pl il; v82 Ag '42 pl p219 (col); v 104 Ag '53 pl p 146-47, 149, 152-53 (col); v 106 D '54 pl p725, 737, 749, 751-55 (col)

AFRICAN TRIBES—*Continued*
Rud pl p60, 98
See also Masai, Swahili; also subdivision African tribes under Bags, purses, etc.; Children; Clowns and jesters; Dancers; Earrings and ornaments; Hair, wigs, etc.; Headdress; Kings and rulers; Medicine men; Necklaces and pendants

AGLETS. See Aiguillettes

AGRICULTURAL LABORERS
LelD p306-07 pl
See also Herdsmen; Milkmaids; Shepherdesses; Shepherds

Argentine Republic
Bac pt4 pl 4 (col) (m)

Egypt, Ancient
Hous2 fig 7-8, 10

England
Early to 1066
AirP il p 13, 45
AirS il p52

1066-1200
AirS il p52

13th century
CunM pl 14 (m)
HousM fig 81-84

14th century
Ab pl p8, 166
CunM pl 21 (m)
Dal v2 fig 192 (col)
Dav v 1 p202-03 fig 567-68, 570 (m)
HousM fig 174-86, 225

15th century
AirM il p57
Norr v3 bk 1 p80-82 il (m)

16th century
Norr v3 bk 1 p305-06 fig 344-46, 355-56; bk 2 p703, 707-08 il

17th century
AirB il p50 (m)

18th century
AirB il p56 (m)
Trev v3 fig 70, 71

19th century
Trev v4 fig 23
Walk pl 7, 15, 19, 23 (col)

France
15th century
BosF pl 2 (m)
Dav v 1 pl p302
EvjD p52 pl 49-50
HousM p 172 fig 300-01 (m)

Germany
Ret pl p51 (f)
RetS pl 54-57

Japan
Haa pl 22-24

Korea
Keit p71 pl p69G (m)

Poland
Stry pl 32 (col) (m)

Scotland
Log p240 pl p238 (col) (m)

Spain
20th century
AnS p78-80 fig 87-88 (m)

United States
19th century
Davi v 1 il p392-93
Part pl p 10-11 il

AHASUERUS (BIBLICAL CHARACTER). See Biblical costume—Ahasuerus

AIGLETS. See Aiguillettes

AIGRETTES
BraF p73, 75, 86 pl p 104
Dal v2 fig 554 (col)
EvnJ p 134-35 pl 30, 90-92 fig 17, 22
Kle p 15 il
Pic il p56

AIGUILLETTES
Bra pl 24
Norr v3 bk 1 p359-60 il; bk 2 p578, 779 il
Pic il p 1
SmU p27 pl p39

AIRPLANE HOSTESSES
AlF pl p 186
Nat v78 D '40 pl p696
RogW p 194 il

ÅKERBO. See Sweden—Öland

ALAND ISLANDS
Nat v77 F '40 pl p247 (f)

ALAVA. See Basque provinces

ALB
Dav v2 fig 1705
EvjD p69 il
HousM p22-23 fig 27 (pat)
Kle p 17 il
NorC p 19-20 il
TiK pl 37 fig 4-8
Wa p61-62 fig 62 II

ALBACETE. See Spain—Murcia

ALBANIA
Brad pl p23
BruK pl 160, 164, 170 (col)
Kle p 140 il (m)
Nat v77 Mr '40 pl p309 (col) (m)
TiK pl 55, 61-64 (col)

La **ALBERCA.** See Spain—León

ALBURQUERQUE. See Spain—Estremadura

ALCANTARINE NUNS
Doy pl 134 (col)

ALDERMEN
England
15th century
Tru il p41
16th century
WilF pl p53

ALEXIAN BROTHERS
Doy pl 51 (col)

ALFRED'S JEWEL
AirB p 14
Jes p87-89 pl B (col)
RogF p66-67 il

ALGERIA
BruK p39 pl 187-88 (col)
GaU pl 12-14 (col)
Nat v83 Ja '43 pl p 123 (m)
Rud pl p 130
TiK pl 30-34 (incl pat) (col)
See also Bedouins; Berbers; Ouled Nails; also subdivision Algeria under Arabs; Dancers; Headdress

ALICANTE. See Spain—Valencia

ALLEGORICAL AND IMAGINARY FIGURES. See Fancy dress and stage costume; Goddesses; Gods; also individual symbolic figures, e.g. Fame, Liberty

ALMERÍA. See Spain—Andalusia

ALMS BAGS
Bra pl 15
Kle p46 il

ALMUCE
NorC p 173-76 pl p 142, 175 (1 col) il (incl pat)

ALPINE COSTUME. See Germany—Bavaria; Switzerland; Tyrol

ALS. See Denmark—Jutland

ALSACE
BluN p49-50, 137 pl p94, 145, 150, 152
CosP p22 pl 23-24
Er p35-36 pl 8 (col)
GaP pl 31 (col) (f)
GiR pl 1-2 (col)
LepF pl 12-13 (col)
Ogr pl p440 (col) (f)
RogD pl 10 (col) (f)
Ten p 18-19 pl 3-4 (col)
See also Lorraine; also Dancers—Alsace; Military costume—Alsace

ALTAR BOYS. See Acolytes

ALTEMBURG. See Germany—Thuringia

ÅLVROS. See Sweden—Härjedalen

AMAGER. See Denmark—Amager

AMAZONS
Dav v 1 p65, 67 2 pl
Gen v 1 fig 292-93
HousG2 p48-50 il

Loud pl 2 (col)
RueG pl 12-13
WilF pl p 11

AMBASSADORS
England
15th century
Dav v 1 p289 fig 785-86
LavE pl 20 (col)
France
16th century
Dav v 1 fig 1150
Gor pl p50
Germany
18th century
Dav v2 p722 il
Hungary
20th century
Hol p20 pl 22b
Mexico, Ancient
DuS p57-58, 61-62 pl 17-19 (col)
Russia
16th century
WilF pl p74

AMBROSIAN NUNS
Doy pl 108-09 (col)

AMERICAN WOMEN'S HOSPITAL RE-SERVE CORPS
Ross p44-45, 48 il (col)

AMERICAN WOMEN'S VOLUNTARY SERVICES
Ross p24-25, 28 il (col)
SmU pl p93 (col)

AMICE
HousM p23-24 fig 28 (pat)
NorC p84-87 il (incl pat)
Pic il p2

AMISH MENNONITES. See Mennonites

AMULETS AND TALISMANS
Ar p32-33 pl 29-31, 33-34 il

AMYCE. See Amice

ANATOLIA
Brad pl p26
Nat v77 Mr '40 pl p395, 399; v94 Jl '48 pl p65, 67-71 (col)
Özb pl 1-22, fig 1-15 (pat) (f)

ANCHORITES
NorC pl p 14

ANCIENT AND HONORABLE AR-TILLERY COMPANY OF BOSTON
Davi v 1 il p57
Nat v70 Jl '36 pl p71 (col) (off)

ANDALUSIA. See Spain—Andalusia

ANDREW, ORDER OF. See Thistle, Order of the

ANDROS (ISLAND). See Cyclades

ANGELS. See Fancy dress and stage costume—Angel

ANGLICAN AND EPISCOPAL CHURCH. See Ecclesiastical costume—Anglican and Episcopal church

ANGLO-SAXON COSTUME. See England—Anglo-Saxon period, 449-1066

ANGOUMOIS. See France—Saintonge and Angoumois

ANJOU. See France—Anjou

ANKLETS

Arabia
Rud pl p 165

Egypt, Ancient
NeE pl 7
NeP pl 12

India
NeN p3-4 pl 17

Indians of North America
MasB p46 il (incl pat)

ANNAM
GaU pl 35 (col) (f)
Nat v69 Ja '36 pl p34 (col) (f)
Pot v2 p39-42 2 pl (col)
See also Tonking

ANNUNCIATE NUNS
Doy pl 115, 138 (col)

ANSÓ. See Spain—Aragon

ANTONIAN MONKS
Doy pl 4-6 (col)

APACHE INDIANS. See Indians of North America—Apache Indians

APOTHECARIES

France
16th century
DeZ pl 49

APPENZELL. See Switzerland—Appenzell

APPRENTICES

England
Norr v3 bk 1 p302-03 il; bk 2 p701-02 il

APRONS
Kle p337-39 il
LelD p396-97 il

Chios
Arg pl 83, 85 (col)

Denmark
WilF pl p94

England
Lint p 177 pl 3
Yar p 195 pl p 194

France
Dav v2 il p552, 858
WilC p315 pl p318

Germany
Pet p50-51 pl
WilF pl p87

Hungary
Palo pl 3, 8-11 (col)

Indians of North America
Hun pl p25
MasB p53 il

Italy
Hea il p41
Lee p40-41 pl

Norway
Hea il p41

Poland
Hea il p43

Rumania
Lee p54-56 pl

Russia
Hea il p43

Spain
AnS p92-93, 283-84 fig 107, 339

Yugoslavia
Lee pl p47

AQUILA DEGLI ABRUZZI. See Italy—Abruzzi e Molise

ARABIA
See also Burnous; Sheiks; also subdivision Arabia under Dancers; Footwear; Headdress; Kings and rulers

Ancient
Dal v 1 p309-47 2 pl il (col)
Pot p41-42 pl 17 (col) (incl pat)
TiK pl 14-15, 21 (col)

Modern
Brad pl p28, 29
BruK pl 191-92 (1 col)
KerM no2 pl 12 (f)
Lee p8-10 pl
Nat v85 F '44 pl p253; v93 Ap '48 pl p497, 499-501, 504-511 (col); v98 D '50 pl p727, 730 (col) (f); v 104 Jl '53 pl p 19, 36, 50 (col)

ARABS
Kle p 11 il (m)

Algeria
BruK pl 187 fig 12, 15 pl 188 fig 16 (col) (m)

Morocco
Rous pl 8-11 (col) (f)

ARAGON. See Spain—Aragon

ARAUCANIAN INDIANS. See Indians of South America—Araucanian Indians

ARBALESTERS. See Crossbowmen

ARCHBISHOPS

Anglican church

MusE pl 41 (col)
Nat v 104 S '53 pl p315, 320

Catholic church

9th-12th centuries

Dav v 1 pl p 102
NorC p 103 pl p 101, 252 (1 col)

13th century—date

AirM il p63
Dav v 1 pl p 174 il
HousM p20, 93 fig 21, 157
MusE pl 16 (col)
NorC p 141-42, 171 pl p47, 140, 172 (1 col)
VanH pl 4

Greek church

HousG2 pl p 175
MusE pl 41 (col)
Nat v91 Ja '47 pl p 134
TiK pl 36 fig 33-34

ARCHDUCHESSES. See Noblewomen

ARCHERS (MILITARY)

See also Crossbowmen

Assyria and Babylonia

Dal v 1 fig 126-27, 133 (col)
Hous2 fig 133-34
LelD p 11 il
TiK pl 6 fig 10
UnW pl 5 (col)

Egypt, Ancient

Hous2 fig 45-48

England

Law v 1 p2-3 il

Europe

WilFo pl p74

France

LelD p 185 il

Germany

Dav v 1 pl p 185

Scotland

Log pl p227 (col)

Scythia

LelD p 11 il

ARCHERS (SPORT)

19th century

Ada v3 il p312
CunA pl 35
Part p 152 il (f)
RogW p 16 il

ARCHITECTS

13th century

HousM fig 62, 76

15th century

Tru il p36

ARGENTINE REPUBLIC

Bac pt 1-6 pl 1-36 (col)
Hal pl 1-4 (col)
Spi pl p21 (f)

See also Fancy dress and stage costume—Argentine; Gauchos; Indians of South America—Argentine Republic; Military costume—Argentine Republic

ARGYLL AND SUTHERLAND HIGHLANDERS (REGIMENT)

BarH pl 9, 16, 24 (col) (off, pte)
Nat v69 Ap '36 il p565 (pte)

ARLES. See France—Provence

ARMADA JEWEL

BraF pl p60
Norr v3 bk 2 p769 il
Yar pl p 136

ARMENIA

Brad pl p30
BruK pl 171 fig 9-11, pl 172 fig 9, 14-15, pl 172 fig 12-15 (col)

ARMENIAN CHURCH. See Ecclesiastical costume—Armenian church

ARMLETS. See Bracelets

ARMOR. See Military costume—Europe—13th-17th centuries

ARMORERS

England

1066-1154

AirS il p38

ARMS AND ARMOR. See Military costume

ARROW CASES
LelD il p70

ARSTAD. See Sweden—Halland

ARTHURIAN COSTUME. See England—449-1066; Kings and rulers—England—449-1066; Military costume—England—449-1066

ARTILLERY. See subdivision Artillery under Military costume — England, France, etc.

ARTISANS

See also names of workers in various trades, e.g. Carpenters, Masons and stonecutters

Egypt, Ancient

Hous2 p60 fig 65-66

England

11th-13th centuries

Lab p38-40 pl (col)

Europe

9th-12th centuries

WilFo il p75

ARTISANS—*Continued*

Italy

18th century

Dav v2 p 723 il

ARTOIS. See France—Artois

ASBY. See Sweden—Östergötland

ASCOT TIES
Pic il p3

ASIA. See various Asiatic countries, e.g. Byzantine Empire; China; Japan; Persia; Phrygia; Turkey; etc.

ASIA MINOR
See Anatolia; Media; Persia; Phrygia; Syria; Turkey

ASSAM. See India—Assam

ASSENDELFT. See Netherlands—North Holland

ASSYRIA AND BABYLONIA
BarC p37-42, 66-74 fig 7-8
BiE p 18-21 pl 5 (m)
Bra p34-35, 39-40 pl 5
BruK p6, 42-43 pl 5-6 (1 col)
Dal v 1 p53-77 8 pl il (col)
Dav v 1 p7-12 il
Dot p 106-08 il
Eli p26-28, 37-40, 58 pl il (incl pat)
Gen v 1 p39-48 10 pl (2 col) table 9 fig 381 (pat)
Gor p8 il
HeuO p63-82 pl 45-49 il
Hous2 p 115-59 17 pl il (incl pat)
LelD pl p349 fig 6 (f)
Loud pl 2 (col)
Nat v99 Ja '51 pl p91, 93, 95, 97-99, 103 (col)
Pot v 1 p 17, 21 pl 5, 7 (col)
TiK pl 1, 6-7
UnW pl 5 (col) (m)
Wa p20-27 pl il (incl pat)
WilC p7-10 2 pl
WilF pl p9
WisF pl 2 (f)
Wrig pt3 p 18-24 pl p29-30 (incl pat)
Yar p6-13 2 pl
See also Hittites; Sumeria; also subdivision Assyria and Babylonia under Archers (Military); Charioteers; Children; Crowns; Footwear; Hair, wigs, etc.; Headdress; Kings and rulers; Military costume; Noblemen; Officials; Priestesses; Priests; Queens and empresses; Umbrellas and parasols

ASTURIAS. See Spain—Asturias

ATHLETIC COSTUME. See Sport costume

ATTORNEYS. See Legal costume

AUBRAC, KNIGHTS OF
Doy pl 148 (col)

AUGSBURG. See Germany—Bavaria

AUGUSTINIAN CANONS
NorC p 160 il

AUGUSTINIAN NUNS
Doy pl 85-88, 115, 132 (col)

AUGUSTINIANS
BruK pl 29 fig 8 (col)
Doy pl 44 (col)
OrM pl 68

AUNIS. See France—Aunis

AUSTRALIA
Brad pl p32 (f)
See also Australian tribes; Military costume—Australia

AUSTRALIAN TRIBES
Nat v93 Mr '48 il p423 (m)
See also Dancers—Australian tribes; Headdress—Australian tribes

AUSTRIA
Brad pl p37 (f)
BruK pl 109 (col)
Lee p 10-12 pl
Nat v99 Je '51 pl p780-81, 784 (col)
See also Czechoslovakia; Hungary; Tyrol; Yugoslavia; Fancy dress and stage costume—Austrian; also subdivision Austria under Dancers; Festival costume; Headdress; Kings and rulers; Military costume; Wedding costume

BY REGION OR PROVINCE

Carinthia
BruK pl 140 fig 1, 5 (col) (f)

Lower Austria
Lep pl 5 (col) (f)

Pfitsch
Lep pl 1, 4 (col)

Salzburg
Breu p 17-18 pl 2 (col)
BruK p35 pl 140 fig 4 (col) (m)
Ham p47-52 3 pl (col)
Kle p 101 il

Salzkammergut
Nat v71 Ap '37 pl p457, 461, 463, 478, 480 (3 col)

Styria
Breu p 17-18 pl 1, 3 (col)
BruK pl 140 fig 6, 10 (col) (f)
Ham p53-60 4 pl (col)
Lep pl 3, 7 (col)

Tyrol
See Tyrol

Upper Austria
BruK pl 140 fig 2-3 (col) (f)

Vienna
BruK pl 113 fig 1-12

Vorarlburg
BruK pl 140 fig 11-12 (col) (f)
Kle p64 il (f)
Nat v73 Ap '38 pl p503, 505, 507 (col)

AUTOMOBILE COSTUME. See Motoring costume

AUVERGNE. See France—Auvergne

AVILA. See Spain—Castile, Old

AXEL. See Netherlands—Zeeland

AZTECS
    KaAz pl 1-12 (col)
    Meri pl 7 (col)
    Nat v71 Je '37 pl p735-42 (col)
    Seto pl 68
    ValM pl 4-5 (col) (f)
        See also Mexico, Ancient; also subdivision Aztec under Footwear; Headdress; Military costume

B

BABIES. See Children; Christening robes; Infants

BABYLONIA. See Assyria and Babylonia

BACCHANALS
    WilF pl p 11

BACCHANTES
    Gor pl p 12
    MusE pl 7 (col)
    Pot v 1 pl 12 (col)
    WilF pl p 10

BADAJOZ. See Spain—Estremadura

BADEN. See Germany—Baden

BAGPIPERS
    Kle p206 il

        Balearic islands
    OrT pl 239

        Czechoslovakia
    Nat v74 Ag '38 pl p 199 (col)

        England
        14th century
    Ab pl p242

        16th century
    Norr v3 bk 1 p306 il

        20th century
    BarH pl 23 (col)

        France
    Nat v84 Ag '43 pl p216 (col)

        Germany
    Dav v 1 p387 il

        India
    Nat v 102 N '52 pl p646 (col)

        Ireland
        15th century
    Mccl p46-48 pl 30-31

        Poland
    Brad pl p 128

        Scotland
    Eyr v 1 pl p224 (col) (m)
    Log pl p246 (col)
    Nat v77 My '40 pl p591, 619 (2 col);
        v89 My '46 pl p569, 580 (1 col)

        Spain
    Agu pl 36, 57, 60
    Gom pl p 142 (col)
    OrT pl 211, 214-15

BAGS, PURSES, ETC.
        See also Alms bags; Chatelaines

        Early to 13th century
    CrO pl 9
    Jes p90-91 pl D (col)
    LelD pl p23
    LesA p415-16 il
    Nat v79 F '41 il p256

        14th-16th centuries
    LelD p 167 pl p23 il
    LesA p417-22 il
    Norr v3 bk 1 p23 il
    Wa p 129, 157 fig 124B, 153A
    WilC pl p62, 80, 85, 114, 134
    WisF pl 9-11

        17th century
    Dav v2 pl p551
    Gor pl p78

        18th century
    Kle p46 il
    Lel v 12 fig 25
    LelD pl p23
    LesA fig 514-15
    WilC pl p235
    WisF pl 15, 18

        19th century
    Chr fig 356 (col)
    Dav v2 p804 il
    Kle p 148 il
    LelD pl p23
    LesA p422-23 il
    WilC pl p270, 318
    WisF pl 19

        20th century
    HaC pl p204
    Kle p 168-69 il
    LesA p424-25 il
    WilC pl p365
    WisF pl 26-27

        African tribes
    Leb pl 29, 31-32 (col)

        Carpathian Ruthenia
    Mak pl 20-21, 50

        Chios
    Arg pl 7-9, 13, 18 (col)

        Indians of North America
    Hun pl 22-23, 27-28, 30
    Lyf p78-87, 102-04 pl 57, 73 il
    MasB p 108-09 il

BAGS, PURSES, ETC.—*Continued*

Mexico

CorA p56-60 pl il
Too p45 il p50

Peru

Zim p20 pl

BAGWIGS
LesA p91 fig 107-08
Pic il p 165
See also subdivision 18th century under Hair, wigs, etc.—England; Hair, wigs, etc.—France

BAILIFFS

England

1066-1154

AirB il p20

BALDRICKS. See Sword belts and baldricks

BALEARIC ISLANDS
Agu pl 37-38, 58, 108-09, 123
CamC pl p52 (f)
D'Iv p 13-16 pl 31-43
Gom p 187-90 pl (col)
Nie pl p221, 225 (1 col)
OrT p30-31 pl 239-53
See also Dancers—Balearic islands

BALI
Cov p 109-19 pl 44 il
See also Dancers—Bali; Fancy dress and stage costume—Balinese; Headdress—Bali

BALKAN STATES. See Albania; Bulgaria; Greece; Macedonia; Rumania; Yugoslavia

BALL DRESSES. See Evening dress

BALLET COSTUME
BroW v2 fig 80
Hea p36-37 pl
Kin pl p64-65, 248-49
Pic il p54
Saun p26-27, 57-95 il (incl pat)

France

16th century

BluE p 17 pl 2
LavR pl p348

India

Am p4 il

Siam

Brad pl p 149

BALMORAL CAPS
WilH p228 pl p235

BALUCHISTAN
AirO il p30 (m)
BruK pl 182 fig 1-4 (col)
Nat v 105 Ap '54 pl p512 (col) (m)
TiK pl 82 (col)

BAND COSTUME

Austria

Nat v99 Je '51 pl p782 (col)

United States

Nat v79 Mr '41 pl 277, 307 (col)

BANYANS. See Dressing gowns—18th century (m)

BAPTISMAL ROBES. See Christening robes

BARA DISTRICT. See Sweden—Skåne

BARBER-SURGEONS

16th-17th centuries

DeZ pl 68-79
Nat v95 Ap '49 pl p463 (col)

BARBERS

Egypt, Ancient

DeZ pl 6, 14

France

17th-18th centuries

DeZ pl 72, 94

19th century

DeZ pl 102 (f)

Germany

15th century

DeZ pl 46

Greece, Ancient

DeZ pl 23

Morocco

OrT pl 272

Netherlands

17th century

Ada v 1 il p 144

Russia

18th century

DeZ pl 85

BARCELONA. See Spain—Catalonia

BARGEMEN

England

16th century

AirT il p 12, 31

BARNABITES
Doy pl 54 (col)

BARTHOLOMITES
Doy pl 13 (col)

BASEBALL COSTUME

19th century

1830-1840

Trai p290 il

1860-1870

Ada v3 il p221
Davi v2 pl p60 il p56

BASEBALL COSTUME—19th century—
Continued
1870-1880
Dur il p89

20th century
AlF pl p68-69
Dur il p 128-30, 176, 178, 180-82, 240-43, 272-73

BASEL. See Switzerland—Basel

BASKET VENDERS
Mexico
Marq pl 27 (m)

BASHKIRS
BruK pl 175 fig 7-8 (col)

BASILIAN MONKS
Doy pl 10-11 (col)

BASILIAN NUNS
Doy pl 80 (col)

BASQUE PROVINCES
Agu pl 56, 84-85
BluN p 138-39 pl p94
CosP pl 31-32
D'Iv p26-27 pl 104-07 (col)
GaE pl 6-7, 17 (col)
GaP pl 40 (col) (f)
Gom p 169-76 pl p24a, 170 (1 col)
LepF pl 23-26 (col)
Nie pl p98 (col)
Ogr pl p358 (col) (f)
OrT p24 pl 1-29
Traj pl 12 (col) (m)
   See also Children—Basque provinces; Dancers—Basque provinces; Musicians—Basque provinces

BATAVIA. See Java

BATHING SUITS
19th century
CunE pl p409 (f)
HaC pl p 198 (f)
RogW p5, 22 il (f)
Walk pl 17 (col)
WisF pl 20 (f)

1870-1880
LavT p218-20 pl (f)
LavT2 p 174 pl p 177-78 (f)
Part p 169 il

1880-1890
CunA pl 39 (f)
Dot p 169 il (f)
LavT p218-20 pl (f)
Wel pl p34
Yar pl p246

1890-1900
Ada v4 il p62 (f)
LavT2 p 175 pl p 178 (f)
VanH pl 11

20th century
HaC pl p 198 (f)
Jen p 134, 165 (f)

1900-1910
BrH pl p 143 fig 2 pl 144 fig 3
Bro20 p24-25 il
Coh p391-95 il
CunPr pl p61, 64b, 78 (f)
Kle p 27 il (f)
LavT p220-21 pl p218, 220 (f)
LavT2 p 175 pl p 178-79 (f)
LelD il p25 (f)
Mo p 155 il (f)
Pic il p 139 (f)
Wom p23 il (f)

1910-1920
Coh p395-400 il (f)
CrO pl 57 (f)
CunPr p 106-07 il (f)
LelD il p25 (f)
Mo p 171 il (f)
WisF pl 25 (f)
Yar pl p254, 257, 259

1920-1930
AlF pl p39-41 (f)
BrH pl p 149 fig 7, 13 (col) (f)
WilC pl p378 (f)
Wom p23 il (f)
Yar pl p269

1930-1940
BrH pl p 151 fig 5 (col) (f)
LavT2 p 176 pl p 179 (f)
Pic il p 139 (f)
WilC pl p391 (f)
WisF pl 28 (f)

1940-1950
LelD il p25 (f)
WisF pl 29 (f)
Wom p24 il (f)

BAVARIA. See Germany—Bavaria; also Dancers—Bavaria; Fancy dress and stage costume—Bavarian

BAYLOR'S CONTINENTAL DRA-GOONS. See Military costume—United States—Colonial period, 1775-1783—Cavalry

BEADLES
17th century
LelD p33 il

BEARDS
Rud pl p90-91

16th century
Dav v 1 pl p396
DeZ p63 pl 64, 67
Hat p281 fig 43-44, 48, 106-09, 112-16
Norr v3 bk 2 p723-26 il

17th century
Dav v2 p622 il
DeZ pl 83-84

19th century
LelD p 175, 223 il

Assyria and Babylonia
WilH pl p 11

BEARDS—*Continued*

Egypt, Ancient

Wa   p8 fig 1, 26C
WilH   p2 pl p5
Wrig   pt3 p 15 pl p26

Greece, Ancient

WilH   p 13-14 pl p 16

Persia, Ancient

WilH   pl p 12

BÉARN. See France—Béarn

BEAU BRUMMELL
Lab   p82-85 pl (col)

BED JACKETS
CrH   p54-55, 58-61 3 pl
Lel   v 11 p58-59 fig 60 (incl pat) (f)

BEDOUINS
BruK   pl 189 fig 1-3, pl 190 fig 17, pl
   191 fig 9, 11, 14 (col)
CamC   pl p28-29, 63
Cyr   pl 2, 14, 21 (col)
Nat   v71 Ja '37 p78 il; v92 D '47 pl
   p758-59 (col); v93 Ap '48 pl p500
   (col)
TiK   pl 13 fig 6-9, pl 14 fig 6, pl 32
   fig 4-5 (col)
Wrig   pt 1 p 13, 21 pl p31 (f)
   See also Headdress—Bedouins

BEEF EATERS. See Yeomen of the Guard

BEEHIVE BONNETS. See Headdress—
19th century—1800-1810

BEGGARS

England

15th century

Norr   v3 bk 1 p 86 il (f)

18th century

Trev   v3 fig 51

BELGIUM

See also Fancy dress and stage costume—Belgian; Festival costume—Belgium; Military costume—Belgium

To 17th century
See Netherlands

19th century
BruK   pl 146 (col)
See also Nineteenth century

BELLACOOLA INDIANS. See Indians of
North America—Salish Indians

BELLBOYS. See Pages

BELLMEN. See Watchmen

BELLS (ORNAMENTS)

13th century
BroW   v 1 p62 fig 25

BELTS, KNIGHTS'. See Sword belts and
baldricks

BELTS AND BELT BUCKLES
CorA   p34-36, 51 pl 4, 8
Dal   v2 fig 170, 581-89 (col)
Dot   il p 118-19
EvnJ   p56-57, 78, 179-80 pl 4, 31-32, 86,
   115, 152-54 fig 2, 5, 33
HousM   p56 fig 103
Hun   pl p23-24, 26
Jes   p69, 135-40 pl 37-38, 40
Lee   pl p27, 55
LelD   p44-45, 78-80, 146 pl il; p303 il
LesA   p237-47 pl il
Lint   p265 pl 20
NeE   pl 6-7, 17
NeM   p2 pl 5
Norr   v3 bk 1 p84-85 il
Ori   pl p24, 30, 34 (col)
Pet   p62-63 pl
RetS   pl 76
Stew   p 134-37 il
WilC   pl p85

BENEDICTINE NUNS
Doy   pl 119, 122-23, 125-26, 128-29 (col)
MusE   pl 19, 23 (col)

**BENEDICTINE NUNS OF MONTE
VERGINE**
Doy   pl 124 (col)

**BENEDICTINE OBLATE SISTERS OF
ST FRANCIS OF ROME**
Doy   pl 128 (col)

BENEDICTINES
BruK   pl 29 fig 9 (col)
Dav   v 1 p 119 il
Doy   pl 57-61, 63-64, 67-68 (col)
EvjD   p66 pl 72b
HousM   p39, 151-52 fig 265
LelD   p376-77 il
MusE   pl 18 (col)

BENGAL LANCERS
AirO   il p28

BERBERS
Rous   pl 1-3, 12-16 (5 col)
TiK   pl 33 fig 8-9 (col) (f)
   See also Algeria; Capes and cloaks—
   Berbers; Kabyles; Tuaregs; Tunisia

BERCHTESGADEN. See Germany—Bavaria

BERETS
LelD   p33-34 il (m)
WilH   pl p84-88

BERGEN. See Netherlands—North Holland

BERN. See Switzerland—Bern

BERNARDINES
OrM   pl 44-45, 47-57

BERRY. See France—Berry

BERTHAS. See Neckwear

BETHLEHEMITE NUNS
Doy   pl 102 (col)

BETHLEHEMITES
Doy pl 49 (col)

BEVELAND. See Netherlands—Zeeland

BEYROUT. See Lebanon

BHUTÁN
Nat v 102 D '52 pl p737-38, 750-52 (col)

BIBLICAL COSTUME
For general costume worn by people of the period see Assyria and Babylonia; Egypt, Ancient; Greece, Ancient; Jews; Rome; also individual aspects such as Footwear, Primitive and early; Headdress—Ancient to 476
Lee p76-77, 86-87 pl
OrM pl 184-87
Saun p61-63 pl (pat)

Abraham
BartC p38, 42 fig 7, 10
Eli p85-91 pl il

Ahasuerus
Eli p 112-13 fig 21

Children
Eli p 144-45 il

Christians (Early Christians)
BartC fig 35

David
Dav v 1 p 130 il

Esther
Eli p 110-11 il
OrM pl 190

Hebrews
BartC p50, 52, 90-92 fig 12-13, 32-33 (f)
Eli p35-37, 44-50, 56-58 front (col) pl fig 4 (pat)
Hea p 12-13 pl

Isaac
Dav v 1 p84 pl

Joseph
Dav v 1 p84 pl
Eli p93-98 il

Judas
OrM pl 203

Madonna
Dab pl 8
Hea p52-53 pl
Lil p 19, 23 il (incl pat)

Pharisees
Eli p 141-43 il (incl pat)

Pharaoh
BartC p58-62 fig 17

Queens (Old Testament)
BartC p70-74 fig 73

Rebecca
Dav v 1 p84 pl

Roman soldier
Eli p65-75 pl (incl pat)

Sarah
BartC p40-41 fig 8
Eli p85-91 pl il

Solomon
OrM pl 181-82

Wise men
Dab pl 8
Eli p 126-29 pl
KerM no2 pl 7
Lil p20-21 il (incl pat)
Wrig pt2 p 15-16 pl p23

BICYCLE COSTUME

19th century
Ada v 4 il p61-63 (f)
BrK pl 45 (f)
CunE pl p351 (f)
Davi v2 pl p67-68 il p65
Dot il p 169 (f)
Jen p 124, 126-27 2 pl il (f)
LavT p227-28 pl (f)
LavT2 p72-74, 180-81 pl p 181 (f)
LelD p 141 il
RogW p5, 18 il
Rud pl p 191 (f)
Trev v4 fig 127
VanH pl 11
WilC pl p327 (f)
WilFo pl p 151 (f)
WisF pl 22 (f)
Yar pl p246 (f)

20th century
1900-1910
BrH pl p 145 fig 8 (col) (f)
Wa p336 fig 258 (m)

BIG HEAD DANCE. See Dancers—Indians of North America—Big head dance

BILLIARD PLAYERS

19th century
Davi v 2 il p30

BINNEN. See Netherlands—North Holland

BIRETTA. See Headdress, Ecclesiastical— Catholic church

BIRGITTINE NUNS
Doy pl 107-08 (col)

BIRGITTINES
Doy pl 53, 90 (col)

BIRRUS. See Capes and cloaks—Rome

BISCAY. See Spain—Biscay

BISHOPS
See also Archbishops

To 9th century
NorC p64 pl p65
TiK pl 36 fig 3, 8-9

9th-12th centuries
NorC p71-75 2 pl

BISHOPS—*Continued*

Anglican and Episcopal churches
16th-17th centuries
AirT il p58
Dav v2 p600-01 il

18th century—date
Dav v2 768, 781 il
MusE pl 41 (col)
Nat v79 Ja '41 pl p83; v 104 S '53 pl p314-17, 320-23 (col)

Armenian church
BruK pl 171 fig 11 (col)

Catholic church
See also Crosiers; Miters

9th-12th centuries
AirB il p22
AirS il p46
Dav v 1 p 109, 123, 137, 148-49 5 pl
EvjD pl 78
LelD p 172 fig 1
WilH pl p30-31

13th century—date
BosF pl 14
BruK pl 30 fig 4, 6 (col)
Dav v 1 pl p 168, 231-32, 235, 291, 339, 426 il; v2 p470-71, 659 il
EvjD pl 83
Gor pl p50
HousM p93-94, 146 fig 158, 261
LavE pl 20 (col)
LavR p34 pl (col)
LelD p 172 il
MusE pl 16 (col)
Nat v 101 Ja '52 pl p87
NorC p81, 83 pl p47, 134 (1 col)
Norr v3 bk 1 p 159 fig 214; bk 2 p690 il
Tru pl p 120 (col) il p 118, 124
WilH pl p31

Coptic church
MusE pl 13 (col)

Greek church
6th century
NorC p63-64 pl p70 (col)

9th century
HousG2 fig 172
WilF pl p 14

1054—date
Dav v 1 p 114 il
HousG2 pl p 173, 177 fig 178a

Syrian church
MusE pl 14 (col)

BISHOP'S RINGS. See Rings, Ecclesiastical

BISHOP'S STAFF. See Crosiers

BJURÅKER. See Sweden—Helsingland

BLACK FOREST. See Germany—Black Forest; Headdress — Black Forest; Waists—Black Forest; Wedding costume—Black Forest

BLACK FRIARS. See Dominicans

BLACK WATCH (REGIMENT)
Lez pl p384 (col) (pte)
VanH pl 8

BLACKFOOT INDIANS. See Indians of North America—Siksika Indians

BLACKSMITHS
Africa
Nat v76 O '39 p544 il

England
16th century
AirT il p30

17th century
Trev v2 p71 il

Netherlands
17th century
Ada v 1 il p 144

United States
19th century
Davi v 1 pl p503

BLEKINGE. See Sweden—Blekinge

BLIAUT. See subdivision 12th century under countries, e.g. France—12th century

BLOOMER COSTUME
Ada v2 il p395 (f)
But pl p 125
CunF pl p 148
Dav v2 p878-79 il
Davi v2 il p377
HaC pl p221
Jen p45 il
LavCl pl p 160
LavT2 pl p 181
May p76-77 il
Rud pl p 183-86

BLOUSES. See Waists

BLUDENS. See Austria—Vorarlberg

BLUE COAT HOSPITAL STUDENTS, CHESTER, ENGLAND
Cla pl p34

BLUE COAT SCHOOL, NORTHAMPTON, ENGLAND
Cla p27-38 pl

BOATMEN
Netherlands
Sit pl p 120

BODICES. See Waists

BOHEMIA. See Czechoslovakia—Bohemia**

BOLERO DANCE. See Dancers—Spain—
Bolero

BOLERO JACKETS
 Hea p22-23, 26-27 2 pl (incl pat)
 Kle p57 il
 Lee pl p5 (pat)
 Pic il p82 (m)

BOLIVIA
 Brad pl p38 (f)
 BruK pl 194 (col)
 CrO pl 25 fig 8 (f)
 Hal pl 5-12 (col)
 Spi pl p23 (col) (f)
  See also Dancers—Bolivia; Footwear—
  Bolivia; Indians of South America—
  Bolivia; Military costume—Bolivia

BOMBAST. See Breeches—Europe—16th
century; Breeches—Europe—17th century

BONNET ROUGE. See Headdress—France
—1789-1795

BONNETS. See Headdress—19th century;
Sunbonnets

BOOTS AND SHOES. See Footwear

BORDEAUX. See France—Guienne and
Gascony

BORDELAIS. See France—Guienne and
Gascony

BORNEO
 Brad pl p39-40
 TiK pl 101 fig 6-7 (col) (m)
  See also Earrings and ornaments—
  Borneo; Headdress—Borneo; Military
  costume—Borneo

BORNHOLM. See Denmark—Bornholm

BOSNIA. See Yugoslavia—Bosnia

BOURBONNAIS. See France—Bourbonnais; also Dancers—Bourbonnais

BOWLING COSTUME

United States

17th century
 Dur il p7 (m)
 Nat v71 Ap '37 pl p437 (col)

19th century
 Ada v3 il p347 (f)
 Part p 152 il

BOXERS. See Pugilists

BOYARINAS. See Noblewomen—Russia

BOYARS. See Noblemen—Russia

BRACELETS
 Bae p 177-78 il
 LelD p49-50 pl il

Ancient
 AirB il p5
 Dal v 1 fig 432, 484-89 (col)
 Dot p 105, 107, 111 il
 Hous2 fig 153
 LesA p314-18 il
 NeE p4 pl 1, 4-5, 10, 17-19
 NeG pl 6
 NeM pl 1, 3
 NeP pl 12-13

10th century—date
 EvnJ p77 pl 8, 154-55, 172 (1 col)
 Flow pl 3 (col) fig 6, 24, 33-44, 82-83,
  86-93, 114-16
 LesA p318-21 il
 NeM pl 19
 NeN p3-4 pl 17
 Yar pl p222

African tribes
 Leb pl 14-16, 18 (col)

BRACES
 CunU p 161 fig 70
 Dav v2 pl p886
 LelD p54 il
 Pet p 12-15 2 pl

BRAID
 LesA p562-68 2 pl il

BRANDENBURG. See Germany—Brandenburg

BRASSIÈRES
 Kle p71, 384 il
 Lib pl p 132-34

BRAZIL
 Hal pl 13-16 (col)
 Spi pl p28 (f)
  See also Carnival costume—Brazil;
  Dancers—Brazil; Indians of South
  America—Brazil; Military costume—
  Brazil

BREECHES
 Lee pl p5 (pat)
  See also Trousers

Europe

16th century
 Bart p20-21 pl (pat) fig 3
 Bin p37-42 pl
 Bra pl 23, 25
 BroH p72-73, 87-89 fig 58, 60, 63-66, 69
 BroW v 1 p 124-29, 134-35 fig 78-79,
  84-89
 CunS p 114-24 pl 45-49
 DeB 188-90 pl p 186, 189-90
 KelF p20-22 pl p83
 LavS p36 pl 15
 LelD p51 il; p213-14 pl; p414-15 il
 Norr v3 bk 2 p403, 528-29, 542-44, 577
  il
 WilC pl p76

17th century
 Bra pl 28
 BroW v2 p46-51 fig 21, 24
 Dot p 152 il

BREECHES—Europe—17th century—*Continued*
  Eth pl p38, 42 (incl pat)
  Gor pl p70
  Kle p308-09 il
  Lecl pl 9 (col)
  LelD p64, 213-14, 346-47, 414-15 pl il
  Roj pl 5, 8-9, 17, 25, 31, 34 (pat)
  Wa p 176, 188-89, 198 fig 160-61, 169-70, 175 (incl pat)
  WilC p 162, 167-68, 175, 184-85 pl p 165, 171, 192

18th century
  Bart p56-57 pl (pat)
  Berg fig 88
  Dav v2 pl p687 (pat)
  Gor pl p 107, 121
  LelD p 139-40 pl
  Wa p212, 222, 229 fig 183 (pat)

BREGENZ. See Austria—Vorarlberg

BRETHREN PENDANT
  RogF p98-100 pl

BREST. See France—Brittany

BREWERS
Egypt, Ancient
  Nat v80 O '41 pl p455 (col)

BRICKLAYERS. See Masons and stonecutters

BRIDAL COSTUME. See Wedding costume

BRIDAL CROWNS. See Headdress, Wedding

BRIDGETTINES. See Birgittines

BRITTANY. See France—Brittany; also Dancers—Brittany; Francy dress and stage costume—Breton; Headdress—Brittany; Wedding Costume—Brittany

BRODDETORP. See Sweden—Vestergötland

BROOCHES
  LelD p55 il
Ancient
  Dal v 1 fig 560-66 (col)
  Jes p60-67, 103, 125-26 pl 10-27, 32
  LelD p 177 il
  LesA p 164-71 il
  Nat v85 Mr '44 il p77
  NeG pl 4, 15, 17, 19
  NeN p2 pl 5
  Pic il p 111
  RogF p62-64, 73, 82-83 pl p66 il
  WilC pl p 17
  WlsC p32-34 2 pl
  See also Tara brooch

10th century—date
  BraF pl p82, 91, 103-04, 113-14, 125, 144-45, 163, 173, 185-86, 188, 205
  CrO pl 25 fig 1
  Dal v2 fig 50-52, 150, 221-22

EvnJ p45-46, 58-66 front (col) pl 1-2, 5-6, 11-22, 44, 115, 125, 130-31, 136-38, 144, 165-70 fig 1
Flow pl 8 (col) fig 6, 10, 12, 26, 28-33, 58, 82, 108, 110-13
HousM p54 fig 99
LesA p 171-76 il
Nat v98 D '50 pl p791 (col)
Pet p62-63 pl
Stew p 137-45 il
Yar pl 91, 106

BRUNSWICK. See Germany—Brunswick

BÜCKEBURG. See Germany—Schaumburg-Lippe

BUCKLES
  Jes p69, 139-40 pl 34, 38-39
  LelD p 176 il
  LesA p280-85 il
  Nat v79 F '41 il p251
  NeN p2, 4 pl 3-4, 21-22
  See also Belts and belt buckles; Shoe buckles

BUCKSKIN SUITS
  Ada v 1 il p215 (m)

BUDDHIST MONKS
  BruK pl 181 fig 2, pl 185 fig 12-13 (col)
  MusE pl 8 (col)
  Nat v73 Mr '38 pl p326-28 (col); v88 O '45 pl p440; v95 Mr '49 pl p344-45 (col)
  NeF p 14 pl 45
  TiK pl 72 fig 1-3, 7-8
  WilFo pl p51, 54

BUDDHIST PRIESTESSES
Korea
  Keit pl p64D

BUILDERS. See Artisans; Carpenters

BUKOVINA. See Rumania—Bukovina

BULGARIA
  Kat p 15-16 pl 1-4 (col)
  Nat v78 O '40 pl p461-62
  TiK pl 60 (col)
  Vel pl 1-60 (col)
  WilF pl p 152 (m)
  See also Dancers—Bulgaria; Fancy dress and stage costume—Bulgarian; Military costume—Bulgaria

BULLFIGHTERS
Crete, Ancient
  HousG2 pl p 1 (f)

Mexico
  Alv pl p401, 408, 417, 440, 449 (col)
  Too p292-93 il

Spain
  Agu pl 10, 13
  BruK pl 155 (col)
  D'Iv p27-28 pl 110 (col)
  Gom front (col)
  LavR pl p233

BULLFIGHTERS—Spain—*Continued*
  LelD p407 il
  Nat v69 Mr '36 pl p411; v99 Ap '51
    pl p529 (col)
  OrT pl 182-83
  Rea p20 pl 30

BUNSCHOTEN.   See   Netherlands—
Utrecht

BURGESSES
        England
        16th century
  Norr v3 bk 1 p296-97 il

BURGOMASTERS. See Mayors

BURGOS. See Spain—Castile, Old

BURGUNDY.   See   France—Burgundy;
  also   Headdress—Burgundy;   Military
  costume—Burgundy

BURIATS
  BruK pl 182 fig 19 (col) (m)

BURMA
  Brad pl p41-45 (1 col)
  BruK pl 181 fig 1-3 (col)
  Nat v84 O '43 il p501, 511
  TiK pl 86-88 (col)
    See also subdivision Burma under
  Ceremonial costume; Children; Dancers

BURNOUS
  BruK pl 187 fig 11 (col)
  LelD p57 il
  Pic il p 167

BUSKINS. See Footwear

BUSKS
  Bra pl 23
  CrC p8-9 pl
  Dav v2 pl p552
  LelD p57-58 il
  Lib pl p30

BUSTLES
  Bra pl 44
  BroH p204-05 fig 133
  CunE p251-52, 364-65 2 pl
  CunP p52-53 il
  CunU p 13, 33, 51-52, 64-65, 91-92, 111,
    133, 149-51, 179, 197 fig 42, 58, 60, 67,
    79
  Dav v 1 fig 443; v2 fig 2383
  Dot p 168 il
  Gor pl p 166, 172
  HaC p52-54 pl p64-65
  LavT p77-79 pl
  LavT2 p63-64 pl
  McP il p38
  Part p 140 il
  Pic il p 16
  Rud pl p83, 85, 87
  WilC pl p318
    See also Nineteenth century—1870-
  1880; Nineteenth century—1880-1890

        Indians of North America
  MasB p28-45 8 pl il(incl pat) (m)

BUTCHERS
        England
        15th century
  HousM p 171 fig 299

BUTTERFLY HEADDRESS. See Headdress—15th century for various European countries, e.g. Headdress—France
  —15th century

BUTTONS
  BroW v 1 p34 pl (col)
  Dal v2 fig 169 (col)
  Dav v2 p700, 702, 707 3 pl (1 col)
  LelD p48-49 pl
  LesA p470-82 pl il

BYZANTINE EMPIRE
  Bra p79-92 5 pl
  BruK p 14-15, 51 pl 27-28 (1 col)
  Dal v 1 p203-33 14 pl il (col) (incl
    pat)
  Dav v 1 p80-82, 85 il
  Dot p 119-20 il
  Gor pl p 16
  HousG2 p 120-61 11 pl (4 col) il
  LelD pl p349 fig 7-9 (f)
  Loud pl 6 (col)
  Pot v 1 p39-40 pl 16 (col)
  TiK pl 36
  UnW pl 19-20 (col)
  VanH pl 2
  Wa p83-86 fig 72, 82, 87
  WilC p33-36 2 pl
  WilF pl p 14
  WisF pl 5 (f)
  Yar p28-33 3 pl
    See also subdivision Byzantine empire
  under Capes and cloaks; Children; Court
  dress; Crowns; Footwear; Headdress;
  Kings and rulers; Military costume; No-
  blemen; Officials; Queens and em-
  presses

C

CABMEN. See Coachmen

CÁCERES. See Spain—Estremadura

CADETS, MILITARY. See Military cadets

CADETS, NAVAL. See Naval cadets

CADIZ. See Spain—Andalusia

CADZAND. See Netherlands—Zeeland

CAESARINE FRIARS
  Doy pl 69 (col)

CAFTANS
  LelD p61 il
  WilF pl p99
  Wrig pt 1 p8 pl p25
    See also Turkey

CALABRIA. See Italy—Calabria

CALASH. See subdivision 18th century under Headdress—England, Headdress—United States, etc.

CALATRAVA, ORDER OF
Doy pl 149 (col)

CALF-PADS
CunU p80-82 fig 35

CAMALDOLESE
Doy pl 120 (col)
OrM pl 28-29

CAMALDOLESE NUNS
Doy pl 60-61 (col)

CAMBODIA
Brad pl p47 (f)
GaU pl 42 (col) (f)
Pot v2 p47-50 pl (col) (incl pat)
See also Dancers—Cambodia

CAMEL DRIVERS
BruK pl 192
LelD p273-74 il
Nat v74 D '38 pl p735, 738 (col); v92 D '47 pl p767 (col)
OrT pl 256

CAMEOS
EvnJ p48-49, 129-30, 186-87 pl 3, 9, 40, 58, 82, 84, 108, 111, 163
Norr v3 bk 2 p769-70 il
RogF pl p 138

CAMERON HIGHLANDERS (REGIMENT)
BarH pl 18, 22 (col)

CAMEROONS, FRENCH
Leb pl 19, 22, 24-25, 28, 30, 37, 39, 44, 47-50 (col)

CAMPANIA. See Italy—Campania

CAMPECHE. See Mexico—Campeche

CANADA. See Indians of North America; Military costume—Canada; Police—Canada

CANARY ISLANDS
Agu pl 121 (f)
Gom p 193-96 pl (col)
OrT p31 pl 254-56

CANDELARIO. See Spain—León

CANES, WALKING STICKS, ETC.
Kle p368 il

Ancient to 1600
LesA p388-92 il

17th century
LesA 392-94 il
WilC pl p 181, 190

18th century
Lel v 11 fig 34; v 12 fig 22
LesA p394-98 il
WilC pl p200, 215, 217, 233
WisF pl 16-17
Yar p 179 il

19th century
LesA 398-99 pl 43 fig 489
WilC pl p242-43, 252-53, 267, 276-77, 288, 289, 301-03

African tribes
Leb pl 42-43 (col)

CANEZOU
CunE il p 181-82, 184, 190-91

CANIONS. See Breeches—Europe—16th century; Breeches—Europe—17th century

CANNING JEWEL
BraF pl p60

CANONESSES OF CHAILLOT
Doy pl 89 (col)

CANONESSES OF COLOGNE
Doy pl 130 (col)

CANONESSES OF HOMBURG
Doy pl 131 (col)

CANONESSES OF MONS
Doy pl 132 (col)

CANONESSES OF NIVELLE
Doy pl 131 (col)

CANONESSES OF REMIREMONT
Doy pl 130 (col)

CANONESSES OF ROUEN
Doy pl 94 (col)

CANONESSES REGULAR OF CHAILLOT
Doy pl 89 (col)

CANONESSES REGULAR OF ST BRIGID
Doy pl 90 (col)

CANONESSES REGULAR OF ST NORBERT. See Premonstratensian nuns

CANONESSES REGULAR OF ST JAMES OF THE SWORD
Doy pl 151 (col)

CANONESSES REGULAR OF ST VICTOR
Doy pl 91 (col)

CANONESSES REGULAR OF THE HOLY SEPULCHER
Doy pl 90 (col)

CANONESSES REGULAR OF THE LATERAN
Doy pl 89 (col)

CANONS REGULAR
Doy pl 18-35, 39-43 (col)
NorC p5-6 pl p 142 (col)
See also Augustinian canons; Premonstrants

CANONS REGULAR OF ST JAMES OF THE SWORD
Doy pl 150 (col)

CAPES AND CLOAKS
Hea p47-51 2 pl (incl pat)
Lee pl p5 (pat)
LelD p262-68 5 pl il
Pic il p22
   See also Burnous; Evening cloaks;
Houppelandes; Ponchos; Serapes; Straw
coats and cloaks

To 1100
Bra pl 5, 14
HousM p2-3 fig 3
LelD pl p263 fig 1-6

12th-15th centuries
Bra pl 16-18, 20-21
BrH pl p39, 41, 45
HousM p5-7 fig 5, 7-8; p81-2 fig 131a,
  137, 139, 167, 192, 194, 211-12 (incl pat)
Kle p 176-77, 249-51, 379 il (m)
LelD p65-66 pl fig 1 (m); p 180 il (m)
LesA p542 il (f)
Wa p 111 fig 117 (incl pat) p 126 fig
  126 (incl pat) (m)
WilF pl p26, 28, 29
WisF pl 7 (f)

16th century
Bart p24-25 pl (pat)
Hea p50-51 pl (m)
KelF p 16-17 pl p69 (m)
LelD p65 pl p66, 264 (m)
Wa p 154 fig 148 (incl pat) 149 (m)
WilC pl p83, 99, 112, 124
WilF pl p72 (f)

17th century
Bra pl 26 (m)
Dal v2 fig 469-78 (col) (incl pat)
Hea p50-51 pl (m)
Kle p251 il (m)
LelD p26, 59 il; p65-66 pl fig 9;
  pl p264 fig 8-10; pl p265 fig 1-2
Wa p 178, 189, 194 fig 157, 158, 161,
  170 (incl pat)

18th century
Bra pl 33, 37
Brk pl 3 (f)
LelD pl p265 fig 3-4 (m)

19th century
Amer pl 1-3, 5 (col) (f)
Bart p62-63 pl (pat) (m)
BruK pl 125 (f)
Kle p76 il (m)
Rud pl p23 (f)

1800-1810
Ada v2 il p 109 (m)
CunE p34-37 pl
Wa p253 fig 202F
WilC pl p270 (f)
WilF pl p 124-26 (f)

1810-1820
Bra pl 38
WilF pl p 127-32

1820-1830
BoeB pl p 112 (col) (m)
CunE p34-37 pl

Pann v3 pl 11 (col)
WilC pl p255 (f)
WilF pl p 132-34

1830-1840
CunE pl p 122 (f)
LavF p26 pl 6 (col) (f)
LelD pl p266 fig 3; il p268 fig 1 (f)
WilC pl p279
WilF pl p 135-36 (f)

1840-1850
Bra pl 40
BroH p 186-88 fig 125-26, 128
CunE p 149-50, 154-55 pl p 136, 144-45
  (il) (f)
LelD il p268 (f)
Pann v3 pl 27 (col) (f)

1850-1860
CunE p 177, 179 pl p 187 il (f)
Dav v2 p889 il (f)
Kle p70 il (f)
LelD p57 il; pl p266 fig 45 (f)
Pann v4 pl 6, 8 (col) (f)
True p44-45 pl il (f)
Vert pl p58 (f)
WilC pl p292 (f)
Yar pl p218 (f)

1860-1870
HaC pl p41b, 48b (f)
KerA pl p 13 (f)
LelD pl p266 fig 6 (f)

1870-1880
CunE il p294 (f)

1880-1890
Bart p82-85 2 pl (pat) (f) fig 33a-33b,
  34c, 34d
CunE p315, 330 il (f)
HaC pl 64b-64c (f)
LelD pl p266 fig 7 (f)

1890-1900
Bart p88-89 pl (pat) (f)
CunE pl p389; il p373, 393 (f)
HaC pl p84 (f)
Trai p325 il (f)
WilC p321 pl p326 (f)

20th century
1900-1910
LelD pl p266 fig 9; il p268 (f)

1920-1930
Hac pl p120c
WilF pl p 179-187 (f)

1930-1940
WilF pl p 188-99 (f)

1940-1950
Kle p76 il (f)
WilF pl p200-20 (f)

Arabia
BartC p42 fig 10, 13, 49
Pot v 1 pl 17 (incl pat)

Berbers
Rous pl 3 (col)

CAPES AND CLOAKS—*Continued*

Bohemia
16th-17 centuries
WilF   pl   p72, 93 (f)

Byzantine Empire
Bra   pl   10-13
WilC   pl   p37 (pat)

Denmark
17th century
WilF   pl   p94 (f)

England
To 1100
BrH   p 16-21   3 pl (col)
CunM   p 10-11, 21-22, 26   2 pl (1 col) il
CunM   p31-32   pl (m)
WilF   pl   p29 (m)

12-14th centuries
BrH   p24-37   7 pl (col)

15th century
WilF   pl   p29 (m)
Yar   pl   p94, 96

16th century
BrH   pl   p83 (m)
BroH   p93 fig 68 (m)
CunS   p30, 68, 103-07   pl 9, 24-25, 37, 41-43, 45 (m)
DeB   p 191-92   pl   p 189, 193 (m)
Norr   v3 bk 2 p416-18, 531, 546-48, 669   pl   il (incl pat) (m)
WilF   pl   p64, 69 (m)

17th century
BrH   pl   p91, 95, 99 (m)

18th century
WilF   pl   p 107 (f)
Yar   p 178, 186, 196, 208   pl p 177, 192, 201

Etruria
Pot   v 1   pl 9 (col)

France
To 1100
EvjD   p3   pl 1a   il (m)

13th century
BroW   v 1   p26 fig 3 (f)
EvjD   p 18-20   pl 16a, 18-19 (m)

14th-15th centuries
EvjD   p32-33   pl 24-25, 28, 30-31   il (pat)

16th century
Bart   p22-23   pl (pat) fig 4c
WilF   pl   p67 (m)

17th century
BluE   p 10-11   pl 8, 32-33, 37 (m)
WilC   p 143, 145   pl   p 148
WilF   pl   p86, 96 (m)

18th century
Lel   v 11   p 19, 57-58, 60-62 fig 13, 57, 61-63 (incl pat)
WilC   pl   p204, 218 (f)
WilF   pl   p 111, 116 (f)

Germany
15th century
Kle   p320-21   il (m)
WilF   pl   p32 (f)

16th-17th centuries
Kle   p320-21   il (m)
WilF   pl   p70-71, 93

Greece, Ancient
Pot   v 1   pl 10 (col)

Indians of Mexico
CorA   p31-33 fig 9 (m)

Indians of North America
Roe   p 105-15   pl 2, 30, 33-34, 38 (col)
WilF   pl   p 113 (m)

Italy
14th-16th centuries
LelD   p 151   il
WilF   pl   p30, 68 (m)

Korea
Keit   p70   pl   p68E (f)

Malta
Nat   v78 Ag '40 p269-70   il (f)

Mexico, Ancient
DuS   pl 20-21 (col) (m)

Netherlands
16th-17th centuries
Kle   p 176-77   il (f)
TiK   pl 124 fig 17-19 (col) (incl pat) (f)
WilF   pl   p87 (f)

Peru
16th century
Zim   p 13   pl (m)

Poland
16th century
WilF   pl   p73 (m)

Rome
Bra   pl 9 (m)
LelD   p238   il (m)
NorC   p22-28, 31-37, 55-62   3 pl   il (incl pat)
Pot   v 1   pl 13-15 (col) (incl pat)
Wa   p54-56, 60 fig 62 A-F
WlsC   p76-129   32 pl (incl pat)

Russia
15th century
WilF   pl   p29 (m)

17th century
WilF   pl   p98-100

Scandinavia
14th century
WilF   pl   p29 (f)

Sicily
16th century
WilF   pl   p71

CAPES AND CLOAKS—*Continued*

Spain
16th century

WilF   pl   p66, 68 (m)

18th century—date

Agu   pl A, C, 40, 66, 76, 86-89 (2 col)
AnS   p240 fig 285-87 (m)
LelD   p220 pl p42 fig 4-5, 8-11, 16
OrT   pl 170, 172 (m)

Sweden
16th century

WilF   pl p71

18th century

Berg   fig 83-85, 97 (incl pat) (m)

CAPOTS. See Capes and cloaks—16th century

CAPPA. See Copes

CAPPA MAGNA
LelD   p64 il
NorC   p 162 pl p 163

CAPS. See Headdress

CAPUCHIN (HEADDRESS). See subdivision 18th century under Headdress —England; Headdress—France; etc.

CAPUCHINESSES
Doy   pl 133 (col)

CAPUCHINS
BruK   pl 29 fig 11 (col)
Doy   pl 72 (col)
MusE   pl 24 (col)

CARABINEERS. See Military costume

CARACO. See subdivision 18th century under Coats and jackets

CARBAJALES. See Spain—León

CARDINALS
To 16th century
HousM   p 150-51 fig 264
NorC   p 162-64 pl il
WilH   pl p30, 31

16th century—date
AirT   il p7
Dav   v 1 464 il; v2 p512 il
MusE   pl 15 (col)
Nat   v75 My '39 pl p607 (col)
Norr   v3 bk 1   p 177-80 il
Trev   v 1 fig 119 il
Tru   pl p 120 (col)
VanH   pl 4
WilF   pl p62

CARINTHIA. See Austria—Carinthia

CARMELITE NUNS
Doy   pl 82-84 (col)

CARMELITES
AirB   il p23
BruK   pl 29, 156 (col)
Doy   pl 14-17 (col)
HousM   p 151 fig 264
MusE   pl 20 (col)

CARPATHIAN RUTHENIA
Mak   pl I-X, 19-21, 50-51, 53-66, 68-91, 99-100 (10 col)

CARPENTERS
Egypt, Ancient
Nat   v80 O '41 pl p457 (col)

England
To 13th century

AirP   il p45
AirS   il p38

France
15th-16th centuries

Dav   v 1 p321 il; v2 p472 il
HousM   p 181 fig 316

CARRICKS. See Coats (Overcoats)—19th century—1810-1820

CARTERS AND DRIVERS
See also Camel drivers; Muleteers
England
Early to 1066

AirS   il p54

13th century

AirM   il p 16

15th century

Norr   v3 bk 1   p 137-40 pl il

19th century

Walk   pl 27 (col)

CARTHUSIAN NUNS
BruK   pl 29 fig 15 (col)
Doy   pl 139-40 (col)

CARTHUSIANS
BruK   pl 29 fig 10, 13-14 (col)
Doy   pl 74 (col)
OrM   pl 6-20, 22-24, 26

CASQUES. See Headdress, Military—Early to 17th century

CASSOCK
McC   p47-57 il
NorC   p 165-67 il
Pic   il p23

CASTELLÓN. See Spain—Valencia

CASTILE, NEW. See Spain—Castile, New

CASTILE, OLD. See Spain—Castile, Old

CASULA. See Capes and cloaks—Rome

CATALONIA. See Spain—Catalonia

CATHOLIC CHURCH. See Ecclesiastical costume—Catholic church

CAUCASUS. See Russia—Caucasus

CAVALIERS. See Noblemen—England—17th century

CAVE DWELLERS
AirP il p7

CELESTINE MONKS
Doy pl 65 (col)

CELESTINE NUNS
Doy pl 105 (col)

CELLARERS
England
Ab pl p63

CELTS
Lab p22-24 pl (col) (m)
See also England—Ancient to 449; France—Early to 511; Scotland—To 1300

CENTRAL AMERICA. See Costa Rica; El Salvador; Guatemala; Honduras; Indians of Central America; Nicaragua; Panama

CENTURIONS. See Military costume—Rome

CEREMONIAL COSTUME
See also Ambassadors; Coronation robes; Court costume; Festival costume; Officials; Parliamentary robes; Wedding costume
Annam
Pot v2 pl 11 (col) (m)
Burma
TiK pl 87 fig 1 (col) (m)
China
BruK pl 184 fig 10 (col) (f)
Camm p3-185 front pl 1-20
Dal v 1 fig 754, 769 (col)
NeF p3-13 pl 1, 16-37, 39-40, 42-44
Pot v2 pl 3 (col) (f)
TiK pl 93 fig 7 (col) (f)
Vu p 13-14, 16-19 pl 1, 7-10, 14 (m)
Egypt, Ancient
HeuO pl 25 (col)
Kle p284, 337-38 il (m)
England
12th-14th centuries
CunM pl 7, 23 (m)
15th century
CunM pl 53 (f)
Norr v3 bk 1 pl 1 (col)
WilF pl p29, 34
16th century
CunS p68-69 pl (f)
Norr v3 bk 1 p 158-59, 182-85, 187-88, 190, 253-55 2 pl (col) fig 211-12, 231 (m); bk 2 p485-87, 610-11 3 pl (f)
17th century
WilF pl p86

20th century
Nat v 103 My '53 pl p703 (f)
France
11th century
EvjD p2 il (m)
14th century
WilF pl p28
16th century
Dav v2 fig 1245 (f)
Gor pl p50
LavR pl p 115-17, 348
Norr v3 bk 1 p 185-89 il
17th century
BluE p20, 22 pl 14, 28 (1 col) (f)
LavR pl 354, 381, 385 (m)
WilF pl p86, 87
18th century
BruK pl 114 fig 3 (col) (f)
Pann v 1 pl 1, 3, 8, 23 (col)
WilF pl p109-11
19th century
Bruh p68-69 pl (col)
Dav v2 p870 il (f)
LelD pl p 184 fig 4 (m)
Pann v2 pl 15, 17 (col) (f) v4 pl 24 (col) (f)
Hungary
18th century
Hol p 14 pl 15-16, 25-26
19th century
Hol p 17-20, pl 18-19, 22, 27-29, 31-32
Indians of North America
Lyf pl 65 (m)
Roe p 109-234 40 pl (col) il
Italy
16th century
WilF pl p56 (f)
18th century
Mora pl 14, 19, 21, 38
Japan
Int v2 pl 94-95
Korea
Keit p47 pl p46, 64, 65 (1 col)
Pot v2 pl 8 (col)
Netherlands
15th century
Dav v 1 fig 882
Norway
UnW pl 3A (col)
Peru
16th century
CrO pl 26 fig 1, 2, 6, 8, 10, 12
Spain
Agu pl 103 (f)
OrT pl 58-59, 131

CEREMONIAL COSTUME—Spain—Continued

15th century

Norr v3 bk 1 p63-64 pl p62 (col) (f)

Sweden

18th century

Berg fig 1 (m)
StocM pl 27 (col) (m)

Tibet

Nat v90 Ag '46 il p209 (f)

CESTUS
LelD p82 il

CEYLON
Brad pl p48, 49
BruK pl 178 fig 13-18 (col)
See also Dancers—Ceylon; Footwear
—Ceylon

CHAINS (JEWELRY)
EvnJ p 105-06 pl 47
LelD il p 128
Norr v3 bk 1 p 119-20 fig 7, 27-29
Vert pl p32 (col)
Wa p 145-46, 150 fig 143, 145-46

CHAIR BEARERS

Egypt, Ancient

Dot il p 106

England

15th century

Norr v3 bk 1 p 135-37 il

16th century

AirT il p31

17th-18th centuries

AirB il p53
AirT il p59
Trev v4 fig 24

CHALDEA. See Assyria and Babylonia

CHAMBERMAIDS. See Servants

CHAMPAGNE. See France—Champagne

CHANCELLORS, LORDS. See Lords
Chancellors

CHANS
BruK pl 182 fig 1-2 (col)

CHAPERON (HEADDRESS). See subdivisions 13th, 14th and 15th centuries
under Headdress—England; Headdress
—France; etc.

CHARACTER DOLLS. See Dolls

CHARIOTEERS

Assyria and Babylonia

CrO pl 1
Gen v 1 fig 184

Egypt, Ancient
BruK pl 4 (col)
Gen v 1 fig 110
HeuO pl 15
Hous2 p45-47 fig 50
Nat v80 O '41 pl p493 (col)

Greece, Ancient
Dav v 1 il p69
Gor pl p 1
HousG2 p58 il
LavS p 18 pl 3
TiK pl 10 fig 5-6

Rome
AirB il p 10
AirP il p39, 55
KerM no 1 pl 1

Sumeria
Hous2 p 112 fig 113

CHARLES, KING. See subdivision under
Kings and rulers—England; Kings and
rulers—France

CHARRO COSTUME. See Riding costume
—Mexico

CHASSEURS D'AFRIQUE

19th century

KnR pl p297

CHASUBLE
Ada v 1 il p 178
Bra pl 16
EvjD p71-74 pl 80 il
HousM p24-27, 144-45 fig 29-34, 259-60
(incl pat)
LelD p93-94 il
NorC p55-83 8 pl (2 col) il (incl pat)
TiK pl 37 fig 15-19
Wa p62 fig 62V

CHATELAINES
BraF p73 pl p 113, 145
Dav v2 fig 2094-95
EvnJ p 175-79 pl 146-51
Lel v 11 fig 33; v 12 fig 24
LelD p94 il
Roj il p22

CHELSEA PENSIONERS. See Pensioners
—England

CHEMISES
LelD p96-97 pl

To 16th century

CunU p31-33 fig 9

16th-17th centuries

CunU p45-47, 62 fig 14, 16-18, 25, 27
DeB p 161 pl p 163
Lint p 189-91 pl

18th century

CunU p82-83, 111 fig 36, 49
Lel v 11 p62-63 fig 64 (incl pat)

19th century

CrH p32-33 pl
CunU p 128, 144 fig 55, 65

CHEMISES—*Continued*

20th century

CunU p224 fig 100, 106
Kle p 171-73

CHETHAM'S HOSPITAL STUDENTS, MANCHESTER, ENGLAND
Cla p 17-18 pl

CHIAPAS. See Mexico—Chiapas

CHIGNONS. See Hair, wigs, etc.

CHILDREN
Bin p 197-219 pl il
  See also Biblical costume—Children; Boy scouts; Headdress, Children's; Infants; also names of individual schools, e.g. Westminster school

19th century

BelQ pl p92 (col)
CrO pl 53
Gor front (col)
Jack p 117-29 il
Jen pl p27
Kle p211-12 il
Lee p 115-16 pl
Lis p71, 73, 81, 85-86 il
Part p 19-20, 24, 99, 134, 139 il
SitC pl 117-22 (1 col)
Trev v4 fig 11
Walk pl 21, 26, 36 (col)
Yar pl p227 (col)

1800-1810

MooC p34-35 pl (f)
Pann v2 pl 21-22 (col) (f)
UnW pl 90, 92 (col)
WilFo pl p 147 (f)

1810-1820

Dav v2 p828 fig 2327 (m)
MooC p36-41 3 pl
Rue fig K1-K2
Trev v4 fig 11
ViN pl 13 (f)
Wa fig 207 (f)

1820-1830

Dav v2 p831 il
LelD pl p336 row 1 (col)
MooC p42-43 pl (f)
Pann v3 pl 13 (col) (m)
Wa fig 213 (f)

1830-1840

Ada v2 il p308
Chr fig 350 (f)
Dav v2 fig 2400-03, 2413-18
LavC p8-9 pl 2-5 (col)
MooC p44-45 pl (f)
Pann v3 pl 23 (col) (f)
UnW pl 98 (col) (f)
WilC pl p305
WilFo pl p 148 (f)

1840-1850

Dav v2 p862-64, 871 il
Gern pl 2 (f)
LelD pl p336 row 2 (col)

MooC p46-49 3 pl
Pann v3 pl 26 (col) (f)
QuV fig 6, 32 (f)
WilH pl p243

1850-1860

Ada v3 il p4, 13, 55
BroF pl p80 (col)
Dav v2 p875-76, 893, 895 pl il
KerA p68-69 1 pl
KerM no4 pl 3 (m)
LavC p9-10 pl 6-10 (col)
Lecl pl 15 (col) (f)
LelD pl p304 (col) (m)
Mer fig 28 (m)
MooC p52-53 front (col) pl (m)
Pann v4 pl 10 (col) (f)
Rud il p87, 161
ViN fig 51-53, 58 (f)
WilC pl p305
WilFo pl p 149 (f)
Yar pl 227

1860-1870

CunP pl p40 (col) (f)
Dav v2 p926, 929 il (f)
Gern pl 32, 44, 50-51
LavC p 10-11 pl 11-14 (col)
Mo p69 pl 25 (f)
MooC p54-63 5 pl
ViN fig 61 (f)

1870-1880

CunP pl p41 (col) (f)
KerA p68-69 1 pl
LavC p 11 pl 15 (col)
LavF pl 13 (col) (f)
MooC p64-73 6 pl
Pann v4 pl 23 (col) (f)
Part il p99, 134, 139
ViN fig 71-72, 74-76, 78

1880-1890

Ada v3 il p384
Bart p86-87 pl (pat) (f)
Bin pl p209
BrH pl p 141 fig 4-5 (col) (f)
Jen pl p26-27
KerA p68-69 1 pl
LavC p8, 12 pl 1, 16 (col)
McP pl p36 (m)
MooC p74-79 3 pl (f)
UnW pl 105 (col) (f)
ViN fig 79-81, 83
Wel pl p34-35
WilC pl p305

1890-1900

Ada v4 il p88
BrH pl p 135 fig 11-12 (col) (m)
KerA p68-69 1 pl
Mo p 137 pl 74 il (f)
MooC p80-87 4 pl
RogW p 122-23 il
Rud il p 199
VanH pl 11
Wa p319, 327 fig 251
WilFo pl p 151 (f)

20th century

Jack p 130-38 il

CHILDREN—20th century—*Continued*

1900-1910

Ada   v4 il p273, 306
Bro20   p 16-17 il
KerA   p68-69   1 pl
MooC   p90-97   5 pl
RogW   p 124, 126 il
VanH   pl 12
Wa   fig 258-59
WilFo   pl p 163 (m)

1910-1920

AlF   pl p8 (f)
KerA   p68-69   1 pl
MooC   p98-101   2 pl (f)
VanH   pl 12 (f)
WilFo   pl p 164 (f)

1920-1930

MooC   p 102   pl (f)

1930-1940

MooC   p 102   pl (f)

1940-1950

Bro20   p81-84 il
WilFo   pl p 170 (f)

African tribes

Nat   v 104 Ag '53 pl p 156 (col)

Assyria and Babylonia

Wa   p26 il

Austria

Nat   v71 Ap '37   pl p457 (col)

Basque provinces

Nat   v 105 F '54   pl p 185 (col)

Burma

Nat   v84 O '43 il p503 (f)

Byzantine empire

Jack   p39-40 il

China

Brad   pl p50

Czechoslovakia

Brad   pl p52 (m)
Nat   v74 Ag '38 pl p 199, 201 (col)

Denmark

AndF   p 14-15   pl 3
Brad   pl p56
Prim   pl p 16 (f)

Egypt, Ancient

VanH   pl 1
Wa   p 16 fig 4C-5 (incl pat)

England

Ancient to 1200

BroF   fig 4 (m)
Jack   p16-19, 41-60 il
Tru   p 14 il (m)

13th century

HousM   p47 fig 64, 74
Jack   p60-65 il

14th-15th centuries

HousM   p 107-08 il (m)
Jack   p65-80 il

16th century

BosE   pl 29 (m)
Dav   v 1 431, 438, 453 il; v2 front (col)
Gor   pl p59 (m)
Hat   fig 50 (m)
Jack   p81-91 il
LavE   pl 42, 44
LavR   pl p 154, 159, 168, 174
Nat   v78 Jl '40 pl p 18 (col) (m)
Norr   v3 bk 2   p527-28, 530, 651-52, 700
   il (m)
Rey   p4, 18 pl 6, 21
Set   il p20 (f)
Tru   il p54 (m)
UnW   pl 38 (col)

17th century

Bin   pl p209 (m)
BrH   pl p83 fig 7 (col) (m)
Dav   v2 p562-63, 573, 576, 578, 581-82,
   593 il
Jack   p92-103 il
LavR   pl p27 (f)
Nat   v70 Jl '36 pl p89 (col) (m)
Rey   p 19 pl 27 (f)
Set   pl p27 (m)
Tru   il p60

18th century

BrH   pl p 123 fig 2, 4 (col)
Dav   v2 p776, 778, 780-81 il
Gor   pl p 117 (m)
Jack   p 104-15 il
MooC   p30-33   2 pl il
Set   p32-36 pl (col) il
SitC   front (col) pl 15, 25, 30, 36, 40,
   42-45, 47-49, 54, 59, 73, 93, 96, 101, 104,
   106-108 (1 col)
Trev   v3 fig 23, 24
Tru   p83-84 il

19th-20th centuries

See Children—19th century; Children
—20th century

Eskimos

Nat   v90 O '46 pl p489 (col) (f)

Europe

13th-14th centuries

Wa   p 101, 104, 115 fig 97, 105, 107, 113-
14, 116A, 119

15th century

Lee   p83-86 pl
Wa   p 131, 136 fig 131-32

16th century

Wa   p 158 fig 147, 152, 155
WisF   pl 11 (f)

17th century

Wa   p 185 fig 162, 166, 173, 174, 178

18th century

Wa   fig 188D, 191, 192, 199

Finland

16th century

WilF   pl p75 (f)

CHILDREN—*Continued*

Flanders

See Children—Netherlands—16th century

France

14th century

Kle p207-09 il (m)

15th century

Dav v 1 p345 il (m)
HousM p 192 il (m)
Kle p207-09 il (f)

16th century

Norr v3 bk 2 p556-57 pl (m)

17th century

BluE p 18-19, 27 pl 7, 11-13, 64 (1 col)
Dav v2 p508, 539-40, 548 il
LavR pl p351, 353, 384 (1 col)
Lib pl p34

18th century

Bruh pl p53 (col) (f)
Dav v2 p665, 673-75, 709 il
Gor pl p 110
Lel v 11 pl 16 fig 84; v 12 p57-59 fig 77-80
Pann v 1 pl 13 (col) (m); v2 pl 2 (col) (f)
UnW pl 83 (col) (f)

19th-20th centuries

See Children—19th century; Children —20th century

Germany

16th century

Bruh pl p37 (col)
BruK pl 77 fig 1 (m)

17th century

KelF pl p97

18th century

Lel v 12 pl 12

19th-20th centuries

See Children—19th century; Children —20th century

Germany, Provincial

Pet p24-25, 64-65 2 pl (f)
Ret il p26, 37, 45, 62 (f)
RetS pl 34-35, 50-51, 65, 89, 103

Greece, Ancient

BiE pl 36 (f)
Eth il p 14 (m)
HousG2 p81-82 fig 84-87
Jack p23-29 pl
KerM no 1 pl 9
Kle p207-08 il (f)
Tru il p4 (m)
VanH pl 1

Hungary

Hol p 10-11 pl 2, 12, 14 (m)
Nat v73 Ja '38 pl p43 (col)
Pif pl p 17, 53 il p20, 43, 46-47 (col)

Iceland

Nat v88 N '45 pl p558 (col) (f)

India

Nat v78 D '40 pl p755-56 (col); v82 O '42 pl p481 (col) (f)

Indians of North America

Nat v72 S '37 pl p306 (col) (f); v78 N '40 pl p596 (col); v96 D '49 pl p795 (col)

Ireland, Ancient

Jack p 16-20 pl

Italy

See also Children—Rome

11th-12th centuries

Kle p207-08 il (f)

16th century

Dav v2 fig 1350 (m)

18th century

Mora pl 58-60
NeEu pl 7 (m)

Japan

Haa pl 1, 69
Nat v73 Ja '38 pl p 121 (col) (f)

Korea

Keit pl p 16, 26, 34 (3 col)
TiK pl 97 fig 46 (col)

Laos

Pot v2 pl 13 (col)

Lapland

Nat v75 Je '39 pl p806; v76 N '39 pl p657, 660, (col); v96 Jl '49 pl p 113, 116 (col); v 106 Ag '54 pl p256-57, 273, 276-77 (col)

Mexico

CorA pl 9 (f)
CovM pl p366 (col)
KaM pl 1-3, 8 (col)
Meri pl 12, 15, 23 (col)
Nat v75 Ja '39 pl p96 (col); v78 S '40 pl p367 (col)

Netherlands

Sit p46-47 pl

16th century

LavR pl p318 (m)

17th century

BruK pl 92
Dav2 p611, 613, 619 il
Nat v94 D '48 pl p735 (col) (f)

Netherlands, Provincial

Hij pl 9-13, 21-27
Int v2 pl 49
Nat v 106 S '54 pl p396, 412 (col)

Norway

Brad pl p 124
Lee pl p51 (f)

CHILDREN—Norway—*Continued*
Nat v75 Ap '39 pl p505, 517-18 (col);
  v94 Ag '48 pl p 199 (col) (f); v 106
  Ag '54 pl p 161 (col) (f)
Prim pl p48 (f)

Palestine, Modern
Nat v89 Mr '46 pl p318 (col)

Persia, Ancient
Hous2 fig 172 (m)

Portugal
Nat v 106 N '54 pl p685, 692 (col)

Rome
BiE pl 52 (m)
Dav v 1 p77 il (m)
Jack p30-34, 36-39 il
Kle p207-08 il (m)
VanH pl 1
Wa p59 fig 59
WlsC p 130-37 8 pl (incl pat)

Rumania
SitR pl p58A (col) (f)

Scotland
Eyr v 1 pl p 152 (col) (m); v2 pl
  p426 (col) (m)
Log pl p 123, 126 (col) (m)
Mccl pl 19 (m)

Spain
Gom pl p 196 (f)
OrT pl 100-03 (f)

15th century
Norr v3 bk 1 fig 72, 73

16th century
Bruk pl 74
Lint pl 4 (f)

17th century
BruK pl 86-87 (1 col)
Dav v2 p638, 645 il
Kle p209 il (f)
LavR pl p249, 252-53 (1 col)

18th century
Bart p56-57 pl (pat) fig 20 (m)
Dav v2 p731 il (m)
NeEu pl 10 (m)

19th century
Agu pl 72-73

Spain, Provincial
AnS p 183-86 fig 222-26

Sudetenland
Mal pl 8-9 (col) (m)

Sweden
MusS pl 2 (col)
Nyl p25-26, 30-31, 76-77 2 pl (col) (f)
Prim pl p76
StocM pl 16-17, 46-47

Switzerland
Kle p208 il (m)
Lee pl p67

Tibet
Nat v90 Ag '46 pl p 190

Tyrol
Ham p 1-2, 5-6, 13-14, 19-20, 33-34, 40,
  46 5 pl (col)
Ori pl p6, 14, 20, 28, 34, 40, 46 (col)

United States
17th century
Ada v 1 il p 121, 335
McP pl p4 (col) (f)

18th century
Ada v 1 il p 152, 154, 170 (m)
Dau pl p68
Dav v2 p740, 764-65 il
Davi v 1 il p87
McP pl p 13 (f)
Nat v94 S '48 pl p304-05
Trai p 114 il
VanH pl 7

19th-20th centuries
See Children—19th century; Children
—20th century

Wends
Ret pl p86, 108 il p89-90 (f)

CHILE
BruK pl 194 (col)
Hal pl 17-20
Spi pl p47 (col) (m)
  See also Gauchos; Indians of South
  America—Araucanian Indians; Military
  costume—Chile

CHILKAT INDIANS. See Indians of
  North America—Chilkat Indians

CHIMERE
NorC p 177 pl p47 il (pat)

CHIMNEY SWEEPERS
Argentine Republic
Nat v76 N '39 il p570

CHINA
Brad pl p50 (f)
BruK p39 pl 183-84 (col)
Camm p3-185 front pl 1-20
Dal v 1 p409-76 il (col)
Lee p 12-15 pl
Loud pl 3 (col)
NeF p3-13 pl 1, 16-37, 39-44, 54
Pot v2 p 11-16 3 pl (col)
RueO pl 1-4
TiK pl 88-93 (col)
Tor p 11-31 front (col) 39 pl (2 col)
Trev v2 fig 59
WilFo pl p48 (f)
  See also Fancy dress and stage cos-
  tume—Chinese; Manchus; Mandarins;
  also subdivision China under Children;
  Coats and jackets; Coronation robes;
  Court dress; Footwear; Hair, wigs, etc.;
  Headdress; Kings and rulers; Military
  costume; Wedding costume

CHIOS
  Arg p 123-250 80 pl (54 col) il (incl pat)
  BruK pl 164 fig 4-5 (col) (f)

CHIPPEWA INDIANS. See Indians of North America—Chippewa Indians

CHITON. See Greece, Ancient

CHLAMYS. See Greece, Ancient

CHOCTAW INDIANS. See Indians of North America—Choctaw Indians

CHOPINS. See division 16th and 17th centuries (c 1550-1625) under Footwear—Europe; Footwear—Venice

CHORISTERS
      England
  SitN pl 9

CHRIST, KNIGHTS OF THE ORDER OF
  Doy pl 157 (col)

CHRISTENING ROBES
      France
  Lel v 11 pl 21, 25 (col)
      Spain
  AnS p 187 fig 227-28

CHRISTIAN BROTHERS
  MusE pl 28 (col)

CHRISTIANS (EARLY CHRISTIANS). See Rome—1st-5th centuries; also Biblical costume—Christians (Early Christians)

CHRISTMAS COSTUMES. See subdivisions under Fancy dress and stage costume, e.g. Christmas Joy, Santa Claus; also Biblical costume—Wise men

CHRIST'S HOSPITAL STUDENTS, HORSHAM, ENGLAND
  Cla p 12-13 pl (col)
  Norr v3 bk 2 p424-25 il

CHURCH OF ENGLAND. See Ecclesiastical costume—Anglican and Episcopal church

CIRCASSIANS
  BruK pl 171 fig 2, 4-6, 8 pl 173 fig 8, 10 (col)

CIRCUS PERFORMERS
  Dav v2 p812 il (f)
  Kou pl 158

CISTERCIAN NUNS
  Doy pl 121-22 (col)
  OrM pl 90

CISTERCIANS
  EvjD p66 pl 72a

CITIZENS SERVICE CORPS
  Ross p20 il (col)

CIUDAD REAL. See Spain—Castile, New

CLARENI FRIARS
  Doy pl 69 (col)

CLASPS. See Belts and belt buckles; Buckles

CLERGYMEN. See Ecclesiastical costume

CLIPS (JEWELRY)
  BraF p 117-18 pl p 173, 175, 185, 205
  Pic il p 111

CLOAKS. See Capes and cloaks

CLOGS AND PATTENS
  Bra pl 20
  Pic il p 108

CLOWNS AND JESTERS
  LelD p 11, 180, 270, 384 il
  Nat v93 Mr '48 pl p315, 319-21 (col)
  Pic il p54
  WilH pl p52
  See also Dolls—Clowns; Fancy dress and stage costume—Clown
      14th-15th centuries
  EvjD pl 61
  Gor pl p27
  HousM p 120, 180 fig 222, 313
      16th century
  Hat fig 133, 160, 164
  Norr v3 bk 1 p300 il
      African tribes
  Nat v79 My '41 pl p659 (col)
      Indians of North America
  Roe p227-33 pl (col)

COACHMEN
      England
      17th century
  AirB il p49
  AirT il p58
  Trev v2 fig 104
      19th century
  Pic il p28
      France
      19th century
  LelD p 105 il
      Rumania
  SitR pl p60A, 78A

COAST GUARD, UNITED STATES
      20th century
  MiI pl p286-87 (off, s)
      Women's Reserve
  RogW p87 il
  Ross p65 il (col)

COATS AND JACKETS
  Hea p22-23, 28-31 3 pl (incl pat) (m)
  Pic p81-83 il
  See also Bolero jackets; Eton jackets; Straw coats and cloaks

COATS AND JACKETS—*Continued*

15th century
LelD p228 il (m)
Wa p 124-26 fig 125-27, 129-31 (incl pat)

16th century
KelF pl p71 (m)
Kle p 170 il (f)
Wa p 142-43 fig 142 (incl pat) 143 (m)

17th century
LelD pl p347 fig 1-2 (m)
Roj pl p9, 16 (pat)
Wa p 188, 196-97 fig 175 (incl pat) 176 (m)
WilC p 174-75, 185-86 pl p 146, 165, 171, 181, 190, 192 (m)

18th century
Bra 31, 36 (f)
BroW v2 p 116-19 il (m)
Kle p76 il (f)
Lel v 11 pl 14 (m)
LelD pl p347 fig 3-7 (m)
LesA fig 590 (m)
Wa p209-10, 220-22, 228-29 fig 183, 187, 195-96, 198 (incl pat) (m)

19th century
ViN fig 8-9, 20, 32, 35, 38, 42, 49, 64, 73-74, 84-85, 88-89, 100 (m)

1800-1810
Kle p75 il (f)
Wa p246, fig 201, 203, 206, 256 (incl pat) (m)

1810-1820
Wa p255 fig 204-06, 211 (incl pat)

1820-1830
BrH pl p 127 (m)

1830-1840
BrH pl p 131 (m)

1840-1850
Wa p267-68 fig 218, 256 (m)
WilC pl p288, 301-03 (m)
WilF pl p 139 (f)

1850-1860
Br pl 41 (f)
CunP p36 il (f)
Gor pl p 150 (f)
Kle p40 il (f)
Wa p276 fig 226-230, 256 (m)
WilC pl p289-90 (m)
WilF pl p 140-41 (f)

1860-1870
BroH p200-02 fig 132 (m)
Pann v4 pl 11-12 (col) (f)
Wa p283 fig 235, 237, 256
WilC pl p288 (m)
WilF pl p 145 (f)

1870-1880
Pann v4 pl 25 (col) (f)
Wa p295-97 fig 241-42, 256 (incl pat) (m)
WilC pl p301, 303 (m)
WilF pl p 144-45 (f)

1880-1890
Mo p 110 pl 52-55 (f)
Wa p309-10 fig 247, 256 (m)
WilC pl 316, 317 (f)
WilF pl p 146-47 (f)

1890-1900
CunE pl p404 (f)
Wa p315-16 fig 251, 256 (m)
WilC pl p326 (f)

20th century
1900-1910
CunPr p44, 57-58, 62 pl p48, 61, 80-81 il (f)
LelD p228 fig 1-2 (f)
Wa p334-35 fig 258, 266 (m)
WilF pl p 165-67

1910-1920
LavT pl p256 (f)
Wa p343-44, 348 fig 266, 268
WilF pl p 168-75

1920-1930
CunPr pl p 162, 174, 192 (f)

1930-1940
KerA pl p59 (f)
LelD p228 fig 3 (m)

1940-1950
Ving pl 104-05 (f)
Yar pl p 276, 279, 280

China
TiK pl 89-90 (col)

Chios
Arg pl 14-17 (col)

Croatia
WilF pl p74 (m)

Denmark
TiK pl 125 fig 11 (col) (m)

England
494-1066
EvnR p22 pl 3 (f)

15th century
WilF pl p31, 37, 42

16th century
CunS p23-26, 31-32, 94-99 pl 2-4, 36-40 (m)
DeB p 183-85 pl p 187, 189 (m)
Lint p 197-204 pl 10, 12, 13 (m)
Norr v3 bk 2 p400, 415, 528-29, 540-42 fig 612, 616-17 il (incl pat) (m)
TiK pl 125 (col)
Vert pl p96 (m)
WilF pl p64, 69, 71

17th century
BrH pl p99, 103, 107 (m)
Dav v2 fig 1482 (f)
Eth p41-42 pl (pat)
LelD il p 134

COATS AND JACKETS—England—17th

century—*Continued*
Lint pl 11, 17 (m)
TiK pl 125 (col)
ViP v 1 pl 2-15
WilF pl p89 (m)

18th century

BrH pl p 111, 115, 119, 123 (m)
Dav v2 fig 2083 (f)
Yar p 196 pl IX (col)

Eskimos

CrO pl 14

France

LelD p332-34 2 pl (m)

14th-15th centuries

EvjD p29-30 il (pat) (m)
Wilf pl p30-32, 35-38, 40

16th century

Dal v2 fig 367-68, 370-71 (col) (incl pat) (m)
WilC pl p99 (m)

17th century

Dav v2 fig 1395-97, 1414-16, 1460 (m)
LelD p217, 232 il
WilF pl p89 (m)

18th century

Dal v2 fig 574, 578-79 (col) (incl pat) (m)
Dav v2 fig 1851-54 (incl pat) (m)
Lel v 11 p9-14 pl 14 fig 1-7 (incl pat); v 12 p42-46 pl 7 (col) fig 52-56 (incl pat)
LelD pl p 184 fig 1-3; p232-33 il (m)
SocC pl p32 (m)
WilC p222 pl p225 (m)

Germany
15th-17th centuries
WilF pl p30, 35, 64, 73, 90, 93
18th century
Kle p26 il (f)

Hungary
Int v2 pl 36-40
15th-16th centuries
Hol p4-6 pl 1-3 (m)
WilF pl p74 (m)
17th-18th centuries
Hol p6-16 pl 4-10, 13-15 (m)
19th century
Hol p 16-17 pl 16-22 (m)

Italy
15th-16th centuries
WilF pl p30, 35-37, 40-41, **73**
18th century
Mora pl 65, 78-82, 84 (m)

Macedonia
TiK pl 57 (col)

Netherlands
15th century
WilF pl p34, 36 (m)

17th century
LavR pl p320 (m)
WilF pl p89, 92

Poland
16th century
WilF pl p73 (m)

Russia
16-17th centuries
WilF pl p63, 74, 98

Siberia
TiK pl 102-06 (col)

Spain
AnS p96-98, 244, 265-68, 273 fig 111, 291-92, 316-17, 325 (m)

Sweden
Sv p37-88 il (incl pat)
16th century
StocM pl 1 (m)
WilF pl p71 (f)
17th century
StocM pl 7 (m)
18th cenutry
Berg fig 48-60, 67-72, 74-75, 82, 93, 98-100, 103-04 (incl pat)

Tyrol
Ham p 1-2, 19-20, 27-28, 31-32, 46, 49-52, 57-60 9 pl (col)
Ori pl p2, 20, 24, 28, 46, 58 (col) (m)

COATS AND JACKETS (FUR)

20th century
WilF pl p 170-72, 174-76, 178-82, 184-220

COATS (OVERCOATS)
Pic p28-30 il

14th-15th centuries
LelD p309-10 il

16th century
Norr v3 bk 2 fig 629 (m)

17th century
Dav v2 p533 il (m)
WilF pl p95 (m)

18th century
Bra pl 33 (m)
Lel v 11 p 16-18 fig 11-12 (incl pat)
LelD p343 il (m)
Pann v2 pl 10 (col) (f)
UnW pl 78 (m)
Yar pl p 177

19th century
LelD p247 il (m)
Pann v2 pl 18, 23-24, 28 (col); v3 pl 18 (col)
WilC pl p243, 253, 267, 277, 289, 304 (m)

COATS (OVERCOATS)—19th century—
Continued

1810-1820
Kle p77, 240 il
Yar pl p201

1820-1830
Gor pl p 139 (m)
WilF pl p 132-34 (m)

1830-1840
BrH pl p 127 fig 4, pl p 131 fig 3 (m)
BroH p 186 fig 123 (m)
Yar pl p207

1850-1860
WilF pl p 142

1860-1870
Brk pl 30 (f)
Kle p252 il (m)

1880-1890
McP pl p37 (m)
WilC pl p304 (m)
WilF pl p 148

1890-1900
ViN fig 92, 100 (m)

20th century
LelD p301 il (m)

1900-1910
Gor pl p 168 (col) (m)
LelD p341, 343 il (m)
WilC pl p342 (m)
Wom p4 il (f)

1910-1920
LavT2 pl p112 (f)
LelD p310 il (m)
WilC pl p343 (m)
WilFo pl p 164 (f)
Wom p4-5 il (f)

1920-1930
Bra pl 51 (m)
WilC pl p343-44 (m)
Wom p5 il (f)

1930-1940
CunPr p219-20, 224, 230, 236, 240-41, 246, 261-62 pl il (f)
WilC pl p341 (m)
Wom p5 il (f)

1940-1950
Bra pl 54-55 (f)
Kle p80, 147-48, 252, 279-80, 296-97, 316, 378 il
WilC pl p342 (m)
Wom p6 il (f)
Yar pl p281 (m)

Hungary
Nat v73 Ja '38 pl p 18 (col) (m)

Poland
Stry pl 7, 10, 25, 27, 29 (col) (m)

Sweden
StocM pl 38, 45

COBBLERS. See Shoemakers

COCKADES
LelD p 105 il

COLDSTREAM GUARDS
BarH pl 13, 18, 20, 22 (col)
LavB p27 pl 2 (col) (pte)
Law v2 p 15-16, 18-19 il (pte)

COLLARS
Nat v79 F '41 il p 167 (m)
Pic p31-33 il

19th century
But pl p 145 (m)
CunU p 138-40, 172 fig 61, 64 (m)
Mer fig 13-20, 29-30, 37-38 (m)

20th century
Rud pl p156 (f)

COLLARS (JEWELRY)
Norr v3 bk 1 p118-19, 350-51 il

COLOBIUM
NorC p 12 front (col) pl p 13 il

COLOMBIA
Hal pl 21-23 (col)
Nat v78 O '40 pl p535 (col)
Spi pl p33 (f)
See also Indians of South America—Colombia

COLOR BEARERS. See Standard bearers

COLSTON'S SCHOOL STUDENTS, BRISTOL, ENGLAND
Cla p 19-20 pl (col)

COLUMBAN MONKS
Doy pl 57 (col)

COMBINATIONS (UNDERWEAR)
19th century
CunU p 176, 195, 209, 222, 224-25, 239 fig 87, 94, 99, 106, 109

20th century
1920-1930
Pic il p34 (f)

1930-1940
Bra pl 52 (f)

COMBS (HEADDRESS)
Chr fig 354 (col)
Dal v2 fig 1041-43
Dav v2 fig 2423
Flow fig 7, 62-63, 70
Lee pl p63
LelD p308 il
LesA p 134-36 il
Nat v69 Mr '36 pl p411; v69 Ap '36 p496 il
RogF pl p 186
WisF pl 18

China
Dal v 1 fig 834 (col)

COMBS (HEADDRESS)—*Continued*
Egypt, Ancient
NeP pl 7
Japan
Dal v 1 fig 876 (col)
Saj p39-40 il
Rome
Lang pl p27

COMMANDOS. See Military costume—England — 20th century — 1939-1945 — Commandos

COMMODE. See Headdress—England—17th century; also Headdress—France—17th century

CONDOTTIERI
LelD il p 122

CONDUCTORS (TRAINS, BUSSES, ETC.)
Finland
Nat v74 O '38 pl p529 (f)

CONFEDERATE SOLDIERS. See Military costume—United States—1860-1865 —Confederate army

CONFIRMATION DRESS
Germany
Pet p24-25 pl (f)
Ret pl p 17, 52, 78-79, 213
RetS pl 46-48
Sweden
StocM pl 55 (m)

CONFUCIANIST PRIESTS
MusE pl 10 (col)

CONOY INDIANS. See Indians of North America—Conoy Indians

CONSTANTINE, ORDER OF
Doy pl 145 (col)

CONSULS
Byzantine empire
Dav v 1 p81 il
HousG2 p 124-25 pl
Rome
KerM no 1 pl 10

CONVENTUALS
Doy pl 71-72 (col)

COOKS AND BAKERS
France
16th century
LelD p 138 fig 1

COPES
HousM p30-32 fig 25-26, 40-41
LelD p84 il
NorC p 157-62 pl (col) il
WilF pl p33

COPTIC PRIESTS. See Ecclesiastical costume—Coptic church

COPTS
Ancient
Dav v 1 p36-39 3 pl
WlsC p56 pl 41

CORN DANCE. See Dancers—Indians of North America—Corn dance

CORDOVA See Spain—Andalusia

CORONATION ROBES
See also Orbs (Regalia); Processions, Coronation; Rings, Coronation; Sceptres
China
18th century
Vu pl 12 (m)
England
13th century
HousM p 12-13 fig 17 (m)
16th century
Norr v3 bk 2 p484-87 pl (col) (f)
19th century
Nat v71 Ja '37 pl p41 (col)
20th century
Bae pl p44
LelD pl p267 fig 1 (f)
Nat v 104 S '53 pl p312-23 (col)
France
17th century
BluE p 19 pl 10
LavR pl p352
18th century
BoeR pl p6-7
19th century
BluN pl p 213-14
Germany
11th century
Dav v 1 pl p 118
16th century
Norr v3 bk 1 p249 fig 286 (m)
18th century
Lel v 11 pl 37
Hungary
18th century
Lel v 12 pl 39 (col)
Sweden
18th century
Lel v 11 pl 37

CORONETS
BraF pl p 163
LelD p 150 il
Pic il p 154
Egypt, Ancient
Hous2 p 13-15 fig 15-16

CORONETS—*Continued*

England

CunM pl 79 (f)
Flow pl 2 (col) fig 16, 57, 95, 98
Norr v3 bk 1 p 118, 349-50 fig 146, 159, 181, 428

Greece, Ancient

NeG pl 7-8

CORPUS CHRISTI MONKS
Doy pl 66 (col)

CORSELETS
Lee pl p5 (pat)

CORSETS
Bin p 122-25 il
Kle p223-26 il
See also Busks

Ancient

CrC p2-3 pl

11th-13th centuries

Bra pl 15
CrC p4-5 pl
CunU p33 fig 10

14th-15th centuries

Lib p 1-8 pl p2, 6, 8, 10 il

16th century

Bin pl p 112
Bra pl 23
CrC p6-7 pl
DeB p 162 pl p 163
Lib p9-22 2 pl il
Lint p 178-79 pl
Nat v77 F '40 il p 175; v 100 S '51 il p423
Norr v3 bk 1 p222-23 il; bk 2 p622-23 il
Rud pl p 158

17th century

CrC p8-11 2 pl
Dav v2 pl p551
Lib p23-38 9 pl il
Wa p202 fig 180
WilC pl p 173, 192
Yar p 173 il

18th century

CrC p 12-17 3 pl
CunU p87-88, 108, 115 fig 36, 38-39, 48, 51-53
Dal v2 fig 612-13
Dav v2 fig 2026-27
Gor pl p 103, 112, 121
Lel v 11 p40-44 fig 39-42
LelD p 124 il
Lib p39-72 11 pl il
Mora pl 59
Pic il p 141
TiK pl 126 fig 21-22
Trai p 163 il
Wa fig 185A, 189
WilC pl p205
Yar p 179 il

19th century

CunU p 115-18, 130-32, 148-49, 163, 179-80, 197-98 fig 66, 78, 88, 96
Dav v2 il p 845, 858
KerA p25, 38 il
LavT p 163-70 pl
LelD pl p 126

1800-1810

CrC p 16-17 pl
Dav v2 il p818

1810-1820

LavT2 p 130 pl p 132
WilC pl p246, 327

1820-1830

Dav v2 il p838
Lib p78-83 pl p78, 172U-172V (1 col)

1830-1840

CrC p 18-19 pl
Dot p 167 il
LavT2 pl p 132
Lib p82-88 pl p82, 86-87, 172W-172W7 (2 col)

1840-1850

CrC p20-21 pl
CunP p27-28 il
Gor pl p 146
Lib p89-93 pl il

1860-1870

CrC p22-23 pl
HaC p46-51 pl
Lib p95-102 3 pl il

1870-1880

CrC p22-23 pl
Lib pl p 121

1880-1890

Ada v3 il p349
CrC p24-25 pl
Lib p 103-10 pl p 104, 107, 121
Mo pl 1
Rud pl p27, 119

1890-1900

Ada v4 il p53 il p 131
Bra pl 45
Gor pl p 172
CrC p26-27 pl
CunE p424-25 pl
Lib pl p 122-23
Rud pl p71
Yar p248 il

20th century

Coh p364-82 il
HaC pl p 194
Kle p 182 il
RogW p 99 il

1900-1910

Ada v4 il p278
CrC p28-31 2 pl
CunP p66-67 il
CunPr pl p95 il p56, 64, 76
CunU p211-12 fig 95, 97
Dot p 170-71 il
LavT2 p 132-33 pl

CORSETS—19th century—1900-1910—*Cont.*
LelD pl p 126 fig 12
Lib pl p 123-25
Rud pl p71-72, 215
Trai p353 il
WilC pl p353
Yar p261 il

1910-1920
CrC p32-35 2pl
CunU p227 fig 101-02
LavT2 p 133-34 pl
LelD pl p 126 fig 13
Lib pl p 126-29
Mo pl 1
Rud pl p71
WilC pl p365
Yar p261 il

1920-1930
AlF pl p58-59
CrC p36-37 pl
CunU p244-45 fig 111-14
LavT2 p 133-34 pl
Lib p 112-18 pl p 112, 114, 129-31
Mo pl 1

1930-1940
CrC p38-39 pl
CunPr pl p247
LavT2 p215-16 pl p214
WilC pl p391

1940-1950
CrC p40-41 pl
Lib pl p 172X-172X8 (1 col)
Rud pl p69
Yar p283 il

CORSETS, MEN'S
Bin pl p52
CunU p43, 106-07, 127-28, 192 fig 47

CORSICA
GaP pl 3 (col) (f)
GiR pl 25-26 (col)
LepF pl 40 (col) (f)
RogD pl 32 (col) (f)

La **CORUÑA.** See Spain—Galicia

COSMETIC CONTAINERS
LesA p 136-50 il

COSSACKS
BruK pl 168 fig 11 (col), pl 123 fig 14 (col)
KnR p445-49 pl
Lez pl p224, 284, 288 (col)
Pic il p37
WilF pl p 153

COSTA RICA
Spi pl p35 (col) (f)

COSTERMONGERS (GALA COSTUME)
Nat v71 Ja '37 pl p47 (col)

CÔTES-DU-NORD. See France—Brittany

COUREUR DE BOIS. See Pioneers and scouts

COURIERS. See Messengers and couriers

COURT DRESS
See also Ambassadors; Coronation robes

Byzantine Empire
HousG2 p 136-39 pl

China
Camm pl 18-20 (m)
LesA fig 596-97
Tor p 11-31 front (col) 39 pl (2 col)

England
15th century
Set pl p8 (col) (f)

16th century
Bae front
LavR p37 (col) (m)
Hat fig 138
KelF pl p32C (m)

17th century
LavR pl p 179
Rey p20 pl 32 (m)

18th century
Dav v2 p768 il
ViP v2 pl 12 (m)

19th century
Flow fig 2 (f)
Mo p 145 pl 80 (f)
WilC pl 266 (m)
Yar pl p205 (m)

20th century
CunP pl p68 (col) (f)
Mo p 145 pl 80 (f)
RogW pl p28

Flanders
15th century
Dav v 1 fig 879
HousM pl 6-7 (col)

France
15th century
HousM pl p 144 (col) (f)

16th century
Bruh pl p39 (col)
Dav v2 p480, 486 il
LavR pl p 106 (m)

17th century
Dav v2 p523, 549 il
LelD pl p354 fig 2 (f)

18th century
Bart p40-41, 44-47, 50-53 5 pl (pat) fig 12, 14-15, 18
BruK pl 111 fig 6-7 (col) (m)
Dav v2 pl p695 (f)
Dot il p 162 (f)
Gor pl p 120
Lel v 11 fig 37; v 12 pl 15, fig 35-36 (f)
LelD pl p265 fig 5; pl p266 fig 2
Loud pl 16 (col) (f)
Wa p238-40 fig 195B (f)
WilF pl p 110-11, 114

COURT DRESS—France—Continued
19th century
Bart p58-59 pl (pat) fig 21 (f)
Dav v2 p806, 815, 818, 821 il
Tik pl 128 fig 13 (col) (f)
Germany
15th century
Gor pl p30
17th century
TiK pl 122-23 (col)
Greece, Modern
At pl 11 (col) (f)
India
Am p91 il
Italy
16th century
BruK pl 83 fig 11-15 (col)
Japan
Tik pl 99 fig 3 (col) (m)
Korea
Bis il p260 (m)
Keit pl p64H, 64N
Lebanon, Modern
Cyr front (col) (f)
Netherlands
17th century
BroW v2 fig 6
Scotland
18th century
Log p298 pl p294 (col) (m)
Spain
17th century
Dav v2 p523, 650 il (incl pat)
18th century
Dav v2 p735 il
19th century
Dav v2 p840 il (f)
Sweden
18th century
StocM pl 19, 25-26, 33
19th century
StocM pl 56 (m)

COURT MUSICIANS
Japan
Haa pl 74

COWBOYS
BruK pl 197 fig 11-15 (col)
Davi v 1 p438-41 pl il
Gor p228-38 9 pl (1 col)
Kle p85 il
Lee p 115-16 pl
LelD pl 131 il
Trai p295-98 il
WilFo pl p 172
See also Gauchos; Herdsmen

COWHERDS. See Herdsmen

CRAVATS. See Neckwear—Europe—**17th** century; Neckwear—Europe—18th **century**

CRETE
Ancient
BiE p21-22 pl 6 (f)
BruK p7-8, 45 pl 11 (col)
Burr p8, 113 pl p9
Dav v 1 p42-44 il
Dot p 108-09 il
Gen v 1 fig 212-16, 223-32 pl 5 (col)
Gor p9 pl p8
Hous2 p65-66 fig 72 (m)
HousG2 p 1-32 front 4 pl (col) il
Kle p237-39 il (f)
LelD pl p349 fig 1-3 (f)
Nat v77 Mr '40 il p304 (f); v85 Mr '44 pl p292 (col)
Pot v 1 p9 pl 1 (col)
TiK pl 8 fig 28-29
UnW pl 7 (col)
Vert pl p43, 48 (f)
WilF pl p 10 (f)
See also Cupbearers—Crete, Ancient; Headdress—Crete, Ancient
Modern
Cros p 18 pl 2 (col) (m)
Nat v77 Mr '40 pl p309 (col) (f); **v79** Ja '41 pl p93 (f); v84 N '43 il p552 (f); v 104 N '53 pl p609 (col) (f)

CRICKET COSTUME
17th century
Dur il p 10
18th century
CunU fig 29
Trev v3 fig 92

CRINOLINE. See Hoop skirts—19th century; also costume of the period, 1855-1870 under Nineteenth century

CRISPIN
BruK pl 102 fig 5 (col)

CROATIA. See Yugoslavia—Croatia **and** Slavonia

CROQUET COSTUME
19th century
Kou pl 151
Part p 150 il

1860-1870
Ada v3 p221
CunF pl p 181
Davi v2 il p63 (f)
Dur il p47
Mo p75 pl 29
RogW p 16 il (f)

20th century
Bro20 p24 il p20
CunPr pl p225 (f)

CROSIERS

To 13th century
NorC p 116-25 2 pl il

13th century—date
AirM il p36
HousM p36, 38, 43 il
LelD p 136 il
LesA p390 il
McC p 139-42 pl
NorC p 124-27 2 pl il

CROSSBOWMEN

14th century
Dav v 1 p202 il

15th century
Gor pl p37

CROSSES (JEWELRY)
BraF pl p70-71, 113, 144
EvnJ p40-41, 49-50, 83 pl 10, 36, 106, 152 fig 3, 6, 31
Flow pl 3 (col) fig 12, 20, 79, 95
Jes p 123-25 pl 30-31
RogF pl p218

CROSSES, PROCESSIONAL. See Cross-staffs

CROSS-STAFFS
HousM p36 fig 21, 47
NorC p 138-45 pl il

CROWN OF THE ANDES
Nat v78 O '40 pl p536 (col)

CROWNS
Eth p59, il p56 (pat)
LelD p 129-30 il

13th century
EvnJ p47-48 pl 7-8 (m)
HousM pl p55

15th century
EvnJ p72-73 pl 24-27 (f)

Assyria and Babylonia
Dot il p 107 (m)
LavS p 13 pl 1

Austria
17th century
Dal v2 fig 555 (col)

Byzantine Empire
Dal v 1 fig 491 (col)
NorC p75-76 il
WilC pl p36
WisF pl 5

China
NeC p2-3 pl 2-4, 6-11, 13-14

Egypt, Ancient
Dot p 105 il (m)
Hous2 p23-24 pl 2 fig 26-30
Lee pl p75
WilH p2-3 pl p5-7
Wrig pt3 p 15 pl p26

England
Nat v 104 S '53 pl p326

449-1066
WilH pl p49

1066-1399
AirB il p 19, 23
HousM p54 fig 97
Wa fig 99-100, 121

14th century
Yar pl p81

15th century
EvnJ p72-73 pl 23 (f)
HousM p205-06 fig 340a-b (m)
Norr v3 bk 1 p 117-18 pl 1, 4 (col) fig 3, 7
Wa fig 137-39

17th century
Nat v 104 S '53 pl p324 (col)

France
11th century
Wa fig 98

12th century
EvnJ pl 5 (f)

13th century
HousM p56 fig 98

14th century
EvjD pl 28-29

19th century
EvnJ pl 158, 161 (f)

Germany
Early to 13th century
HousG2 p 159 fig 167d

Hungary
Nat v73 Ja '38 p4 il

Scotland
16th century
Norr v3 bk 1 p349

Spain
Dal v2 fig 154, 305 (col)

CROWNS, ECCLESIASTICAL
Nat v 103 Mr '53 pl p383 (col)

CROWNS, PAPAL. See Papal tiara

CROWNS, WEDDING. See Headdress, Wedding

CROZIERS. See Crosiers

CRUSADERS
BruK pl 32 fig 2, pl 37 fig 6-7
Dot p 125-26 il

12th century
Lis il p35
TiK pl 117 fig 13

13th century
EvjD pl 9a

CUCULLUS. See Headdress, Ecclesiastical

CUENCA. See Spain—Castile, New

CUFFS AND HANDRUFFS

16th century
DeB p 170, 175, 195 pl p 177
LelD p260 fig 1

17th century
Gor pl p94
LelD p260 fig 2-7; pl p302 fig 1-8
WisF pl 12

18th century
Gor pl p 105
LelD p260 fig 8-11; pl p302 fig 9-21
Pic p40 il

19th century
LelD p260 fig 12-14; pl p302 fig 22-29
  (m)

Carpathian Ruthenia
Mak pl IV (col)

Chios
Arg pl 23-25 (col)

Indians of North America
MasB pl 56, 60 (incl pat)

CUIRASSIERS. See Military costume—
Austria—Hungary; Military costume—
England; Military costume—France;
Military costume—Germany

CUMMERBUNDS
Pic il p41

CUPBEARERS

Crete, Ancient
Dot il p 109
HousG2 p 11-12 il

CURLING COSTUME
Nat v96 O '49 pl p445 (col) (m)

CYCLADES
Nat v85 My '44 il p594, 622

CYPRUS

Ancient
BruK p45 pl 11 (col)
Dav v 1 pl p58
TiK pl 8 fig 24-27

Modern
Nat v 101 My '52 pl 633, 663 (col) (f)

CZECHOSLOVAKIA
Brad pl p51
Int v2 p 14-18, 94-96 pl 57-62
Nat v74 Ag '38 pl p 183-85, 197, 199,
  201, 203-04, 213-14, 216-20 (col); v88
  D '45 il p669 (f)
  See also Fancy dress and stage cos-
tume — Czechoslovakian; Sudetenland;
also subdivision Czechoslovakia under
Bagpipers; Children; Dancers; Military
costume

BY REGION OR PROVINCE
Bohemia
BruK pl 142 fig 1-6 (col)
Er p51-54 pl 14 (col)
Lep pl 28, 30 (col) (f)
Lub p 18 pl 2 (col)

16th century
Rud pl p21 (f)
WilF pl p72, 74

17th century
Dav v2 pl p617

Moravia
Brad pl p52, 53 (1 col)
BruK pl 142 fig 7-11 (col)
Hor pl 1-24 (col)
Lee p 15-18 pl
Lep pl 23-25 (col)
Lub p 16, 18 pl 1, 3-4 (col)
Nat v74 Ag '38 pl p204 (col) (f)

Ruthenia
Brad pl p55
WilF pl p 153

Slovakia
BruK pl 142 fig 12-16 (col)
Lep pl 21-22, 26-27, 29 (col)
Lub p 17 pl 2a (col)

D

DAGGING. See subdivision 14th century
under Europe, particularly the period
1330-1400

DAIRYMAIDS. See Milkmaids

DAKOTA INDIANS. See Indians of North
America—Dakota Indians

DALARNE. See Sweden—Dalarne

DALECARLIA. See Sweden—Dalecarlia

DALMATIA. See Yugoslavia—Dalmatia

DALMATICS
Bra pl 10, 14, 16
EvjD p69-71 il
HousM p7, 27-28 fig 9, 35-39 (incl pat)
Kle p88 il
LelD p 142-43 pl
NorC p42-54 2 pl il (incl pat)
TiK pl 37 fig 1-3
Wa p62 fig 63 III

DAMASCUS. See Syria

DANCERS
  See also Bacchantes; Ballet costume
Nat v76 O '39 pl p548; v79 My '41 pl
  p649 (m) v82 D '42 pl p751 (col);
  v96 Jl '49 pl p62 (m) v 101 Mr '52
  pl p352, 355, 358 (col); v 106 O '54
  pl p516-17 (col) D '54 pl p740 (col)

Algeria
BruK pl 188 fig 1-3 (col) (f)

DANCERS—*Continued*

African tribes
CamC pl p 12-13, 114 (m)

Alsace
Ten pl 3-4 (col)

Annam
Pot v2 pl 11-12 (col)

Arabia
Kin p 196-208 10 pl

Australian tribes
Nat v70 D '36 p729 il (m)

Austria
Breu pl 1-3 (col)

Balearic Islands
Agu pl 123

Bali
Cov p224-28, 230-5 pl 49-55 and pl p226-27, 230 (1 col) il
Nat v75 Mr '39 pl p323, 329, 345 (1 col); v99 Ja '51 pl p9-11, 13 (col) (f); v99 Mr '51 pl p360-62

Basque provinces
LepF pl 23-25 (col)
Nat v 105 F '54 p 174 pl p 148-49, 161, 163 (col)
OrT pl 28-29 (m)

Bavaria
Kin pl p 187

Bhután
Nat v 102 D '52 pl p734, 748-49 (2 col)

Bolivia
Nat v98 N '50 pl p489, 493 (col)

Bourbonnais
Marce p 19-22 pl 3-4 (col)

Brazil
Spi pl p29 (col) (f)

Brittany
Marce p9-15 2 pl (col)

Bulgaria
Kat pl 1-4 (col)

Burma
BruK pl 181 fig 3 (col)

Cambodia
Ving pl 42 (f)

Ceylon
Am p88-89 2 pl
Brad pl p49
Nat v 105 Ap '54 pl p522 (col)

Costa Rica
Nat v90 O '46 pl p433 (col)

Cuba
Spi front (col) (f)

Czechoslovakia
Brad pl p53 (col)
Lub p 17-18 pl 1-4 (col)
Nat v88 D '45 pl p661 (f)

Denmark
LorD p 18-19 pl 1 (col)

Egypt, Ancient
Hous2 p 18-19 fig 25 (f)

Egypt, Modern
Kin pl p210-13, 216-17

England
Int v2 pl 78 fig 1 (m)
Ken pl 2, 8, 17

England
14th century
Ab pl p244 (f)

18th century
Gor pl p 111

Maypole dance
Kar pl 3 (col)
Ken front pl 6

Morris dance
Hat p 172-74, 274, 296-97 fig 90-91, 136
Kar p 10-11 front (col)
Ken pl 6 (m)
Nat v 103 Je '53 pl p825 (col)
Norr v3 bk 1 p300-02 il (m)

Sword dance
Ab pl p244 (m)
Int v2 pl 78 fig 2 (m)
Kar pl 2 (col) (m)
Ken pl 10-14 (m)

Estonia
Nat v76 D '39 il p807

Finland
Heik p7-15 pl 1-4 (col)

Formosa
Nat v87 Ja '45 pl p 13; v97 F '50 pl p 166-67, 169

France
GiR pl 15 (col) (m)
LepF pl 37 (col) (m)
Ten p 10-11 pl 1-2 (col)

15th century
EvjD pl 66

17th century
Bruk pl 102 fig 7-17 (col)
Kin pl p48, 54-55

18th century
Dav v2 p669 il

Germany
Ret il p34-35
RetS pl 66-68 (f)

Gilbert Islands
Nat v83 Ja '43 pl p81

DANCERS—*Continued*

Greece, Ancient
Dav v 1 p63 il (f)
Gor pl p 12 (f)

Greece, Modern
Cros pl 1-4 (col)
Nat v77 Mr '40 pl p317, 319 (col)

Guatemala
Nat v92 O '47 pl p561 (col)

Hawaiian Islands
Nat v96 N '49 pl p591 (col) (f); v 105 My '54 pl p584, 590, 613 (col)

Hungary
Buda pl 2 (col) (m)
Karo p 26
Nat v73 Ja '38 pl p30, Ap '38 pl p520 (col)
Rud pl p33 (f)

Incas
Nat v73 F '38 pl p261

India
Am p 16-22, 58-87 front 10 pl il
Brad pl p87, 93 (1 col)
KerM no2 pl 6 (f)
Nat v78 D '40 pl p741 (col) (f); v85 Je '44 pl p744; v99 N '47 pl p625 (col) il p612
RueO pl 16 (f)
TiK pl 25 fig 3, pl 84 fig 11-12 (col) (f)
See also Dancers—Burma; Nautch girls

Indians of North America
Hun pl p21
Lyf pl 2
Nat v96 O '49 pl p483, 494 (col), D '49 pl p822
Seto p26 pl 8 (m)

Big head dance (Kuksu dance)
Nat v93 F '48 pl p 187 (col)

Buffalo dance
Roe p 184-90 pl 21-22 (col) il

Corn dance
Nat v78 N '40 pl p576 (col); v96 D '49 pl p815, 817 (col)

Deer dance
Roe p 196-200 pl 25-28 (col) (m)

Devil dance
Nat v78 N '40 il p583

Eagle dance
Nat v78 N '40 pl p570
Roe p 194-96 pl 23-24 (col)

Fire dance
Nat v78 N '40 pl p592 (col)

Pipe dance
Ada v2 il p230, 233

Rain dance (Kokochi dance)
Roe p 224-27 pl 37 (col) (m)

Scalp dance
Nat v86 Jl '44 pl p93 (col)

Snake dance
Nat v78 N '40 p580, 583-85 pl (col)

Sun dance
Nat v86 Jl '44 pl p85 (col)

Tablet dance
Roe pl 19-20 (col)

Tomahawk dance
Ada v2 il p230

White deerskin dance
Nat v93 F '48 pl p 190 (col)

Indians of South America
Nat v83 Mr '43 pl p314-15, 317 (col); v84 O '43 pl p470 (col)

Indo-China
Nat v99 Ap '51 pl p474, 479 (col) (f); v 102 S '52 pl p305 (col)

Ireland
Kin pl p 174-75

Italy
16th century
BluL p23 pl 46

Italy
18th-19th centuries
Kin pl p 160-61

Furlana dance
Gal p 17 pl 3 (col)

Sword dance
Gal p 17 pl 1 (col) (m)

Tarantella
Gal p 16 pl 2 (col)
Kin pl p 156-57, 159

Japan
CamC pl p9
Ema p31 pl
Int v2 pl 90-93, 96-97
Kin pl p226-27 (f)

Devil dance
Nat v 104 N '53 pl p632 (col) (m)

Java
BruK pl 181 fig 14 (col) (f)
Kin pl p222 (f)
Nat v99 Ja '51 pl p31 (col)

Korea
Keit p25 pl p64M (f)
Nat v97 Je '50 pl p781, 787 (col) (m)

Mexico
Alv pl p 192, 208, 224, 233, 240, 265, 272, 304, 313, 320 (col)
CorA p 12-18 fig 2-8
CovM p 16-21, 360 il
Marq pl 1-2, 10, 21-22, 36-42, 38-39, 41, 44-53, 55-58, 60, 68-69, 78-90
MeriC pl 4-10 (col)

DANCERS—Mexico—_Continued_
MeriF pl 1-3, 5-6, 8, 10 (col)
Spi pl p 11 (col) (f)
Too p312-376 2 pl (col) il
Val p3 pl 5-6, 8-10 (col)

The flying pole
Alv pl p281 (col) (m)
Marq pl 61-63
Nat v71 Mr '37 p388, 396 il
Too p317-23 fig 146-50, 152-54 il

The little old men
Alv pl p201 (col)
Marq pl 18, 20
Nat v71 My '37 pl p643
Too p356-57 il
Val p2 pl 12 (col)

The Moors and Christians
Alv pl p249 (col) (m)
Marq pl 17 (m)
MeriF pl 9 (col) (m)
Too p347-49 fig 77, 151, 155-57
Val pl 4 (col)

The plumes
Alv pl p217 (col) (m)
Marq pl 76-77
MeriF pl 7 (col)
Val pl 1 (col)

Spur dance
Nat v82 N '42 pl p656 (col)

The tlacololeros
Alv pl p329 (col) (m)
Marq pl 64-65 (m)
MeriF pl 4 (col)
Too p360 fig 78

Panama
Nat v80 N '41 pl p604 (col)

Peru
Nat v82 Ag '42 pl p 191 (col); v98
O '50 pl p433 (col) (m)
TooP p60, 81-82, 139-41, 152-53 pl 53-
59, 64, 70

Poland
Bene p 137-42 pl p 173
Glin pl 1-20 (col)
Wol p 15-16 pl 1-3 (col)

Portugal
Arms p7-15 pl 1-4 (col)
CamC pl p42-43

Pyrenees mountains
Nat v72 O '37 pl p435-36, 439, 450
(col)

Rumania
Gri pl 1-4 (col)
Nat v74 N '38 pl p565

Samoa
Nat v79 My '41 pl p625, 630 (f); v81
Ja '42 pl p39 (col)

Sardinia
Gal p 16-17 pl 4 (col)

Scotland
Kin p 171 pl p 168
MilJ pl 3-4 (col)

Highland fling
Nat v77 My '40 pl p577

Reel
Kin p 170 pl p 165
MilJ pl 1 (col)
Nat v89 My '46 il p547

Sword dance
Kin pl p 164
Nat v77 My '40 pl p591 (col)

Serbia
Kin pl p 190

Siam
Brad pl p 149-50 (f)
Nat v 100 D '51 p739 (f)
Pot v2 pl 15 (col)

Spain
Agu pl F, 4, 15, 26, 44, 99, 110, 115,
122 (1 col)
AnS p35-58 pl il
Arm v 1 pl 1-4 (col); v2 p9-11, 15-16
pl 1-4 (col)
Brad pl p152 (f)
D'Iv pl 48, 66-67 (col)
Int v2 pl 76 (m)
Nat v69 Mr '36 pl p428 (f); v97 Ap
'50 pl p445 (col) (f)
OrT pl 30-31, 117, 136-38, 176, 198-203

Maypole dance
Traj pl 5 (col)

Bolero
Kin pl p 138

Flamenco
Agu pl 74 (f)

Sweden
Salv p 16 pl 1-4 (col)

Switzerland
Wit pl 2-4 (col)

Syria, Modern
BruK pl 191 fig 6 (col) (f)

Tahiti
Nat v95 Ja '49 pl p41, 43 (col) (f)

Tibet
Nat v95 My '49 pl p680 (col)

Devil dance
MusE pl 38 (col)
Nat v99 My '51 pl p632-33 (col)

Trinidad
Nat v 103 Ja '53 pl p65 (col)

Tyrol
Breu pl 4 (col)
Nat v71 Ap '37 pl p463, 477 (1 col)

Wales
Kar p20 pl 4 (col) (f)

DANCERS—*Continued*

Wends

Ret pl p 110 (f)

Yap

Nat v 102 D '52 pl p816-17 (f)

Yugoslavia

Nat v85 Ap '44 pl p509

DANCING MASTERS

France

18th century

Bruh pl p83 (col)
BruK pl 104 fig 3 (col)

DANZIG

18th century

Nat v76 N '39 il p678 (m)

DAUPHINÉ. See France—Dauphiné

DAUGHTERS OF THE DEFENDERS OF THE REPUBLIC

Ross p29 il (col)

DAVAO. See Philippine islands

DAVID (BIBLICAL CHARACTER). See Biblical costume—David

DEACONS

MusE pl 17 (col)

Catholic church

9th-12th centuries

Dav v 1 p 102, 123 2 pl

13th century

EvjD pl 75
HousM p22 fig 22
NorC p49 pl p50 fig 229

14th century

NorC p51-53 pl il

15th century

BruK pl 30 fig 1-2 (col)
EvjD pl 76-77
NorC p54 pl p 161 (col)

DEACONS (SUBDEACONS)

Catholic church

10th-13th centuries

NorC p28, 49 pl p30, 50

DEANS

Anglican church

20th century

Nat v 104 S '53 pl p316-17 (col)

DEER DANCE. See Dancers—Indians of North America—Deer dance

DELAWARE INDIANS. See Indians of North America—Delaware Indians

DELECARLIA. See Sweden—Dalarne

DELSBO. See Sweden—Helsingland

DENMARK

Brad pl p56(f)
Lee p 18-19 pl

See also Faroe islands; Frisian islands; also the subdivision Denmark under Capes and cloaks; Children; Coats and jackets; Dancers; Headdress; Military costume; Mourning costume; Queens and empresses

16th century

AndD p6-8 pl (m)

18th century-date

AndD p9-35 15 pl il
BruK pl 129-30 (col)
Prim p 10-24 11 pl (1 col)

BY REGION OR PROVINCE

Amager

AndD p34 pl p24, 35 (f)
AndF p 14-16 pl 3-4, 27 (1 col)
Dan pl 9 (col) (f)
Int v2 pl 1 (f)
Ras p33-41 3 pl (col)

Bornholm

AndF p 19 pl 10 (f)
Ras p42-57 2 pl (col) (f)

Drejoe

AndF p21 pl 12 (f)

Falster

AndD pl p 23 (f)
AndF p22-23 pl 14, 32 (1 col) (f)
Dan pl 8 (col) (f)
Ras p42-57 2 pl (col) (f)

Fanoe

AndD pl p21 (f)
AndF p28 pl 35 (col) (f)
Dan pl 5 (col) (f)
LorD p 17-18 pl 4 (col) (f)

Fyn

AndF p20 pl 29-30 (col)
Dan pl 1, 3 (col)
Ras p60-68 pl (col)

Hedebo

AndF p 13-14 pl 25-26 (col)
Dan pl 11, 12 (col)

Jutland

AndD p32-34 pl p 15, 27, 33 (f)
AndF p24-27, 29-30 pl 7, 16-20, 22-24, 33-34 (2 col)
Dan pl 6 (col)
Int v2 pl 1
LorD p 17 pl 2 (col) (m)
Ras p69-108 5 pl (col)

Laaland

AndF p22 pl 13 (f)

Laesoe

AndD pl p 19 (f)
AndF p23-24 pl 15 (f)

Lyoe

AndF p22 pl 31 (col) (f)
Dan pl 10 (col) (f)

DENMARK—*Continued*

Roesnaes

AndF p 16-17 pl 5-6 (f)

Samsoe

AndF p 17-18 pl 7 (f)

Taasinge

AndF p 21 pl 11 (f)

Zealand

AndD p34-35 pl p 18, 25
AndF p 12-13, 18-19 pl 1, 8-9, 28
(1 col)
Dan pl 4 (col) (f)
LorD pl 3 (col) (f)
Ras p 11-32 4 pl (col)

DENTISTS

Italy

18th century

Mora pl 91

Netherlands

17th century

Ada v 1 il p 144

DERVISHES

BruK pl 170 fig 5, pl 174 fig 18, pl 175
fig 1 (col)
Nat v82 S '42 il p390; v83 Ja '43 pl
p 121

DEVIL DANCERS

BruK pl 178 fig 15 (col)
See also Dancers—Indians of North
America—Devil dance; Dancers—Japan
—Devil dance; Dancers—Tibet—Devil
dance

DEVIL MASKS

Austria

Nat v99 Je '51 pl p783 (col)

Guiana, Dutch

Nat v83 Ap '43 pl p471 (col)

Nigeria

AirO il p47

DIADEMS. See Coronets

DIPLOMATIC COSTUME. See Ambassadors; Court dress

DIRECTOIRE COSTUME. See France—
Directory, 1795-1799; also similar periods
under other countries

DIVERS (SUBMARINE)

Jen p93 il (f)

DOCTORS. See Physicians

DOGES

Venice

BruK pl 55 fig 14 (col); pl 59 fig 1-8
Dav v 1 p273 il
LelD p 151, 300-01 il
Mora pl 1
WilF pl p22
WilH pl p28, 49

DODECANESE ISLANDS

Nat v 103 Mr '53 pl p365, 381-82, 388
(col) (f)

DOLLS

Only dolls representing types or characters indexed here. For correct costume of dolls in
national dress, see country headings, e.g. England,
France, etc.

Abbess

Sub pl p496

Alice in Wonderland

Faw p 103-04 pl il

Amelia Bloomer

Faw p55-56 fig 39
SaiT pl p 181

Amish

Joh p265-67 il
Mls pl 59

Antonia Slagboom Bronck

Nat v94 Jl '48 pl p31 (col)

Archbishop

Joh il p251

Beau Brummel

SaiY pl p 188i

Belle Hervey

Joh il p89

Bridal party

Lew p54-67, 116-21 4 pl

Bride

Eld p76-79 3 pl (incl pat)
Faw p68-70 pl il
Lew p2-53, 72-77, 108-15, 122-29, **136-61,**
168-83 25 pl
SaiT pl p75, 161

Catherine II, empress of Russia

Faw fig 119

Catherine Adams

RobC pl p 105

Child Jesus

SaiT pl p 136

Clara Barton

Faw p62 fig 44

Clowns

Faw pl p 18 (incl pat) (f)
Fras p51-52 pl il (pat)

Court lady of England

SaiT pl p88

Crèche

Go p 12-14 il
Joh p205-09 il
Mls p22-32 pl 20-27
RobC pl p 168-69

Cyrano de Bergerac

RobC pl p 160

Dancer

Fras p39-43 3 pl (incl pat)

DOLLS—*Continued*

    Deanna Durbin
Joh il p272

    Ed Wynn
RobC pl p 161

    Edith Roosevelt
RobC pl p 105

    Eleanor of Toledo
Faw pl p 103

   Elizabeth I, queen of England
Mls pl 101

  Elizabeth, consort of George VI
Joh il p250

Elizabeth, princess of Great Britain
SaiT pl p30

  Eugénie, empress of the French
Faw fig 118

    Flower girl
Go il p41

  George VI, king of England
Joh p250-52 il

   George Washington
Joh il p243
SaiT pl p 171

    Gipsy
Joh p 187 il

    Goldilocks
RobC pl p 123

    Jenny Lind
Joh p 126-28 il p 127, 129, 136
Lew p50-53 pl
SaiT pl p73, 121

    John Bull
Joh il p252

 Joséphine, empress of the French
Faw pl p 100

    Judy Garland
Joh il p272

    Katcina
Joh p 13-14 il
Mls p63-64 pl 43
Roe pl 2 (col)

   Katrina Van Tassel
Nat v94 Jl '48 pl p31 (col)

    Kewpie
Lew p 130-35 pl

   Knight in armor
Fras p44-46 pl

    Letitia Penn
Ada v 1 il p234
Joh p63 pl p62

   Liberty doll, 1864-1865
Rob pl p201-02

    Little Bo-Peep
RobC pl p 122

   Little Lord Fauntleroy
Faw pl p 107

   Little Miss Muffet
Go pl p 14 (col)
RobC pl p 124

   Little Red Riding Hood
Go il p42
RobC pl p 122
SaiT pl p5
SaiY pl p 188j

    "Little Women"
Joh il p203

   Louise, queen of Prussia
Faw pl p 100
Joh p 129 il p 133

    Lucy Stone
SaiT pl p 181

    Mandarin
RobC pl p 187
SaiT pl p 12

Margaret, princess of Great Britain
SaiT pl p 30

   Marie Antoinette
Faw pl p 100, 103

   Marie of Burgundy
SaiT pl p 103

   Martha Washington
Faw p 111-12
Joh p 130-31 il p 122, 243
SaiT pl p 171
SaiY pl p 189

   Mary, Queen of Scots
Joh il p250

   Mary and the lamb
RobC pl p 124, 209

   Mary Todd Lincoln
RobC pl p 105

    Medieval lady
Mls pl 62

    Mennonite
Joh p265-66 il

    Monk
Go il p37

    Mormon
SaiY pl p60k

    Moses
SaiT pl p 128

    Mozart
SaiT pl p 119

    Negro
SaiY p 65-68 pl p 188e-f (f)

DOLLS—*Continued*
Negro minstrel
Fras p 20-23 2 pl (incl pat)
Nun
Joh p209 il
RobC pl p83
SaiY pl p 188d
Nurse
Go p 118-19 il
Joh il p278
Old woman who lived in a shoe
RobC p 120 il (incl pat)
Organ grinder
SaiT pl p 15
Papal guard
Go il p36
Peddler
Go p30 il
Joh p 113-14 il
Mls p74-75 pl 53
RobC pl p219 (f)
SaiT p 162-66 2 pl il
SaiY p 157-60 pl p 141, 188
Puritan
Go il p 125
SaiT p 191 il p 193
Quaker
RobC pl p213 (f)
Rhadames
Joh il p 194
Rajah
Fras p28-31 2 pl (incl pat)
Richard II, king of England
Mls pl 62
Sailor
Go pl p51
SaiT p 191 il p 193
Santa Claus
Lee p 119-20 pl
Sarah Josepha Hale
Joh il p297
SaiT pl p 181, 183
Scarlett O'Hara
Faw pl p 103
Sherlock Holmes
Joh p253-54 il
Shirley Temple
Joh il p276
Mls pl 64
Soldier
Go p43 il
Soldier (U.S. 1860-1865)
Faw p44-46 il (incl pat)
Stanley Baldwin
Joh il p252

Susan B. Anthony
SaiT pl p 183
Thomas Jefferson
RobC pl p 159
Tin soldier
Mls p50-51 pl 29-32
Tommy Tucker
SaiY pl p 188i
Victoria, queen of Great Britain
SaiT pl p 137
SaiY pl p60n
Washington Irving
Nat v94 Jl '48 pl p31 (col)
White House ladies
Faw p 109-38 il
Joh pl p200, 248-49

DOMINICAN NUNS
Doy pl 99-100 (col)
HousM p39-40 fig 50
MusE pl 23 (col)

DOMINICAN REPUBLIC
Spi pl p39 (f)

DOMINICANS
AirB il p23
BruK pl 29 fig 6 (col)
Doy pl 46 (col)
EvjD p68 il 73
HousM p38-39 fig 49
OrM pl 63-65

DOMINOES. See Fancy dress and stage costume—Domino

DOUARNENEZ. See France—Brittany

DOUBLETS. See Coats and jackets

DRAGON ROBES. See Ceremonial costume—China

DRAGOONS

Austria-Hungary
18th century
KnR pl p223

19th century
KnR pl p233 (off)
Lez pl p309, 311 (col)

England
17th century
BarH p47-48 pl 3 (col)
Law v 1 p 106-13 il

18th century
BarH p52-53 pl 4-5 (col) (off, pte)
KnR pl p369
Lez pl p 198 (col) (pte)
Law v 1 p 110 fig 74; v2 p 118-34, 145-50 il (off, pte)

DRAGOONS—England—*Continued*

19th century

BarH   p 105-06, 118, 121, 137-38   pl 8-11, 13-14 (col) (off, pte)
LavB   p31, 33-34   pl   12, 15-16   (col) (off, pte)

20th century

BarH   pl 18, 20, 23-24   (col)

France

17th century

LelD   p 153 fig 1 (pte)

18th century

BruK   pl 119 fig 8 (col)
KnR   p274-79   pl p275
LelD   p 153 fig 2 (off)

19th century

BluN   pl p204, 207, 210
Dav   v2 p821-22 il (off)
KnR   p274-79   pl p275
LelD   p 153 fig 3-5 (off)
Lez   pl   p272-73, 304 (1 col)

Germany

17th century

KnR   pl p5

18th century

KnR   pl p37, 103, 121

19th century

KnR   p35-41 pl p37, 121, 131, 139, 181, 193, 203
Lez   pl p298 (col)

Prussia

18th century

BruK   pl   120 fig 4

Russia

18th century

Lez   pl p223 (col)
KnR   pl p437

19th century

KnR   pl p437

United States

1775-1783

Kre   pl 2 (col)
Kre2   pl 3 (col)
MusM   pl 3, 26 (col)

1812-1860

Ada   v2 pl p 150
Kre   pl 13 (col) (pte)
Kre2   pl 15 (col) (pte)

DRAWERS

13th-15th centuries

CunU   p25-31 fig 2-8 (m)

16th-18th centuries

CunU   p60-61, 78, 105 fig 15, 21, 33, 46 (m)

19th century

CrH   p20-27   3 pl (f)
CunU   p 105, 110, 112-14, 127, 143, 148, 168, 176 fig 46, 50, 63, 74
LavT2   pl p140-41 (f)

20th century

Bra   pl 48 (f)
CunU   p229-31 fig 90, 104-06, 110, 116-17

DRAYMEN. See Carters and drivers

DRENTE. See Netherlands—Drente

DRESSING GOWNS

Kle   p 103 il (m)

17th century

Bart   p38-39   pl (pat) (f) fig 11
Dav   v2 p533, 535 il
LelD   p309 pl p362 fig 3-4
WilF   pl p95 (m)

18th century

Dav   v2 fig 1406 (f)
LelD   p309 il (f) pl p362 fig 5-6 (m) pl p363 fig 1 (m)
Pic   il p 167 (m)

19th century

Dav   v2 fig 2446, 2594, 2739
LelD   pl p363 (m)
Nat   v94 S '48 pl p315 (col) (m)

20th century

Kle   p 261 il (f)
LelD   p309 il (f)

DRIVERS. See Carters and drivers

DROVERS

Hungary

Lep   pl 11 (col)

DRUGGISTS. See Apothecaries

DRUIDS

AirB   il p6
AirP   il p31
Dal   v 1 p242 fig 500 (col)
Nap   il p31
VanH   pl 2

DRUM MAJORS

England

BarH   p 143   pl 12, 23 (col)
Law   v 1 p25-26 il

France

BluN   pl p 172
LelD   p400 il

Germany

Erl   pl p 128 (col)
Lez   pl p255 (col)

Russia

Lez   pl p285 (col)

Scotland

Nat   v89 My '46 pl p580

DRUMMERS

England

17th century

Law v 1 p26-28 il

18th century

BarH p75, 79 pl 5-6 (col)

France

18th century

VanH pl 9

19th century

Fro pl 14 (col)

Germany

19th century

BruK pl 123 fig 4 (col)

Lez pl p332 (col)

Indians of North America

MasB il p80

United States

18th century

Cra pl p7

19th century

Kre2 pl 6-7, 10 (col)

DRUSES

BruK pl 191 fig 3, 5 (col)

Cyr pl 8, 13 (col)

Nat v 104 Jl '53 pl p 18 (col)

TiK pl 14 fig 8 (col) (f)

DULWICH COLLEGE STUDENTS, ENGLAND

Cla pl 16

DUNGANS. See Turkestan

DUTCH CAP. See Headdress—Netherlands

DUTCH COSTUME. See Netherlands; also Fancy dress and stage costume—Dutch

DUTCH GUIANA. See Surinam

DYAK PRIESTESSES

MusE pl 2 (col)

DYAK PRIESTS

MusE pl 2 (col)

DYAKS. See Borneo

E

EAGLE DANCE. See Dancers—Indians of North America—Eagle dance

EARRINGS AND ORNAMENTS

Kle p277 il

LelD p44-45 il

Ancient

Dal v 1 fig 416-25, 481-83 (col)

Dot il p 107, 114

Hous2 fig 153

LesA p106-12 il

NeE pl 16, 20

NeG pl 1-3, 9, 14, 16, 21-23

NeM pl 2, 6

NeN p2-3 pl 6, 8, 9

RogF p26 pl

10th century—date

BraF p86 pl p82, 93-94, 173

Chr fig 355 (col)

Dal v2 fig 58-60, 151-53, 768-72 (col)

EvnJ pl 118, 138-39, fig 29

Flow pl 1 (col) fig 7, 9-12, 18-19, 52, 56-61, 64-69

LesA p 112-16 il

Norr v3 bk 2 p778 il

Pet p 62-63 pl

RogF pl p 186

African tribes

Leb pl 9 (col)

Nat v 106 O '54 il p492, 494, 500, 511 (1 col)

Borneo

Nat v88 S '45 pl p310-11

Caroline islands

Nat v81 Je '42 pl p781

Hainan

Nat v74 S '38 p400, 402 il

Indians of North America

Nat v72 N '37 p555 il

Mexico

Too il p58

Peru, Ancient

Zim p21 pl

Savage and primitive races

Rud pl p 53

Spain

AnS p57-59, 90-91, 201-02, 218-21, 258-59 fig 66-67, 105, 187, 240-41, 262-64, 311-12

EvnJ pl 118, 138-39

Sub pl p466-76

Tibet

Bin il p240 (m)

Nat v95 My '49 pl p671, 674-75 (col)

EARLY CHRISTIANS. See Rome—1st-5th centuries

ECCLESIASTICAL COSTUME

See also Buddist monks; Buddist priestesses; Jewish priests; Lamas; Mohammedan officials; Rabbis; Shinto priests; Taoist priests; also names of individual articles of attire (e.g. Footwear, Ecclesiastical; Gloves, Ecclesiastical; Headdress, Ecclesiastical)

To 9th century (Early Christian church)

AirS il p 11

HousG2 p 126, 128 il

NorC pl 3-4, 13 (2 col) fig 32, 74-76, 81, 95-96

Wa p61-62 fig 62 no 1-5 (incl pat)

ECCLESIASTICAL COSTUME—*Cont.*

Anglican and Episcopal
See also Archbishops—Anglican church; Bishops—Anglican and Episcopal churches

16th-17th centuries
Gor il p85

18th century—date
AirH il p 10
MusE pl 41, 44 (col)

Armenian church
Nat v98 D '50 pl p717 (col); v 106 D '54 il p846
See also Bishops—Armenian church

Catholic church
BruK pl 30 (col)
See also Abbesses; Abbots; Cardinals; Popes; also subdivision Catholic church under Archbishops; Bishops; Deacons; Monks; Nuns; also names of individual articles of attire (e.g. Alb, Copes, Papal tiara)

9th-12th centuries
AirB il p 15
AirS pl p47
Dav v 1 p93, 102, 110, 119, 123 4 pl il
EvjD p76 pl 82
Wa p 100 fig 95

13th century
Dav v 1 pl p 168
EvjD pl 79
HousM p 19-40 6 pl il (incl pat)
LelD p393 il

14th century
Dav v 1 p210, 230, 235 2 pl il
HousM p91-94 il
NorC p81 pl p82 fig 66, 86, 108
Wa p114 fig 112

15th century
EvjD p74-77 pl 81
HousM p 144-53 il
Nat v 101 Ja '52 pl p90-91
NorC pl 14-16 (col) fig 250
TiK pl 37 (incl pat)

16th century
TiK pl 37 (incl pat)

17th century—date
Kle p205 il
MusE pl 15-17 (col)
Nat v94 S '48 pl p314 (col)
Tru p 118-26 pl (col) il

Church of England
See Ecclesiastical costume—Anglican and Episcopal churches

Coptic church
MusE pl 13 (col)
Nat v77 Ap '40 il p468
See also Bishops—Coptic church; Monks—Coptic church; Nuns—Coptic church

Eastern church
See Ecclesiastical costume—Greek church

Ethiopic church
See Monks—Ethiopic church; Nuns—Ethiopic church

Greek church
See also Archbishops—Greek church; Bishops—Greek church; Monks—Greek church; Patriarchs—Greek Church

To 1054
BruK pl 28 fig 11-14
Gor pl p 16
Yar pl p29

1054—date
HousG2 p 162-77 4 pl il
LelD p328-29 il
MusE pl 11, 40 (col)
Nat v94 D '48 il p803, 809
TiK pl 37 fig 20

Jacobite church
See Ecclesiastical costume—Syrian church

Protestant churches
LelD p304 il
MusE pl 42-43 (col)

England—17th-18th centuries
Trev v3 fig 58, 59

Germany—16th century
BruK pl 68 fig 12 (col)

United States—17th century
Ada v 1 il p73, 113, 124
VanH pl 6

United States—18th century
Davi v 1 il p 123

Syrian church
MusE pl 14 (col)
See also Monks—Syrian church

ECCLESIASTICAL FOOTWEAR. See Footwear, Ecclesiastical

ECCLESIASTICAL GLOVES. See Gloves, Ecclesiastical

ECCLESIASTICAL HEADDRESS. See Headdress, Ecclesiastical

ECCLESIASTICAL RINGS. See Rings, Ecclesiastical

ECCLESIASTICAL VESTMENTS. See Ecclesiastical costume

ECUADOR
See also Indians of South America—Ecuador
CrO pl 26 fig 4 (f)
Hal pl 25-28 (col)
Spi pl p41 (col) (f)

EDWARD, KING. See subdivision under Kings and rulers—England

EGERLAND. See Czechoslovakia—Bohemia

EGYPT
Ancient
BartC p54-66 fig 15-21
BiE p 17 pl 3-4
Bra p 13-28 4 pl
BruK p5-6, 41-42 pl 1-4 (3 col) table 1 (pat)
Burr p4, 109-11, 184, 249, 295, 321-22 pl p5
CrO pl 2
Dal v 1 p 15-52 11 pl il (col)
Dav v 1 p 15-40 18 pl il
Dot p 103-06 il
Gen v 1 p 17-35 19 pl (2 col) table 9 fig 379 (pat)
Gor p3-7 3 pl
HeuO p 1-41 pl 1-30 (3 col) il
Hous2 p5-64, 74-106 21 pl (1 col) il (incl pat)
KerM no 1 pl 2-5
Kle p200 il (f)
Lecl pl 1 (col)
Lee p74-76 pl
LelD pl p349 fig 4-5 (f)
Lis p 13-16 il
Loud pl 1 (col)
Nat v80 O '41 p436-67, 484-510, 514 31 pl (col)
NeP p3 pl 9-10
Pot v 1 p 11-16 pl 2-4 (col)
RueG pl 18-23
TiK pl 2-4 (2 col)
UnW pl 2-4 (col)
VanH pl 1
Wa p3-18 2pl il (incl pat)
WilC p 1-6 3 pl
WilF pl p8
WisF pl 1 (f)
Wrig pt3 p 13-17 pl p26-28 (incl pat)
Yar p 1-6 3 pl
See also subdivision Egypt, Ancient under Ceremonial costume; Children; Dancers; Footwear; Hair, wigs, etc.; Headdress; Jewelry, Ancient; Kings and rulers; Military costume; Noblemen; Noblewomen; Officials; Priestesses; Priests; Queens and empresses; also under occupations (e.g. Barbers; Carpenters; Charioteers)

Modern
Brad pl p60
BruK pl 189 (col)
Nat v77 Ap '40 pl p453, 455, 461, 465, 473 (col)
TiK pl 20 fig 7, 9; pl 22-24 (col)

ELAM
HeuO pl 40-41, 43

ELEPHANT ORDER, KNIGHTS OF THE
Doy pl 151 (col)

ELIZABETHAN COSTUME. See England —Elizabeth, 1558-1603; Fancy dress and stage costume—English, 16th-17th centuries; Queens — England — Elizabeth, 1558-1603

EMBROIDERY
LesA p483-506 fig 595-97 il
Carpathian Ruthenia
Mak pl VI-VIII, X, 68, 70-88, 90-91, 99 (4 col)
Chios
Arg p73-103 pl 5-31 (col)
England
Dav v 1 fig 1194-98; v2 fig 1899, 2074, 2083
HousM p68-71, 131-38, 212-18 3 pl fig 347, 349
France
Dav v2 fig 1890-95, 1897-98, 1902, 2079-81, 2084, 2249-51, 2253
Germany
Dav v2 fig 2082
Greece, Modern
At p23-24 pl 1-49 (col)
Italy
Dav v2 fig 1896, 2075-78, 2252
United States
18th century
Dav v2 fig 2080, 2085-86

EMILIA. See Italy—Emilia

EMIRS
AirO il p45

EMMENTAL. See Switzerland—Bern

EMPERORS. See Kings and rulers

EMPIRE STYLE. See Nineteenth century —1800-1810; Nineteenth century—1810-1820

EMPRESSES. See Queens and empresses

ENGLAND
See also Fancy dress and stage costume—English; also subdivision England under Ceremonial costume; Children; Coronation robes; Court dress; Dancers; Evening dress; Hair, wigs, etc.; Military costume; Mourning costume; Naval costume; Parliamentary robes; Processions; Riding costume; Wedding costume; also names of occupations (e.g. Blacksmiths, Merchants, Physicians, Police, Servants) and individual articles of attire (e.g. Coats and jackets, Footwear, Headdress)

Ancient to 449
AirB pl p3-4, 6, 8-9
AirP pl p50
Dot p 118-19 il
VanH pl 2
Wel p 1-2 pl
WilC pl 32 (f)
Yar p34-38 3 pl
See also Druids

ENGLAND—*Continued*

Anglo-Saxon period, 449-1066

AirB pl p 12-16
Bra p 105-07 pl 14
BruK pl 35-36 (1 col)
CunM p9-19 3 pl
Dav v 1 p 113, 115, 119 il
Dot p 118-19, 122-23 il
Tru p 11-15 il
Wa p78-83 fig 79-80 (incl pat)
Wel p 1 pl p3-5
WilC pl p61 (f)
Yar p38-43 2 pl
  See also Kings and rulers—England—
  Anglo-Saxon period, 449-1066; Noble-
  men—England — 449-1066; Noblewomen
  —England—449-1066; Queens and em-
  presses—England—449-1066

Norman period, 1066-1154

AirB pl p 18-22
BrH p 16-25 4 pl (col)
BroF p 14-17 fig 6 (f)
BroH p 1-8 fig 1-3, 5, 7
BruK p54 pl 35
CunM p20-27 3 pl (1 col)
Dot p123-24 il
Gre p 18-29 2 pl
KerM no3 pl 12 (f)
Lab p34-36 pl (col) (m)
Nat v95 Ap '49 pl p452 (col)
Tru p 16-19 il
Wel p 1 pl p6
WilF pl p22-23 (m)
Yar p42-50 3 pl
  See also Kings and rulers—England—
  Norman period, 1066-1154; Noblemen—
  England—11th-12th centuries; Noble-
  women—England—11th-12th centuries;
  Queens and empresses—England—1066-
  1154

1154-1199
Henry II, 1154-1189
Richard I, 1189-1199

AirM pl p9
BrH p28-29 pl (col) (f)
BroF fig 6 front (col)
BroH p 1-18 fig 4, 6-13
BruK pl 36 fig 4-5 (col) (f)
CunM p28-41 5 pl
Dav v 1 p 130-33 2 pl il
Dot p 126-27 il
Gre p30-35 pl
HousM fig 1-2 (pat)
Wel p 1 pl p7
Yar p51-57 3 pl
  See also Kings and rulers—England—
  12th century; Noblemen—England—11th-
  12th centuries; Noblewomen—England—
  11th-12th centuries; Queens and em-
  presses—England—12th century

13th century

BroF fig 7-9
BroH p 18-28 pl p39 (col) fig 14-17
BruK pl 36 fig 6 (col) (f)
CrO pl 41
CunM p42-54 7 pl
Dav v 1 p 175-76 il
Dot p 129-31 il

HousM p 1-17, 41-53 pl 1-2 (col)
  il (incl pat)
Tru p20-25 il
Wel p 1 pl p8
Yar p54-57 1 pl
  See also subdivision England- –13th
  century under Kings and rulers; Noblemen; Noblewomen; Queens and empresses

John, 1199-1216

BrH p30-33 2 pl (col)
Gre p30-35 pl
Nat v95 Ap '49 pl p457 (col)
Tru p20-21 il
  See also Kings and rulers—England—
  John, 1199-1216

Henry III, 1216-1272

BrH p30-33 2 pl (col)
Gre p36-40 pl
Tru p21-23 il
Yar p57-63 3 pl
  See also Kings and rulers—England—
  Henry III, 1216-1272

Edward I, 1272-1307

BrH p34-37 2 pl (col)
Tru p25-28 il
Yar p63-69 2 pl
  See also Kings and rulers—England—
  Edward I, 1272-1307; Queens and em-
  presses—England—1272-1307

14th century

Ab p 152-72 2 pl
AirB pl p27
BroH p28-42 fig 18-29 (1 col)
BruK pl 36 fig 7-13 (col)
CunM p55-97 22 pl
Dav v 1 p 192-215 18 pl il
Dot p 133-34 il
HousM p72-88, 95-121 10 pl (3 col)
  (incl pat)
Nat v95 Ap '49 pl p459 (col)
TiK pl 118 fig 28-29 (f)
Wel p 1 pl p9
WilC p57-61 2 pl
  See also subdivision England—14th
  century under Kings and rulers; Noble-
  men; Noblewomen; Queens and em-
  presses

Edward II, 1307-1327

BrH p38-41 2 pl (col)
Gre p41-47 pl
Yar p63-69 2 pl
  See also Kings and rulers—England—
  Edward II, 1307-1327

Edward III, 1327-1377

BrH p42-45 2 pl (col)
BroF fig 10-11
Gre p41-47 pl
Tru p24-28 il
Yar p67-82 5 pl (1 col)
  See also Kings and rulers—England—
  Edward III, 1327-1377

Richard II, 1377-1399

BrH p46-49 2 pl (col)
Gre p48-53 pl

ENGLAND—14th century—Richard II, 1377-1399—*Continued*
HousM p 109-21 2 pl (1 col) il
Tru p29-33 il
Yar p74-82 5 pl (1 col)
See also Kings and rulers—England—Richard II, 1377-1399

15th century

Ab p 152-72 2 pl
AirB pl p27
BroH p46-61 pl (col) fig 37-46, 53
BruK pl 36 fig 14-20 (col)
Burr p 14, 119-20, 324 pl p 15
CunA front (col)
CunM p98-168 37 pl (2 col)
Dav v 1 p349-59 8 pl il
Dot p 137-38 il
HousM p 139-42, 159-98 4 pl (1 col) il (pat)
Pric p 14-20 pl (m)
Set p 14-17 il
Tru p34-48 2 pl (1 col) il
Wel p 1 pl p 10
WilC pl p60-61
WilF p44-45 il (m)
Yar p95-99 4 pl
See also subdivision England—15th century under Kings and rulers; Noblemen; Noblewomen

Henry IV, 1399-1413

BrH p50-53 2 pl (col)
Gre p53-55 fig 6
Tru p34-38 il
Yar p83-92 2 pl
See also Kings and rulers—England—Henry IV, 1399-1413

Henry V, 1413-1422

BrH p54-57 2 pl (col)
Gre p53-55 fig 6
Yar p83-92 2 pl

Henry VI, 1422-1461

Ab p 158-62 2 pl
BrH p58-61 2 pl (col)
BroF pl p 16 (col) fig 12
CunA pl 5
Gre p56-61 pl
Yar p83-92 5 pl
See also Queens and empresses—England—1422-1461

Edward IV, 1461-1483

BrH p62-65 **2 pl** **(col)**
Gre p60-66 pl
Yar p93-99 5 pl (1 col)

Richard III, 1483-1485

BrH p66-69 2 pl (col)
Gre p67-69 pl
LavR pl p21 (f)
Yar p93-99 4 pl

Henry VII, 1485-1509

BrH p70-73 2 pl (col)
Gor p40-43, 46-48 5 pl (1 col)
Gre p67-74 pl
LavE pl 7-8
LavR pl p25 (m)

Norr v3 bk 1 p72-87 il
Tru p44-48 pl (col) il
WilC p 118-20 pl p 123-24
Yar p 100-07 3 pl
See also Kings and rulers—England—Henry VII, 1485-1509; Queens and empresses—England—1485-1509

16th century

BroH p61-69 fig 47-65, 70
CrO pl 41
Dav v 1 p426-54 3 pl il
Dot p 143-47 il
Pric p21-32 2 pl (m)
Wel p 1 pl p 11-12
WilF pl p58-59
See also subdivision England—16th century under Kings and rulers; Noblemen; Noblewomen

Henry VIII, 1509-1547

BosE pl 28
BrH p74-77 2 pl (col)
BroF pl p33 (col) fig 16
BruK pl 71
Burr p20, 78-79, 123-24, 202, 258-59, 298 pl p21
CunA pl 7a (f)
CunS p 17-86 pl 1-33, 56, 59
Eth p27-31 pl
Gor p42-43 pl p49-50
Gre p75-83 pl
LavE pl 21-22, 25-26, 31-41, 44-46, 49, 51 (5 col)
LavR pl p6-9, 45-47, 52, 54, 56 (2 col)
Nat v95 Ap '49 pl p463 (col)
Norr v3 bk 1 p 154-62, 166-67, 176-80, 187-88, 190-91, 194-98, 207-17, 232-40, 253-72, 278-310 12 pl (5 col) il (incl pat)
Set p 18-20 pl il (f)
Tru p49-53 il
UnW pl 32-36 (col)
Vert pl p51 (col) (f)
WilC p 120-24 2 pl
Yar p 107-17 6 pl (1 col)
See also Kings and rulers—England—Henry VIII, 1509-1547; Queens and empresses—England—1509-1547

Edward VI, 1547-1553

BrH p78-81 2 pl (col)
CunA pl 9 (m)
CunS pl 36 (m)
Gor p43 pl p52
Gre p81-85 pl
LavR pl p53
Norr v3 bk 2 p389-96, 414-19, 424-29 3 pl (1 col) il (incl pat)
Set pl p9 (col) (m)
Yar p 118-23 2 pl
See also Kings and rulers—England—Edward VI, 1547-1553

Mary, 1553-1558

BrH p78-81 2 pl (col)
Gre p81-85 pl
LavR pl p53, 60 (f)
Norr v3 bk 2 p438-45 3 pl (1 col) il

ENGLAND—16th century—Mary, 1553-1558
—*Continued*
WilC p 126-27 pl p 133 (f)
Yar p 118-23 2 pl

See also Queens and empresses—England—Mary, 1553-1558

Elizabeth, 1558-1603

BosE pl 26, 28
BrH p82-85 2 pl (col)
BroF fig 20-21
BroH p77-99 fig 57-65, 70
BruK pl 82
Burr p22, 80-81, 125-26 pl p23
CunS p87-189 front (col) pl 37-55, 57-58, 60-72
DeB p 141-207 21 pl (incl front)
Eth p31-36 2 pl (incl pat)
Gor p43-44 pl p56-62
Gre p86-92 pl
Hat p23-24, 198-204 fig 145-56
KelF p8-49 pl p63, 65
LavR p 129-37, 150-73 24 pl (5 col)
Lee p94-97 pl
Lint p 176-215 front pl 6-8, 10, 12, 14
Nat v93 Ap '48 pl p443 (col); v95 Ap '49 pl p465, 467
Norr v3 bk 2 p690-720 il
Pic il p48 (f)
Rey p5-13, 15-20 pl 1-26, 29, 31 (6 col)
Set p20-24 il (f)
Tru p54-58 il
UnW pl 38-46
WilC p 127-33 2 pl
WilF pl p68 (f)
Yar p 123-37 6 pl (1 col)

See also Queens and empresses—England—Elizabeth, 1558-1603

17th century

Ada v 1 il p53, 84, 87, 90, 123
AirB il p49 (f)
BroH p 100 fig 66-69, 71
Burr p34, 212-13, 329-30 pl p35
Dav v2 p560-600 11 pl il
Dot p 153-56 il
KerM no5 pl 1
KerR pl 12
NeEu pl 11 (f)
Pric p33-49 4 pl (m)
Set p24-30 2 pl (1 col)

See also Noblemen — England — 17th century; Noblewomen — England — 17th century

James I, 1603-1625

AirT pl p45
BosE pl 8 (m)
BrH p86-89 2 pl (col)
Dav v 1 front (col) (m)
Gor pl p71
Gre p92-96 pl
Hat fig 141-44 (m)
LavR pl p173-88 (2 col)
Rey p7-13, 19-21 pl 26-38 (3 col)
Roj p2-5 3 pl il (incl pat)
TiK pl 125 fig 1-2, 5, 7 (col)
Tru p56-58 il
ViP v 1 pl 1-7

WilC p 149-56 2 pl
Yar p 138-46 3 pl

See also Kings and rulers—England—James I, 1603-1625; Queens and empresses—England—1603-1625

Charles I, 1625-1649

AirT pl p45
BrH p 90-93 2 pl (col)
BroF pl p48 (col) fig 23-24
BroH p 101-13 fig 72-79A
Bruh p42-43 pl (col)
BruK p23-24, 70 pl 96 (f)
CunA pl 7b, 14
Gor p66 pl p74-75, 77, 80
Gre p96-98 fig 13
Loud pl 13 (col)
Roj p6-27 17 pl il (incl pat)
Tru p59-63 pl (col) il
UnW pl 47-51 (col)
ViP v 1 pl 8-11 (m)
Wel p 1, 26 pl p 13
WilC p 149-56 2 pl
WilFo p 115 (f)
Yar p 146-54 4 pl (1 col)

See also Kings and rulers—England—Charles I, 1625-1649; Puritans; Queens and empresses—England—1625-1649

Commonwealth, 1649-1660

BrH p94-97 2 pl (col)
Gre p99-104 pl
Roj p28-31 3 pl il (incl pat)
Tru p64-67 il
UnW pl 52 (col)
WilC p 158-60 pl
Yar p 154-59 2 pl

See also Kings and rulers—England—Cromwell, 1649-1660; Puritans

Charles II, 1660-1685

AirT pl p58
BrH p98-101 2 pl (col)
BroF fig 26-27
BroH p 114-24 fig 79-86
Eth p37-43 3 pl (incl pat)
Gre p 104-08 pl
Roj p32-35 3 pl il (incl pat)
SitC pl 4-5
Tru p68-71 pl (col) il
UnW pl 53-64 (col)
VanH pl 4
ViP v 1 pl 14-15 (m)
Wel p26 pl p 14
WilC p 184-91 2 pl
Yar p 159-67 3 pl

See also Kings and rulers—England—Charles II, 1660-1685; Queens—England—1660-1685

James II, 1685-1689

AirT pl p58
BrH p 102-05 2 pl (col)
BroF fig 28 (f)
BroH p 125-33 fig 87-88
Gre p 108-11 pl
Lab p54-56 pl (col) (m)
Nat v95 Ap '49 pl p470 (col) (m)

ENGLAND—17th century—James II, 1685-1689—*Continued*
Roj p36-39 3 pl il (incl pat)
WilC p 184-91 2 pl
Yar p 159-67 3 pl

William and Mary, 1689-1702
AirT pl p58
Bart p34-37 2 pl (pat) (f) fig 10
BrH p 106-09 2 pl (col)
BroF pl p65 (col) fig 29-30 (m)
BroH p 130-33 fig 90, 92
Dav v2 p599 il (f)
Gre p 110-13 pl
Lab p50-60 pl (col) (m)
Roj p40-42 2 pl il (incl pat)
Tru p72-75 il
Wel p26 pl p 15
Yar p 167-73 3 pl
See also Queens and empresses—England—1689-1702

18th century
Burr p42, 93-94, 135-39, 214-17, 331-32 pl p43 (m)
Dav v2 p736-68, 770, 772-86 10 pl il
Dot p 159-63 il
Eth p43-45 pl
Lab p69-77 2 pl (col) (m)
Nat v95 Ap '49 pl p491-92
NeEu pl 12-13, 16 (f)
Set p30-36 3 pl (2 col) il
SitC 104 pl (2 col)
SitN pl 2, 25-27, 29-35, 39-40, 43, 52-56, 58-65, 67-77, 79-81 (1 col)
Trev v3 pl p30 (col) fig 36-37
See also Noblemen—England—18th century; Noblewomen—England—18th century

Anne, 1702-1714
AirT pl p58
BrH p 110-13 2 pl (col)
Gre p 114-19 pl
Lab p62-64 pl (col) (m)
Lis il p63 (f)
Tru il p74 (f)
Yar p 167-72 2 pl
See also Queens and empresses—England—Anne, 1702-1714

George I, 1714-1727
AirB pl p52
AirH pl p 10
BrH p 110-13 2 pl (col)
BroF fig 31 (f)
BroH p 133-37 fig 91, 93-94
Gor pl p 104
Gre p 119-20 fig 17
Lab p66-68 pl (col) (m)
Tru p74-75 il (f)
ViP v2 p 1-2 pl 1 (m)
Yar p 174-80 4 pl (1 col)

George II, 1727-1760
AirH pl p 10
BrH p 114-17 2 pl (col)
BroF fig 32, 34
BroH p 136-44 pl p 151 (col) fig 95-97
CunA pl 17-20
Gor p98 pl p 108, 110-11, 113

Gre p 120-25 pl
Lel v 11 pl 3, 15, 21, 35, 39 (2 col)
Tru p76-80 pl (col) il
ViP v2 pl 2-8
Wel p26 pl p 16
Yar p 180-88 4 pl
See also Queens and empresses—England—1727-1760

George III, 1760-1820
AirB pl p56
AirH pl p 19
BrH p 118-25 4 pl (col)
BroF fig 35, 37-40
BroH p 145-72 fig 98-111
BruK p29 pl 118
CunA pl 21-23, 25
Dav v2 p770, 772-88, 790-92 il
Gor p 100-01 pl p 117, 119-20, 123
Gre p 126-36 2 pl
Lab p74-85 3 pl (col) (m)
Lel v 12 pl 1, 18-19, 30, 32, 38 (2 col)
Lis p67-76 il
MooC p26-29 2 pl (f)
Pric p60-81 4 pl (m)
Tru p81-84 il
ViP v2 p 1-2 pl 9-20
Wel p26 pl p 17
WilC p257-69 4 pl
WilF pl p 117-18
Yar p 189-211 10 pl (2 col)
See also Macaronis; Nineteenth century—1800-1810; Nineteenth century—1810-1820; Queens and empresses—England—1760-1820

1820—date
See Kings and rulers—England—Edward VII, 1901-1910; Nineteenth century—1820-date; Queens and empresses—England—Victoria, 1837-1901; Queens and empresses—England—Elizabeth II, 1953-

EPAULETS
LelD p 161-62 il

EPISCOPAL CHURCH. See Ecclesiastical costume — Anglican and Episcopal churches

EQUESTRIAN COSTUME. See Riding costume

ERIE INDIANS. See Indians of North America—Erie Indians

ESCOFFION. See Headdress—Europe—16th century

ESKIMOS
Brad pl p78-79, 113
BruK p96 pl p 200 (col)
CrP pl 4 (f)
EvnH p48-53 pl il (pat)
Gen v 1 fig 30 (m)
Nat v82 S '42 pl p376 (col) (f); v90 O '46 il p470 (f) pl p496 (col) (f); v96 O '49 pl p486, 564; v 100 O '51 pl p479 (col) (f)

ESKIMOS—*Continued*
  Prim p26-32 4 pl
  Seto p 15-19 pl 3-4 (incl pat)
  WilF pl p 163-64

    See also Lapland; also subdivision Eskimos under Children; Coats and jackets; Footwear; Headdress

ESTHER (BIBLICAL CHARACTER).
  See Biblical costume—Esther

ESTONIA
  Brad pl p62 (f)
  BruK pl 166 fig 2, 7, 14 (f)
  Int v2 pl 29-30
  Nat v76 D '39 p 815-16, 820, 832 pl il

    See also Dancers—Estonia; Headdress —Estonia

ESTREMADURA. See Spain—Estremadura

ESTUNA. See Sweden—Uppland

ESTRUN NUNS
  Doy pl 127 (col)

ETHIOPIA
          Ancient
  Brad pl p 17-18

    See also Priests—Ethiopia, Ancient

          Modern
  TiK pl 24 fig 3, 5-6 (col) (m)

ETHIOPIC CHURCH. See Ecclesiastical costume—Ethiopic church

ETLA. See Mexico—Oaxaca

ETON COLLEGE STUDENTS
  Cla p25-27 pl
  Kle p 111 il

ETRURIA
  BruK p9, 47 pl 16
  Dav v 1 p54-55 il
  Dot p 112 il
  HousG2 p83-86 il
  Nat v90 N '46 p570, 572 (col)
  Pot v 1 p25 pl 9 (col)
  RueG pl 10-11 (m)
  WilFo p26 pl p27

    See also subdivision Etruria under Hair, wigs, etc.; Headdress; Jewelry, Ancient; Military costume

EUBOEA ISLAND
  At pl 30-33 (col) (f)

EUNUCHS
          Assyria and Babylonia
  BartC p 68 fig 22

          Korea
  Keit pl p64E

EUROPE
    See also various European countries, e.g. England, France, Germany; also subdivision Europe under Breeches; Children; Footwear; Hair, wigs, etc.; Headdress; Military costume; Musicians; Noblewomen

          To 476
  BruK table 5 (pat)
  CrP pl 3
  Dal v 1 p279-307 2 pl il (col)
  Dot p 116-18 il
  Kle p258 il (m)
  Lab pl 2-3 (col) (m)
  May pl p 10 (m)
  VanH pl 2
  Wa p66-83 2 pl (incl pat) il

          8th century
  VanH pl 2

          9th century
  Gor p 19-20 pl p23 (m)

          10th century
  Lis p28-33 il (m)

          11th century
  BruK table 6 (pat)
  Dal v2 p9-21 il (col)
  Gor p20 pl p2, 23
  TiK pl 117 fig 4 (f)
  Wa p95-97, 101-02 fig 90-92, 103 (incl pat)

          12th century
  Bra p 117-24 pl 15-18
  BruK table 6 (pat)
  Dal v2 p21-57 4 pl il (col)
  LelD p36 il
  Lis p28-33 il (f)
  Pic il p 132 (f)
  TiK pl 117 fig 10-12
  UnW pl 21-24 (col)
  VanH pl 3
  Wa p98-100, 102-03 fig 92C, 104 (incl pat) pl p 106
  WisF pl 6 (f)

          13th century
  Bra p124-29 pl 15-18
  BroW v 1 p 17-41 11 pl (3 col) il
  BruK table 6 (pat)
  Dal v2 p59-98 3 pl il (col)
  HousM front (col)
  Lis p34-37 il (m)
  TiK pl 118 (incl pat)
  VanH pl 3
  Wa p 100-01, 103-04 fig 90, 96
  WisF pl 7 (f)

          14th century
  Bra p 137-42 pl 19-22
  BroW v 1 p42-63 16 pl (3 col) il
  BruK table 7 (pat)
  Dal v2 p99-142 2 pl il (col)
  EvnR p30-31 pl 6 (incl pat) (f)
  Gor p20-21 pl p27
  HousM p72-82 2 pl il (pat)
  Kle p414 il (m)
  Lis p34-37 il (f)
  Pic il p98, 132 (f)

EUROPE—14th century—*Continued*
TiK pl 120 (col)
UnW pl 25-28 (col)
VanH pl 3
Wa p 107-19 2 pl (incl pat) il
WisF pl 8 (f)

15th century
Bra p 142-47 pl 19-22
Brow v 1 p64-105 24 pl (5 col) il
BruK table 7 (pat)
BruM p9-16 4 pl (3 col)
Dal v2 p 143-200 pl il (col) (incl pat)
Eth p20-26 2 pl
EvnR p30-31, 34-36 pl 6, 8 (incl pat) (f)
Gor p21-22 pl p28-33
HousM p 139-42 il (pat)
Kle p414 il (f)
Lis p38-42 il
TiK pl 120 (col)
UnW pl 29-30 (col)
VanH pl 3
Wa p 122-36 2 pl il (incl pat)
WisF pl 9 (f)

16th century
Bra p 153-76 4 pl
BroW v 1 p 106-51 36 pl (5 col) il
BruK table 7 (pat)
BruM p 16-24 3 pl (1 col) (f)
Dal v2 p201-58 pl il (col) (incl pat)
EvnR p36 pl 8 (incl pat) (f)
Gor p41-44 pl p46-54
Kle p 142 il (m)
LavE pl 11-52 (7 col)
LavR p 21-60, 63-126 75 pl (8 col)
Lis p43-51 pl il
Pic il p 132 (f)
Wa p 139-69 3 pl il (incl pat)
WisF pl 10-11 (f)

17th century
Bra p 176-206 7 pl
BroW v2 p26-72 5 pl (col) il
BruK table 7 (pat)
BruM p24-32 pl p23, 25-26, 28, 33 (3 col)
Dal v2 p259-341 il (col)
EvnR p50 pl 11 (incl pat) (f)
Gor p65-94 23 pl il
LelD pl p353-54 (f)
Lis p52-61 2 pl il
Wa p173-204 5 pl il (incl pat)
WisF pl 12-13 (f)

18th century
Bra p207-255 10 pl
BroW v2 p86-129 9 pl (col) il
BruK table 7 (pat)
Dal v2 p343-414 2 pl il (col) (incl pat)
EvnR p50 pl 11 (incl pat) (f)
Gor p96-126 23 pl (1 col) il
Lel v 11 pl 5-6 (1 col); v 12 pl 10, 25 (col)
Lis p62-71 il
TiK pl 126 (col) (incl pat)
Wa p209-40 2 pl il (incl pat)
WisF pl 14-17 (f)

19th century
See Nineteenth century

20th century
See Twentieth century

EVENING CLOAKS
19th century
HaC pl p 64b
Kou pl 13 (f)
WilF pl p 148, 150-51

20th century
WilF pl p 183, 185, 187, 189, 194-95, 197, 207

1900-1910
CunPr pl p50, 72 il p61
Mo p 159 il (f)
WilC pl p352 (f)
WilF pl p 166 (f)

1910-1920
Mo p169, 173 il (f)
WilC pl p363 (f)

1920-1930
AlF pl p55-57 (f)
KerA pl p57 (f)
WilC pl p376 (f)

1930-1940
Bra pl 42

1940-1950
Kle p 13 il (f)

EVENING DRESS
Kle p91-95 pl il
LavT p 181-92 pl (f)

16th century
BluL p24, 26 pl 50-52, 64 (1 col)
LavR pl p 112-13, 123 (1 col)

17th century
BluE p26 pl 54

18th century
Dav v2 p677-78 il (f)
Lis il p63 (f)
Pann v 1 pl 16-17, 21 (col)

19th century
Amer pl 1, 4, 7-8, 12 (col) (f)

1800-1810
BroH fig 111 (f)
CunA pl 23
CunE p38-43, 45-46, 48 pl p33, 38-39, 42-43, 49 (f)
ViN fig 12 (f)

1810-1820
CunE p44-50 pl p 16, 51, 63, 66 (1 col) (f)
Dav v2 fig 2242 (f)
LavT pl p 114 (f)
LavT2 pl p97 (f)
ViN fig 14, 17-18 (f)
WilC pl p250 (m)

1820-1830
CunE p51-52, 79-80, 82-89 pl p67, 78-79, 86-87, 91, 96 (f)
CunP pl p 11 (col) (f)
LavF p24 pl 3 (col) (f)

EVENING DRESS—19th century—1820-
1830—*Continued*
LavT2 pl p39 (f)
ViN fig 27 (f)
WilC pl p250 (m)
Yar pl p201

1830-1840
CunE p 111-21 pl p 119, 129 (f)
Dot p 167 il
LavF p25-26 pl 5 (col) (f)
LavT2 pl p42
Pann v3 pl 19 (col) (f)
ViN fig 33, 37 (f)

1840-1850
BrH pl p 135 fig 3 (col) (m)
CunE p 137-44, 149-54 3 pl (f)
CunP pl p24 (col) (f)
Flow fig 4 (f)
LavT2 p 46-47, 146-47 pl p 46
Rue fig N 1 (f)
ViN fig 43
WilF pl p 137 (f)

1850-1860
Ada v3 il p56
Bruh pl p79 (col)
CunE p 172, 175, 178-79, 185-86, pl
    p 181, 189, 193 il (f)
Dav v2 p883 il (f)
Flow fig 5 (f)
LavF p27 pl 9 (col) (f)
NeV pl 17 (f)
ViN fig 55-56, 58
WilC pl p288, 302 (m)

1860-1870
CunE p209, 213-14, 220-23, 225, 228-29,
    232 3 pl il (f)
Dav v2 p899-901, 932 4 pl
Flow fig 48 (f)
Mer fig 39 (f)
Mo p73, 80 pl 27, 33 (f)
NeV pl 17-18, 20, 22-23 (f)
Pann v4 pl 14 (col) (f)
ViN fig 60, 62-63, 67-68 (f)

1870-1880
Bart p78-79 pl (pat) (m)
BruK pl 126 (f)
CunA pl 38 (f)
CunE p260, 263, 269, 272, 274, 278, 281,
    285, 288-89, 294 pl p258, 270, 304 il
    (f)
CunP p48 pl (col) (f)
KerA pl p 19 (f)
LavF p29 pl 14 (col) (f)
QuV fig 143 (f)
Trev v4 fig 105
Wa fig 241 (m)

1880-1890
CunE p319-20, 323-24, 327, 329-30, 332-
    33, 337-38, 341-42, 345-48, 350-51 2 pl
    il (f)
CunU fig 83 (m)
HaC pl 56b (f)
Mo p 106, 116 pl 50, 59 (f)
Rud pl p58 (f)
Tru il p 103 (f)
WilC pl p302 (m)

1890-1900
Bart p90-93 2 pl (pat) (f) fig 37-38
CunE p372-74, 377-78, 383, 388-89, 393,
    397-98, 401-02, 405-06, 410 pl p373,
    381, 397, 404, 412-13 il (f)
Flow fig 96 (f)
Gern pl 66-67 (f)
HaC pl p80
Lab pl 22 (col) (m)
Mo p 123-24, 130, 133, 141 pl 63-64,
    70-72, 78 (f)
VanH pl 11
ViN fig 90, 96 (f)
WilC pl p324, 326 (f)
WilF pl p 149 (f)

20th century
1900-1910
Ada v4 il p333 (f)
BrH pl p 145 fig 9 (col) (f)
Bro20 p 19 il
CunPr p34-35, 43-45, 50, 56-57 pl p31,
    60, 96 (1 col) il (f)
HaC pl p92 (f)
KerA pl p44
Kle p29 il (f)
LavS p55 pl 29 (f)
LavT2 p 148-49 pl p 160 (f)
LelD p209 il (m)
Mo p 145, 150, 154, 159 pl 80, 85, 89,
    93 il (f)
NeV pl 53, 56-60 (f)
Rud pl p37
VanH pl 12
WilC p336 pl p339 (m)

1910-1920
CunPr p 100-94, 109, 122, 131, 135, 138,
    143-44, 154-55 pl p96-97, 108, 120,
    152 il (f)
Mo p 164, 169 pl 100-01 (f)
VanH pl 12 (f)
WilC pl p362 (f)
Yar pl p250, 254

1920-1930
BroW v2 fig 73, 76 (f)
CunA pl 45 (f)
CunPr p 160-62, 166, 170, 174, 178, 185,
    193, 196-97, 203-04 2 pl il (f)
HaC pl 120b, 128b, 128d (f)
KerA pl p57 (f)
Kle p 12 il (f)
Mo p 174 pl 107 (f)
WisF pl 27 (f)
Wom p2-3 il (f)
Yar pl p265 (f)

1930-1940
BrH pl p 147 fig 10 (m)
Bro20 p62-63, 75-77 il
CrP front (f)
CunPr p212-14, 218, 222-24, 229-30, 234-
    37, 241, 244-46, 252, 255-56, 261 7 pl
    il (f)
HaC pl p 144-45, 153, 160-61 (f)
Kle p 13 il (f)
LavT2 p 150-51 pl p 160 (f)
Nat v76 N '39 pl p616 (col) (f)
WilC p336 pl p338-39 (m)
WisF pl 28 (f)
Yar pl p267, 269, 271, 273

EVENING DRESS—20th century—*Continued*
1940-1950
CunA pl 48 (f)
CunPr p267, 271, 273-74, 280, 286-87, 289-90, 292 4 pl (f)
Kle p 12, 59, 125, 401 il
WilC p336 pl p339 (m)
WisF pl 29 (f)
Yar pl p275-76, 278

United States
18th century
VanH pl 8

19th century
KerM no4 pl 6 (f)
Kou pl 79, 228
Part pl p64-65 il

EVZONES. See Military costume—Greece, Modern

EXORCIST
Catholic church
NorC p31 pl p30

EYE SHADES
LelD p 1 il

EYEGLASSES AND LORGNETTES
LelD p34, 246 il
Norr v3 bk 2 p570-71 il
Rud pl p46-47, 96-97, 99

F

FAIRIES. See Fancy dress and stage costume—Fairy

FALCONERS
England
14th century
Ab pl p231
19th century
Walk pl 30 (col)
India
RueO pl 15

FALLING BANDS. See Neckwear—Europe—17th century (m)

FAME (SYMBOLICAL FIGURE)
BluE p27 pl 66

FAN BEARERS
Egypt, Ancient
Hous2 p61-63 fig 69

FANCY DRESS AND STAGE COSTUME
See also Biblical costume; Shakespearian costume
Angel
BartC p 114-16 fig 40
Hea p 12-13 pl
NorC pl p28
Wrig pt2 p 14-16 pl p20-21 (incl pat)

Animal
Hea p66-69 2 pl (pat)
Arabian Nights characters
Lee p68-70 pl
Bird
Dab pl 2
Hea p 70-71 (pat)
Lil p28 il (incl pat)
Bishop
Hea p50-51 pl
Brownie
Lil p33 il (incl pat)
Butterfly
Dab pl 6
Hea p72-73 (pat)
Cat
Dab pl 7
Christmas Joy
Dab pl 4 (f)
Christmas tree
Dab pl 4 (f)
Clown
Dab pl 1, 3
Hea p52-53, 80-81 2 pl (incl pat)
Lee p5, 118-19 2 pl (incl pat)
Lil p 1 il (incl pat)
See also Clowns and jesters; Dolls—Clown
Courtier (English)
Wel pl p23
Crusader
Wel pl p 18
Cyrano de Bergerac
Lee p98-99 pl
Daniel Boone
Lee p 109-11 pl
Devil
Lee p86-87 pl
Dickens' character
Barnaby Rudge
Wel pl p29

David Copperfield
Wel pl p29

Mr Bumble
Wel pl p29

Mr Pickwick
Wel pl p29

Mrs Gamp
Wel pl p29
See also period divisions under Nineteenth century from 1800 to 1830
Dolly Varden
CunE p262 il
Pic il p43

FANCY DRESS AND STAGE COSTUME
—Continued

Domino

LelD p 152 il (m)
Pic   il p98

Donkey

Lil   p30-31 il (incl pat)

Dormouse

Lil   p29 il (incl pat)

Dwarf

Hea   p20-21 pl
Lee   p 121-22 pl
Pic   il p54

Elf

Dab   pl 7
Lee   p 121-22 pl

Fairy

Dab   pl 6
Hea   p80-81 (pat)
Lee   p 121-22 pl
Lil   p34 il (incl pat)

Fairy tale character

Lee   p 113-14, 120-23 2 pl
Saun p69-79 il (incl pat)

Fairy tale prince

Lee   p94-95 pl

Flower

Dab   pl 2
Hea   p74-77 2 pl (incl pat)

Folly

LelD p 179 il (f)

Friar Tuck

Lee   pl p87

George Washington

Lee   p 108-09 pl

Ghost

Lee   p 119-20 pl

Gilbert and Sullivan character

Wel   pl p32-33

Gipsy

Dab   pl 25

Gnome

Dab   pl 3

Goblin

Dab   pl 3

Green Mountain boy

Dab   pl 18

Guinevere

Lee   p83-84 pl

Hansel and Gretel

Lee   p83-85 pl

Harlequin

BruK pl 102 fig 3 (col); pl 103 fig 4
Hea   pl p83 (pat)
Lee   p 118-19 pl

Heidi

Lee   pl p67

Herald

Dab   pl 7

Hiawatha

Lee   p 104 pl p 101

Jack Frost

Hea   p80-81 (pat)

Joan of Arc

Pic   il p54

John Bull

LelD p57 il

Kate Greenaway child

Dab   pl 10
Lee   p 113-14 pl
Pic   il p85 (f)

King

Dab   pl 9

King of Hearts

Dab   pl 7

Knight

Hea   p52-3 pl
Lil   p2-3 il (incl pat)

Little Lord Fauntleroy

WilFo pl p 150

Little Red Riding Hood

Pic   il p55

Lord Dundreary

QuV   fig 98

McGuffey boy and girl

Dab   pl 10

Maid Marian

Lee   pl 91

Medieval king

Hea   p 12-13 pl
Wel   pl p 18

Medieval lady

Lil   p4-5 il (incl pat)

Medieval queen

Hea   p 12-13 pl
Wel   pl p21

Mermaid

Saun p 125-27 il (pat)

Miss Liberty

Dab   pl 5

Miss United States

Dab   pl 5

Mrs Santa Claus

Dab   pl 4

Morris dancer

Wel   pl p22

Moth

Dab   pl 2

Mother Goose character

Lee   p 113-14 pl

Negro mammy

Dab   pl 15

FANCY DRESS AND STAGE COSTUME
—Continued

Negro uncle
Dab pl 15

Neptune
Nat v76 N '39 pl p578 (col)

Page, Medieval
Hea p 10-11 pl
Wel pl p22

Peasant
Hea p 10-11, 18-19 2 pl
Pic il p 109 (f)

Peter Pan
Lee p 123 pl p 121
Pic il p54, 72

Pied Piper of Hamelin
Lee p83-85 pl

Pierrette
Hea pl p83 (pat)
Lee p 118-19 pl
Pic il p55

Pierrot
BruK pl 102-03 (1 col)
Dab pl 1
Hea pl p83 (pat)
Kin pl p64
Lee p 118-19 pl
LelD p317 il

Pioneer
Dab pl 14, 18
Hea p 18-19 pl
Lil p 12-13 il (incl pat)

Pirate
Lee p 123 pl 121
Lil p26-27 il (incl pat)

Pocahontas
Lee p 104 pl p 101
Pic il p55

Polichinelle
BruK pl 103 fig 7
LelD p325 il

Prince
Dab pl 9

Prince Charming
Dab pl 7

Princess
Dab pl 9

Puritan
Lil p6-9 il (incl pat)
Wel pl p22, 23

Robin Hood
Dab pl 9
KerM no 3 pl 7
Lee p85, 90-93 pl p87, 91
Lil p 18-19 il (incl pat)
Pic il p55, 73

Rooster
Hea p70-71 (pat)

Sailor
Saun p 115 pl p 116

Santa Claus
Pic il p55

Scapin
BruK pl 103 fig 8

Scaramouche
BruK pl 103 fig 1

Shepherd
Hea p 10-11 pl
Lil p 19, 22 il (incl pat)

Sir Walter Raleigh
Tru il p54
Wel pl p21

Snow White
Pic il p55

Soldier
Saun p94-98, 114-15 il

Soldier (Celtic)
Hea p 10-11 pl

Soldier (Confederate States)
Dab pl 18 (off)

Soldier (Saxon)
Hea p 10-11 pl

Soldier (Union soldier)
Dab pl 18 (off, pte)

Strawberry
Hea p78-79 (pat)

Tiger
Lil p32 il (incl pat)

Tin soldier
Dab pl 3

Tom Jones
Dav v2 p784-85 il

Toy soldier
Hea p 18-19 pl

Uncle Sam
Dab pl 5

Valentine
Saun p 139-40 il

Vegetable
Hea p78-79 (pat)

Venetian princess
Jen p54 il

Witch
Lee p 121-22 pl

Wood nymph
Dab pl 6

Regional types
This heading is used for illustrations of costumes suggestive of the countries listed, usually peasant dress. For additional illustrations for costumes of these types, see such headings as France, Germany, Switzerland, etc.

Argentine
Saun p 149-50 (pat) (m)

Austrian
Dab pl 19 (f)

FANCY DRESS AND STAGE COSTUME
—Regional types—*Continued*

Balinese
Cov   p243-49 il

Bavarian
Hea   p20-21   pl (m)

Breton
Hea   p42-45   2 pl

Bulgarian
Dab   pl 24

Chinese
CamC   pl   p54-55 (f)
Dab   pl 22
Hea   p 14-15, 18-19   2 pl (incl pat)
NeF   p 15-16   pl 50-53

Czechoslovakian
Dab   pl 25
Hea   p26-27   pl

Danish
Dab   pl 20 (f)
Hea   p20-21   pl (m)

Dutch
Dab   pl 26
Hea   p30-31, 34-35   2 pl

English
Dab   pl 23

11th-13th centuries
Wel   pl   p 18

14th-15th centuries
Wel   pl   p20

16th-17th centuries
Hea   p24-25   pl (m)
Wel   pl   p20-23

18th-19th centuries
Wel   pl   p23-24, 27-28

Finnish
Dab   pl 20 (f)

French
Dab   pl 30

17th century
Dav   v2   p526 il

German
Dab   pl 28

Greek, Ancient
Dab   pl 8
Hea   p 10-13, 89   3 pl (incl pat)
Lil   p 16-17 il (incl pat) (m)

Greek, Modern
Dab   pl 23

Indian (East Indian)
Dab   pl 29

Indians of North America
Dab   pl 11-12
Hea   p 18-19   pl
Lil   p 10-11 il (incl pat)

Irish
Dab   pl 30
Hea   p44-45   pl (f)

Italian
Dab   pl 27
Hea   p40-41   pl (f)

Japanese
Dab   pl 22

Mexican
Dab   pl 19 (f)
Hea   p26-27, 40-41, 44-45   3 pl
Saun   p 118   pl   p 117 (f)

Norse
Lil   p 14-15 il (incl pat)

Norwegian
Dab   pl 21

Polish
Dab   pl 26
Hea   p30-31, 42-45   3 pl

Russian
Dab   pl 21
Hea   p42-43   pl

Scottish
Dab   pl 29

Siamese
Nat   v91 F '47   p211   pl   p201-08 (col)

Spanish
Dab   pl 27
Hea   p 18-19   pl
Lil   p24-25 il (incl pat)

Swedish
Dab   pl 24
Hea   p40-41   pl (f)

Swiss
Dab   pl 28
Hea   p44-45   pl (f)

Tyrolean
Hea   p30-31, 34-35, 40-41   3 pl
Nat   v70 Ag '36   pl   p201-08

United States
Colonial period (to 1775)
Dab   pl 14
Hea   p24-25, 34-37   3 pl
Saun   p99-100, 130 il (f)

1800-1860
Dab   pl 13

1860-1865
Dab   pl 16

FANOE.   See Denmark—Fanoe

FANS
Bin   p 187-96   pl   p208 il
Kle   p 112-14 il
LelD   p 171-72   pl

Ancient and early
Dal   v 1   fig 837-39
Hous2   fig 69
LelD   p 178 il
LesA   p436-39   fig 528-33
NorC   p 149-56   pl il
WilC   pl   p6, 10

FANS—*Continued*

14th-15th centuries
LesA p440-44 il
WisF pl 9

16th century
LesA p443-44 pl 45 il
Norr v3 bk 1 p223-24 fig 244, 248, 252;
bk 2 p505-07, 628-30 il
Rey pl 14, 25
WilC pl p76, 101, 114, 134

17th century
LesA p444-47 fig 541
Rey pl 30, 34
Trai p70 il
WilC pl p 148, 157

18th century
Dav v2 p689, 877 2 pl
Davi v 1 il p302
LesA p447-52 il
WisF pl 18

19th century
Agu pl 106-07
Dal v2 fig 782 (col)
Dav v2 p877-78 pl
LesA p452-53 il
Sub p 129-30 pl p433-37
WilC pl p256
WilF pl p318
WisF pl 23
Yar p234 il

20th century
WilC pl p365, 378
WisF pl 24, 26

Indians of North America
MasB p88 il (incl pat)

FARMERS. See Agricultural laborers

FAROE ISLANDS
Ras p 109-15 2 pl (col)

FARTHINGALE. See Hoopskirts—16th
century; also period subdivisions 1558-
1625 under various countries, e.g. England—Elizabeth, 1558-1603

FELLINGSBRO. See Sweden—Västmanland

FENCING COSTUME

Europe
16th century
Hat p 183 fig 94

FERNEBO. See Sweden—Västmanland

FERRARA. See Italy—Emilia

FESTIVAL COSTUME

Ainos
Nat v69 Ap '36 p471 il

Austria
Nat v99 Je '51 pl p783 (col)

Belgium
Nat v93 My '48 pl p592-94, 613 (col)

Brazil
Nat v76 S '39 pl p307-14 (col)

Euboea Island
At pl 32 (col) (f)

Germany
Pet p86-87 pl

Black Forest
Ret pl p212, 216 il p 190 (f)

Hesse
Er pl 37 (col)
Ret il p32 (f)
RetS pl 88-89 (f)

Silesia
Ret pl p 123, 128 (f)

Thuringia
Ger pl 6, 15 (col)

Greece, Modern
At pl 14, 17, 23 (col) (f)
Nat v77 Mr '40 pl p313 (col) (f)

Hawaii
Nat v96 N '49 pl p587 (col)

Hungary
Bud pl 6, 8-9, 13, 18, 22-23, 26 (5 col)

India
Nat v78 D '40 pl p734-35 (col)

Italy
Nat v71 Mr '37 pl p289, 315 (col);
v 100 Ag '51 p230-44 7 pl (6 col) il

Venice
18th century
Bruh pl p55 (col)
Kle p41 il (m)

Macedonia
At pl 49 (col) (f)

Mexico
CorZ p50-60 pl il
CovM p262-63 pl (col) pl 78, 85, 88-
89 il
Marq pl 72 (f)
MeriC p 1-2 pl 1-10 (col)

Morocco
OrT pl 261 (f)

Panama
Nat v80 N '41 pl p601, 605 (col) (f)

Peru
Spi pl p69 (col) (f)
TooP pl 23, 68-69

Puerto Rico
Nat v76 D '39 pl p713, 731 (col)

FESTIVAL COSTUME—*Continued*

Spain

Agu pl F, 28, 63, 95-97 (1 col)
AnS fig 55, 70, 74-76, 95-99, 102-04, 117-19, 124, 174-77, 189-92, 195, 206-13, 220-26, 234, 273-76, 283, 288-89, 301-02, 304-05, 323-26, 332-33, 363-64, 383-84
Nat v97 Ap '50 pl p439 (col) (f); v99 Ap '51 pl p523, 526, 530 (col)
OrT pl 86-87, 95, 119, 124, 139, 145, 167 (f)

Sweden

MusS pl 2-3, 5-9 (col)

Switzerland

Nat v70 Ag '36 pl p 147, 162 (col)

Trinidad

Nat v 103 Ja '53 pl p60

Tyrol

Pes p 15-16 pl (col) (f)

United States
Louisiana

Ada v3 il p271
Nat v 103 F '53 pl p 159-63 (col)

New Mexico

Nat v96 D '49 pl p794

North Carolina

Nat v80 Ag '41 pl p 189, 213 (col)

Texas

Nat v92 D '47 pl p818-19, 822-24 (col)

West Indies

Nat v93 Ja '48 pl p26 (col)

FEUILLANTS
Doy pl 62 (col)

FEZ. See Headdress—Albania; Headdress—Dalmatia; Headdress—Turkey

FIBULAS. See Brooches—Ancient

FICHUS
AnS p227 fig 273-75
Bra pl 31, 41
CunE p 183-84, 189-91 il
Gor pl p 150
Kle p 120 il
LelD p 177 il
Pic il p57

FIELD MARSHALS
England
20th century

BarH pl 17 (col)

FILIPINOS. See Philippine Islands

FINISTÈRE. See France—Brittany

FINLAND
Brad pl p63 (f)
Bruk pl 166 fig 4-6, 8, 11-13
Heik p 16-17 pl 1-4 (col)
Prim p78-96 16 pl (1 col)

TiK pl 53 fig 1-3 (col)
WilF pl p75 (f)
See also Dancers—Finland; Fancy dress and stage costume—Finnish; Headdress—Finland

FIRE DANCE. See Dancers—Indians of North America—Fire dance

FIREMEN
Chile

Nat v72 D '37 pl p751, 753 (col)

England
17th century

AirT p63 il

United States
19th century

Kou pl 136
McP p21-22 pl (col)

FISHERMEN
Basque provinces

OrT pl 8-9, 14, 16, 22

Denmark

AndD p32 pl p9

England
19th century

Walk pl 5 (col)

Japan

Haa pl 33
Nat v69 Ap '36 pl p476 (m)

Mexico

Alv pl p89 (col)
Meri pl 12 (col)

Newfoundland

AirO il p 15

Poland

Lep pl 35 (col)

FISHERWOMEN
Denmark

AndD pl p 15

Netherlands

Nat v77 F '40 pl p284 (f)

FISHMONGERS
Argentine Republic

Bac pt4 pl 5 (col) (m)

Basque provinces

OrT pl 17 (f)

Netherlands

Hij pl 42 (f)

FISHWIVES
See also Fishmongers; Newhaven fishwives

Denmark

AndF p 14 pl 2

FLABELLUM. See Fans—Ancient and early

The **FLAMENCO.** See Dancers—Spain— Flamenco

FLANDERS. See Netherlands—13th-16th centuries; Belgium—17th century—date

FLANDERS, FRENCH. See France— Flanders, French

FLODA. See Sweden—Dalarne

FLORENCE. See Italy—Tuscany

FLOWER VENDERS
France
GiR pl 54 (col) (f)
Germany
Vert pl p 101 (f)
Mexico
CovM il p274 (f)
Pr pl 5 (col) (m)
Spain
Agu pl 1, 8 (f)

The **FLYING POLE.** See Dancers—Mexico—The flying pole

FÖHR. See Frisian islands

FOIX. See France—Foix

FOLK COSTUME
Folk costume will generally be found under provincial subdivisions of European countries, e.g. France—Brittany, Germany—Bavaria.

FONTANGE. See subdivisions 17th century (from 1650 to 1700) under Headdress — England; Headdress — Europe; Headdress—France; etc.

FONTEVRAUD, NUNS OF THE ORDER OF
Doy pl 123 (col)

FOOTBALL COSTUME
19th century
Dur il p62-69
1850-1860
Kou pl 25
1870-1880
Ada v3 il p312
1890-1900
Part p 156 il
20th century
Dur il p 144-45, 163, 218-22
RogW p 172

FOOTMEN, ROYAL
India
Nat v71 Ja '37 p 1 il; v92 N '47 pl p615 (col)

FOOTWEAR
Faw p 138-44 2 pl
Hea p 62-64 pl (incl pat)
Nat v70 Jl '36 pl p72 (col)
Pic p 11-12, 129-31, 137-38 il
See also Clogs and pattens; Gaiters; Garters; Hose; Leggings; Overshoes; Riding boots; Sabots
Primitive and early
CrO pl 13 fig 1
Eli p61-65 il
Jae p9-32 12 pl
LesA p250-57 il (m)
See also Footwear—Assyria and Babylonia; Footwear—Egypt—Ancient; Footwear — Greece — Ancient; Footwear — Rome, etc.
Amazons
WilFo p 19 pl p25
Arabia
CrO pl 12 fig 16
Dal v 1 fig 615, 645-46 (col)
Rud pl p165
Assyria and Babylonia
BroF p4 fig 1 D-E, 2 G
Dot p 107 il
Gen v 1 fig 206-07
WilC pl p 10
WilFo p9-10 pl 13-14 (m)
Aztec
WilFo pl p98
Bolivia
Hal pl G (col)
Byzantine empire
Dal v 1 fig 471-72 (col)
Dot il p 119
Wa p84 fig 88E, 88F
WilC pl p36
WilFo p62 pl p73
Ceylon
CrO pl 12 fig 6
China
CrO pl 12 fig 14
Dal v 1 p463-69 fig 831-32 (col)
WilFo p44-47 pl p48, 172
Cyprus, Ancient
Dav v 1 p58 fig 175-76
Egypt, Ancient
BroF p2-3 fig 1 A-C
Dot p 105 il
Gen v 1 fig 166-67
Gor p7 il
Hous2 p96-97 fig 103 (m)
KerM no 1 pl 4
Loud pl 1 (col)
Wa p6, 12 fig 8L, 11A-B, 12
WilFo p 1-7 2 pl
England
To 499
BroF p8-11 fig 3
WilFo p56-57 pl p60 (m)

FOOTWEAR—England—*Continued*

499-1066

CunM p 12-14 pl
Dot il p 122 (m)
Tru p 13 il
WilFo p57 pl p60 (m)

1066-1154

BroF p 14 fig 4 (m)
Tru p 17-18 il (m)
WilFo pl p76 (m)

12th century

BrH pl p22, 26 (m)
CunM p 33, 38-39 pl 8
Dot p 127 il

13th century

BroF p20-23 fig 4, 8-9
Dot p 130 il (m)
WilFo pl p76 (m)

14th century

BrH pl p47 (m)
BroF p28-31 fig 10-11
CunM p60-62, 87-88 pl 22, 35
Dot p 134 il (m)
HousM p 126-28 fig 233-34 (m)
Tru p30-31 il
WilC pl 63
WilFo pl p77 (m)

15th century

Ab pl p 158
BrH pl p63 (m)
BroF p32-38 fig 13-15
CrO pl 12 fig 3, 8
CunM p 109-11, 144-48 3 pl (m)
HousM p214-15 fig 348 (m)
Norr v3 bk 1 p 113-16 il (m)
Tru pl p43
WilFo pl p78 (m)
Yar pl p91, 106

16th century

BroF p39-53 pl p33 (col) fig 16-20
CunS p32-39, 114-31, 180-82 pl 7-9, 16, 45-50
Dot p 145 il
Lint p238-64 pl 10
Norr v3 bk 1 p343-46 (m); bk 2 p456-58, 756-62 il
WilC pl p 134
WilFo pl p94, 96-98
Yar pl p 117, 124

17th century

BrH pl p87 (m)
BroF p54-68 pl p48 (col) fig 22-29
CrO pl 12 fig 9-10; pl 13 fig 7
Dot p 156 il (f)
Lint p238-64 pl 16-18
Rey p 11 pl 33, 36
Tru p60-61 il (m)
WilC p 152, 185 pl p 157, 192
WilFo p 108-10 pl p113-16
Yar pl p 144, 153, 158, 166, 173

18th century

BroF p70-84 fig 32-38
CrO pl 13 fig 8

Dav v2 fig 1836 (f)
Dot p 160 il
WilFo pl p 128-30
Yar pl p 179, 187, 197

Eskimos

May pl p 18 (f)
WilFo pl p 172

Etruria

WilFo p26-27 pl

Europe

Kle p332-36 il
Pic p75-76 il
WilFo p 131-46 pl p 147-51

3rd-6th centuries

NorC p39-40 il (m)

9th-12th centuries

Dal v2 p33-39 2 pl il (col)
LelD pl p385 fig 1-3 (m)
LesA p257-58 il
NorC p40-41 il
WilFo p64-66 pl p75, 76
WisF pl 6 (f)

13th century

BroW v 1 p30, 35 fig 8 (m)
Dal v2 p97-98 fig 165 (col)
NorC p41 il
WilFo p66-67 pl p76-77

14th century

Bra pl 20-21
BruK pl 51
Dal v2 p 140-42 il (col) (m)
LelD p317 il (m)
NorC p41-42 il
Wa p 110-11 fig 111 (m)
WilFo p67-70 pl p74-75, 77
WisF pl 8 (f)

15th century

Bra pl 20-21
BruK pl 51
CrO pl 13 fig 2-4 (m)
Dal v2 p 196-200 il (col)
Eth pl p23 (incl pat) (m)
Gor pl p31, 33
Kle p32, 66, 109-10, 330 il
LelD pl p385 fig 5, 7-10, 12-21; pl p386 fig 1-2
LesA p259-61 il
Wa p 126-27 fig 136
WilFo p70-72 pl p73-75, 77
WisF pl 9 (f)

16th century

BroW v1 p 120-21 fig 75 (m)
Dal v2 p254-58 pl il (col)
Gor pl p48 (m)
Jae p33-44 6 pl il
KelF p25-27 pl p79 (m)
LelD p41 fig 2-9 (m) pl p386 fig 3-12 (m) p398 il (m)
LesA p261-62 il
Wa p 144, 154 fig 149, 154 (m)
WilFo p83-93 pl p94-98
WisF pl 11 (f)

FOOTWEAR—Europe—*Continued*

17th century
Bra   pl 26-27
CrO   pl 49 (f)
Dal   v2 p339-41 fig 559-70 (col)
Gor   pl p70, 73, 78, 82-83, 86, 92, 94
Jae   p45-77   16 pl il
Kle   p43 il (m)
LelD   p41, 43, 305, 398-99   pl p386 fig
  13-23; pl p387 fig 1-9
LesA   p262-69 fig 328-335, 341
Pic   p 11 (m)
Roj   il p 14, 28, 32, 36
Wa   p 178, 183, 189, 195 fig 167, 181
WilC   p 168, 177   pl p 173, 183
WilFo   p 102-11   pl p 113-16
WisF   pl 12-13 (f)

18th century
CrO   pl 13, 49 fig 6 (f)
Dal   v2 p367-68, 413-14 fig 618-23, 774-
  76 (col) (f)
Gor   pl p 103, 105, 107, 112, 118, 121,
  124
LelD   pl p387 fig 11-27; pl p388 fig 1-
  2; p398-99 il
LesA   p266-69, 310-11 fig 333-34, 336-40,
  342
May   pl p64 (m)
Wa   p212-13, 217, 226, 230 fig 194, 195,
  198 (m)
WilFo   p 117-27   pl p 128-30
WisF   pl 14-15 (f)

19th century
Dal   v2 p497-98 fig 1060-80
Jae   p78-113   8 pl
Kle   p59 il (m)
LelD   p43-44 il;   pl p388 fig 3-5
LesA   p269-75 il
WisF   pl 20 (f)

1800-1810
Wa   fig 201 (m)
WilC   p237-38   pl p246 (m)
WilFo   pl p 147

1810-1820
Chr   p 180 fig 352 (f)
CunE   pl p 167 (f)
Gor   pl p 135, 137 (f)
Wa   p257 fig 204 (m)
WilC   p251, 259   pl p270 (f)
WilFo   pl p 147-48

1820-1830
BroF   p83-100 fig 39
WilC   p275   pl p280 (f)
WilFo   pl p 147-48
Yar   pl p209 (f)

1830-1840
CunE   pl p 167 (f)
Dav   v2 p845-46   2 pl
Gor   pl p 140, 142 (f)

1840-1850
Chr   fig 357 (f)
Gor   pl p 146, 157 (f)
WilFo   pl p 148-49
Yar   pl p222 (f)

1850-1860
CrO   pl 13 fig 5, 17
WilFo   pl p 149

1860-1870
CunE   pl p237 (f)
Dav   v2 pl p904-05 (f)
Gor   pl p 157 (f)
WilC   pl p293 (f)
WilFo   pl p 149-50
Yar   pl p234 (f)

1870-1880
Wa   p298, 304 fig 241, 255
WilC   pl p311 (f)
WilFo   pl p 150

1880-1890
Chr   p 183 fig 362 (f)
Gor   pl p 165 (f)
HaC   pl p 180 (f)
KerA   p31 il (f)

1890-1900
CunE   pl p387 (f)
Gor   pl p 172 (f)
WilC   p314 pl p318 (f)
WilFo   pl p 150-51

1890-1900
Dot   p 169 il (f)
WilFo   pl p 151
WisF   pl 22-23 (f)
Yar   pl p248 (f)

20th century
BroF   p 101 fig 49-55
HaC   pl p 180-81 (f)
LelD   pl p389 fig 6-18
LesA   p275-79 il
Rud   pl p74-75, 78, 210-11
WilFo   p 152-62   pl p 163-72

1900-1910
CunPr   pl p83 (f)
WilC   pl p353 (f)
WilFo   pl p 163-64

1910-1920
AlF   pl p9 (f)
WilC   pl p365 (f)
WilFo   pl p 163-64
Yar   pl p261 (f)

1920-1930
CunPr   il p 190, 206 (f)
WilC   pl p378 (f)
WilFo   pl p 165, 167
WisF   pl 27 (f)
Yar   pl p273 (f)

1930-1940
CunPr   p242, 248, 253 il (f)
WilC   pl p391 (f)
WilFo   pl p 165-66, 168
WisF   pl 28 (f)

1940-1950
Bra   pl 54 (f)
CunPr   p274   pl p279, 285 il (f)
Kle   p59 il (f)
WilFo   pl p 165-66, 169-71
WisF   pl 29 (f)
Yar   pl p283

FOOTWEAR—*Continued*
France
To 511
LelD   p373 il (m)
WilFo   p56 pl p59

511-987
May   il p 17 (m)
WilFo   pl p76 (m)

11th-13th centuries
WilC   p48 pl p54
WilFo   p66 pl p76-77 (m)

14th century
Dot   p 135 il (m)
WilFo   pl p77 (m)

15th century
WilC   p48 pl p54
WilFo   pl p75, 78 (m)

16th century
CrO   pl 13 fig 14 (m)
WilC   pl p93, 101, 140
WilFo   p89-91 pl p94, 96-98 (m)

17th century
BluE   p 10 pl 51 (col) (m)
CrO   pl 13 fig 11, 13, 19
Dav   v2 fig 1714 (f)
SocC   pl p51 (f)
WilC   p 168, 177 pl p 148, 173, 183
WilFo   p 103-08 pl p 113-16

18th century
CrO   pl 13 fig 18
Dav   v2 fig 1847 (m)
Lel   v 11 p23-26, 65-66 fig 17-20, 67;
  v 12 p 18, 47-48 fig 13, 61
SocC   pl p51 (f)
WilC   p 199, 214, 232 pl p205, 219, 235
WilFo   p 117-18, 121-25 pl p 128-30

Germany
Kle   p 103 il (m)

7th century
LelD   il p241

12th century
HousG2   fig 167g
WilFo   pl p76 (m)

16th century
CrO   pl 13 fig 15, 16 (m)
WilC   pl p80
WilFo   pl p94, 96-98 (m)

18th century—date
Pet   p32-33 pl
RetS   pl 76 (m)

Greece, Ancient
Bra   pl 7
BroF   p5-6 il
BruK   p48-49 pl 21
Dal   v 1 p 129-39 fig 235-53 (col)
Dot   p 111 il
Gen   v 1 pl p94
Gor   pl p 13
LelD   p373, 378 il (m)

May   pl p 12 (m)
Pic   p 11 il (m)
Pot   v 1 pl 12 (col)
Wa   p37-38, 45 fig 56
WilC   pl p 17
WilFo   p 15-25   4 pl

Greece, Modern
Nat   v77 Mr '40 pl p294
WilFo   pl p 172 (m)

Greenland
WilFo   pl p 172

Hungary
Bud   pl 127 (col) (f)
Buda   pl 4 (col)

India
CrO   pl 12 fig 11, 12, 15
WilFo   p40-42 pl p43, 172

Indians of Mexico
WilFo   pl p 172

Indians of North America
CrO   pl 12 fig 1, 3, 7, 17
EvnH   p7-13 il (incl pat)
Hun   pl p29-31
Lyf   p 104-06 il (incl pat)
MasB   p48-49 il (incl pat)
Roe   p 126-31 pl 8 (col) (m) il
Rud   pl p210
Seto   p63 pl 15 (pat)
TiK   pl 113-14
Trai   p 17 il
WilFo   p 101-02 pl p98, 116, 166, 172

Ireland
WilFo   pl p 128 (m)

Italy
WilFo   pl p 172

10th-11th centuries
WilFo   pl p76 (m)

13th century
WilFo   pl p76 (m)

14th century
WilC   p40-41 pl p44
WilFo   pl p77 (m)

15th century
WilC   p40-41 pl p44
WilFo   pl p78 (m)

16th century
Kle   p231 il (f)
Rud   pl p169-70
WilC   pl p76 (f)

17th century
Dav   v2 fig 1715 (f)

Japan
Pic   il p 151
WilFo   p52-53 pl p54, 172

Korea
TiK   pl 97 fig 13 (col) (f)
WilFo   p49-51 pl

FOOTWEAR—*Continued*

Lapland
TiK   pl 53 fig 15 (col) (m)

Mayan
WilFo   pl   p98 (m)

Media
WilFo   pl   p 14 (m)

Mesopotamia
WilFo   p8-14   2 pl (m)

Mexico, Ancient
DuS   fig 27-28

Mohammedan
WilFo   pl   p 172

Mongolia
WilFo   p45   pl   p48

Morocco
TiK   pl 29 fig 4 (col)

Netherlands
Int   v2   pl 51

15th century
WilFo   pl   p75 (m)

17th century
WilFo   pl   p 113-14, 116

Orient
BruK   pl 180 (col)
Kle   p330 il
LelD   p24 il
May   pl   p 14

Palestine, Modern
Wrig   p25   pl 1 fig 9-10 (m)

Persia, Ancient
Wa   p27 fig 42
WilC   pl   p28
WilFo   p 10   pl   p 13 (m)

Philippine Islands
Nat   v78 O '40   pl   p445 (col)
WilFo   pl   p 172

Phrygia
WilFo   p 11   pl   p 13-14 (m)

Poland
WilFo   pl   p 172 (f)

Portugal
WilFo   pl   p 172

Rome
AirP   p50 il
BroF   p6-7 fig 2 A-F, H
BruK   p48-49   pl 21
Dal   v 1   p 194-96 fig 365-73 (col)
Dav   v 1 fig 272
Dot   p 114 il
Gor   pl   p 15
HousG2   fig 101-03, 111, 128
KerM   no 1   pl 12
LelD   p55-56, 61-63, 373, 378 il (m)
May   pl   p 12 (m)
NorC   p38-39 il (m)

Tru   p8-9 il
WilC   pl   p23
WilFo   p28-39   4 pl
WisF   pl 4 (f)
Wrig   pt2   pl   p 17, 19

Russia
Lee   pl   p57
WilFo   pl   p98, 128, 172

Scotland
WilFo   pl   p 116, 172

Spain
AnS   p73-74, 86-87, 92-93, 149, 242, 269-70, 315 fig 82, 101, 108, 185-86
WilFo   pl   p 172

16th century
Dav   v2 fig 1713 (f)
WilFo   pl   p95

19th century
LelD   il   p382 (f)

Sweden
Berg   fig 87, 90 (m)
Sv   p231-42 il

Syria
Rud   pl   p 171

Turkey
WilFo   pl   p 172

16th century
LelD   p382 fig 5 (f)
WilFo   pl   p95 (f)

18th century—date
Özb   fig 19 (f)
Pic   il   p 137 (m)
TiK   pl 17 fig 5, 11a (col)

Tyrol
Ori   pl   p50 (col)

United States
18th century
Ada   v 1 il   p267, 358; v2 il   p7
Trai   p 193 il

19th century
1850-1860
Ada   v3 il   p4 (m)

1880-1890
Ada   v3 il   p364-65
McP   il   p39 (f)

1890-1900
Ada   v4 il   p53, 131

Venice
16th century
Dal   v2 fig 443-45 (col)
Jae   pl 17 (f)
LelD   p304-05 fig 4 (f)   p382 fig 2-3 (f)
WilFo   p89   pl   p95 (f)

17th century
BroF   p48-50 fig 22

FOOTWEAR—Venice—*Continued*

18th century

Mora pl 87 (f)

Yugoslavia

Kle p277 il

FOOTWEAR, CHILDREN'S
Jack p 139-54 5 pl

FOOTWEAR, COWBOY
WilFo pl p 172

FOOTWEAR, ECCLESIASTICAL
HousM p35-36 fig 120
McC p 111-13 il
WilFo p62-63 pl p73

FOOTWEAR, MILITARY

20th century

WilFo pl p 166

England
17th century

Law v 1 fig 71

Etruria

WilFo pl p27

Europe
5th-12th centuries

WilFo pl p59, 74

14th-15th centuries

WilFo pl p74

France
18th century

LelD p206 il
WilC pl p246

19th century

LelD p206 il

Germany
16th century

WilFo pl p94

20th century

Erl p54-55 il

Greece, Ancient

WilFo p 18-19 pl p22-23

India
19th century

WilFo p42 pl p43

Persia, Ancient

WilFo pl p 14

Phrygia

WilFo pl p 13

Rome

WilFo p34-35 pl p36, 38

FOREIGN LEGION (FRENCH ARMY)
BluN pl p 184 (pte)
LelD p242 il

FORESTERS

Scotland

Log p253 pl p251 (col)

FORMOSA
Brad pl p64
Nat v87 Ja '45 il p 18 (f)
See also Dancers—Formosa

FORSSA. See Sweden—Helsingland

FOURRAGÈRE
SmU p27 il

FRAGA. See Spain—Aragon

FRANCE
See also Fancy dress and stage costume—French; also subdivision France
under Ceremonial costume; Children;
Coronation robes; Court dress; Dancers;
Hair, wigs, etc.; Hunting costume; Military costume; Mourning costume; Officials; Parliamentary robes; also under
occupations (e.g. Barbers; Carpenters;
Police) and individual articles of attire
(e.g. Capes and cloaks; Coats and jackets; Footwear; Headdress)

Early to 511 (Gaul)

BluC p 10-13 pl
Bra p 100-02 pl
BruK p 13, 50 pl 24 (col)
Dal v 1 p236-50 pl il (col)
Pot v 1 p43 pl 18 (col)
WilC pl 32 (m)

511-1000

Bra p 103-05 pl 14
BruK p50 pl 24 fig 13-15 (col) (m)
Dot p 121-22 il
Loud pl 7 (col)
WilC pl p53 (f)
See also Kings and rulers—France—
Early to 987; Noblemen—France—Early
to 987; Noblewomen—France—Early to
987; Queens and empresses—France—
Early to 987

11th century

BruK pl 34 fig 1-6 (m)
Dot p 125-26 il
EvjD p2-4 pl 1a, 2, 5, 7 il

12th century

BluC p 15-17 pl p 19-20
Burr p 12, 116-17, 192-93, 252-53, 296-**97**
pl p 13
Dav v 1 p 133-37 4 pl
Dot p 128-29 il
EvjD p2-9 pl 1b, 3-8, 10 il
Lecl pl 3 (col)
See also Kings and rulers—France—
Philip II, 1180-1223; Queens and em-
presses—France—12th century

FRANCE—*Continued*

13th century

Louis VIII, 1223-1226
Louis IX, 1226-1270
Philip III, 1270-1285
Philip IV, 1285-1314

BluC p 18-24 pl p21, 49
BroW v 1 p20-26 fig 2-3, 5 (f)
CrO pl 41
Dav v 1 p 165-73 9 pl
Dot p 131-32 il
EvjD p 10-25 pl 4a, 9, 12-19
HousM p 1-17 pl 1-2 (col) il (incl pat)
Kle p85 il (f)
Lecl pl 4 (col)
Loud pl 8 (col)
WilC p46-52 pl

See also Kings and rulers—France—13th century; Kings and rulers—France—Louis IX, 1226-1270; Noblewomen—France—13th century; Queens and empresses—France—13th century

14th century

Louis X, 1314-1316
Philip V, 1316-1322
Charles IV, 1322-1328
Philip VI, 1328-1350
John II, 1350-1364

BluC p 18-31 2 pl
BruK pl 45
Dot p 131-35 il
EvjD p21-58 front pl 11, 20-25, 27b-29, 32, 37 fig 3-5 (incl pat)
TiK pl 118 fig 27
UnW pl 25-28 (col)
WilC p46-51 pl p53 (f)

See also Kings and rulers—France—14th century; Noblemen—France—14th century; Noblewomen—France—14th century

Charles V, 1364-1380

Loud pl 9 (col) (f)
Vert pl p29 (f)

See also Kings and rulers—France—Charles V, 1364-1380; Queens and empresses—France—1364-1380

Charles VI, 1380-1422

Lib pl p2 (f)

See also Kings and rulers—France—Charles VI, 1380-1422

15th century

BluC pl p27-28
BruK pl 46-47 (col)
Burr p 14, 117-19, 194-95, 323-24 pl p 15
Dav v 1 p297-345 22 pl il
Dot p 138-40 il
EvjD p38-66 pl 26-27, 30-31, 37-41, 44-66
Gor pl p27-28, 32
HousM p 139-42, 159-98 4 pl (1 col) il (pat)
KerM no3 pl 2 (f)
LavE pl 2-3
Lecl pl 4-5 (col)
LelD pl p350 (f)
Lib pl p6, 10

UnW pl 29-30 (col)
Vert pl p22 (col)
WilC p46-53 2 pl
WilF p36-37, 39 il

See also France—Burgundy—15th century; Noblemen—France—15th century; Noblewomen—France—15th century

Charles VII, 1422-1461

Loud pl 9 (col) (f)

Louis XI, 1461-1483

EvjD p59-60 pl 58-61

Charles VIII, 1483-1498

EvjD p62-64 pl 62-63 (m)
Gor pl p46 (f)
Pro v 1 pl 1 (col) (f)
WilC p81-84 2 pl

16th century

Bart p20-23 2 pl (pat) fig 3, 4a, 4c (f)
BluC p26-46 4 pl
BroW v 1 p 115, 128, 138, 142 front, pl 130 (col) fig 62, 69-71, 73-75, 77, 82, 84-86, 89B, 91-92
Burr p 18, 24, 77-78, 122-23, 198-201, 206-07, 297-99, 325-27 pl p 19, 25
Dav v2 p469-89 pl il
Dot p 147-48 il
KelF p46-47 pl p37, 65
KerM no 5 pl 8-9
KerR pl 5-6
LelD pl p351 (f)
Norr v3 bk 2 p396-99, 431-36, 556-69, 654-68 5 pl (1 col) il
VanH pl 4
Vert pl p99 (f)

See also Noblemen—France—16th century; Noblewomen—France—16th century

Louis XII, 1498-1519

EvjD p64-66 pl 64-71
LavE pl 10 (f)
LavR pl p27 (f)
Norr v3 bk 1 p 191-92, 308 il
WilC p81-84 2 pl

See also Kings and rulers—France—Louis XII, 1498-1515; Queens—France—1498-1515

Francis I, 1515-1547

BluL p7-9, 18 pl 1-6, 17 (2 col)
BosF pl 21, 27
BruK pl 73 (col)
LavR pl p65-67, 87-90, 95 (2 col)
Pro v 1 pl 2-4 (col) (f)
SocC pl p 13 (f)
WilC p86-92 2 pl
WilF pl p53-59

See also Kings and rulers—France—Francis I, 1515-1547; Queens—France—1515-1547

Henry II, 1547-1559

BluL p9-10, 18-19 pl 7-15, 25 (1 col)
LavR pl p67-68, 91-94, 99 (1 col)
Pro v 1 pl 5 (col) (f)
WilC p89-90 pl p92 (f)

See also Kings and rulers—France—Henry II, 1547-1559; Queens and empresses—France—1547-1559

FRANCE—16th century—*Continued*

Francis II, 1559-1560

LavR   pl   p96-98

Charles IX, 1560-1574

BluL   p 10-11, 20-22   pl 19-34, 48, 53, 57 (4 col)
BruK   pl 75 (col)
LavR   p 68-69, 100-05   6 pl (1 col)
Pro   v 1   pl 6-7 (col) (f)
WilC   p94-100   2 pl
WilF   pl p60, 66-67
   See also Kings and rulers—France—
Charles IX, 1560-1574; Queens and empresses—France—1560-1574

Henry III, 1574-1589

BluL   p 11-14, 22-27   pl 34-71 (1 col)
BruK   pl 76 (col)
KelF   pl   p44
LavR   p69-72, 105-26   12 pl (1 col)
LelD   p297   fig 2-3 (m)
Pro   v 1   pl 8-9 (col) (f)
TiK   pl 124   fig 1-8 (col) (f)
Vert   pl   p28 (f)
WilC   p94-100   2 pl
   See also Kings and rulers—France—
Henry III, 1574-1589; Queens and empresses—France—1574-1589

Henry IV, 1589-1610

BluE   p8-9, 17-18   pl 1-8 (1 col)
BruK   pl 84 fig 1-7 (col)
LavR   p326-27, 347-51   5 pl (1 col)
Lib   pl   p24 (f)
Loud   pl 12 (col)
Pro   v 1   pl 10-14 (col) (f)
WilC   p 135-39   pl
   See also Kings and rulers—France—
Henry IV, 1589-1610; Queens and empresses—France—1589-1610

17th century

Burr   p26-31, 81-86, 127-29, 206-09, 261-63, 299-300,   3 pl
Dav   v2   p508-59, 640   5 pl il
Dot   p 151-53 il
Lecl   pl 9 (col)
LelD   pl   p352 fig 3
Vert   pl   p39 (f)
WilF   p86-89   4 pl
   See also France—Burgundy—17th century-date; Noblemen—France—17th century; Noblewomen—France—17th century

Louis XIII, 1610-1643

BluC   p45-56   2 pl
BluE   p9-13, 19-27   pl 9-66 (7 col)
BroW   v2   p29 fig 1-2, 7   pl   p34 (col)
BruK   pl 84 fig 8-16 (col)
DeZ   pl 88 (m)
Gor   pl   p71, 74, 76-77, 81
LavR   p327-32, 352-83   32 pl (6 col)
Lib   pl   p26 (f)
Pro   v 1   pl 15-20 (col) (f)
WilC   p 141-47   2 pl
   See also Kings and rulers—France—
Louis XIII, 1610-1643; Queens and empresses—France—1610-1643

Louis XIV, 1643-1715

Bart   p32-33   pl (pat) fig 9a-9b (m)
BluC   p57-65   2 pl
BroW   v2   p39-46 fig 13, 18-19, 23-24, 30, 42   pl   p60, 72, 86, 92 (col)
Bruh   p44-47   pl (col)
BruK   p25-26, 70-71   pl 98-101 (1 col)
Dal   v2   p316-27 il (col) (incl pat)
Gor   pl   p80, 84, 87-88, 90-91, 93, 102
Kle   p87, 198, 299-300 il
Lecl   pl 10 (col)
LelD   pl   p354 (f)
Lib   pl   p172B-172F (f)
Loud   pl 14-15 (col)
May   pl   p40
Pann   v 1   pl 1 (col)
Pro   v2   pl 1-20 (col) (f)
SocC   pl   p28
TiK   pl 128 fig 6 (col) (f)
UnW   pl 53-64 (col)
Wa   pl   p187 (m)
WilC   p 161-83   6 pl
WilF   pl 95-97
WilFo   pl   p 115-16
   See also Kings and rulers—France—
Louis XIV, 1643-1715; Queens and empresses—France—1643-1715

18th century

Dav   v2   p652-721, 769   16 pl il (incl pat)
LelD   pl   p272 (col) (f)
   See also Noblemen—France—18th century; Noblewomen—France—18th century

Louis XV, 1715-1774

BluC   p66-78   6 pl
Brk   pl 1-5 (f)
BroW   v2   fig 44-53   pl   p98, 102, 118 (col)
Bruh   p48-53   3 pl (col)
BruK   p26-28   pl 101-05, 108 (2 col)
BruM   p34-41   5 pl (3 col) (f)
Burr   p32, 129-32, 210-11, 263-64, 301   pl p33
Dot   p 158 il
Gor   pl   p 104, 106, 108, 110, 113, 117, 119
Kle   p310-13 il
Lecl   pl 11 (col)
Lel   v 11   p 1-77   pl 1-2, 4, 7-11, 15, 18-20, 22, 24, 26, 28-31, 35-36, 38 (11 col) fig 1-84 (incl pat)
LelD   pl   p355-56 fig 1 (f)
Lib   pl   p42, 172G-172K (1 col) (f)
Loud   pl 16 (col) (m)
NeEu   pl 14 (f)
Pann   v 1   pl 2-18 (col)
Pic   il   p 115 (f)
SocC   pl   p37, 42, 47
TiK   pl 128 fig 7-8 (col) (f)
UnW   pl 65-74 (col)
WilC   p 193-205   4 pl
WilF   pl   p 107-10
YoR   p45-53 il (f)
   See also Kings and rulers—France—
Louis XV, 1715-1774; Queens and empresses—France—1715-1774

FRANCE—18th century—*Continued*

Louis XVI, 1774-1789

BelQ front (col) (f)
BluC p79-90 6 pl
BoeR p530-55 pl p354, 402, 432, 466 (col) il (f)
Brk pl 6-9 (f)
Bruh p56-59 2 pl (col)
BruK p28-29, 72-73 pl 110-12, 114 (2 col)
Burr p36, 132-33, 218-19, 266-68, 301-02 pl p37
CrO pl 46
Dal v2 p372-74, 379-91 il (col) (incl pat)
Gor pl p96, 119-20, 123, 125 (1 col)
Kle p87 il (f)
LavS p42 pl 19 (f)
Lecl pl 12 (col)
Lel v 12 p8-14 pl 2-6, 11, 13-14, 16-17, 21, 24, 26-30, 40 (9 col) fig 1-9, 26-48 (incl pat)
LelD p226, 326 il; pl p356-57 (f)
Lib pl p58, 172L-172Q (2 col)
NeEu pl 3-6, 8-9, 15, 17-20
Pann v 1 pl 19-28 (col)
Pic il p98, 132 (f)
SocC pl p56 (f)
TiK pl 128 fig 9 (col) (f)
UnW pl 75-81 (col)
Vert pl p69-70 (f)
WilC p206-18 4 pl
WilF pl p 111, 114-16
WisF pl 15-16 (f)
YoR p53-60 il (f)

See also Kings and rulers—France—Louis XVI, 1774-1789; Queens and empresses—France—1774-1789

Assemblies to Directory, 1789-1795

BluC p91-100 3 pl
BluN p9-11, 97-100 pl p25-27, 113-14
Brk pl 10-12 (f)
Bruh p62-65 2 pl (col)
BruK p29-30, 74 pl 116-17 (col)
Dal v2 p374, 378 il (col)
Kle p 137-38 il (f)
Lel v 12 p 14-15, 40-41 pl 8, 31, 33-35, 37 (4 col) fig 8-11, 49
LelD p69 il (m)
Pann v2 pl 1-15 (col) (f)
TiK pl 127 fig 10-14, 20-23 (col) (incl pat)
WilC p220-26 2 pl
YoR p61-63 il (f)

Directory, 1795-1799

BluN p 11-13, 100-02 pl p27-28, 114-15
Bruh p66-67 pl (col)
BruM pl p42-43 (col) (f)
Burr p38, 90-91, 133-34, 220-21, 302 pl p39
CrO pl 51
Dav v2 fig 1999, 2001-02
Kle p99-100, 188-89 il
LavT2 pl 1 (col) (f)
LelD p223 il; p274 il (f); pl p357 fig 4-7 (f)
Pann v2 pl 6-10 (col)

Pic il p43 (f)
UnW pl 82-85 (col)
Vert pl p93 (col) (f)
Wa p230-31 il (f)
WilC p228-34 2 pl
WisF pl 18 (f)
YoR p64-66 il (f)

19th century

See Nineteenth century; also Kings and rulers—France—Napoleon 1799-1814; Queens and empresses—France—1804-1814; Queens and empresses—France—1852-1817

BY REGION OR PROVINCE

CrO pl 27

Anjou

GaP pl 6, 9 (col) (f)
GiR pl 5-6 (col)
RogD pl 14 (col) (f)

Artois

GaP pl 24 (col) (f)
GiR pl 7-8 (col)
RogD pl 15 (col) (f)

Aunis

GaP pl 19 (col) (f)
GiR pl 10 (col) (f)
RogD pl 22 (col) (f)

Auvergne

Brad pl p67 (f)
BruK pl 150 fig 5-12 (col)
CosP p9-11 pl 7-9
GaP pl 26 (col) (f)
GiR pl 11-12 (col)
LepF pl 20 (col) (f)
LhA 27 pl (col)
Ogr pl p302 (col) (f)
RogD pl 24 (col) (f)

Basque provinces

See Basque provinces

Béarn

CosP pl 26-30
GaP pl 36 (col) (f)
GiR pl 13-14 (col)

Berry

GaP pl 33 (col) (f)
GiR pl 15-16 (col)

Bordeaux

Brad pl p66
LepF pl 22 (col) (f)

Bourbonnais

Brad pl p67 (f)
GaP pl 34 (col) (f)
GiR pl 17-18 (col)
LepF pl 19 (col) (f)
LhA 21 pl (col)
Marce p23-24 pl 3-4 (col)
RogD pl 23 (col) (f)

Brittany (Bretagne)

BluN p75-79, 131-37, 139-40 pl p62-63, 145-46, 152
Brad pl p68 (f)
BruK pl 149-50 (col)

FRANCE—Brittany—*Continued*
CosP   p 14-16   pl 1-6, 12, 15-16 (4 col)
GaP   pl 1 (col) (f)
GiR   pl 21-22 (col)
Lee   p20-22   pl
LepF   pl 1-5 (col)
LhB   99 pl (col)
Marce   p 15-16   pl 1-2 (col)
Nat   v71 Je '37   pl   p751, 765 (f); v84
   Ag '43   pl   p213 (col)
Ogr   pl   p232 (col) (f)
RogD   pl 13 (col) (f)

Burgundy (Bourgogne)

Int   pl 32-33
LepF   pl 18 (col) (f)
Ogr   pl   p266 (col) (f)

14th century

Bruh   p 18-20   pl (col)
Kle   p 182   il (m)

15th century

Bruh   p20-22   pl (col)
BruK   p 17-19, 58-59   pl 48-50 (1 col)
Kle   p67-69   il

17th century—date

BruK   pl 148 fig 13;   pl 150 fig 4, 13-15;
   pl 151 fig 2-4 (col)
CosP   pl 36-39
GaP   pl 27 (col) (f)
GiR   pl 19-20 (col)
LepF   pl 16-17 (col)
RogD   pl 19 (col) (f)

Champagne

GaP   pl 36 (col) (f)
GiR   pl 23-24 (col)
LeID   il p262 (f)
LepF   pl 10 (col) (f)
Ogr   pl   p250 (col) (f)
RogD   pl 17 (col) (f)

Corsica

See Corsica

Dauphiné

BruK   pl 148 fig 10-11 (col)
GaP   pl 5 (col) (f)
GiR   pl 27-28 (col)
RogD   pl 27 (col) (f)

Flanders, French

GaP   pl 11 (col) (f)
GiR   pl 29-30 (col)

Foix

GaP   pl 10 (col) (f)
GiR   pl 31-32 (col)

Franche-Comté

GaP   pl 25 (col) (f)
GiR   pl 33-34, 51-52 (col)
LepF   pl 14-15 (col)
RogD   pl 20 (col) (f)

Guienne and Gascony

BruK   pl 148 fig 6-8 (col)
CosP   pl 25 (m)
GaP   pl 4, 38 (col) (f)

GiR   pl 35-38 (col)
Ogr   pl   p342 (col) (f)
RogD   pl 30 (col) (f)

Île de France

BluN   pl 151
GaP   pl 32 (col) (f)
GiR   pl 39-40 (col)
Ogr   pl   p 194 (col) (f)
RogD   pl 9 (col) (f)

Languedoc

GaP   pl 2 (col) (f)
GiR   pl 41-42 (col)
LepF   pl 39 (col) (m)
Ogr   pl   p382 (col) (f)
RogD   pl 29 (col) (f)

Limousin

GaP   pl 16 (col) (f)
GiR   pl 43-44 (col)
Ogr   pl   p314 (col) (f)

Loire valley

Ogr   pl   p284 (col) (f)

Lorraine

See Lorraine

Lyonnais

GaP   pl 7 (col) (f)
GiR   pl 47-48 (col)
RogD   pl 25 (col) (f)

Maine

GaP   pl 13 (col) (f)
GiR   pl 49-50 (col)

Marche

GaP   pl 14 (col) (f)

Nice

BluN   pl   p58, 150
GaP   pl 21 (col) (f)
GiR   pl 53-54 (col)
LepF   pl 38 (col)
Ogr   pl   p416 (col) (f)

Nivernais

BluN   pl 52
GaP   pl 28 (col) (f)
GiR   pl 55-56 (col)

Normandy

BluN   pl   p58, 62, 64, 96, 150
Brad   pl   p65 (f)
BruK   pl 148 (col)
CosP   p 19-20   pl 17-22 (3 col)
GaP   pl   p8 (col) (f)
GiR   pl 57-58 (col)
LeID   il   p262 (f)
LepF   pl 6-9 (col) (f)
Ogr   pl   p216 (col) (f)
RogD   pl 12 (col) (f)

Orléanais

GaP   pl 22 (col) (f)
GiR   pl 59-60 (col)
RogD   pl 18 (col) (f)

Paris

See France—Île de France

FRANCE—*Continued*

Picardy
GaP pl 20 (col) (f)
GiR pl 61-62 (col)
RogD pl 16 (col) (f)

Poitou
BluN p79-80, 137-38 pl p60, 96, 150
CosP pl 40 (f)
GaP pl p 12, 17 (2 col) (f)
GiR pl 63-64 (col)
LepF pl 21 (col) (f)
Ogr pl p326 (col) (f)
RogD pl 21 (col) (f)

Provence
BluN p72-75 pl p60
BruK pl 148 fig 12 (col) (f)
CosP p24-26 pl 10-11, 13-14
GaP pl 30 (col) (f)
GiR pl 65-66 (col)
LepF pl 35-38 (col)
Ogr pl p396 (col) (f)
RogD pl 28 (col) (f)
Ten p 14 pl 1-2 (col)

See also France—Nice

Pyrenees
See Pyrenees mountains

Roussillon
GaP pl 29 (col) (f)
GiR pl 67-68 (col)

Saintonge and Angoumois
GaP pl 35 (col) (f)
GiR pl 3-4, 9 (col)

Savoie
CosP p27-28 pl 10
GaP pl 18 (col) (f)
GiR pl 69-70 (col)
LepF pl 31-34 (col) (f)
Ogr pl p412 (col) (f)
RogD pl 26 (col) (f)

Touraine
GaP pl 39 (col) (f)
GiR pl 71-72 (col)

Venaissin
GaP pl 23 (col) (f)
GiR pl 73-74 (col)

Vendée
See France—Poitou

FRANCHE-COMTÉ. See France—Franche-Comté

FRANCIS, KING. See subdivision under Kings and rulers—France

FRANCISCAN OBSERVANTS
Doy pl 73 (col)

FRANCISCAN SISTERS
Doy pl 135-37 (col)
MusE pl 23 (col)

FRANCISCANS
Ab pl p77
BruK pl 29 fig 7 (col)
Dav v 1 p 178 il (m)

Doy pl 70 (col)
HousM p37-38 fig 48
MusE pl 21 (col)
OrM pl 70-72
Trai p 51 il p40

FRANCONIA. See Germany—Franconia

FRÄNKE. See Sweden—Bohuslän

FRENCH EQUATORIAL AFRICA
GaU pl 9-10 (col)

FRENCH GUIANA. See Guiana, French

FRENCH HOODS. See Headdress—England—16th century; Headdress—France—16th century

FRIARS, BLACK. See Dominicans

FRIARS, GRAY. See Franciscans

FRIARS MINOR. See Franciscans

FRIARS PREACHERS. See Dominicans

FRIBOURG. See Switzerland—Fribourg

FRIENDS, SOCIETY OF. See Quakers

FRIESLAND. See Netherlands—Friesland

FRINGES AND TASSELS
LesA p532-39 il

Indians of North America
MasB p 100-01 il (incl pat)

FRISIAN ISLANDS
AndD pl p 13 (f)
AndF p29 pl 36 (col) (f)
BruK p34 pl 131 fig 1-10 (col) (f)
Kle p 158-59 il (f)
Nat v90 N '46 pl p643 (col) (f)
Ret p69-73 pl p73, 76-77 il

FROCK COATS

18th century
Yar p 198 pl p 199

19th century
Kle p 125 il
Trai p327 il
WilC p258 pl p266, 276
Yar p211, 223 pl p214, 226

20th century
WilC pl p338
Yar p251 pl p254

FRONTIERSMEN. See Pioneers and scouts

FUNERAL PROCESSIONS. See Processions, Funeral

FUR GARMENTS
Kle p283-85 il
LavT p208-15 pl (f)
LesA p541-54 2 pl il
WilF many pl il

FUR GARMENTS—*Continued*
19th century
Brk pl 22, 27, 34, 40 (f)
LavT2 p 167-68 pl p 161 (f)
20th century
AlF pl p7 (f)
Brk pl 47 (f)
CunPr il p38, 41 pl p51, 61 (f)
LavT2 p 168-69 pl p 161 (f)
WilC pl p343, 376
Wom p 10-12 il (f)

FUR TRAPPERS. See Pioneers and scouts

FUSILIERS
England
18th century
LavB p27-28 pl 3 (col) (pte)
Germany
18th century
KnR pl p 16, 17 (off, pte)
Lez pl p204 (col) (pte)
19th century
KnR pl p 17, 23, 125 (off, pte)
Lez pl p238 (col)

FYN. See Denmark—Fyn

G

GABLE HEADDRESS. See Headdress—England—15th and 16th centuries

GAGNEF. See Sweden—Dalarne

GAITERS
AnS p206-07 fig 248
LelD p389 il
LesA p311-12 il
Pic il p64, 139
WilFo p 107 pl p 116, 147, 150-51, 166

GALICIA. See Spain—Galicia

GARDE DU CORPS. See subdivision Guards and household troops under Military costume—France

GARDENERS. See Agricultural laborers

GARRALDA. See Spain—Navarre

GARTER, ORDER OF THE
BosE pl 5
Dav v 1 fig 916, 1151, 1201, 1210; v2 fig 1512
Doy pl 158 (col)
LelD p229 il
Norr v3 bk 1 p 160-62; bk 2 p531-34 il

GARTERS
Kle p 142 il
LelD p229 il
LesA p302-09 il
See also Leg-bands—Indians of North America

15th-16th centuries
CunS p37, 124 pl 50
DeB p 191 pl p 186 (m)
Lint p263-64 pl 16 (m)
WilC pl p 134
WilFo pl p78 (m)

GASCONY. See France—Guienne and Gascony

GÄSTRIKLAND. See Sweden—Gästrikland

GAUCHOS
Bac pt2 pl 5 (col)
CrO pl 26 fig 3
Hal pl 1, 3 (col)
Nat v74 N '38 pl p645, 649 651 (col); v76 N '39 pl p595 (col); v86 O '44 pl p490 (col); v94 N '48 pl p639-40 (col)
Spi pl p 16-17, 47 (col)
TiK pl 116 fig 22-23 (col)
See also Cowboys

GAUL. See France—Early to 511

GAUNTLETS (ARMOR)
Dav v 1 pl p 155
LelD p 190, 193 il

GEISHA GIRLS
Haa pl 5, 82
Saj pl p87

GELDERLAND. See Netherlands—Guelders

GENDARMES. See Police—France

GENERALS
Germany
17th-18th centuries
Lez pl p 200 (col)
WilF pl p88
19th century
Lez pl p263 (col)
20th century
Lez pl p381 (col)
Italy
14th century
Dav v 1 fig 609
Korea
Pot v2 pl 8 (col)
Netherlands
18th century
Lez pl p232 (col)
Rome
Loud pl 5 (col)
UnW pl 17 (col)
Russia
19th century
BruK pl 123 fig 10 (col)

GENEVA. See Switzerland—Geneva

GENOA. See Italy—Liguria

GENTLEMEN-AT-ARMS

England

16th century

Norr v3 bk 1 p31 il

19th century—date

BarH pl 23 (col) (off)

GENTLEMEN PENSIONERS, ENG-LAND. See Pensioners—England

GEORGE, KING. See subdivisions under Kings and rulers—England

GEORGIA. See Russia—Georgia

GERMANY
> *See also* Fancy dress and stage costume —German; also subdivision Germany under Children; Coronation robes; Court costume; Dancers; Festival costume; Hair, wigs, etc.; Military costume; Mourning costume; Naval costume; Wedding costume; also names of occupations (e.g. Agricultural laborers; Barbers; Musicians) and individual articles of attire (e.g. Capes and cloaks; Coats and jackets; Footwear; Headdress)

Early to 843

Bra p 102-03 pl 14
Bruh p 10-13 (2 pl col)
BruK p 11-12, 49-50 pl 22-23
Dal v 1 p250-57 pl il (col)
Kle p 148-50 il
Ni p 1-16 pl 1-3
TiK p25 pl 38
WilC pl p32 (f)

843-1300

BroW v 1 front (col) pl p 18 (col) fig 1, 4, 7, 9
Bruh p 14-16 pl (col)
BruK p53-54 pl 31-33 (1 col)
Dav v 1 p 123, 140-42, 184-89 7 pl
Dot p 123, 126, 132 il
Ni p 17-44 pl 4-9, 12
Tik pl 117 fig 1 (m)
WilC p63-67 2 pl
> *See also* Kings and rulers—Germany— 10th century; Kings and rulers—Germany—11th-12th centuries; Noblemen—Germany—13th-14th centuries; Queens and empresses — Germany — 13th-14th centuries

14th century

Bruh p 16-17, 22-23 2 pl (col)
Dav v 1 p228-33 6 pl
Dot p 135-36 il
KerM no3 pl 10 (f)
Ni p44-52 pl 10-11, 13-14
WilC p63-67 2 pl

15th century

BroW v 1 fig 26-27, 36, 38, 42-43, 52, 55-56
BruK pl 60-61 (1 col)

BruM p pl 15 (col) (f)
Dal v2 fig 283-85 (col) (m)
Dav v 1 p367-73 il
Dot p 140-41 il
Gor pl p29-30, 32
KerM no3 pl 3 (m)
LavE pl 5, 9
Ni p52-71 pl 15-23
WilC p63-67 2 pl
WilF pl p38-45
> *See also* Noblewomen—Germany—15th century

16th century

BroW v 1 p 124, 128, 142 pl p 110, 118 (col) fig 66, 68, 74D, 76B-81B, 83, 87, 89C-90
Bruh p28-33, 36-37 4 pl (col)
BruK p20-21, 62-63, 65-66 pl 60-65, 68-70, 77-80 (4 col)
BruM pl p 17, 19, 21 (1 col) (f)
Dav v 1 p384-403, 407-13 6 pl il; v2 p501 il (f)
Dot p 149 il
Gor pl p46, 49, 52, 54, 57-58, 61
Kle p297-98 il (f)
Ni p72-107 pl 24-33
TiK pl 121 (col)
UnW pl 37 (m)
VanH pl 4
WilC p77-79 pl
WilF pl p53-56, 59, 70
> *See also* Kings and rulers—Germany—16th century; Noblemen—Germany—16th century; Noblewomen—Germany—16th century; Queens and Empresses—Germany—16th century

17th century

BroW v2 fig 9, 29 (m)
BruK p23-24 pl 85, 94 (1 col)
Dav v2 p630 fig 1680 (f)
Ger fig 15 (m)
Hat fig 157
KelF pl p97
Kle p 179 il (m)
Ni p 108-39 pl 34-38
TiK pl 122 (col)
> *See also* Noblemen—Germany—17th century; Noblewomen—Germany—17th century

18th century—date

BroW v2 fig 58-59, 65-67, 69-70 pl p 110, 124 (col)
BruK p29 pl 109, 115 (1 col)
Dav v2 fig 2042-53
Gor pl p 106, 119
Kle p47-49 il
Lel v 11 pl 8, 13, 17, 25, 34-35, 39-41 (5 col); v 12 pl 12 (f)
Ni p 140-212 p39-56
> *See also* Nineteenth century; Twentieth century

BY REGION OR PROVINCE

Baden

BruK pl 138 (col)
Kle p41 il (f)
> *See also* Germany—Black Forest

GERMANY—*Continued*

Bavaria

16th century

BruK pl 68 fig 1-4 (col) (f)
Kle p64 il (f)
WilF pl p65, 66 (f)

17th century

BruK pl 94 fig 11 (f)
Kle p32-36 il

18th century—date

Brad pl p74 (f)
BruK p36 pl 137 (col)
Er p40-42 pl (col)
Kle p42-43, 65, 301-02 il
Lee p22-25 pl (f)
Ret p 149-55, 163, 166-73   5 pl il

Black Forest

Brad pl p69-71 (1 col)
BruK pl 138 (col)
CamC pl p22-23, 32 (f)
Er p48-50 pl (col)
Kle p339-41 il
Pet p 12-27, 30-37, 40-89   37 pl (7 col)
front (col)
Ret p 185-216 16 pl il

Brandenburg

BruK pl 132 fig 15-17 (col)

Brunswick

BruK pl 133 fig 14-19 (col)

Franconia

Er p55-59 pl 15-16 (col)

Frisian islands

See Frisian islands

Hamburg

BruK p34 pl 133 (col)
Er p 16-18 pl (col)
Kle p400 il (f)
Ret p64-70 2 pl il (f)
Vert pl p 101 (f)

Hanover

BruK pl 133 fig 1-7 (col)

Harz mountains

BruK pl 135 (col)

Helgoland

See Helgoland

Hesse

Brad pl p73 (f)
BruK p35 pl 135 (col)
Er p37-39 pl (col)
Kle p58, 174-76 il
Ret p 17-55 18 pl il
RetS pl 36-41, 44, 46-51, 54-57, 101-12

Mecklenburg

BruK pl 132 fig 13-14 (col)

Palatinate

WilF pl p68 (f)

Pomerania

BruK p34-35 pl 132 fig 7-12 (col)
Er p 19-20 pl (col)

Saxe-Altenburg

Er p23-24 pl 4 (col)

Schaumburg-Lippe

BruK pl 134 (col)
Er p31-34 pl (col) (f)
Kle p65 il (f)
Ret p56-64 2pl il (f)

Schleswig-Holstein

BruK p34 pl 131 fig 12-16 (col)

Silesia

BruK pl 136 (col)
Er p28-30 pl (col) (f)
Ret p 113-28 9 pl il
WilF pl p72

Spreewald

BruK pl 136 (col)
Kle p365 il (f)
Nat v71 F '37 p 166 il
See also Wends

Swabia

Ret p 155-623 pl il

Thuringia

BruK pl 135 (col)
Ger p 11-131 18 pl (16 col) il

Vierland

See Germany—Hamburg

Westphalia

BruK p35 pl 134 (col) (f)
Dav v 1 fig 1103 (f)
Er p31-34 pl (col) (m)

Württemberg

BruK p36 pl 139 (col)
See also Germany—Black Forest

GERONA. See Spain—Catalonia

GIBSON WAISTS. See Waists—20th century—1900-1910

GILBERT ISLANDS. See Dancers—Gilbert Islands

GILBERTINE NUNS
Doy pl 92 (col)

GILDSMEN

England

Trev v 1 fig 54-57 il
WilF pl p62

GIPSIES
See also Fancy dress and stage costume—Gipsy

Hungary

Nat v73 Ja '38 p 18 (col) (f)

Spain

Agu pl 105 (f)
Gom pl p53, 61
OrT pl 224-25, 229

GIRL SCOUTS
    Turkey
  Nat v87 My '45 pl p589 (col)

GIRONDE. See France—Guienne and Gascony

GLADIATORS
  AirP p39 il
  Dal v 1 fig 400-01
  Gor pl p 14
  LelD p201-02 il

GLASSBLOWERS
    16th century
  AirT p30 il

GLEANERS. See Agricultural laborers

GLENGARRY BONNETS
  WilH pl p204

GLOBES, IMPERIAL. See Orbs (Regalia)

GLORY (SYMBOLICAL FIGURE)
  OrM pl 188

GLOVES
  Kle p 165-68 il
  Pic p66 il
  See also Mitts and mittens
    Early to 1200
  Coll p4-7, 48-52 2 pl
  HousG2 fig 167f
  LesA p351-57 il
  Rud pl p218
  WisF pl 6 (f)
    13th-15th centuries
  Coll p34 pl p33
  LelD pl p 192 fig 3-6
  WisF pl 7 (f)
    16th century
  Coll p 19-27 front, pl p 17, 20, 25, 28, 35, 37
  CunS p50, 143-44, 182 pl 69
  KelF p34 pl p83 (m)
  LelD p 192-93 pl fig 7-10
  LesA p359-64 pl il
  Norr v3 bk 1 p260-61 il; bk 2 p551-53 il
  WilC pl p 140
  WisF pl 10-11 (f)
  Yar pl p 117, 136
    17th century
  Coll pl p 10 (m)
  Dal v2 fig 459 (col)
  Dav v2 fig 1476-78
  Gor pl p83, 89
  LelD p 136 fig 2; pl p 192 fig 11-18
  LesA p364-68 pl 41 il
  Lint p266-70 pl
  TiK pl 124 fig 20
  ViP v 1 pl 17
  Yar pl p 173

    18th century
  Coll pl p20
  Dav v2 fig 1848
  Gor pl p 114
  Lel v 11 p33, 73 fig 32, 78 (incl pat)
  LelD il p 136 (f)
    19th century
  Dal v2 fig 783
  Dav v2 p847 il
  HaC p 175-76 pl (f)
  LesA p368-70 pl il
  WisF pl 20 (f)
    20th century
  Coll p66-79 3 pl
  HaC pl p 176 (f)
  LelD p 136 fig 3; pl p 192 fig 20-24
  LesA p370-74 il
  Rud pl p218
  WisF pl 27, 29 (f)
    Byzantine Empire
  Dal v 1 fig 470 (col)
    Estonia
  Int v2 pl 30 (f)
    Indians of North America
  Hun pl p34
    Latvia
  Int v2 pl 44
    Norway
  Prim pl p52
    Peru
  CrO pl 25 fig 3
    Sweden
  Sv p214-21 il

GLOVES, ECCLESIASTICAL
  Coll p40-47 2 pl
  LelD pl p 192 fig 1-2, 6, 10-11
  LesA p354-55 il
  McC p 114-16 il
  NorC p 185-87 pl

GNOME. See Fancy dress and stage costume—Gnome

GOBLIN. See Fancy dress and stage costume—Goblin

GODDESSES
    Assyria and Babylonia
  Hous2 p 124 fig 124
    China
  Nat v85 Je '44 pl p736
    Crete
  Vert p38
    Egypt
  Gen v 1 fig 97, 115 pl 2 (col)
  HeuO pl 20
  Hous2 pl 1 (col) fig 35-36, 78
    Greece
  Dav v 1 p66, 69-70 3 pl
  Gen v 1 fig 263, 277, 294, 296, 307, 322-23, 328 pl 6 (col)

GODDESSES—Greece—*Continued*
HousG2 pl p61
TiK pl 10 fig 9
Vert pl p72
WilFo pl p24

Hittites
Hous2 p71-72 fig 77a

Persia
Hous2 p 175-77 fig 173, 177

GODS
Assyria
Gor pl p8
Aztec
KaAz pl 10-12 (col)

Egypt
Gen v 1 fig 115
Hous2 p22-23 pl 2 fig 26
Wa p 13-15 fig 13-25
Wrig pt3 p 14 pl p26

Greece
Dav v 1 p60, 62, 68-69 il
Gen v 1 fig 263-64, 267, 306
HousG2 p68-69 il
TiK pl 10 fig 1
Wa p47-48 fig 45C
WilF pl p 10
WilFo pl p22

Mexico
DuS p21-24, 37 pl 5, 15 (col)

Persia
Hous2 p 171-74 fig 169

GÖINGE. See Sweden—Skåne

GOLD MINERS. See Miners and prospectors

GOLDEN FLEECE, ORDER OF THE
BraF pl p 17
BruK pl 30 fig 13 (col)
Dav v 1 p309-11 fig 826, 832, 1216, 1220
EvnJ pl 133

GOLF COSTUME
17th century
Dur il p8 (m)

18th century
Dav v2 fig 2223 (m)
Lel v 12 pl 18

19th century
Ada v4 il p59, 94 (f)
Davi v2 il p68
Jen p 132 il (f)
Kou pl 229
Pic il p 134 (f)
Trai p343 il (f)

20th century
CunA pl 31b

1900-1910
Ada v4 il p306 (f)
LavT2 p 180 pl p 189 (f)
VanH pl 12 (f)
Wom p 19 il (f)

1910-1920
CunPr pl p 119 (f)
Dur il p 140 (m)
WilC pl p364 (f)

1920-1930
AlF pl p76 (m)
Bro20 il p59
Dur pl p 193 (f)
LavT2 p 180 pl p 189 (f)
Wom p 19 il (f)

1930-1940
CunPr p218 pl p209 (f)
LavT p 180 pl p 189 (f)
Wom p 19 il (f)

1940-1950
Wom p 19 il (f)

GONDOLIERS
Mora pl 100, 102

GORDON   HIGHLANDERS   (REGI-MENT)
BarH pl 16, 20 (col) (pte)
Nat v78 S '40 pl p389

GORGETS. See Wimples and gorgets

GOTHIC PERIOD. See entries for costume of various European countries during the period 1200-1450

GOTHS
See Europe—To 476

GOWNS, COLLEGE. See Academic costume

GRANADA. See Spain—Andalusia

GRAND BIGARD NUNS
Doy pl 127 (col)

GRANDMONTINES
Doy pl p74 (col)

GRAUBÜNDEN. See Switzerland—Graubünden

GRAY FRIARS. See Franciscans

GREAT BRITAIN. See England; Ireland, Scotland; Wales

GREECE
Ancient
BartC p86-98 fig 30-39
BiE p23-44 pl 11-42, 54 il
Bra p45-62 3 pl
BruK p8-9, 45-47 pl 12-15, table 2 (pat)
Burr p8, 114, 188-89, 295-96 pl p9
Dal v 1 p99-146 19 pl il (col)
Dav v 1 p40-72 21 pl il
Dot p 109-12 il

GREECE—Ancient—*Continued*
Eli p28-32, 40-43, 58-60 pl il (incl pat)
Eth p7-16 3 pl il
Gen v 1 p65-94 26 pl (3 col) fig 265-66, 295, 297, 304-05, 314-17, 320, 382-89 (incl pat)
Gor p9-13 3 pl
HousG2 p33-82 7 pl (1 col) il (incl pat)
KerM no 1 pl 6-9
Kle p 19, 81-83, 98-99, 110 il
Lecl pl 2 (col) (f)
Lee p78-80 pl
LelD p 100-01, 173, 216, 312 il
Lis p22-24 il (f)
Loud pl 4 (col)
Nat v85 Mr '44 p314-35 11 pl (col)
NorC p 11, 21-22 il (incl pat)
Pic il p26 (f)
Pot v 1 p27-32 pl 10-12 (col) (incl pat)
RueG pl 5-9 (f)
TiK p13-14 pl 10
Tru p3-6 il
UnW pl 8-12 (col)
Wa p32-48 pl il (incl pat)
WilC p 11-17 3 pl
WisF pl 3 (f)
Yar p 13-21 3 pl
    See also Amazons; Bacchantes; Chios; Euboea Island; Fancy dress and stage costume—Greek; Macedonia; also subdivision Greece—Ancient under Charioteers; Children; Dancers; Hair; Wigs, etc.; Gods; Military costume; Priests; also under individual articles of attire (e.g. Footwear, Headdress)

Modern

    See also Dancers—Greece, Modern; Fancy dress and stage costume—Greek; Festival costume — Greece, Modern; Military costume—Greece, Modern

        16th-17th centuries
Nat v96 D '49 pl p727 (col) (f)
TiK pl 65 (col)

        18th century—date
At pl 2-29, 34-45 (col)
Brad p76-77
Bruk pl 164 (col)
CrO pl 32
Cros p 17-18 pl 1, 3 (col)
Int pl 35
Lee p26-28 pl
Nat v75 Je '39 il p793; v77 Mr '40 pl p307-11, 313, 317, 320-21 (col); v79 Ja '41 pl p95; v85 Mr '44 pl p258, 266
TiK pl 65 (col)
    See also Fancy dress and stage costume—Greece, Modern

GREEK CHURCH. See Ecclesiastical costume—Greek church

GREEN MOUNTAIN RANGERS
MusM pl 24-25 (col) (off, pte)

GREENLAND. See Eskimos

GREMIAL
McC p 146-47 il

GRENADIERS

        Austria-Hungary
        18th-19th centuries
KnR pl p221, 229

        England
        17th century
BarH p44, 47 pl 2-3 (col)
Law v 1 p28-32 il (off, pte)

        18th century
BarH p48 front pl 3, 5 (col) (pte)
KnR pl p357
Law v2 p 1-4, 14-16, 28, 114-16, 136-37, 140-44 fig 1-5, 13, 15, 29-30, 32, 38 il (off, pte)

        19th century
BarH p 188-90 pl (col) (off, pte)
KnR pl p361

        20th century
Nat v 104 S '53 pl p295, 331 (col)

        France
        18th century
KnR pl p259 (pte)

        19th century
BluN pl p 172 (pte)
BruK pl 123 fig 17 (col)
Fro pl 2, 8-9 (col) (off, pte)
KnR pl p293
LelD p204-05 il
Lez pl p273 (col) (off, pte)

        Germany
        17th-18th centuries
BruK pl 119 fig 3 (col) pl 120 fig 11
KnR pl p 13, 95, 151 (off, pte)
Lez pl p 188-89, 194-95, 197, 205-06, 219 (col) (off, pte)

        19th century
BruK pl 123 fig 3 (col) (pte)
KnR pl p23
Lez pl p238, 240, 341 (col) (off, pte)

        Poland
        19th century
Lez pl p313 (col)

        Spain
        19th century
Lez pl p291 (col)

GRONINGEN. See Netherlands—Groningen

GROOMS

        Egypt, Ancient
Hous2 fig 67

        Egypt, Modern
Nat v89 Mr '46 pl p335 (col)

        England
        19th century
Gor pl p 134

GRUYÈRE. See Switzerland—Fribourg

GUADALAJARA. See Spain—Castile, New

GUADELOUPE (ISLAND)
    GaU pl 27 (col) (f)

GUANAJUATO. See Mexico—Guanajuato

GUATEMALA
    CrO pl 25 fig 5 (f)
    Spi p46-51 pl il
        See also Dancers—Guatemala

GUELDERS. See Netherlands—Guelders

GUERRERO. See Mexico—Guerrero

GUIANA, DUTCH. See Surinam

GUIANA, FRENCH
    GaU pl 28-29 (col) (f)
    Nat v79 My '41 pl p639-46 (col)

GUIENNE.   See France—Guienne and
    Gascony

GUIPÚZCOA. See Basque provinces

GUNSMITHS
        19th century
    Kou pl 64

GYMNASIUM SUITS
    Chr p 184 fig 366
    Jen pl p 142-43 (f)
    Rue pl P

GYPSIES. See Gipsies

H

HABIT SHIRTS
    CunU p83-87 fig 37, 56 (f)

HADERSLEV. See Denmark—Jutland

HAIR, WIGS, ETC.
    Bin p85-113 4 pl il
    Kle p36-39, 159-63, 232-35 il
    LelD p 107-14 5 pl il; p312-14 pl il;
        p312-14 pl il
    Pic p 165-66 il
        See also Bagwigs; Beards; Headdress;
    also costume of different countries and
    periods, e.g. France—17th century
        19th century
    AirB pl p58-63 (m)
    KerA p64-65 pl (f)
    LavT p 140-49 pl (f)
    Nap p62-73 il (f)
    Rud pl p92-93
        1800-1810
    Gor pl p 135
    LelD p99 fig 7, pl p 113 fig 1-2 (f)
    Wa p248, 253 fig 202
    WilH p201-10 10 pl

        1810-1820
    But pl p52-53 (m)
    LavT2 pl p 124 (f)
    LelD p 109 fig 12 (m) pl p 113 fig 3-4
        (f)
    Wa p257-58 fig 202, 207
    WilC p259 pl p270

        1820-1830
    BroH p 181 fig 121 (f)
    LavT2 p 117-18 pl p 124 (f)
    LelD pl p 113 fig 5-6 (f)
    Wa p261 fig 213, 223
    WilC p250 pl p256
    WilH p221, 258 pl il

        1830-1840
    Lang p 119-26 11 pl (2 col) (f)
    LelD p99 fig 8 (f) p 109 fig 13 (m)
        pl p 113 fig 7-9 (f)
    Wa p266 fig 224F
    WilC p274 pl p280
    WilH pl p217, 224

        1840-1850
    Gor pl p 146 (f)
    LavT2 p 118 pl p 124 (f)
    LelD p7 il (f) p99 fig 9 (f) p 109
        fig 14-16 (m) pl p 113 fig 10-13 (f)
    QuV fig 138 (f)
    Wa p269, 271 fig 218, 220
    WilH pl p238-39, 242

        1850-1860
    Gor pl p 150
    LavT2 p 118-19 pl p 124 (f)
    LelD pl p 113 fig 14-15 (f)
    Wa p278, 281 fig 231, 234, 256

        1860-1870
    Kle p80 il (f)
    Lang p 126-30 pl (f)
    LavT2 p 119 pl p 124 (f)
    LelD p99 fig 10 (f) p 109 fig 17 (m)
        pl p 113 fig 16 (f)
    Trai p328 il (m)
    Wa p285, 288-89 fig 237 (f)

        1870-1880
    LavT2 p 120 pl p 124 (f)
    LelD pl p 113 fig 17-20 (f)
    QuV fig 139-40 (f)
    Wa p298 fig 241 (m)

        1880-1890
    Gor pl p 165 (f)
    LavT2 p 120 pl p 124 (f)
    LelD p99 fig 11 (f) p 109 fig 18-19
        (m) pl p 113 fig 21 (f)
    Part p 143 il
    Wa p313-14 fig 249A (f)
    WilC p314 pl p318 (f)

        1890-1900
    Ada v4 il p53
    Wa p325 fig 253 (f)

        20th century
    KerA p64-65 pl (f)
    LavT p 155-59 pl (f)
    Nap p74-96 19 pl il

HAIR, WIGS, ETC.—20th century—_Continued_

1900-1910
Bro20 p25-27 il (f)
LavT2 p 120-21 pl p 124 (f)

1910-1920
LavT2 p 123-24 pl p 125 (f)
LelD pl p 113 fig 23-25 (f)
Wa p349 fig 267-68 il (f)
WisF pl 26 (f)

1920-1930
LavT2 p 124-25 pl p 125 (f)
LelD pl p 113 fig 26-27 (f)
Wa p355 fig 275 (f)

1930-1940
LavT2 p 126-27 pl p 125 (f)
LelD pl 113 fig 28-30
WilH pl p309

1940-1950
CunPr p271 pl p273 il (f)
Kle p80 (f)

African tribes
Nat v73 S '38 pl p359 (f); v81 Mr '42
il p373, 385 (f); v97 Mr '50 pl p337
(col) (m)

Annam
Pot v2 pl 12 (col)

Assyria and Babylonia
Dot p 107 il
LelD pl p 108 fig 5 (m)
Wa p22, 24 fig 29, 30A, 32A, 33A, 34A
WilC pl p 10
WilH pl p 11

Burgundy
15th century
BruK pl 50 (m)

Byzantine empire
Nap p29-30 il (f)

China
Dal v 1 fig 801-03 (col) (f)
Nap p 18-19 il (f)
Nat v71 Ap '37 p506 il (m)

Crete, Ancient
WisF pl 3D (f)

Egypt, Ancient
Bra pl 3-4
DeZ pl 8-9, 16-17 (m)
Dot p 104-05 il
Hous2 p 10-11 fig 12-14, 17-18
Kle p287 il (m)
Lang p 13-17 2 pl (1 col) (f)
LelD pl p 108 fig 3-4 (m) pl p 110
fig 3-5 (f) pl p313 fig 1-2
LesA p83-84 fig 96-100
NeP p3 pl 8
Wa p6, 12 fig 1
WilH pl p5-7
WisF pl 1 (f)

England
To 449
Nap p31 il

1066-1200
BrH p 16-27 6 pl
CunM p23-24 il
Tru p 18 il p 16, 17
Yar pl p49

14th-15th centuries
CunM p74-76, 116-17 (3 pl)
Norr v3 bk 1 p88-89, 101-02, 108 il

16th century
CunS p48-50, 84, 141-43, 179-80 pl 14-
15, 43-44
Nap p40-43 il (f)
Norr v3 bk 1 p311-13 il (m); bk 2
p447-49, 721-22, 735-38 il
Rey p 10 pl 12-13, 43, 47-50, 52-56

17th century
AirB pl p42-47 (m)
BroH p 129-31, 139 fig 89-90, 93-95
Kle p287 il (m)
Roj pl p26-27
Tru p61-62, 68-75 il
WilC pl p 157, 192
Yar pl p 153, 158, 166, 173

18th century
AirB pl p52-55 (m)
AirH p 10 il (f)
BroH p 139, 141, 143, 159 fig 91, 93, 95,
101-01, 103-06, 154-58
Dav v2 p763 il
Dot p 159, 161 il
Yar p 191, 195 pl p 173, 179, 187, 192,
197

Etruria
WilH pl p22

Europe
Early to 1200
LelD pl p 108 fig 117 (m)
WilH pl p49

13th-14th centuries
LelD pl p 108 fig 18-21 (m) pl p 110
fig 17-19 (f)

15th century
BroW v 1 p78-81, 100-05 fig 57-61 (f)
Lang p38-45 4 pl il (f)
LavR pl p26
LelD pl p 108 fig 22-24 (m) pl p 110
fig 20-23 (f)
Nap p32-38 il (f)
Wa p 127 fig 131

16th century
KelF p31-33 pl p73 (m)
LelD pl p 108 fig 25-28 (m) pl p 110
fig 24-26; pl p 110 fig 1-2 (f)
WilH p93-103 9 pl (f)

17th century
Bra pl 27, 29
BroW v2 p59-64 fig 31-36
Gor pl p70, 73, 78, 82-83, 86, 89, 92,
94
Kle p 17 il (m)
Lang p46-51 5 pl il (f)
LelD p99 fig 1-4; pl p 108 fig 29-32;
p 109 fig 1; pl p 111 fig 3-22

HAIR, WIGS, ETC.—Europe—17th century
—*Continued*
LesA p85-88 il
Wa p 178, 183-84, 190, 195, 198 fig 156,
165G, 168, 171
WilH p 126-36 11 pl

18th century

Bra pl 33, 36
Gor pl p 103, 105, 107, 112, 114, 118,
121-22, 124
Kle p 16, 77-78 il (m)
Lang p51-115 36 pl (8 col) il (f)
LelD p99 fig 5-6; p 109 fig 2-11
LesA p88-96 il (m)
Wa p213, 217, 222-23, 226-27, 229, 232
fig 182, 183C, 199
WilH p 161-77 11 pl

France

Early to 1200

LelD pl p 108 fig 13-14 (m)

14th century

Dav v2 fig 1395-97

16th century

Norr v3 bk 2 p725, 738-40 il

17th century

BluE pl 6, 43, 45, 55 (1 col)
DeZ p75-77 pl 95
LelD p60 il (m) p221 il (f) pl p313
fig 3-9 (m)
Nap p44-50 il (f)
WilC p 138, 144, 168, 176, 179 pl p 140,
148, 173, 183

18th century

BruK pl 112 (f)
Dal v2 p395-409 pl il (col)
Lang p67-109 16 pl (4 col) (f)
LelD p78, 338 pl p 112, 313 fig 10-27
il
Nap p51-61 3 pl il (f)

1715-1774

Dav v2 p688 il (f)
Lel v 11 p26-29, 66-68 fig 21-26, 68-69;
v 12 p20-21, 49-51, pl 9 fig 16, 62-65
(1 col)
WilC p 195, 198 pl p205

1774-1789

WilC p208, 212 pl p219

1789-1795

WilC p222 pl p227

1795-1799

WilC p231 pl p235
WilH p 191-95 5 pl

Germany

16th century

DeZ pl 54 (m)

18th century

DeZ pl 94
Kle p420 il (f)
Lang pl p81 fig 12, 14 (1 col)

Greece, Ancient

BruK p48 pl 20
Dal v 1 fig 228-34 (col) (f)
DeZ pl 24-25 (m)
Dot p 111 il
HousG2 p78-80 il
Lang p 18-23 5 pl (col)
LelD pl p 108 fig 1-2, 6-8; pl p 110
fig 1-2, 6-7
Nap p21-24 pl il (f)
Pot v 1 pl 11 (col) (f)
Tru p4-5 il
Wa p38, 45 fig 45
WilC pl p 17 (f)
WilH pl p5
WisF pl 3 (f)

Hungary

Bud pl 78 (m)

Indians of North America

MasB p 116 il
Nat v78 N '40 pl p590 (col) (f)

Italy

15th century

Kle p420 il (f)
WilC p72 pl p76

16th century

Norr v3 bk 2 p725-26, 740-41 fig 662-
64, 761-64
WilC p72 pl p76

17th century

DeZ pl 90

Japan

Nap p 19-20 il (f)
Nat v 100 D '51 p741 (f)
SaJ p9-88 33 pl il
Tik pl 100 fig 4 (col) (f)

Laos

Pot v2 pl 13 (col) (f)

Netherlands

17th century

BruK p69-70 pl 95

New Guinea

Nat v86 O '44 il p453 (m)

Palestine, Ancient

Wrig pl p 25

Persia, Ancient

Wa p27 fig 29

Peru, Ancient

Zim p6 pl il

Philippine Islands

Nat v86 N '44 pl p548 (col) (f)

Rome

BruK p48 pl 20
Dal v 1 fig 307-12, 315-21 (col) (f)
DeZ pl 35-39 (m)
Dot p 113 il
HousG2 p 111-17 il (f)
Lang p24-27 5 pl (f)
LelD pl p 108 fig 9-12 (m) pl p 110
fig 8-15 (f)

HAIR, WIGS, ETC.—Rome—*Continued*
Nap p25-28 il (f)
Tru p9 il p8, 9
Wa p60 fig 57 (f)
WilC p20 pl p23 (f)
WilH pl p23, 24
Yar pl p27

Russia
18th century
Lang pl p78 (f)

Savage and primitive races
Bra p6-7 pl

Spain
16th century
Norr v3 bk 2 p726, 741 fig 772-73, 843, 886

19th century—date
Agu pl 112 (f)
AnS p 102-04, 129-33 fig 120-23, 157-58

Sweden
18th century
Lang pl p79 (f)

Tibet
Nat v95 My '49 pl p667 (col) il p689 (f)

United States
18th century
But pl p 16-17 (m)
LesA pl 21 fig 102
Trai p 160 il (m)
WilH pl p 161

Venice
18th century
Mora pl 2-11 (m)

HAIR ORNAMENTS
Lee pl p41
See also Aigrettes; Combs (Head-dress); Hair pins

16th century
WilH pl p93-97

19th century
Flow pl 9 (col) fig 99, 100
WisF pl 23G

20th century
Coh p323-25 il

Cameroons, French
Leb pl 1 (col)

China
NeC pl 5, 18, 20-21

France
LelD p 176 il

HAIRDRESSERS
France
18th century
BoeR il p536 (m)

Japan
SaJ pl p43 (f)

HAIRPINS
Ancient
Dot il p 114
Jes p56-57, 101-03 pl 9
LesA p 116-19 il
WilC pl p23
WilH p 14, 21 pl p 17

Modern
EvnJ fig 35
Flow fig 17, 63, 100, 223
Kle p 158 il
LesA p 119-21 il

HAITI
Spi p52, 55 il
See also Military costume—Haiti

HALLAND. See Sweden—Gothland

HALLINGDAD. See Norway—Hallingdad

HAMBURG. See Germany—Hamburg

HANDBAGS. See Bags, purses, etc.

HANDKERCHIEFS
Dav v2 p635-36, 867 il
HaC pl p204
LesA p426-35 pl il
Norr v3 bk 1 p261 fig 244, 289; bk 2 p549-50 il
Rey pl 34 (f)

HANDRUFFS. See Cuffs and handruffs

HANOVER. See Germany—Hanover

HANOVERIAN REGIMENTS
18th century
Law v2 p229-58 il (off, pte)

HARDANGER. See Norway—Hardanger

HARLEQUINS. See Fancy dress and stage costume—Harlequin

HARPISTS
Egypt, Ancient
Dal v 1 fig 35 (col) (f)
Hous2 fig 59 (m)

Ireland
17th century
Mccl p57 pl 44

England
19th century
QuV fig 125 (f)

Sumeria
Hous2 p 109-10 fig 109 (m)

HARZ MOUNTAINS. See Germany—Harz mountains

HAT ORNAMENTS
EvnJ p88-91, 98-99, 128-29 pl II, III (col) pl 28, 42-43, 45, 48, 51, 56-57, 59, 69, 82, 84, 132
LelD p 161 il
NeR p 1-2 pl 1, 3, 20
Norr v3 bk 1 p 122, 353-54 il; bk 2 p776-77 il

HATS. See Headdress

HAUDRIETTE SISTERS. See Hospitaler sisters of the Assumption

HAUSAS
GaU pl 8 (col) (m)
Nat v85 My '44 pl p545 (col) (m)

HÄVERÖ. See Sweden—Uppland

HAVERSACKS
LelD p214 il

HAWAIIAN ISLANDS
Lee p28-29 pl
Nat v74 O '38 pl p440-41 (col) (f)
TiK pl 101 fig 13-19 (col) (m)
    See also Dancers—Hawaiian Islands; Festival costume—Hawaiian Islands

HAWKERS. See Street venders and peddlers

HAWKING COSTUME. See Falconers; Hunting costume

HEADDRESS
Hea p54-61 4 pl (incl pat)
Kle p 183-87, 324-26 2 pl il
Pic p 18-22, 70-78 il
Pric p 145-59 pl (m)
    See also Aigrettes; Berets; Combs (Headdress); Hair, wigs, etc.; Hair ornaments; Hennins; Hoods; Kerchiefs; Nightcaps; Sombreros; Tricorns and bicorns; Turbans

      Ancient to 476
Bra pl 5
BruK pl 8
LelD pl p86 fig 1-2
Nap p 10-11 il (f)

      13th century
Pic il p31 (f)

      19th century
Chr p 182 fig 360
Dal v2 p478-91, 1000-49 (col) (f)
Dav v2 p807, 861, 871, 875 il
Dot il p 166
GiMi p 19-20 (col) (f)
Gor pl p 135, 137, 140, 142, 146, 150, 157, 162, 165, 172
Kle p426-27 il (m)
LavT p 143-49 pl p 152 (f)
LesA p46-56, 80-82 pl 15, 19-20 il
Part p 154 il (m)
Pic il p 10-11 (f)
Yar pl p209, 222, 234, 248

      1800-1810
Brk pl 13, 14 (f)
CunE p55-61 il (f)
Dav v2 p807 il
Gor pl p 135 (f)
LelD pl p40 fig 14-16, pl p89 fig 8 (f)
ViN fig 1-12
Wa p248-49, 253 fig 201-02

WilC p237, 240, 263-64 pl p246, 256, 270
WilH p201-10 10 pl

      1810-1820
Ada v2 il p 109 (m)
Brk pl 15-16 (f)
CunE p64-69 il (f)
Gor pl p 137
LelD pl p87 fig 19; pl p89 fig 9-12
ViN fig 14-22
Wa p258-59 fig 204, 207, 221
WilC p237, 240 pl p246 (f)
WilH pl p218, 220

      1820-1830
Brk pl 17, 18 (f)
CunE p90-98 il (f)
Dav v2 p836-38 il (f)
Gor pl p 140 (f)
Loud pl 17 (col)
ViN fig 23-31
Wa p261-62 fig 209, 211-13
WilC pl p256
WilH pl p217-18

      1830-1840
BoeB pl p601 (m)
Brk pl 20 (f)
CunE p99-103, 122-23 il (f)
Dav v2 p849-51 il
Gor pl p 142
LelD pl p40 fig 17-19, 21; pl p87 fig 20-21; pl p89 fig 15-17
ViN fig 34-39
Wa p264, 266 fig 214-15, 220, 225
WilC p272, 274 pl p280, 306
WilH pl p216-17, 222

      1840-1850
Brk pl 21-22 (f)
CunE p 156-62 il (f)
Dav p860-61, 871 il
Gern pl 1, 10 (f)
Gor pl p 146
LavT2 p 118 pl p 117 (f)
LelD pl p87 fig 25; pl p89 fig 18-19
ViN fig 40-49
Wa p271 fig 220 (f)
WilH pl p218, 232-33, 235, 237-38

      1850-1860
Bra p299 pl 43 (f)
Brk pl 23-25 (f)
CunE p 196-204 il (f)
Dav v2 p873-76 pl il
Gor pl p150 (f)
Kle p84 il (f)
LelD p32 il; pl p87 fig 26; pl p89 fig 20-23
Tru p96 il (f)
Wa p281 fig 230, 232-34, 257 (f)
WilC p283, 298-99 pl p293, 306
WilH pl p232-33, 238

      1860-1870
Brk pl 26-31 (f)
BroH p 198-200 fig 131 (f)
CrO pl 11
CunE p238-43 il (f)
CunP p36 il (f)

HEADDRESS—19th century—1860-1870—
Continued
Gor pl p 157, 187
LelD pl p40 fig 22 (f)
Wa p289-90 fig 237 (f)
WilC p285, 295-96 pl p293, 306
WilH pl p233-34, 239-42

1870-1880

Brk pl 32-36 (f)
CunE p296-301 il (f)
Gor pl p 162, 191
Kle p79 il (f)
LavT2 p 119-20 pl p 117 (f)
LelD pl p40 fig 23-24; pl p89 fig 24-26; pl p90 fig 1-4 (f)
WilC pl p311 (f)
WilH p244-53 6 pl

1880-1890

Brk pl 37-40 (f)
CrO pl 11
CunE p352-57 il (f)
CunP p54-55 il (f)
Gor pl p 195-97
LelD pl p90 fig 5-7 (f)
Wa p314 fig 248 (f)
WilC p314 pl p306, 318
WilH p254-263 7 pl

1890-1900

Ada v4 il 130-31 (f)
Brk pl 41-44 (f)
CunE p414-19 il (f)
Gor pl p 172, 200
HaC p 169-73 2 pl (f)
Kle p202 il (f)
LavT2 p 120 pl p 117 (f)
LelD pl p90 fig 8-9 (f)
Lis pl p59
Wa p318, 326 fig 251, 254
WilH p264-273 6 pl

20th century

LavT p 149-59 pl (f)
Pic p70-74 il
Yar pl p261, 273

1900-1910

Ada v4 il p 178-79
Brk pl 46-49 (f)
Bro20 p26-27 pl (f)
Coh p329-342 il (f)
CunPr p36, 58, 62, 68-69, 74, 79 pl p45, 63, 75, 83, 93 (f)
Dot p 171 il (f)
Kle p402 il (f)
LavT2 p 120-22 pl p 117 (f)
LelD pl p90 fig 10-12 (f)
LesA p56-60 il (f)
Tru p 115 il (f)
Wa p337, 342 fig 258-65
WilH p274-82 5 pl
WisF pl 24 (f)
Wom p 13 il (f)

1910-1920

BrH pl p 147 (m)
Bro20 p42-44 pl (f)
Coh p344-53 il (f)

CunPr p 100, 109, 116, 124, 140, 156 pl p 100, 108, 117, 125, 157 il (f)
Gor pl p245-47 (f)
HaC p 103-04 pl p96-97, 100-01, 104a, 104c, 112a, 173
LelD pl p90 fig 13-23 (f)
Wa p345, 349 fig 266-69
WilH p283-93 7 pl
WisF pl 26 (f)
Wom p 13-14 il (f)

1920-1930

AlF pl p57 (f)
Bro20 pl p55 (f)
CunPr p 161-62, 170, 178-79, 193-94 pl il (f)
Gor pl p248 (f)
LavT2 p 124-26 pl p 117 (f)
LelD pl p90 fig 24-28 (f)
Wa p355 fig 274-75
WilC pl p378 (f)
WilH p294-302 5 pl
Wom p 14 il (f)

1930-1940

Bro20 p72-73, 75-76 pl (f)
CunPr p214, 224-25, 230-31, 236, 241-42, 246, 252, 256-57, 262 pl il (f)
LelD pl p87 fig 29-32; pl p90 fig 29-30
LesA p56-60 il (f)
WilC pl p391 (f)
WilH p303-13 6 pl
WisF pl 28 (f)
Wom p 14-15 il (f)

1940-1950

Bra pl 53
Bro20 pl p88 (f)
CunPr p272 pl p281 il (f)
Kle p84 il (f)
LelD pl p90 fig 31-35 (f)
WilH p314-27 10 pl
Wom p 15 il (f)

African tribes

GiMi p31-32 pl (col) (f)
Nat v85 My '44 il p565 (m); v97 Mr '50 pl p319 (col) (f); v 101 Mr '52 pl p327 (col) (m); v 106 O '54 pl p497, 509 (col) (m)

Aland islands

Nat v77 F '40 pl p247 (f)

Albania

Kle p 119 (f)

Algeria

Kle p 173-74 il (f)
LelD p273 il (m)
Nat v95 F '49 pl p219 (col)

Annam

Pot v2 pl 12 (col)

Arabia

CamC pl p 111 (m)
KerM no2 pl 2
Nat v82 S '42 il p402 (f)
Pic il p20 (m)
Pot v 1 pl 17

HEADDRESS—*Continued*

Argentine Republic
Bac pt3 pl 2-6 (col); pt5 pl 1-6 (col)

Armenia
Nat v89 Mr '46 il p388 (f)

Assyria and Babylonia
Dal v 1 p72-77 il (col)
Eli p52-54 il (incl pat) (m)
GiMi p7-8 pl (col) (f)
Lis p 16 pl p30 (m)
Nap p 15-17 il (f)
Wa p22, 24-25 fig 29 il
WilC pl p 10 (m)
WilH pl p 11
WisF pl 2 (f)

Australian tribes
Nat v70 D '36 p729 il

Austria
Nat v71 Ap '37 p467, 469 il (f); v99
  Je '51 pl p784 (col) (f)

Aztec
KaAz pl 9 (col)

Bali
Nat v75 Mr '39 pl p329, 331, 333, 335
  (col); v89 F '46 pl p261 (f)

Basque provinces
Kle p40 il (m)

Bavaria
Kle p56, 142 il

Bedouins
Nat v78 O '40 il p486; v 104 Jl '53
  pl p42

Black Forest
Kle p27, 51, 56-57, 330, 341 il (f)
Pet p 12-27, 34-37, 42-43, 46-49, 54-61,
  66-73, 76-84 26 pl (7 col) front (col)
Ret pl p203-04, 214 il p 189-90, 192,
  198, 205-11

Borneo
Brad pl p40
Nat v88 S '45 pl p306 (m)

Brittany
BluN p71-72 pl p95
CamC pl p74-75 (f)
Lee pl p5 (pat)
Marce p 16 pl 1-2 (col)
Nat v84 Ag '43 pl p211, 213, 215 (col)

Brunswick
Kle p45 il (f)

Burgundy
BruK pl 50
Kle p239, 329, 344-45 il
LelD pl p88 fig 6 (f)

Byzantine empire
Bra pl 12
Dal v 1 p227 fig 477-79 (f)
Dot p 119-20 il (f)
Pot v 1 pl 16 (col)
WilH pl p29

Cambodia
Pot v2 pl 14 (col) (f)

Cameroons, French
Leb pl 2-4, 6, 50 (col)

Canary Islands
Agu pl 121 (f)

Carpathian Ruthenia
Mak pl 66

Chaldea
Pot v 1 pl 7 (col)

China
CrO pl 10
Dal v 1 fig 796-807, 823 (col)
GiMi p 1-2 pl (col)
KerM no2 pl 2
Loud pl 3 (col)
NeC p2-4 pl 1, 6, 15-17
Pic il p97 (f)
Pot v2 pl 1-3 (col)
TiK pl 92 (col) (m)

Chios
Arg p21-22, 195, 198-99, 206-07, 210-12,
  216-17, 219-20, 226-27, 230-31, 234-35,
  238, 240-44, 247, 249-50 pl 36-37, 39,
  41-48, 51-110 (51 col)

Crete, Ancient
Dot p 109 il
Vert pl p48 (f)

Dalmatia
Kle p 119 il (m)

Denmark
AndD p8, 14-22 il
AndF p27-28 pl 21, 23 (f)
GiMi pl p 18 (col) (f)
Int v2 pl 2 (f)
Prim pl p 18

Druses
Nat v90 D '46 pl p744, 755 (col) (m)

Egypt, Ancient
Bra pl 3-4
Dal v 1 p38-45 pl il (col)
Dav v 1 p 19 il (f)
Dot p 104-05 il
Eli p50-52 il (incl pat) (m)
Gen v 1 fig 122-29, 131-32, 134
GiMi p5-6 pl (col) (f)
Gor p 7 il
HeuO p6 pl 22-24 (f)
Hous2 p23-39 fig 26-43
KerM no 1 pl 4
Kle p 148 il
LelD p236 il
LesA p2-5 pl 1-2 il
Lis p 14 pl p30
Loud pl 1 (col)
Nap p 12-14 il (f)
Nat v80 O '41 pl p466, 470, 478 (1 col)
NeE p3 pl 8 (f)
Pot v 1 pl 2-3 (col)
RogF p 10-11 pl (f)

HEADDRESS—Egypt, Ancient—*Continued*
Wa   p8, 12-15 fig 1, 13-25 il
WilC   pl   p6
WilH   pl   p 1, 5-7   pl   il
Yar   pl   p5

Egypt, Modern
TiK   pl 23 fig 2-3, 6-7 (col)

England
GiMi   p23-24   pl   (col) (f)

449-1066
CunM   p 18   pl 3 (f)
LesA   p9-10 fig 12
Lis   pl   p30 (f)
Tru   p 13 il

1066-1200
CunM   p26-27, 32-34, 38-40   3 pl (1 col)
Tru   p 18 il   p 16-17
Yar   pl   p56

13th century
CunM   p47, 50   pl 13, 17-18
Dot   il   p 129-30
Tru   p26-27 il
WilC   pl   p62 (f)
Yar   pl   p62, 68

14th century
BroH   p36-42 fig 27-28
CunM   p62-66, 72-76, 87-89, 94-96   7 pl
Dot   p 133 il
HousM   p82-88   pl   (f)
Loud   pl 10 (col)
Tru   p30-33 il
WilC   p57   pl   p62
Yar   pl   p81

15th century
Ab   p 158-60   pl   (f)
AirB   il   p31 (m)
BrH   p50-73   10 pl
CunA   pl 11 (m)
CunM   p 111-17, 124-32, 147-51, 159-66
   15 pl
Dav   v 1 fig 833, 931, 933 (f)
Dot   p 137-38 il
GiMi   pl   p 18   (col) (f)
LavE   p6   pl 1 (f)
LavR   pl   p21 (f)
Norr   v3 bk 1   p90-112   3 pl il (incl pat)
Set   p 16-17 il (f)
Tru   p35-38, 40-43, 46-47   pl   p38 (col)
   il
WilC   pl   p62 (f)
Yar   pl   p91, 98-99, 106 (1 col)

16th century
AirB   il   p32, 34
AirO   il   p 16
BrH   p76-85   5 pl
BroH   p42, 57-61, 77-80, 97 fig 30-32,
   46-47, 57, 60 (f)
CunS   p40-47, 70-84, 131-41, 172-79
   pl 10-15, 17-33, 51-54, 66-68
Dav   v 1 fig 1134-35, 1140-45, 1152-55,
   1157-60, 1176, 1178
DeB   p 175, 180, 195   pl   p 178-79, 196-
   97

Dot   p 145-46 il
Eth   p28-30   pl   il
Gor   pl   p60
KerR   pl 11 (f)
LavE   pl   p21-22, 31-32 (f)
LavR   pl   p35, 38, 42-43, 45-47, 50-51,
   53 (f)
LavS   p30   pl 11 (f)
LelD   pl   p408 fig 9 (m)
Lint   p216-37   pl 8, 10
Loud   pl 12 (col)
Norr   v3 bk 1   p313-27 il; bk 2   p448-56,
   617-18 il
Rey   p8, 10   pl 11, 19-20, 42, 45, 51
Set   il   p 19 (f)
Tru   p51-52, 56 il
WilC   p 119-21   pl   p 125, 134
Yar   pl   p 117, 124, 136

17th century
BroH   p 118-19, 127-29 fig 85-86, 89
Dot   p 155-56 il
KerR   pl 11 (f)
LelD   pl   p88 fig 1-2, 5, 7, 9 (f)
Roj   pl   p27
Tru   p74-75 il (f)
ViP   v 1   pl 16
WilC   p 151-53, 188   pl   p157, 192
Yar   pl   p 144, 153, 158, 166, 173

18th century
AirH   p 10 il (m)
BrH   p 110-25   8 pl
BroH   p 139-40, 143, 147-49, 159-60 fig
   96-97, 107
Dav   v2   p568 il (m)
Kle   p426-27 il (m)
Lel   v 12   pl 20 (f)
LelD   pl   p88 fig 14, 18, 22 (f)
LesA   p80   pl 14 (f)
Tru   p79 il (m)
Yar   pl   p 187, 197

Eskimos
Prim   pl   p31 (f)

Estonia
Nat   v76 D '39 il   p816 (f)

Etruria
GiMi   p 15-16   pl   (col) (f)
Pot   v 1   pl 9 (col)
WilH   pl   p22

Europe
LelD   p85-91   5 pl

Early to 1200
Dal   v2   p27-34 il (col) (f)
Kle   p 144 il (f)
LelD   pl   p39 fig 1 (m)
LesA   p 10-11 il
Wa   p96 fig 89B, 90
WilH   pl   p49

13th century
Bra   pl 15-18
BrH   pl   p35, 37
BroW   v 1   p26, 36-40 fig 2, 12
Dal   v2   p76-82   pl fig 124-39, 143-44
   (col)

HEADRESS — Europe — 13th century —
Continued
LelD   pl   p39 fig 2-4;   pl   p86 fig 3-4
  (m)
LesA   p76 il (m)
Lis   p34-35 il (m)
WilH   pl   p50-51

14th century

Bra   pl 20-21
BrH   pl   p35, 37, 39, 43, 45
BroW   v 1   p52-56 fig 21-22 (f)
Dal   v2   p 127-31 fig 201-11 (f) (col)
Kle   p 154-55 il (f)
LelD   p28 il;   pl   p86 fig 5-6;   p 106 fig
  2-3;   p222 il; il p416
LesA   p 11-22   pl 5 il
Lis   p34-35, 44-45 il
Wa   p 112, 117-18 fig 106-07, 113, 117,
  124, 131A (incl pat)
WilH   pl   p51, 52, 57-59

15th century

Bra   pl 20-21
BroW   v 1   p72-75, 81, 94-102 fig 32-33,
  38-39, 51, 54-56
Dal   v2   p 172-81 il (col)
Gor   pl   p31-32
HousM   p 164-66 fig 284-91
KerM   no5   pl 2 (f)
LavS   p25   pl 9 (f)
LelD   pl   p39 fig 5;   pl 86 fig 7-9, 11-
  18;   p91-92 fig 2-6;   p 106 fig 4;   p 168
  il
LesA   p22-28, 76-77   pl   il
Lis   p38-39, 44-45   pl   il
Norr   v3 bk 1   p90-112   3 pl   il (incl
  pat)
Wa   p 127-28, 134-35 fig 122, 124, 126-
  27, 129, 131, 133
WilH   p52-64, 84-85   12 pl
WisF   pl 9 (f)

16th century

BosF   pl 28 (m)
Bra   pl 23-25
Dal   v2   p236-44 fig 393-423 (col)
EvnJ   pl 49-52 (f)
Gor   pl   p48, 51, 53, 58, 60
KelF   p27-29, 39-41   pl   p75, 77
KerM   no5   pl 2 (f)
Kle   p32, 219 il
LavE   pl 16-17
LelD   pl   p39 fig 6-12;   pl   p86 fig 10,
  19-25, 29 (m)
LesA   p22-28 il
Lis   p44-45   pl
Loud   pl   p 11 (col)
Norr   v3 bk 1   p313-42   pl   il (incl pat);
  bk 2   p452-54, 726-35, 741-56 il (incl
  pat)
Vert   pl   p46
Wa   p 145, 150, 156, 162-63 fig 140-44,
  146, 148-49, 151
WilH   p84-97   24 pl
WisF   pl 10-11 (f)

17th century

Bra   pl 29-30
BroW   v2 fig 36

Dal   v2   p292-98, 327-34 fig 537-49 il
  (col)
Dav   v2   p617 il (f)
Gor   pl   p70, 73, 78, 82-83, 86, 89, 92, 94
KerM   no5   pl 2 (f)
Kle   p 124 il (f)
LavS   p37   pl 17 (f)
LelD   pl   p39 fig 13-14;   pl   p86 fig 26-
  28, 31-35;   pl p87 fig 1-2 (m)   p 180-
  81 il
LesA   p28-39   2 pl   il
Lis   p52-54   pl
Pic   il   p35 (f)
Roj   pl   p39 il   p40
Wa   p 178, 184, 190, 195, 198-99, 201-02
  fig 156, 165, 168, 171
WilH   p 123-36   13 pl
WisF   pl 13 (f)

18th century

Bra   pl 34, 36
Dot   p 159, 161 il
Gor   p97-99   pl   p 103, 105, 107, 112,
  114, 118, 121-22, 124
Lel   v 11   pl 12 (f); v 12   pl 23 (col)
  (f)
LelD   p 180-81 290,   pl   p39 fig 15-16
  (m)   pl   p40 fig 1-12 (f)   pl   p89 il
LesA   p39-46   4 pl   il (f)
Lis   pl   p59
Wa   p213, 218-20, 227, 229 fig 182, 194,
  196, 198-99
WilH   p 161-84   24 pl
WisF   pl 14-17 (f)

Finland

Prim   pl   p86, 93
TiK   pl 53 fig 4-9 (col)

Flanders
15th century

Dav   v 1 fig 817-21, 856-59, 890

France
See also Headdress—Brittany; Headdress—Normandy, etc.

Early to 1200

Pot   v 1   pl 18 (col)
WilC   pl   p54 (f)

13th century

Dot   il   p 131
EvjD   p21-24   pl 15-16a

14th century

Dav   v2 fig 1394-97
EvjD   p34-35   pl 23, 25, 29, 42
EvnJ   pl 29 (f)
WilC   p49   pl   p54

15th century

BroW   v 1   pl   p98 (col) (f)
Dav   v 1 fig 794, 903 (f)
Dot   p 139 il
EvjD   p50-52, 55-58   pl 44-48, 51a-65
EvnJ   pl 41 (f)
HousM   p 177-80 fig 308-12 (f)
Kle   p 15, 173-74 il (f)
LelD   il   p416 (f)
Norr   v3 bk 1   p 110-11 il (incl pat) (f)
WilC   p49   pl   p54, 85

HEADDRESS—France—*Continued*

16th century

BosF pl 33, 35, 40 (f)
BroW v 1 p 115 fig 69-71, 82 (f)
Dav v2 p477, 480 il (m)
KerR pl 11 (f)
LelD p21 il (f) pl p408 fig 1-3, 10-12
(m) pl p409 fig 1 (m)
LesA p77 pl 18 (m)
WilC p 101 pl p85, 93, 140

17th century

BluE pl 20-22 (m)
Dav v2 fig 1368 (f)
GiMi p 19-20 pl (col) (f)
LelD p 137, 293 il
WilC p 143-45, 176, 179-80 pl p 148,
173, 183

18th century

BruK pl 112 (f)
Dal v2 p395-409 pl il (col)
GiMi p 19-20 (col) (f)
Vert pl p74 (f)

1715-1774

Brk pl 1-5 (f)
Lel v 11 p30-31, 68-73 fig 27-29, 70-77
pl 33
LelD p31, 59, 239 pl p87 fig 3-5 il
WilC p 196, 199 pl p205

1774-1789

BluC pl p84 (f)
Brk pl 6-9 (f)
Dav v2 p695, 704 il (f)
Lel v 12 p21-25, 50-54 fig 17-21, 64-71
pl 20 (f)
LelD p61 il; pl p87 fig 6-9; p216 il
WilC p208, 212-13 pl p219

1789-1795

Brk pl 10, 11 (f)
BruK pl 117 (col)
Lel v 12 p53-55 fig 68-73 (f)
LelD pl p39 fig 17-18; p87 fig 10-17
(m)
WilC pl p227

1795-1799

Brk pl 12 (f)
LelD p290 il (m)
WilC p231-32 pl p235
WilH p 191-95 5 pl
WisF pl 18 (f)

Germany

GiMi p27-28 pl (col) (f)
See also Headdress—Bavaria; Headdress — Black Forest; Headdress—
Schaumburg-Lippe; Headdress—Thuringia; Headdress—Tyrol

11th-12th centuries

WilC pl p68 (f)

13th century

Dot p 132 il (f)
WilC pl p68 (f)

14th century

Kle p 183 il (f)

15th century

BroW v 1 pl p98 (col) (f)
Dot p 140-41 il
WilC pl p68

16th century

BroW v 1 p 114 fig 68 (f)
BruK pl 70, 77, 79
Dav v 1 fig 1005-07, 1009, 1034, 1043-45,
1067-71
DeZ pl 63
LelD pl p88 fig 4 (f) pl p409 fig 4, 7
(m)
WilC pl p80

17th century

LelD pl p88 fig 8 (f)

18th century

Kle p58, 426-27 il
Lel v 11 pl 33 (f)

Greece, Ancient

Bra pl 6-7
Dal v 1 p 120-29 fig 223-27 (col)
Dot p 111 il
Eli p54-55 il (f)
Gen v 1 pl p89 (f)
GiMi p 13-16 pl (col) (f)
Gor pl p 13
Kle p287 il (m)
LelD p315 il (m)
LesA p7-8 il
NorC p95-96 il
Tru p5 il p4-6 (incl pat)
Wa p39, 45 fig 47A
WilC p 13 pl p 17
WilH pl p 16-17

Greece, Modern

At p23 pl 1-49 (col)
Lee p26-27 pl

Guatemala

Nat v88 Jl '45 pl p 96 (f); v92 O '47
p554-55, 560 (col) (f)

Hesse

Kle p46 il (f)
Ret pl p21-24, 38, 49, 54-55 il p28, 36,
40-41, 43, 46, 48 (f)

Hungary

Bud pl 76-77, 84-85 (1 col)
Palo pl 2-3, 7-9 (col) (f)
Pif p26-27 il (f)

India, Ancient

Dal v 1 p383-91 fig 654, 658, 686, 694,
705-09, 712-19 (col)
GiMi p 11-12 (col) (f)

India, Modern

AirO il p26 (m)
BruK pl 179
KerM no2 pl 2
Nat v78 D '40 pl 772 (col) (f)

Indians of North America

Lyf p 112-16 pl il
MasB p2-27 5 pl il (incl pat) (m)

HEADDRESS—Indians of North America
—Continued

Nat v72 N '37 p554-55, 561 2 pl (col)
il; v86 Jl '44 pl p81, 96 (col) (m);
v91 Je '47 pl p769 (col) (m)
Roe p 18-19 pl 9-10 (col) il
Seto p47 pl 27 (m)

Indians of South America

Hal pl 8, 12, 16 E-H
TiK pl 116 (col)

Indo-China

Nat v69 Ja '36 pl p36 (col) (f)
Pot v2 pl 9 (col) (f)

Italy

LelD p5 il (f)

Early to 1200

WilC pl p45 (f)

13th-14th centuries

Dav v 1 p220 fig 612 (m)
Kle p200-01 il (f)
WilC p39 pl p45

15th century

BroW v 1 pl p98 (col) (f)
BruK pl 58 (f)
Dav v 1 pl p260 (col) fig 673, 703-06,
712-13, 715, 722-23, 728, 762-68, 776,
778
DeZ pl 53 (m)
Dot p 141-42 il
GiMi p 17-18, 25-26 2 pl (col) (f)
KerR pl 11 (f)
Kle p 173-74, 344 il (f)
Lang pl p38 (f)
Norr v3 bk 1 p 101 il (f)
Vert pl p21, 23, 102-03 (1 col)
WilC pl p45, 76 (m)

16th century

BroW v 1 fig 89, 95
BruK p63 pl 67
Dav v2 p495, 497 2 pl
Kle p29 il (m)
LelD pl p408 fig 5 (m)
Norr v3 bk 2 p753-54 il (f)
WilC pl p76 (f)

17th-18th centuries

Dav v2 p568 il (m)
Lee p40-42 pl

Japan

CrO pl 10
Dal v 1 fig 850-53 (col) (f)
GiMi p3-4 pl (col) (f)
Haa pl 81 (f)
Pot v2 pl 7 (col) (f)

Java

Brad pl p58, 59 (f)

Kirghiz

Nat v69 Ja '36 pl p35 (col) (f)

Korea

CrO pl 11
Keit p66 pl p64J, 69G (m)

Pot v2 pl 8 (col)
TiK pl 96 (col)

Laos

Pot v2 pl 13 (col) (f)

Lapland

Nat v74 O '38 pl p507 (m); v76 N
'39 il p669
Prim pl p 102 (f)
TiK pl 53 fig 10 (col) (m)

Libya, Ancient

LesA fig 91

Malta

Nat v78 Ag '40 il p269 (f)

Manchuria

Pot v2 pl 4 (col) (f)

Mayas

Nat v70 N '36 pl p625, 628 (col) (m)

Mexico

Brad pl p 116
CorZ p86-92 pl il (f)
CovM p260-62 pl (col) il
DuS pl 1-24, 27-32 (col)
Lee p48-50 pl
Marq pl 14-15
Meri pl 16 (col) (f)
See also Headdress—Tehuantepec

Mongolia

Nat v69 Ja '36 pl p28-29 (col) (m)
Pot v2 pl 5 (col)
TiK pl 78, 94 fig 2-4 (col)

Morocco

TiK pl 28 fig 7, pl 29 fig 11-12 (col)
(m)

Moslem

Nat v83 Ja '43 il p 117 (f)
Pic il p 21, 158 (m)
WilH p33-37 3 pl
Wrig pt 1 pl p26 fig 15

Netherlands

GiMi p 17-18 pl (col) (f)
Hea p58-59 pl (incl pat)
Lee pl p5 (pat)
Pic il p71 (f)

11th-13th centuries

WilC pl p68 (f)

14th-16th centuries

BroW v 1 pl p98 (col) (f) p 112 fig
67-68
Dav v 1 p306-07, 326, 340 4 pl; v2
p568 il
HousM p 164-65 il
LelD pl p408 fig 8 (m)
Nat v94 D '48 pl p721 (col)
Norr v3 bk 1 p 111-12 il (incl pat) (f)
WilC pl 68

17th century

BruK p69-70 pl 95
KerR pl 11 (f)

HEADDRESS—**Netherlands**—17th century
—*Continued*
LavR pl p299 (col) (f)
ThiG p8-9 pl 2-3, 6, 9-11, 16, 20-21, 30, 35-36, 44-45, 49, 55 (5 col)

18th century—date
Hij p22-23 front, pl 4, 18-20, 34, 36-39, 40-41, 46-53, 59, 62, 64 (1 col)

New Guinea
Nat v81 Je '42 il p709 (m); v96 D '49 pl p840, 843-44; v 100 N '51 pl p683, 685 (col); v 103 Ap '53 pl p423, 425, 435, 438, 442-43, 445, 455, 462, 469-71, 481, 487

Normandy
Nat v84 Ag '43 pl p215 (col) (f)

Norway
CrO pl 10
Nat v75 Ap '39 pl p504-05, 518 (col) (f)
Prim pl p42, 54

Orient
BruK pl 179 (m)

Palestine, Ancient
Pic il p70 (f)
Pot v 1 pl 8 (col) (f)

Palestine, Modern
Wrig pt 1 p25-26

Paraguay
Spi p65 il (f)

Persia, Ancient
GiMi p9-10 (col) (f)
Pot v 1 pl 6 (col)
WilC pl p28
WilH pl p 12, 35-37

Peru
CrO pl 26 fig 6, 8, 12-13
TiK pl 112 (col)
Zim p7-8, 10 3 pl

Philippine Islands
Brad pl p 127
CrO pl 10
Nat v87 Mr '45 il p307 (f)

Phrygia
Bra pl 5-6
Kle pl p288 il
LesA p7 il
Loud pl 2 (col) (f)
NorC p96 il
WilH pl p 182 (f)

Poland
Stry pl 1-13, 15-18, 21-22, 25, 27-33, 35-40

16th century
WilF pl p75 (f)

Polynesia
Nat v79 My '41 pl p621 (m)

Portugal
Nat v94 N '48 pl p613 (col)

Rhodes
Nat v79 Ap '41 il p467 (f)

Rome
Dav v 1 fig 274 (f)
Dot p 113 il
Eli p55-56 fig 8 (f)
Gor pl p 15
KerM no 1 pl 12
LesA p8 il
Pot v 1 pl 13 (col) (f)
Tru p9 il p8, 9
Wa p57-58, 61 fig 57, 60 (incl pat)
WilH pl p23

Rumania
Lee p55-56 pl

Russia
CrO pl 10
LelD p234 il (f)
TiK pl 47 fig 6-9, 11; pl 49 fig 1-5; pl 50 fig 10-12, 18-19 (col) (f)
WilF pl p75 (m)

Sardinia
GiMi pl p24 (col) (f)

Saxony
Kle p58 il (f)

Scandinavia
GiMi pl p 18, 21-22 (col) (f)
See also Headdress—Denmark; Headdress—Norway; Headdress—Sweden

Schaumburg-Lippe
CamC pl p40-41 (f)
Ret il p59, 63-64 (f)

Scotland
Lee p59-61 pl
Pic il p20-21
See also Balmoral caps; Glengarry bonnets

Siam
Brad pl p 150 (f)

Silesia
Kle p39 il (f)

Solomon islands
Nat v81 Je '42 il p712 (m); v82 D '42 pl p827 (m); v87 Ja '45 il p93 (m)

Spain
AnS p92, 117-35 fig 109, 137, 144-54, 160-66, 174-75, 208, 212-13, 220-21
GiMi p 17-18, 25-26 2 pl (col) (f)
OrT pl 62, 80, 114-16, 121, 123, 128-29, 150-55, 160-61, 234-35
WilC pl p 107
See also Headdress—Basque provinces; Mantillas

15th century
Dav v 1 p366 il (f)
Norr v3 bk 1 p 109-10 il (f)

HEADDRESS, ECCLESIASTICAL—*Continued*

Catholic church
AirS p 16 il
Kle p31 il (f)
LelD p29 il
McC p61-72, 79-82, 117-20 il
Pic il p 19
Tru p 123-25 il
WilH pl p84
See also Papal tiara

HEADDRESS, FUR
20th century
WilF pl p 199, 202, 209, 215

HEADDRESS, MILITARY
Early to 17th century
AirB il p6, 14, 48
AirM il p25
BruK pl 43
Dal v2 fig 83-93 (col)
Dav v 1 p56-57, pl p 154 il
Dot il p 123
KelF pl p85
LavS p 19 pl 5
LelD p3, 12, 24, 32, 34, 46-47, 59, 71-77,
  102, 214-15, 275, 279, 285 il
LesA 76-77 il
Pic il p 100, 107
Wa p 114 fig 106D
WilC pl p 140
WilH pl p71-72

18th century
WilH pl p 171

Assyria and Babylonia
Dal v 1 p75 fig 135
KerM no2 pl 3

Australia
20th century
WilH pl p288

Austria
19th century
WilH pl p219

Belgium
20th century
WilH pl p288

Byzantine empire
WilH pl p29-30

Canada
20th century
WilH pl p288

Colombia
Nat v78 O '40 il p527

Egypt, Ancient
Dal v 1 fig 91-98 (col)

England
Pic il p 19-21

Ancient-449
Yar pl p39

11th century
Lis pl p30

17th-18th centuries
Law v 1 p20-21, 28-31 il; v2 p20-21,
  25-27, 29-32 il

19th century
WilH pl p203-05

20th century
WilH pl p288, 325-27
Yar pl p283 (f)

Etruria
WilH pl p22

France
Pic il p20

Early to 511
Dal v 1 fig 501-04 (col)

15th-16th centuries
WilF pl p42, 140

19th century
BluN pl p 175
LelD pl p39, 374, 381; il p 118, 231,
  235, 323, 326, 399
WilH pl p201, 203-05, 219, 235

20th century
WilH pl p288, 325-27

Germany
15th century
WilF pl p42

19th century
WilH pl p204, 235

20th century
Erl p36-41 pl p48 (col)
WilH pl p288, 325-27

Greece, Ancient
Dal v 1 fig 275-82 (col)
Eth pl 12, il p 16 (incl pat)
Gor pl p 13
Lis pl p30
Pot v 1 pl 12 (col)

Italy
20th century
Nat v71 Mr '37 p325 il
WilH pl p288, 325-27

Persia
Ancient
Dal v 1 fig 142-50 (col)

15th century
WilH pl p36

Poland
19th century
LelD p92 il
WilH pl p219

HEADDRESS, MILITARY—*Continued*
Rome
Dal v 1 fig 377, 383-85, 406
Eli p70-75 fig 15 (incl pat)
Eth il p 18
WilC pl p23
WilH pl p23
Yar pl p27
Russia
19th century
WilH pl p219

20th century
WilH pl p288, 325-27
Saracenic
LavS p24 pl 7
Turkey
16th-17th centuries
LelD pl p418 fig 3-4
United States
18th century
Pic il p71
19th century
WilH pl p204-05, 234, 236
20th century
Kle p203 il (m)
Nat v84 O '43 pl p432 (col) (f)
SmU pl p7, 9 (col) (off, pte)
WilH pl p325-27

HEADDRESS, MOURNING
France
16th century
WilC pl p93 (f)
17th century
WilH pl p133
19th century
WilH p256 pl p258

HEADDRESS, NAVAL
England
20th century
GrA pl 2, 13 (off)
France
19th century
WilH pl p235
Germany
20th century
Erl p84-86 pl p88 (col) il
United States
19th century
WilH pl p234

20th century
Nat v83 Je '43 p695-96 pl p681, 683 (col)
SmU pl p39-42, (col) (off, s)
UnN p2-5 to 3-5 il (off)
WilH pl p288 (s)

HEADDRESS, OFFICIAL
France
17th-19th centuries
LelD p279 il
HEADDRESS, PURITAN
17th century
Lis pl p54
HEADDRESS, WEDDING
19th century
WilH p256 pl p236, 257, 272
20th century
WilH pl p323
Carpathian Ruthenia
Mak pl 63a-64 (f)
China
NeC pl 16 (f)
France
19th century
WilH pl p222
Germany
Ger fig 39, 62 (f)
Kle p61, 319-20 il (f)
Pet 22-23, 84-85 2 pl (1 col) front (col)
Ret pl p61, 163, 165, 196 il p45, 191 (f)
RetS pl 80-85, 87 (f)
Hungary
Pif p60-61 il
Poland
Stry pl 8, 11, 35 (col)
Wends
Ret pl p94 il p92-93, 95, 97, 102-03

HEBREWS. See Jews; Palestine; also Biblical characters

HEDEBO. See Denmark—Hedebo

HEDESUNDA. See Sweden—Gästrikland

HELGOLAND
BruK pl 131 fig 11 (col) (f)
Nat v90 N '46 pl p643 (col) (f)
Ret pl p75 (f)

HELMETS. See Headdress, Military—Early to 17th century; also Headdress, Military—Greece, Ancient; Headdress, Military—Rome

HENNINS
Dav v 1 fig 710, 859
Kle p 173-74 il
LelD p215-16 il
Pic il p76
Tru pl p43
WilC pl p45, 61
WilH p46 pl p60-63
Yar p97, 99 pl p89, 91, 94, 96, 98, pl IV (1 col)
See also entries under Headdress—Europe—14th and 15th centuries; Headdress—France—14th and 15th centuries

HENRY, KING. See subdivisions under Kings and rulers—England; Kings and rulers—France

HERALDIC COSTUME
Dot p 133-35 il
HousM p 108, 168 pl (col) il
Norr v3 bk 1 p288-89 il (f); bk 2 p444 il (f)

HERALDS
See also Fancy dress and stage costume—Herald

England
16th century
Hat p292 fig 99-101

Greece, Ancient
WilF pl p 11

HERDSMEN
Hungary
Brad pl p83
Bud pl 66-67
Palo pl 6 (col)

Spain
AnS p36-38, 265-69, 273-74 fig 37-38, 315-20, 323-26
Nat v69 Mr '36 pl p414
OrT pl 218, 220

Switzerland
Nat v79 Ap '41 pl p491, 493; v98 Ag '50 pl p217 (col)

HERMELINS, KNIGHTS OF
Doy pl 159 (col)

HERMITS OF CORDOVA
OrM pl 60-62

HERZEGOVINA. See Yugoslavia—Herzegovina

HESSE. See Germany—Hesse; Headdress —Hesse; Wedding costume—Hesse

HESSIAN MERCENARIES
VanH pl 8

HIANACATO INDIANS. See Indians of South America—Hianacato Indians

HIERONYMITE NUNS
Doy pl 107 (col)

HIERONYMITES
Doy pl 53 (col)

HIGH PRIESTS. See Jewish priests

HIGHLAND FLING. See Dancers—Scotland—Highland fling

HINDELOOPEN. See Netherlands—Friesland

HINDUS
Lee p36-37 pl (f)

HITTITES
BruK pl 8
HeuO p87-97 pl 54-55 il
Hous2 p70-73 fig 66-67
TiK pl 8 fig 15-19

HOBBLE SKIRTS. See Skirts—Twentieth century—1900-1910

HOLLAND. See Netherlands

HOLY CHARITY MONKS. See St Chariton monks

HOLY GHOST, ORDER OF THE
BluE p27 pl 61
BluL p22, 27 pl 37, 71
Doy pl 155-56 (col)
LelD p371 pl p264 fig 5
MusE pl 34 (col)

HOMESTEADERS
United States
18th century
But pl p38

19th century
Gor pl p220
Jen p35 il (f)

HONDURAS
Spi p56 il (f)

HONFLEUR. See France—Normandy

HONOURABLE ARTILLERY COMPANY
England
BarH p48-49 pl 3 (col) (pte)
Law v2 p206-09 il (off, pte)
Nat v 103 Je '53 pl p824 (col)

HOODS
HousM p 10-11 fig 13-16 (pat)
Kle p203 il (f)
Pic p77-78 il (f)
See also Headdress

HOOP SKIRTS
Gor pl p 112, 157
Lee pl p5 (pat)
Pic p78 il

16th century
Bra pl 25
BroH p80-84 fig 60, 62
CunS p 159-62 pl 58-61
CunU p50-51 fig 19
DeB p 162-68 3 pl
Dot p 146-47 il
KelF p35-36 pl p81
Lib pl p 172A
Lint p 179-82 pl 6
Norr v3 bk 1 p 199-200; bk 2 p503-04, 618-22 il
Rey p9, 17, 19 pl 16, 28-29
Rud pl p80-83
WilC pl p 101

HOOP SKIRTS—*Continued*

17th century

BroH   p 136-37 fig 94-95
Kle   p302 il
Trai   p 109-10 il

18th century

Bra   pl 35
BroH   p 145 fig 98
CrH   p8-9 pl
CunU   p88-91 fig 40-41
Dal   v2 fig 614, 643 (col)
Dav   v2 p749 il
Gor   pl p 112
Kle   p302 il
Lel   v 11 p36-40 fig 38
LelD   p295-97 il
NeEu   pl 12-20

19th century

AirB   il p59
BroF   fig 43
CrH   p8-9 pl
CunE   p249-51 pl il
CunP   p30-32 pl (col)
CunU   p 163-66 fig 71-73
Dav   v2 p902-03 il
Gor   pl p 157
HaC   p34-37 pl p48
Kle   p424-25 il
LavS   p48 pl 23
LavT   p59-71 pl p64, 68, 78
LavT2   p49-58 pl p50-51, 63
LelD   p 135 il
Tru   p93-95 il
ViN   fig 56, 58, 63
WilC   p283 pl p293, 311
WisF   pl 20

HOORN. See Netherlands—North Holland

HOPE DIAMOND NECKLACE
Nat   v98 D '50 pl p791 (col)

HOPI INDIANS. See Indians of North America—Hopi Indians

HOPLITES. See Military costume—Greece, Ancient

HORNBLOWERS
Nat   v71 Je '37 p801 il

HORSE GUARDS

England

LavB   p27, 32 pl 1, 13 (col) (off, pte)

HOSE
Kle   p 178-80, 371-76 il
May   p 10-80 14 pl il
   See also Leggings

To 16th century

BroW   v 1 p35-36 fig 8, 10 (m)
CunM   p22-24, 30-31, 106-09, 144-45 4 pl (m)
LelD   p29-30 il (m)
LesA   p286-92 fig 363-70, 372, 375-76
Norr   v3 bk 1 p115-16 il (m)
WilFo   p63, 68, 71, 85 pl p75-77

16th century

BroW   v 1 p 120 fig 73-74 (m)
Lint   p204-09 pl 10 (m)
May   p32-38 pl il
Norr   v3 bk 1 p 169-70 il (m); bk 2 p545-46 fig 625, 627, 635
Rey   p8 pl 19 (m)
Wa   p 153-54 fig 144B, 148-49, 153 (incl pat)
WilFo   p86-88, 90 pl p97 (m)

17th century

Dav   v2 p634-35 pl
Gor   pl 78, 94 (m)
LelD   p29-30 il (m)
LesA   p293-96 il (m)

18th century

May   pl p66 (f)
Wa   p212, 222 fig 198 (m)

20th century

Ada   v4 il p 179 (f)
Coh   p354-63 il
Rud   pl p 111

Egypt, Ancient

Rud   pl p208-09

Germany

Ger   pl 7 (col) fig 25 (m)

Scotland

Lee   pl p61

Spain

AnS   p 149, 180, 201, 255-56, 284 fig 101, 182, 215-17, 239, 309, 342-43

Tyrol

Ham   p31-32, 57-58 2 pl (col)
Ori   pl p32, 58 (col)

Yugoslavia

Lee   pl p47

HOSE, ECCLESIASTICAL
McC   p 108-10 il

HOSPITAL SISTERS
Doy   pl 54, 93-94, 98, 143, 146, 191, 236 (col)

HOSPITALERS OF ST JOHN OF JERU-SALEM, ORDER OF THE. See Malta, Knights of

HOTTENTOTS
Gen   v 1 fig 33 (f)

HOUPPELANDE
Brad   pl p 181
BrH   p46-59 6 pl
BroH   p42-46 fig33-34
BroW   v 1 p90 fig 40, 48-49
CunM   p82-84, 100-05, 120-22 4 pl (1 col)
Dal   v2 fig 252 (col)
Dav   v 1 p 190-91, 295, 301, 307, 350-51 fig 801, 820, 913, 917
EvjD   p34, 49, 54-55 pl 26-27, 38-41, 44, 53

HOUPPELANDE—*Continued*
  Kle p 182 il
  LelD p218-19 pl
  UnW pl 28 (col)
  WilC pl p52, 66
  WilF pl p27-28, 30-37
  Yar p80, 83-84 pl p85 pl III (1 col)
    See also subdivisions 14th and 15th centuries (chiefly in the period from 1380 to 1450) under Europe and under names of individual countries, e.g. England—14th century; France—15th century

HUELVA. See Spain—Andalusia

HUESCA. See Spain—Aragon

HUIZEN. See Netherlands—North Holland

HULA-HULA DANCERS. See Dancers—Hawaiian Islands

HUMILIATI
  Doy pl 64 (col)

HUMILIATI NUNS
  Doy pl 124 (col)

HUNGARY
  BruK table 8 (pat)
  Buda p 18-19 pl 1-4 (col)
  CrP pl 8 (m)
  Int v2 p45-53 pl 36-40
  Karo pl p 10, 66, 68, 70, 72, 78, 80, 82, 84, 86, 92, 100
  Ret p 142-48 3 pl il (f)
  TiK pl 41-42 (col) (m)
  WilF pl p 152
    See also subdivision Hungary under Ceremonial costume; Children; Coats and jackets; Coronation robes; Dancers; Festival costume; Footwear; Headdress; Military costume; Shepherds; Wedding costume

      16th century
  BruK pl 89 (col)
  Hol p3-5 pl 1-3 (m)

    17th century—date
  Brad pl p83-85
  BruK pl 89, 162 (col)
  Bud pl 1-33, 38, 40-42, 45, 47-48, 50-56, 63, 65-67, 70-71, 75-78, 84-85, 127 (26 col)
  Hol p5-19 pl 4-25, 27-32
  Lee p32-35 pl
  Lel v 12 pl 39 (col)
  Lep pl 11-20 (col)
  Nat v73 Ja '38 pl p 17, 22-23, 45-48 (col) (f)
  Palo pl 2-3, 7-12 (col)
  Pif p7-63 23 pl (col)

HUNS. See Europe—To 476

HUNTING COSTUME
  See also Falconers
      19th century
      1840-1850
  WilC pl p290 (m)

      1880-1890
  WilC pl 317 (f)

    Assyria and Babylonia
  Dot il p 107

      Austria
  Lep pl 7 (col) (m)

      England
    13th-14th centuries
  Ab pl p231 (f)
  HousM p50 fig 85 (incl pat)

    16th-17th centuries
  Hat fig 97
  Trev v2 fig 106-11

      18th century
  Lab pl 15 (col)
  Set pl p33 (col) (m)
  Trev v3 fig 117

      19th century
  SitC pl 124, 129 (m)
  Trev v4 front (col)

      France
      15th century
  EvjD pl 48 (m)
  HousM p 169-70 fig 294-95 (m)

      17th century
  WilC pl p 166 (f)

      18th century
  WilFo pl p 129 (m)

      19th century
  WilC pl p290, 317

      Germany
      16th century
  Norr v3 bk 1 p41 il (m)

    Greece, Ancient
  Burr p8 pl p9 (f)

      Italy
      15th century
  WilF pl p42

      Japan
  Ema pl p33, 35 (m)

    Persia, Ancient
  Hous2 fig 175-76
  TiK pl 9 fig 12 (m)

    United States
      19th century
  Dav v2 fig 2539 (m)

HUNZA
  Nat v 104 O '53 pl p489, 491, 494, 498, 501, 507-09, 511, 514-16 (col)

HUPA INDIANS. See Indians of North America—Hupa Indians

HUSSARS
Austria-Hungary
18th-19th centuries
KnR pl p235
WilF pl p 112

England
19th century
BarH p 118, 137-39, 188-89 pl 9, 11, 13, 24 (col)
KnR pl p369
LavB p34, 36 pl 17, 22 (col)

20th century
BarH p202-08 pl 16-17, 19 (col) (off, pte)

France
18th century
BruK pl 123 fig 15 (col)
KnR p279-85 pl p281

19th century
BluN pl p 172, 174, 182, 207
Fro pl 15, 17
KnR p279-85 pl p281
LelD p 151 il; p222 fig 4-6
Lez pl p272 (col) (off)

Germany
18th century
BruK pl 120 fig 7, 9(off, pte)
KnR p41-49 pl p45
Lez pl p210-11, 214-15

19th century
KnR p41-49, 85-86 pl p45, 83, 103, 147, 159, 181, 193, 207
Lez pl p293, 295, 299, 354 (col)

Russia
18th-19th centuries
KnR p440-43 pl

I

IBIZA. See Balearic islands

ICELAND
Nat v80 Jl '41 pl p88 (f)
See also Children—Iceland; Eskimos

ÎLE DE FRANCE. See France—Île de France

ÎLE-ET-VILAINE. See France—Brittany

IMAMS
BruK pl 90 fig 14

IMMACULATE CONCEPTION NUNS
Doy pl 138 (col)

INCARNATE WORD, SISTERS OF THE
Doy pl 117 (col)

INCAS
BruK pl 193 (col)
Nat v73 F '38 pl p228-36 (col)
TiK pl 111 (col)
See also Dancers—Incas

INCROYABLES
BluN pl p 115
BruK pl 116 fig 14 pl 117 fig 15-16 (col)
Dav v2 p823 fig 2308-09
LelD p223 il
WilC p228-29 pl p232
WilFo pl p 128-29
See also France—Directory, 1795-1799

INDIA
Brad pl 90-93, 95
CrO pl 37
TiK pl 82-88 (col) (incl pat)
See also Fancy dress and stage costume—Indian (East Indian); Hindus; Nagas; Natal; Nautch girls; Rajas; Rajputs; Saris; Sikhs; and also subdivision India under Children; Court dress; Dancers; Festival costume; Footwear; Headdress; Musicians; Noblemen; Wedding costume

Ancient
Dal v 1 p349-408 8 pl il (col) (incl pat)
RueO pl 14-21

16th century-date
Am p90-94 2 pl il
BruK p38-39, 87-88 pl 176-78 (col)
Ind pl p29, 64-65, 69, 79, 85, 87, 89, 93, 103, 113, 121 (col)
KerM no2 pl 4-6
Nat v78 D '40 pl p765 (col) (m); v91 Mr '47 pl p319-22, 324 (col)
Rud pl p 130-33 (m)

BY REGION OR PROVINCE
Assam
Brad pl p31 (f)
TiK pl 86, 88 (col)
See also Nagas

Kashmir
Brad pl p94 (f)
BruK pl 176 fig 9 (col) (m)
Nat v93 Ap '48 pl p529, 534-35, 538-39 (col)
TiK pl 83, 85 fig 6-8 (col)
See also Hunza

Nepal
See Nepal

Punjab
Nat v92 N '47 pl p604 (f)

INDIANS OF CANADA. See names of individual tribes such as Nootka Indians under the heading Indians of North America

INDIANS OF CENTRAL AMERICA
BruK pl 196 (col)
See also Mayas; San Blas Indians

Guatemala
Nat v70 O '36 pl p437, 439-41 (col);
v92 O '47 pl p526, 533, 542-45, 551,
554-57, 560, 563 il p540, 562, 564 (col)

Panama
Nat v80 N '41 pl p620-21, 623 (col)

INDIANS OF MEXICO
Alv pl p 16, 24, 32, 40, 73, 96, 137 (col)
CorA pl 9, 28, 43
CorZ p70-97 9 pl il
DuS pl 1-32 (col)
Lee p48-50 pl
Marq pl 3-7, 25, 28-30, 32-34, 94, 97
Meri pl 2-4, 6, 8-12, 14-24 (col)
Nat v70 N '36 pl p604 (col); v78 S
'40 pl p361 (col)
Pr pl 6, 8-9 (col)
Too p 76-83 pl p46, 108, 140, 172, 236,
486 (col) fig 7-20, 25, 28-40, 42-44, 59-
63, 131-40, 143-45
ValM p 1-15 (col)
See also Aztecs; Mayas; also regional
divisions under Mexico, e.g. Mexico—
Michoacán; Mexico—Tehuantepec

INDIANS OF NORTH AMERICA
AirB il p53
BruK p40, 95-96 pl 198-99 (col); table
12 (pat)
Lee p 101-04 pl
TiK pl 113-15 (col)
VanH pl 5, 6
WilF pl p 113
See also subdivision Indians of North
America under Bags, purses, etc.; Capes
and cloaks; Ceremonial costume; Chil-
dren; Dancers; Fancy dress and stage
costume; Footwear; Hair, wigs, etc.;
Headdress; Leggings; Masks; Snow-
shoes

Apache Indians
Nat v78 N '40 pl p557 (col) (m)
Seto pl 51 (f)

Chilkat Indians
Seto p40-41 pl 9
Lyf p 107-20 pl 2, 15, 61, 64-65 il
MasB p61-65 3 pl il (incl pat)
Nat v72 N '37 p549, 586, 595 pl (col)
il
Seto p62-65 pl 14
TiK pl 113 fig 2 (col) (m)

Choctaw Indians
Nat v79 Mr '41 pl p301 (col) (f)

Conoy Indians
MusI pl 11 (col)

Dakota Indians
Brad pl p24
EvnH p23-36 pl il (pat)
Mer fig 126-27

Nat v86 Jl '44 pl p89 (col); v88 N
'45 il p588 (f); v98 Ag '50 il p229
(m)
Seto p82-106 pl 21, 28-29, 31 (incl pat)
TiK pl 113 fig 3, pl 114 fig 9-10, pl
115 fig 4 (col)
Trai p 18-21 2 pl

Delaware Indians
MusI pl 2 (col)

Erie Indians
MusI pl 4 (col)

Hopi Indians
Ada v3 il p67
Brad pl p25 (f)
EvnH p41-46 pl il (pat)
Seto p 164-74 3 pl (incl pat)

Hupa Indians
Seto p 139-43 pl

Iroquois Indians
EvnH p2-15 pl il (incl pat)
Nat v72 N '37 p539, 551-52, 558 3 pl
(col) il
Seto p55-56 pl 12 (m)

Kutchin Indians
Nat v96 O '49 pl p479

Micmac Indians
Nat v77 My '40 pl p597 (col) (f)

Mohawk Indians
Nat v92 Jl '47 il p92, 95

Mohegan Indians
MusI pl 7 (col)

Nanticoke Indians
MusI pl 13 (col)

Navaho Indians
EvnH p37-41 pl il (pat)
Nat v73 My '38 pl p541 (col); v78 N
'40 pl p596 (col) (f)
Seto p 196-98 pl 59, 62-63

Nez Percés Indians
Nat v93 F '48 pl p 177 (col) (m)

Niska Indians
Nat v87 Ja '45 pl p40 (col) (m)

Nootka Indians
Nat v87 Ja '45 il p26 (m)

Northwest
Brad pl p26

Ojibwa Indians
See Indians of North America—Chippewa Indians

Oneida Indians
MusI pl 8 (col)

Salish Indians
Nat v87 Ja '45 pl p41 (col) (f)

Sauk Indians
Ada v2 il p231

INDIANS OF NORTH AMERICA—*Continued*

Seminole Indians
Ada v2 il p274 (m)
BruK pl 197 fig 7 (col)
EvnH p 16-22 pl il (pat)
Nat v89 Ja '46 il p55; v93 F '48 pl p 164-65 (col)
Seto p 148-53 2 pl

Seneca Indians
MusI pl 6 (col)

Shawnee Indians
MusI pl 1, 5 (col)
Nat v72 N '37 pl p590 (col)

Siksika Indians
EvnH p23-36 pl il (pat)
Seto p82-106 pl 28-30 (incl pat)

Sioux Indians
See Indians of North America—Dakota Indians

Southwest
TiK pl 108, 113-15 (col)

Susquehanna Indians
MusI pl 3 (col)

Tlingit Indians
Nat v87 Ja '45 pl p33 (col) (m)

Tuscarora Indians
MusI pl 10 (col)

Tutelo Indians
MusI pl 12 (col)

Virginia
AirO il p3 (m)
Nat v89 Ja '46 pl p65 (col) (f)

Wenrohronon Indians
MusI pl 9 (col)

Yakima Indians
Nat v93 F '48 pl p 192 (col) (f)

Yuma Indians
Nat v78 N '40 pl p593, 594 (col)

Zuñi Indians
Nat v78 N '40 pl p564 (col) (m)
Roe p 17-18 pl 1 (col) (f)

INDIANS OF SOUTH AMERICA
TiK pl 116 (col)
See also Incas; also subdivision Indians of South America under Dancers; Hair, wigs, etc.; Headdress

BY COUNTRY
Argentine Republic
Hal pl 4 (col) (f)

Bolivia
Hal pl 5-7, 9, 12 (col)
Nat v83 Mr '43 pl p 310, 321, **323**, 325 (col)

Brazil
Hal pl 13-14, 16 (col)

Colombia
Nat v78 O '40 pl p534 (col)

Ecuador
Brad pl p61 (m)
Hal pl 25-28 (col)
Nat v80 D '41 pl p726, 730-31, 733-34 (col)

Patagonia
Hal pl 30 (col) (m)

Peru
Hal pl 31-39 (col)
Nat v82 Ag '42 pl p 189-90, 193-95 (col); v98 O '50 pl p429, 436-39, 453, 459 (col)
TooP pl 21-30, 51-52, 79, 113
Zim p23-24 2 pl
See also Incas

BY TRIBE
Araucanian Indians
Hal pl 18 (col)
Nat v80 Jl '41 pl p 101 (col)

Hianacato Indians
Hal pl 23 (col) (m)

Kechua Indians
Brad pl p 126

INDO-CHINA
Nat v99 Ap '51 il p464, pl p471, 475, 479, 481; v 102 S '52 pl p324, 326 (col)
See also Annam, Cambodia, Laos, Tonking

INDONESIA
TiK pl 101 (col)
See also Borneo, Java, Sumatra

INFANTS
See also Children; Christening robes; Swaddling bands

18th century
Lel v 11 p76-77 fig 82-83; v 12 fig 77

19th century
MooC p24-25, 88-89 2 pl

Indians of North America
Lyf pl 15

INGELSTAD DISTRICT. See Sweden—Skåne

INSTITUTE DE FRANCE. See Academicians—France

IRAN. See Persia

IRAQ
Nat v99 Ja '51 pl p73, 75, 77, 79-80, 82, 84, 86, 88 (col)
TiK pl 13 (col)

IRELAND
See also Bagpipers—Ireland; Children—Ireland; Dancers—Ireland; Fancy dress and stage costume—Irish

IRELAND—*Continued*

Early to 1500
Mccl p 1-29 7 pl

16th century
Mccl p30-49, 74-88 front (col) pl 17-32 (1 col)

17th-19th centuries
Brad pl p96
Lee p38-39 pl
Mccl p49-62, 89-94 11 pl

IROQUOIS INDIANS. See Indians of North America—Iroquois Indians

ISAAC (BIBLICAL CHARACTER). See Biblical costume—Isaac

ISCHL. See Austria—Upper Austria

ITALY
See also Etruria; Fancy dress and stage costume—Italian; Rome; also subdivision Italy under Academic costume; Capes and cloaks; Ceremonial costume; Children; Coats and jackets; Court dress; Dancers; Festival costume; Hair, wigs, etc.; Headdress; Kings and rulers; Military costume; Musicians; Noblemen; Noblewomen; Queens and empresses; Riding costume

To 1200
Dav v 1 p 139 pl
Dot p 122, 126, 129 il (f)

13th century
Dot p 132-33 il (f)
WilC p37-42 pl p44 (f)

14th century
BroW v 1 p42-46 pl p42, 50 (col) fig 10, 13-16
BruK p59-60 pl 52-53 (col)
Dav v 1 p216-27 9 pl il
Dot p 136 il
HousM p 116-17 fig 214-15 (m)
TiK p52 pl 119 (col) (incl pat)
WilC p37-44 2 pl
WilF pl p26-27

15th century
BroW v 1 pl p78, 102 (col) fig 30, 33-35, 40, 45, 49, 57-61
BruK p 19, 60-61 pl 53-58 (4 col)
Burr p 16, 76-77, 121-22, 196-97, 297 pl p 17
Dav v 1 p242-90 front (col) 19 pl (1 col) il
Dot p 141-42 il
Gor pl p29 (m)
KerM no5 pl 12
Kle p304-07 il (m)
Nat v78 Jl '40 pl p12, 19 (col) (m)
TiK p52 pl 119 (col) (incl pat)
UnW pl 31 (col)
Vert pl p45 (f)
WilC p37-43, 69-75 3 pl
WilF pl p43-45 (m)

16th century
BroW v 1 p 124, 130, 148 pl 13 (col) fig 64-66, 74, 77, 81, 88, 95
BruK p 19-20, 61 pl 59, 66-67, 83 (3 col)
Dav v2 p490-503 8 pl il
Dot p 149-50 il
Gor pl p50, 56-57, 61
KerM no5 pl 10-11
Kle p256-57 il (m)
LavE pl 28 (m)
Nat v 101 Ja '52 pl p88 (col) (m)
Norr v3 bk 1 p 167-70 il (m); bk 2 p568-72, 669-73 il
VanH pl 4
WilC p69-75 3 pl
WilF pl p55, 61 (f)

17th century
BroW v2 fig 8, 27, 38

18th century
BroW v2 fig 43, 54-55
BruK pl 157-59 (col)
Lee p40-42 pl
Lel v 11 pl 32
NeEu pl 1 (m)

BY REGION OR PROVINCE
Abruzzi e Molise
Brad pl p97, 99 (f)

Brescia
See Italy—Lombardy

Calabria
Brad pl p97-98
BruK pl 158 fig 7, 10; pl 159 fig 12-15 (col)

Campania
Brad pl p99 (f)
Gal p 16 pl 2 (col)

Emilia
BruK pl 56 fig 1-8, 15-16 (col)

Ferrara
See Italy—Emilia

Florence
See Italy—Tuscany

Genoa
See Italy—Liguria

Liguria
15th-16th centuries
Arg pl 33, 48
19th century
BruK pl 157 fig 1-5 (col) (m)

Lombardy
15th century
BruK pl 55 fig 6-11 (col) (m)
16th century
Dav v2 p502 fig 1347 (f)

Sardinia
See Sardinia

Siena
See Italy—Tuscany

ITALY—*Continued*

Tuscany
14th century
Kle   p299-300 il

15th century
Bruh   p24-25 pl (col)
BruK   pl 57 (f)
KerR   pl 1

16th century
Dav   p492, 497-99 4 pl
Norr   v3 bk 2 p572, 670-71 il
WilF   pl p66 (f)

Venice
See also Doges; Gondoliers; also the
subdivision Venice under Footwear;
Noblemen; Noblewomen; Officials

14th century
WilF   pl p26

15th century
BruK   pl 54 fig 20-21, pl 55 fig 4, 12-16,
   pl 56 fig 9-13 (col)
LavR   pl p24 (f)

16th century
BroW   v 1 p 148 fig 93, 95
Dav   v2 p491, 498, 500-01 il (f)
KerR   pl 2-3
Norr   v3 bk 2 p671-72 il (f)
Rud   pl p 169 (f)
WilF   pl p64, 68, 75
WilFo   pl p95 (f)

17th century
BruK   pl 83 fig 6-10 (col)
Dav   v2 p637 il

18th century
Arg   pl 39 (col) (m)
BroW   v2 fig 43, 55
BruK   pl 107, 113 fig 13-17
Dav   v2 p722-27, 749 il
Gor   pl p 110
Mora   p9-101 pl 1-34, 36-40, 44-108

Verona
15th century
Bruk   pl 55 fig 1-2 (col) (m)

16th century
Norr   v3 bk 2 p669 il (incl pat) (m)

IVIZA. See Balearic islands

J

JABOTS
Kle   p 191 il (f)
LelD   pl p 117 fig 17; p227 il

JACK-BOOTS. See Footwear—England—
17th century; Footwear—England—18th
century

JACKETS. See Coats and jackets

JACOBITE CHURCH. See Ecclesiastical
costume—Syrian church

JAÉN. See Spain—Andalusia

JAGERS
France
18th-19th centuries
KnR   p285-91 pl
Lez   pl p272-73 (col)

Germany
19th century
KnR   p27-29 pl p55, 89, 121, 125, 159,
   163, 167, 199

JALISCO. See Mexico—Jalisco

JAMAICA
Brad   pl p 102-03 (1 col) (f)

JAMES, KING. See subdivision under
Kings and Rulers—England

JÄMTLAND. See Sweden—Jämtland

JANISSARIES. See Military costume—
Turkey

JANITZIO. See Mexico—Michoacán

JAPAN
Brad   pl p 104-05, 107-08 (1 col)
BruK   p 39, 91 pl 185-86 (col)
Dal   v 1 p477-502 il (col)
Ema   p5-41 18 pl (f)
Haa   pl 9, 48, 55, 60 (f)
Kaw   p9-63 front (col) 20 pl il (f)
Kle   p207 il (f)
Kou   pl 45 (m)
Lee   p42-45 pl
Nat   v73 Ja '38 pl p 119 (col) (f)
Pot   v2 p23-28 2 pl (col)
RueO   pl 5-9
SaJ   pl p 11, 14, 21, 25, 30-31, 35, 43,
   46-47, 49, 81, 85, 87
TiK   pl 98-100 (col)
See also Fancy dress and stage cos-
tume—Japanese; Geisha girls; Samurai;
Shinto priests; Taoist priests; also sub-
division Japan under Actors; Ceremo-
nial costume; Children; Court dress;
Dancers; Fishermen; Footwear; Hair,
wigs, etc.; Headdress; Masks; Military
costume; Officials; Pugilists

JARACUARO. See Mexico—Michoacán

JÄRRESTAD DISTRICT. See Sweden—
Skåne

JAVA
Brad   pl p58-59 (f)
BruK   pl 181 fig 7-16 (col)
CrO   pl 3
See also Dancers—Java

JERKINS. See Coats and jackets

JESTERS. See Clowns and jesters

JESUITS
Doy   pl 51, 75 (col)

JEWELRY
Bin   p 131-54 il

See also Anklets; Bracelets; Brooches; Cameos; Chains (Jewelry); Coronets;' Crosses (Jewelry); Earrings; Necklaces and pendants; Nose ornaments; Rings; Watches; also names of famous jewels (e.g. Alfred's jewel; Armada jewel; Hope diamond necklace; Kohinoor diamond)

JEWELRY, ANCIENT
CrO   pl 8
Dal   v 1 fig 596-604 (col)
Gen   v 1 pl p6, 9, 13, 25, 32, 48, 53, 59-61, 94
Nat   v79 F '41 il p263
NeM   p 1-4 pl 1-20
WlsC   p32-35   4 pl

Assyria and Babylonia
Hous2   p 156-59 pl 8 fig 153
WilC   pl p 10

Byzantine Empire
Dal v 1 fig 481-93 (col)
RogF   p58-59 pl il

China
Dal   v 1 p451-57 fig 808-22, 835-36 (col)

Egypt
Dal   v 1 fig 40-45 (col)
Dav   v 1 p 19, 34-35   3 pl
KerM   no 1 pl 4
RogF   p 9-29 pl il

England
RogF   p61-69 pl il

Etruria
Dav   v 1 p55 il
Nat   v90 N '46 il p548
RogF   p40-42 il

Europe
AirS   pl p8-10
Dal   v 1   fig 505-15 (col)
Dav   v 1 p91-92   2 pl

Greece
BiE   pl 38
Dal   v 1 p 140 fig 255-56, 258, 260, 262-73 (col)
RogF   p32-39 pl p42 il
WilC   pl p 17

India
Dal   v 1 p393-400 il (col)

Mesopotamia
NeN   p 1-2 pl 1

Persia
Pot   v 1 pl 6 (col)

Rome
Dal   v 1 p 198-201 fig 416-33 (col)
HousG2   p 112-13 il
RogF   p42-58   2 pl il
WilC   pl p23

Scythia
Dav   v 1 fig 253-59
NeN   p 1-2 pl 2

Spain
Dal   v 1 fig 559-72 (col)

JEWELRY, MEDIEVAL AND MODERN
Asia
Int   v 1 pl 46-47
NeN   p4 pl 16-20
Özb   fig 19

Europe
10th-15th centuries
Ab   p 163-70 pl
BroW   v 1 p32-33 fig 9
Dal   v2 p40-47, 83-91, 132-37, 182-86 fig 50-61, 216-21, 315-25 (col)
Norr   v3 bk 1 p 117-26 il
RogF   p70-100 il

16th-18th centuries
BraF   p27-76 14 pl
Dal   v2 p245-53, 335-39 fig 426, 551-58 (col)
Hij   pl 2, 44B
Int   v 1 pl 57
Norr   v3 bk 1 p347-65 pl il; bk 2 p458-63, 762-86 il
RogF   p 103-33 pl p99, 106 il
Roj   il p22

18th century—date
Ar   p25-34 pl 8-34 il
BraF   p77-119 pl p81-82, 114-16, 125-26, 143-46, 163-64, 173-76, 185-88, 205
Dal   v2 p409-13, 490-96 il (col)
Int   v 1 pl 21, 69-70
Prim   pl p45, 49, 82, 94
RogF   p 134-35 pl il
Sub   p 117-27 pl p459-79
WisF   pl 29

Savage and primitive races
Hal   pl E (col)
Nat   v79 My '41 pl p641, 644; v97 Mr '50 pl p337, 341, 347 (col); v 106 O '54 pl p501, 511 (1 col)

JEWELRY, ECCLESIASTICAL
McC   p 148-49 il

See also Pectorals; Rings, Ecclesiastical

JEWELRY, ENAMEL
BraF   p68-73, 85-86, 139-51 pl   57-58, 60

JEWELRY, FRATERNAL
Bae   p 186-87 pl

JEWELRY, MEMORIAL
BraF   p74, 87-88 pl p57
EvnJ   p 155-56, 182 pl 114-15, 156
RogF   p 119-20, 149-55 pl il

JEWISH PRIESTS
BartC   p48 fig 11
BruK   pl 7   fig 14-15 (col)
Eli   p 137-41 il (incl pat)
Gen   v 1 fig 171

JEWISH PRIESTS—*Continued*
  Gor pl p8
  LelD p215 il
  MusE pl 5 (col)
  Wa p26-27 fig 37 (incl pat)
  WilH pl p31
  Wrig pt 1 p 14-16 pl p28
    See also Rabbis

JEWS
    See also Biblical costume—Hebrews;
  Jewish priests; Palestine; Rabbis
      Ancient times to A.D. 70
  Bra p36-38 pl
  BruK p6, 44 pl 7
  Dal v 1 p93-97 pl il (col)
  Gen v 1 fig 173-74
  Gor p8 il (m)
  Lis p 19-21 il
  Pot v 1 p23 pl 8 (col)
  TiK pl 8 fig 1 (m)
  Wa p26-27 fig 40 (incl pat)
  Wrig pt3 p9-12 pl p25 (incl pat)
      England
      11th century
  AirS p46 il
      Germany
      12th-13th centuries
  BruK pl 32 fig 5, 12 (m)
      17th century
  BruK pl 94 fig 2 (m)
      Morocco
  GaU pl 17 (col) (f)
      Poland
  Nat v75 Je '39 pl p751 (m)
      Tunisia
  BruK pl 188 fig 13-15 (col)

JOCKEYS
      16th century
  Norr v3 bk 1 p299 il
      19th century
  DuR il p57
  LelD p230 il

JODHPURS
  Bra pl 54
  LelD p230 il (f)
  Pic il p84
  WilFo pl p 171
    See also Riding costume

JÖLSTER. See Norway—Jölster

JOHN, KING. See subdivisions under
  Kings and rulers—England; Kings and
  rulers—France

JOSEPH (BIBLICAL CHARACTER).
  See Biblical costume—Joseph

JUDAS (BIBLICAL CHARACTER). See
  Biblical costume—Judas

JUDGES. See Legal costume

JUGOSLAVIA. See Yugoslavia

JUNSELE. See Sweden—Ångermanland

JUTLAND. See Denmark—Jutland

K

KABYLES
  TiK pl 32 fig 2 (col) (m)

KACHINS. See Burma

KAISERS. See Kings and rulers—Germany

KALMUCKS
  BruK pl 167 fig 10 (col), pl 175
    fig 15-16 (col)
  TiK pl 72 (col)

KAMCHATKA. See Siberia

KASHGAI
  Nat v 101 Je '52 pl p814-15, 820-21,
    823, 826-27 (col)

KASHMIR. See India—Kashmir

KATE GREENAWAY COSTUME. See
  Fancy dress and stage costume—Kate
  Greenaway child

**KATCINA COSTUME (PUEBLO IN-
  DIANS)**
  Roe p 177-78 pl 29-30, 35, 38 (col)
    See also Dolls—Katcina

KAZAKHS
  Nat v 106 N '54 pl p629-36, 641-45
    (col)

KAZÁR. See Hungary

KECHUA INDIANS. See Indians of
  South America—Kechua Indians

KENNEL HEADDRESS. See Subdivisions 16th century under Headdress—
  England; Headdress—France; etc.

KEPIS. See Headdress, Military—France—
  19th century

KERCHIEFS
  Kle p222 il (f)
      Chios
  Arg pl 10, 20, 26-28, 31 (1 col)

KHIOS. See Chios

KIEV. See Russia—Ukraine

KILTS
  Eyr front (col)
  Kle p206 il
    See also Scotland—Clans and tartans

KIMONOS
Kaw p9-38 front (col) 8 pl il
Lee p42-45 pl
LelD p235 il
Pic il p85 (f)
Pot v2 pl 7 (col)
TiK pl 98-99 (col)
See also Japan

KINGS AND RULERS
See also Coronation robes; Crowns; Queens and empresses; Sceptres

African tribes
Nat v74 S '38 pl p335

Arabia, Modern
Nat v88 O '45 il p465

Assyria and Babylonia
BartC p68 fig 22
BruK pl 5-6 (1 col)
CrO pl 1
Dal v 1 fig 112-13, 115, 117 (col)
Dav v 1 p4, 7-12 il
Gen v 1 fig 180-81 pl 4 (col)
HeuO pl 45-49 fig 47-50
Hous2 p 128-36 pl 6 fig 118-19, 128-30, 148
KerM no 2 pl 8
LelD p21 il (m)
MusE pl 4 (col)
Nat v80 O '41 pl p514 (col)
Pot v 1 p 17 pl 5 (col)
RueG pl 17
TiK .pl 6 fig 2-5, 7-8
UnW pl 5 (col)
WilC pl p9
WilFo pl p 13
Yar pl p7

Austria
16th century
Norr v3 bk 1 p 180-83 pl p 180 fig 369

Aztec
KaAz pl 5 (col)

Bahrein
Nat v89 F '46 pl p201 (col)

Byzantine empire
Dal v 1 p204 fig 446, 458, 460 (col)
UnW pl 19 (col)

4th-5th centuries
BruK pl 27 fig 1, 4 (col)
Dav v 1 p80 il
TiK pl 36 fig 1

6th century
BruK pl 27 fig 9 (col)
Dav v 1 p85 il
Dot p 119-20 il
HousG2 p 136-37 pl
Kle p71-73 il
Loud pl 6 (col)
TiK pl 36 fig 2, 6
WilC pl p35
WilFo p61-62 pl p73

10th century
Dot il p 122

11th-12th centuries
BruK pl 27 fig 13 (col)
Dav v 1 p 114 il
HousG2 p 150-53 pl p 151, 154 (1 col)
WilF pl p 14

13th century
HousG2 p 155-56 pl

China
Ancient
Loud pl 3 (col)
Pot v2 pl 1 (col)

14th-17th centuries
Camm pl 3

Egypt
Ancient
BruK pl 2-4 (col)
Dav v 1 p29, 31-33 il
Gen v 1 fig 101-03, 109, 111, 158 pl 1-2 (col)
Gor pl 5
HeuO pl 2-3, 5, 9-12, 14-15 (1 col) fig 9, 18
Hous2 p5-6, 31-32 fig 1, 6, 34, 41, 45-47, 102
KerM no 1 pl 2
Lee p74-76 pl
MusE pl 3 (col)
Nat v80 O '41 pl p438, 440, 482, 508 (2 col)
Pot v 1 pl 4 (col)
TiK pl 2 fig 7, pl 3 fig 1-2, 8 (col)
WilC pl p5
WilFo p 3-4 pl p6
Wrig pt 3 p 15 pl p28

England
Early to 499
KerM no3 pl 6

Anglo-Saxon period, 449-1066
Covers Alfred the Great, Athelstan, Canute, Edgar, Edward the Confessor, Harold, etc.
AirS il p6, 14, 30
Dot il p 123
VanH pl 2
Wel pl p5
WilC pl p60

Norman period, 1066-1154
Covers William I the Conqueror, William II, Henry I, Stephen
AirS il p46
Wel pl p 6
WilFo pl p76

12th century
Wel pl p7

Henry II, 1154-1189
Dot il p 123
Yar pl p52

Richard I (Coeur de Lion) 1189-1199
LelD pl p263 fig 8

KINGS AND RULERS—England—*Cont.*

13th century
HousM p 12-17 il
Wel pl p8

John, 1199-1216
Ab pl p 158
Yar pl p52

Henry III, 1216-1272
HousM p 14 fig 19
Yar pl p60

Edward I, 1272-1307
Dot il p 130

14th century
Dav v 1 fig 545, 547-48, 602
Gor pl p27

Edward II, 1307-1327
HousM p89-91 fig 152
Yar pl p64, 66

Edward III, 1323-1377
Dav v 1 p212 pl
HousM p89-91 fig 153
Yar pl II (col)

Richard II, 1377-1399
AirM il p29
HousM p 114-15 fig 210, 212
Yar pl p75

15th century
Henry IV, 1399-1413
Gor pl p24
Pric pl p 17

Henry VII, 1485-1509
Dot p 144 il
Norr v3 bk 1 p 15-18 pl 1 (col)
   fig 6-7, 111

16th century
Henry VIII, 1509-1547
AirB il p32
BosE pl 1
Dav v 1 p430, 434 il
Dot p 144 il
EvnJ p 106-07 pl 63
Gor pl p40 (col)
LavE pl 33 (col)
LavR pl p44 (col)
Nat v70 Jl '36 pl p88 (col)
Norr v3 bk 1 p 182, 184-85, 187-88, 190,
   232-33, 236-37, 253-60 pl p 185, 197,
   237, 254, 256 (2 col) fig 254, 256
Pric pl p24
Trev v 1 pl 167
UnW pl 36 (col)
Wel pl p 11
WilF pl p57
Yar pl p 110, 114

Edward VI, 1547-1553
BruK pl 82
LavR pl p55
Norr v3 bk 2 p392-93 front (col) pl
Trev v 1 pl 140
Yar pl p 119, 121

17th century
James I, 1603-1625
BosE pl 10
BruK pl 82
CunA pl 8b (f)
Dav v2 p561 il
Hat fig 86

Charles I, 1625-1649
Dav v2 p572 il
Dot p 154 il
Gor pl p72
Lint pl 17
Tru pl p58 (col)
WilF pl p86
Yar pl p 151

Cromwell, 1649-1660
Dot p 154 il

Charles II, 1660-1685
Tru pl p70 (col)

19th century
See Coronation robes—England—19th
century; Queens and empresses—England, 1830-1837; Queens and empresses—
England—Victoria—1837-1901

20th century
See also Coronation robes—England—
20th century; Queens and empresses—
England—Elizabeth II, 1953-

Edward VII, 1901-1910
Mer fig 34

Europe
11th century
UnW pl 21 (col)

13th century
VanH pl 3

France
Early to 987
Covers Merovingian and Carlovingian kings,
Clovis, Charlemagne, etc.
Dot p 121 il
LeID pl p349 fig 10
WilC pl p52

12th century
Philip II, 1180-1223
Dot il p 128

13th century
Dav v 1 p 169 il
HousM p 12 pl 2 (col)

Louis IX (St Louis) 1226-1270
Dot il p 128

14th century
WilF pl p25
Charles VI, 1380-1422
EvjD pl 26

16th century
Louis XII, 1498-1515
Norr v3 bk 1 pl p35, fig 113

Francis I, 1515-1547
BluL p 18 pl 1, 17 (1 col)
BosF pl 16
Dav v2 p473-74 il

KINGS AND RULES—France—16th century—Francis I, 1515-1547—*Continued*
Dot il p 147
LavE pl p23
LavR pl p36, 89, 95 (1 col)
LelD pl p263 fig 10
LesA pl 18
Loud pl 11 (col)
Norr v3 bk 1 p 185-87, 242-45 pl p 171, 244 (1 col) fig 228
Ogr pl p52
Pric pl p 12

Henry II, 1547-1559
BluL p 18-19 pl 7, 9
BosF pl 29
Dot il p 147
LavR pl p91-92
Norr v3 bk 2 p396-99 2 pl il

Charles IX, 1560-1574
BluL p21 pl 26-27
BosF pl 38
Dot il p 148
LavR pl p 100
LesA pl 50
Norr v3 bk 2 p556-58 2 pl (1 col) il

Henry III, 1574-1589
BruK pl 76 fig 1 (col)
Gor pl p59
LavR pl p37
Norr v3 bk 2 p654-55 il

Henry IV, 1589-1610
BluE p 18-19 pl 7-8
BosF pl 41
BruK pl 84 fig 1, 4 (col)
Dav v2 p508 il
LavR pl p347-349, 351
Loud pl 12 (col)
Norr v3 bk 2 p659-61 il

17th century
See also Coronation robes—France—17th century
Louis XIII, 1610-1643
Blue p23 pl 36
LavR pl p353

Louis XIV, 1643-1715
BruK pl 99 fig 7, 15 (col)
Loud pl 14-15 (col)
Ogr pl p53

18th century
See also Coronation robes—France—18th century
Louis XV, 1715-1774
Dot il p 158

Louis XVI, 1774-1789
BoeR pl p 198, 546 (1 col)

Napoleon, 1799-1804 (Consulate)
Dav v2 p719 il

19th century
See also Coronation robes—France—19th century

Napoleon, 1804-1814 (Empire)
Dot p 164 il

Germany
10th century
Dav v 1 p 111-12 2 pl

11th-12th centuries
BruK pl 31 fig 11, 14 (col)
HousG2 p 156-58 fig 167a, b, c
Ni pl 4
See also Coronation robes—Germany—11th century

16th century
Norr v3 bk 1 p37-42, 247-50 2 pl il; bk 2 p400-01, 403 il

Greece, Ancient
Pot v 1 pl 12 (col)

Hunza (Kingdom)
Nat v 104 O '53 pl p 508 (col)

India
See also Rajas
20th century
Nat v78 D '40 pl p740 (col)

Italy
14th century
WilFo pl p77
20th century
Nat v77 Mr '40 il p392

Korea
19th century
Bis pl p430

Macedonia
Nat v85 Mr '44 pl 344 (col)

Mayas
Nat v70 N '36 pl p628 (col)

Mexico
Ancient
Alv p296 pl p284a-284b (col)
DuS p65-69 pl 20-24 (col) il
16th century
BruK pl 195 fig 17 (col)

Nepal
Nat v97 Ja '50 pl p 11 (col)

Nigeria
Nat v83 Ap '43 pl p508

Palestine, Ancient
Dal v 1 fig 171 (col)
Pot v 1 pl 8 (col)
Wrig pt3 pl p25

Persia
Ancient to A.D. 640
BartC p78-82 fig 79
BruK pl 9
Dal v 1 fig 136, 139-40
Dav v 1 p 14 il
Hous2 p 162, 171, 175, 177-80 pl 9 fig 155, 168, 171, 174-76
Pot v 1 pl 6 (col)
TiK pl 9 fig 1-4

KINGS AND RULERS—Persia—Ancient to A.D. 640—*Continued*
UnW pl 6 (col)
WilC p24-25 pl p 27
Wrig pt 3 p22 pl p31
Yar pl p 12

Rome
BiE pl 51
Dal v 1 fig 333 (col)
Dav v 1 fig 262, 296
TiK pl 11 fig 1, 6; pl 35 fig 1
Tru p8 il
VanH pl 1
WilFo p33-35 pl p38-39

Russia
17th century
BruK pl 88 fig 13 (col)

18th century
Dot il p 164

Scotland
13th century
AirB il p24

14th century
Yar pl II (col)

15th-16th centuries
Norr v3 bk 1 p 175 fig 225-26, p251-53 pl
See also Queens and empresses—Scotland—16th century

Siam
BruK pl 181 fig 5 (col)

Spain
To 11th century
Dal v 1 fig 627-28 (col)

12th century
Dav v 1 p 148 il

13th century
Dal v2 fig 157 (col)

15th century
Norr v3 bk 1 p42-43 pl

16th century
BruK pl 74, 86 fig 7 (col)
Dav v 1 pl p459, 461
LavE pl 30, 50
LavR pl p41, 215
Norr v3 bk 2 p404-11, 573-76, 673-74, 677-78 pl p404, 408, 442, 673 (2 col) il
Rea p 15 pl 1
Rey p 14 pl 1
Yar pl p 121

17th century
BruK pl 86 fig 11 (col) pl 87 fig 1
Dav v2 p644, 649 il
LavR pl p239, 241-42, 250 (1 col)
Rea p22-24 pl 44, 46-47, 56 (1 col)

18th century
Gor pl p 126

Sweden
18th century
Berg fig 1, 3, 13, 76-77, 130, 140
See also Coronation robes—Sweden—18th century

Trans-Jordan
Nat v92 D '47 pl p754 (col)

Turkey
BruK pl 169 fig 14 (col)

Uganda
Nat v71 Ja '37 p 118 il

Zanzibar
Nat v 101 F '52 pl p265 (col)

KINGSTON BROOCH
Jes front (col) pl 24

KIRGHIZ
BruK pl 175 fig 9-12, 17 (col)
CrO pl 34 (f)

KLONDIKE PIONEERS
Gor pl p225-26

KNICKERBOCKERS
Kle p217-18 il
Pic il p85

KNIGHTS, MEDIEVAL
Dav v 1 fig 519, 555, 914
HousM p44-45 fig 68
KerM no3 pl 1
Loud pl 8 (col)
See also Military costume—England—14th and 15th centuries

KNIGHTS OF MALTA. See Malta, Knights of

KNIGHTS OF RHODES. See Malta, Knights of

KNIGHTS OF THE GARTER. See Garter, Order of the

KNIGHTS OF THE HOLY SPIRIT
LavR pl p 126

KNIGHTS OF THE WINETASTERS
Nat v98 Jl '50 pl p52 (col)

KNIGHTS OF WINDSOR
BarH pl 23 (col)

KNIGHTS TEMPLARS (MONASTIC AND MILITARY ORDER). See Templars

KNOTS, ORNAMENTAL
CrO pl 44

KOHINOOR DIAMOND
RogF p208-13 il

KOLOBUS
NorC p 11-12 il

KOREA
Bis il p81, 120
Brad pl p 109, 110
Keit p 13-16, 63-72 34 pl (14 col)

KOREA—*Continued*
Nat v88 O '45 pl p431, 444
Pot v2 p29-32 pl (col)
TiK pl 96-97
WilFo pl p51
See also subdivision Korea under
Capes and cloaks; Ceremonial costume;
Children; Court dress; Dancers; Foot-
wear; Headdress; Military costume

KORYAKS
CrO pl 34

KU KLUX KLAN
Ada v3 il p241
But pl p 191
Gor pl p218
Kou pl 108

KURDS
Brad pl p 111-12
BruK p 173 pl 16-17 (col) (m)
Nat v69 Ja '36 pl p22 (col) (m)
TiK pl 18, 19 fig 4 (col) (m)

KUTCHIN INDIANS. See Indians of
North America—Kutchin Indians

KYJOV. See Czechoslovakia—Moravia

L

LAALAND. See Denmark—Laaland

LA ALBERCA. See Spain—León

LABORERS. See Agricultural laborers;
Artisans; etc.

LABRADOR
Brad pl p 113 (f)

LABRETS
Leb pl 12 (col)
Nat v99 F '51 il p264

LACE
Dav v2 p684, 867 il
Int v2 pl 22-27
LesA p509-31 3 pl il
Norr v3 bk 1 p230-31; bk 2 p420, 589-
92 il
Pic p86-91 il

LACERNA. See Capes and cloaks—Rome

LADY WASHINGTON'S DRAGOONS.
See Military costume—United States—
Colonial period, 1775-1783—Cavalry

LAENA. See Capes and cloaks—Rome

LAESOE. See Denmark—Laesoe

LAGARTERA. See Spain—Castile, New

LAMAS
BruK pl 182 fig 7-8, 12 (col)
MusE pl 38 (col)

Nat v70 D '36 pl p784 (col); v87 Je
'45 pl p680 (col); v95 My '49 pl
p665 (col); v 97 Ja '50 pl p 13
(col); v99 My '51 pl p611, 627
(col); v 102 D '52 pl p721 (col)
Tik pl 79 fig 3-4, pl 80 fig 6, 12-13,
pl 95 (col)

LAMPLIGHTERS
United States
Davi v2 il p 162

LANCERS
England
19th century
BarH pl 13-14 (col) (off)
LavB p32-33 pl 14 (col) (off)
20th century
BarH p260-61 pl 17 (col) (off)

France
19th century
BluN pl p 174 (off)
Fro pl 5-6, 19 (col)
KnR p291-95 pl (off)
LelD p237, 240 il (off)
Lez pl p303 (col)

Germany
17th century
KnR pl p5

Naples (Kingdom)
19th century
Lez pl p307 (col)

LANDES. See France—Guienne and Gascony

LANDSKNECHTS. See Military costume
—Germany—16th century

LANGUEDOC. See France—Langudoc

LÄNNA. See Sweden—Uppland

LAOS
GaU pl 38 (col) (f)
Nat v 105 My '54 il p675 (m)
Pot v2 p45-46 pl (col)

LAPIDARIES
RogF p76-80 il

LAPLAND
Brad pl p 114
BruK pl 127 fig 1-6 (col) pl 128 fig
1-5 (col)
Nat v76 N '39 pl p657-64 (col); v96
Jl '49 pl p 109-16 (col); v 106 Ag
'54 pl p253, 256-57, 262-63, 273-77,
280 (col)
Prim p98-103 4 pl (1 col)
TiK pl 53 fig 10-17 (col)
WilF pl p 154, 163
See also Children—Lapland; Head-
dress—Lapland; Wedding costume—
Lapland

LATERAN CANONESSES. See Canonesses regular of the Lateran

LATVIA
Brad pl p 115
BruK pl 166 fig 1 (f)
Int v2 p11-13 pl 43 (f)

LAWYERS. See Legal costume

LAZARISTS
Doy pl 147 (col)

LEBANON, MODERN
Cyr pl 1-2, 4-5, 7, 12-13, 16, 18, 20-21,
23-24 (col)
See also Court dress—Lebanon, Modern

LECTORS
NorC p31 pl p30

LEG-BANDS
Indians of North America
MasB p47 il (incl pat)

LEGAL COSTUME
England
14th century
Ab pl p4
15th century
AirM il p63
Dav v1 p354 fig 928
Norr v3 bk 1 p76 fig 80
16th century
Hat p295-96 fig 135
Norr v3 bk 1 p295 il; bk 2 p690-91 il
18th century
Nat v95 Ap '49 pl p496 (col)
Trev v3 fig 30
19th century—date
Nat v71 My '37 pl p612
France
16th century
BruK pl 76 fig 4 (col)
17th century
LelD p247 il; pl p362 fig 2
Nat v 101 Ja '52 pl p84 (col)
18th century
LelD p233 il
Italy
15th century
WilF pl p30
Rome
Dav v 1 p76 il
Lab p26-28 pl (col)
United States
18th century
Ada v 1 il p 113; v2 il p67

LEGGINGS
See also Footwear
Primitive and early
WilFo pl p60
15th century
WilFo pl p74
19th century
LelD p278 il
Pic il p94 (m)
Indians of North America
LyF p 108-11, 114-16 il
MasB p52-53 il
WilFo pl p 116
Spain
19th century—date
AnS fig 82, 293, 320, 386-87

LEGIONNAIRES. See Military costume—
Rome

LEKSAND. See Sweden—Dalarne

LEÓN. See Spain—León

LÉRIDA. See Spain—Catalonia

LIBERIA
Nat v93 F '48 pl p211-17 (col)

LIBERTY (SYMBOLICAL FIGURE)
BruK pl 117 fig 2 (col)
See also Fancy dress and stage cos-
tume—Miss Liberty

LIBYA, ANCIENT
TiK pl 8 fig 20-22 (m)

LICTORS AND FASCES
Dal v 1 fig 333 (col)
LelD p243 il
UnW pl 16 (col)

LIEUVIN. See France—Normandy

LIFE GUARDS
Part of the household cavalry of the army
England
17th century
Law v 1 p83-99 il
20th century
Nat v 104 S '53 pl p304 (col)

LIGURIA. See Italy—Liguria

LILLHÄRDAL. See Sweden—Härjedalen

LIMBURG. See Netherlands—Limburg

LIMOUSIN. See France—Limousin

LINZ. See Austria—Upper Austria

LIP ORNAMENTS. See Labrets

LIRIPIPE. See subdivisions 14th and 15th
centuries (about 1375-1445) under Headdress — England; Headdress — France,
etc.

LITTER BEARERS. See Chair bearers

The **LITTLE OLD MEN.** See Dancers—Mexico—The little old men

LITTLE RUSSIA. See Russia—Ukraine

LIVERY
France
14th-15th centuries
EvjD p27-28, 39-43 pl 20b
18th century
LelD p215, 245 il
19th century
Dav v2 p806 il (m)
LelD p245 il
Italy
18th century
Mora pl 99, 101 (m)
19th century
Dav v2 p806 il (m)

LIVONIA. See Estonia; Latvia

LJUSDAL. See Sweden—Helsingland

LOCKETS. See Necklaces and pendants

LOGROÑO. See Spain—Castile, Old

LOLOS
Nat v91 Ja '47 pl p 117
Pot pl 9 (col) (f)

LOMBARDY. See Italy—Lombardy

LORDS CHAMBERLAINS
England
19th century
Hat p296 fig 106, 117
20th century
Nat v90 Ag '46 pl p241 (col); v 104 S '53 pl p315 (col)

LORDS CHANCELLORS
Sweden
18th century
StocM pl 27 (col)

LORDS TREASURERS
England
13th century
Dav v 1 p454 il
16th century
Norr v3 bk 2 p532-33, 642 il

LORGNETTES. See Eyeglasses and lorgnettes

LORRAINE
BruK pl 151 (col)
CosP p20-21 pl 33-35 (1 col)
GaP pl 15 (col) (f)
GiR pl 45-46 (col)
LavR pl p 120-21, 357
LepF pl 11 (col) (f)
RogD pl 11 (col) (f)
See also Alsace; Noblemen—Lorraine; Noblewomen—Lorraine

LOUIS, KING. See subdivisions under Kings and rulers—France

LÖVÅNGER. See Sweden—Västerbotten

LOVELOCKS
Bra pl 29
WilF pl p89, 95
WilH p 109 pl p 124, 126-27

LOWER AUSTRIA. See Austria—Lower Austria

LUCERNE. See Switzerland—Lucerne

LUGO. See Spain—Galicia

LUMBERJACKS
Gor pl p211, 226
Nat v72 Jl '37 pl p23 (col)

LYOE. See Denmark—Lyoe

LYONNAIS. See France—Lyonnais

M

MACARONIS
Dav v 1 p773 il; v2 p772-73 il
Lab p74-77 pl (col)
Pic il p96
Yar p 189 pl p 190
See also England—George III, 1760-1820

MACE BEARERS
England
AnS p318 fig 391
HousM pl 5 (col)
Nat v90 Ag '46 pl p237 (col)
France
LelD p272 il
Spain
OrT pl 206-07

MACEDONIA
At pl 46-55 (col)
Brad pl p 165-69 (1 col)
BruK pl 170 fig 2 (col) (m)
Jan p 15-16 pl 4 (col)
TiK pl 57-59 (col)
See also Coats and jackets—Macedonia; Kings and rulers—Macedonia

MACES
AirB il p48
LelD il p46
Nat v92 N '47 pl p575 (col)

MÂCON. See France—Burgundy

MADAGASCAR
Brad pl p21 (f)
GaU pl 22-25 (col)

MADRID. See Spain—Castile, New

MAGDALENA, MONKS OF THE ORDER OF
Doy pl 50 (col)

MAGICIANS AND SORCERERS. See Medicine men; Shamans

MAGISTRATES. See Legal costume

MAHARAJAS. See Rajas

MAHARANIS. See Ranis

MAINE. See France—Maine

MAJORCA. See Balearic islands

MALAGA. See Spain—Andalusia

MALAGASY. See Madagascar

MALLORCA. See Balearic islands

MALTA
Nat v78 Ag '40 p269-70 il (f)

MALTA, KNIGHTS OF
Doy pl 141-42 (col)

MAMELUKS (FRENCH ARMY)
BluN pl p 174
LelD p250 il

MANCHURIA
Pot v2 p 17-20 pl (col)
TiK pl 95 (col)

MANCHUS
Camm p20-34 pl 8, 12-14, 18

MANDARINS
BruK pl 183 fig 11-12 pl 184 fig 2 (col)
Dal v 1 fig 765-69
KerM no2 pl 1
Lee p 12-15 pl
Nat v96 S '49 pl p354-55 (col)
Pic il p29
Pot v2 pl 2, 11 (col)
TiK pl 91 fig 4, pl 92 fig 11, pl 93 fig 6 (col)
WilFo pl p48

MANDARIN'S WIFE
Dal v 1 fig 753 (col)
Lee p 12-15 pl

MANDEVILLE. See subdivisions 16th and 17th centries under Coats and jackets— Europe and under specific countries

MANDILION. See subdivisions 16th and 17th centuries under Coats and jackets —Europe and under specific countries

MANIPLE
HousM p28-30 fig 21-24
NorC p92-94 il
Wa p62 fig 62 IV

MANTELLETA
McC p94-97 pl

MANTELLONE
McC p98-99 il

MANTILLAS
Spain
Agu pl D, 41-42, 92, 106-07 (1 col)
Gom pl p 197
Lee p62-63 pl
LelD p269 il
Nat v99 Ap '51 pl p513 (col)
OrT pl 180-81, 189, 198-201, 223, 237
Pic il p97

MANTLES. See Capes and cloaks

MAORIS
AirB il p62
AirO il p59
Nat v69 F '36 pl p 182-83 (col); v 101 Ap '52 pl p427, 440, 442 (col) (f)

MARABOUTS
Nat v81 Mr '42 pl p388

MARAGATOS
Agu pl 124
D'Iv p25 pl 96-97 (col)
Gom pl p70, 134 (1 col)
Int v2 pl 6
OrT pl 174-77

MARCHE. See France—Marche

MARDI GRAS. See Festival costume— United States—Louisiana

MARIMBA PLAYERS
Spi il p46

MARINE CORPS
England
Nat v 101 Ap '52 pl p538 (col)
18th century
LavB p28 pl 5 (col) (pte)
Law v2 p22-25 il (off, pte)
19th century
BarH pl 9 (col) (pte)
LavB p34-35 pl 18 (col) (off)
20th century
BarH p259 pl 20 (col) (pte)
United States
1775-1783
Cra pl p6-7, 10 (off, pte)
Met p25-26 pl p40 (off, pte)
VanH pl 9 fig 17
1783-1812
Cra pl p 12 (off, pte)
Met p39-41 pl (off, pte)
1812-1860
Met front (col) pl p69 (off, pte)
VanH pl 14 fig 3-6, 11-12

MARINE CORPS—United States—Continued

1860-1898
Cra pl p 15-16 (pte)
Met pl p227, 249-51 (off, pte)
VanH pl 14 fig 13-14, 17-18

1898-1917
Cra pl p 17-20 (off, pte)
Met pl p256-57, 292, 327, 444 (off, pte)
VanH pl 14 fig 21-22

1917-1939
Cra pl p22-24
Met pl p477 (off, pte)

MARKEN. See Netherlands—Marken

MARKET WOMEN
England
16th century
Norr v3 bk 1 p310 il; bk 2 p717 il

MARRIAGE COSTUME. See Wedding costume

MARSHALS
France
19th century
BluN pl p202-03, 214

Germany
17th century
Ni pl 37

MARTINIQUE
GaU pl 26 (col) (f)
Nat v79 Ja '41 pl p50 (f); v93 Ja '48 pl p41 (col) (f)

MARYKNOLL FATHERS
MusE pl 36 (col)

MASAI
Nat v 106 O '54 pl p490, 496-97, 499, 506, 508-09 (6 col); v 106 D '54 pl p722-23 (col)

MASKS
Eth p60-62 pl (incl pat)
LelD p245, 271-72 il
WilC pl p 101, 183
WilH p80 pl p 103
See also Devil masks

Bhután
Nat v 102 D '52 pl p747, 749

China
Nat v70 D '36 p774-75 il

Europe
Bra pl 27
Dav v 1 p443 il
Int v 1 pl 4-5
LesA p 102-04 fig 106-07
Lint p271-72 pl 6 (f)
WilC pl p 101, 183

Greece, Ancient
LesA p 101 fig 105

Indians of North America
Ada v 1 il p351
MasB p 112-13 il (m)
Nat v72 N '37 pl p570 (col); v78 N '40 pl p590 (col)
Roe p 158-74 pl 3-7, 11-18, 24-38, 40 (col)

Italy
Int v 1 pl 49

Japan
Int v2 pl 87
LesA fig 114

Mexico
DuS pl 2, 5, 7, 11-14, 29 (col)
Too p63-64 fig 65, 124

Peru
Hal pl E (col)
TooP pl 40, 42, 46

Rome
Dal v 1 il p201

Solomon Islands
CrO pl 5-6

United States
Trai p211 il (f)

MASMÜSTER NUNS
Doy pl 120 (col)

MASONS AND STONECUTTERS
Egypt, Ancient
Nat v80 O '41 pl p460 (col)

England
11th century
AirS il p38

15th century
Dav v 1 fig 924

MASQUERADE COSTUME. See Fancy dress and stage costume

MATADORS. See Bullfighters

MAURITANIA
GaU pl 4-5 (col)

MAYAS
DuS pl 17, 24, 31
Nat v70 N '36 pl p626-40 (col)
ValM p 15-16 pl 12 (col) (f)

MAYORESSES
Spain
Nat v69 Mr '36 pl p427
OrT pl 66-67

MAYORS
England
16th century
Dav v 1 fig 1139
Hat p296 fig 118
LavR p30 (col)
Norr v3 bk 2 p698 il

17th century
AirT il p45

MAYORS—England—*Continued*

20th century

Nat v 104 S '53 pl p312 (col)

Netherlands
17th century

Dav v2 p629-30 il
LavR pl p308 (col)

Peru

Nat v98 O '50 pl p455

Spain

OrT pl 33-34, 41, 73, 188

MAYPOLE DANCE. See Dancers—England—Maypole dance; Dancers—Spain—Maypole dance

MECKLENBURG. See Germany—Mecklenburg

MEDIA
Bra p38-39 pl 5

MEDICI COLLARS. See Neckwear—Europe—16th century (f)

MEDICINE MEN
See also Shamans

African tribes
AirO il p49
CrO pl 11
MusE pl 1 (col)

Indians of North America
Nat v78 N '40 p578 (col)

MEDIEVAL COSTUME. See period subdivisions 5th-15th centuries under various countries

MEN-AT-ARMS. See Military costume

MENNONITES
Ada v 1 il p276
Nat v80 Jl '41 pl p39, 48 (1 col) (f)
Sit pl p 104
Trai p 193 il (m)

MENORCA. See Balearic islands

MERCERS
England
14th-15th centuries
Ab pl p96

MERCHANTS
England
14th century
Ab pl p4
BrH pl p47 fig 6
Wel pl p9

15th century
BrH pl p75 fig 4 (col)
Norr v3 bk 1 p79 fig 86
Tru pl p48 (col)

16th century
Norr v3 bk 1 p295-96 il; bk 2 p697-700 il
WilF pl p64

17th century
BrH pl p95 fig 5

18th century
AirB il p52
Lab p78-81 pl (col)

19th century
AirB il p58

Germany
17th century
BruK pl 94 fig 1, 7

Netherlands
16th century
WilF pl p73

Portugal
16th century
Rea p 19 pl 21

Syria
Cyr pl 5 (col)

Turkey
16th century
BruK pl 90 fig 9

MERCIA. See Spain—Mercia

MERMAIDS. See Fancy dress and stage costume—Mermaid

MERVEILLEUSE
BruK pl 116 fig 13, 15; pl 117 fig 13-14 (col)
Dal v2 fig 781
Dav v2 fig 2310-14 (f)
Lecl pl 14 (col)
LelD il p274
WilC p231 pl p234
WilF pl p 118
See also France—18th century—Directory, 1795-1799 (f)

MESOPOTAMIA. See Iraq

MESSENGERS AND COURIERS
England
15th century
Norr v3 bk 1 p80 il

France
18th century
LelD p 129 il

MEXICO
See also Aztecs; Bullfighters; Fancy dress and stage costume—Mexican; Indians of Mexico; Mayas; Serapes; also subdivision Mexico under Ambassadors; Bags, purses, etc.; Children; Dancers; Festival costume; Fishermen; Flower venders; Footwear; Gods; Headdress;

MEXICO—*Continued*

Kings and rulers; Masks; Military costume; Musicians; Noblewomen; Pottery venders; Priestesses; Priests; Riding costume; Wedding costume

Ancient

Alv   p 293-300   pl   p284-85, 288-89, 292-93 (col)
BruK   pl 193 (col)
DuS   p73-86   pl 25-32 (col) (il) (f)
TiK   pl 107 (col)

Modern

Alv   pl   p64, 112, 300-01 (col)
Brad   pl   p 117, 119 (1 col)
BruK   pl 196 (col)
KaM   pl 1-12 (col)
Lee   p48-50   pl
TiK   pl 109-10 (col)

BY REGION OR PROVINCE

Campeche

MeriT   p8   pl 1 (col) (f)

Chiapas

MeriT   p8-9   pl 3-5 (col)
Pr   pl 6 (col)

Chihuahua

Meri   pl 2 (col)
MeriT   p9   pl 6 (col) (f)

Guanajuato

MeriT   p 10   pl 7 (col) (m)

Guerrero

MeriT   p 10   pl 8 (col) (f)

Jalisco

Alv   pl   p 169 (col) (f)
Marq   pl 8-14
Meri   pl 4 (col)
MeriT   p 10   pl 9 (col) (f)

Mexico, D.F.

Meri   pl 6-7 (col)
MeriT   p 11   pl 10 (col) (f)

Michoacán

MeriT   p 11   pl 11-12 (col)
Pr   pl 1-3 (col)
Valm   p 11   pl 3, 5 (col) (f)

Nayarit

Meri   pl 4 (col)
MeriT   p 12   pl 13 (col) (m)
ValM   p 10-11   pl 2 (col)

Oaxaca

Alv   pl   p 185 (col) (f)
Marq   pl 70-92
Meri   pl 14-22 (col) (f)
MeriT   p 12-13   pl 14-16 (col) (f)
Pr   pl 5, 7-9 (col)
ValM   p 13-14   pl 8-9 (col) (f)

Puebla

Marq   pl 42-58
Meri   pl 6, 8-10 (col) (f)
MeriT   p 13   pl 17 (col) (f)
ValM   p 11-12   pl 4, 6 (col)

San Luis Potosí

Meri   pl 3 (col) (f)
MeriT   p 13-14   pl 18-19 (col) (f)
ValM   p 10   pl 1 (col) (f)

Sonora

MeriT   p 14   pl 20 (col) (m)

Tabasco

MeriT   p 14   pl 21 (col) (m)

Tehuantepec

Alv   pl   p 128, 176 (col) (f)
Brad   pl   p 116 (f)
CovM   p43-44, 52-54, 60-63   pl   p50, 246, 262, 310 (col)   pl 56-57, 59
Marq   pl 83-84, 86-91
Meri   pl 20-21 (col) (f)
Nat   v75 Ja '39   pl   p68 (col) (f); v80 S '41   pl   p312-13 (col) (f)
Pr   pl 8-9 (col) (f)
ValM   p 15   pl 11 (col) (f)

Tlaxcala

MeriT   p 15   pl 22 (col) (m)

Vera Cruz

Meri   pl 13 (col) (f)
MeriT   p 15   pl 23-24 (col) (f)
ValM   p 13-15   pl 7, 10 (col) (f)

Yucatán

Alv   pl   p 144 (f)
Meri   pl 25 (col)
MeriT   p 16   pl 25 (col) (f)
ValM   p 15-16   pl 12 (col) (f)

MICHOACÁN. See Mexico—Michoacán

MICMACS. See Indians of North America —Micmacs

MIDDLE AGES. See period divisions from 5th to end of 15th centuries under various European countries, e.g. France—14th century

MIDSHIPMEN. See Naval cadets

MILAN. See Italy—Lombardy

MILITARY CADETS

United States

Kre   pl 7 (col)
Kre2   pl 8 (col)
Nat   v69 Je '36   pl   p779, 781, 786 (col); v 101 My '52   pl   p601, 603 (col)

MILITARY COSTUME

Where no subdivision of an army is designated uniforms of infantry may be assumed

See also Amazons; Crossbowmen; Crusaders; Footwear, Military; Headdress, Military; Marine corps; Military cadets; Naval cadets; Naval costume; Volunteer troops

Early-1100

BruK   pl 37

Afghanistan

AirO   il p27 (pte)

MILITARY COSTUME—*Continued*

African tribes

Nat   v74 S '38   pl   p340-47   (col)
TiK   pl 25 fig 3-5, 7, 13-14 (col)

Alsace

12th century

Dav   v 1   p 143 il

Annam

Pot   v2   pl 12 (col)

Argentine republic

20th century

MiI   pl   p6-7 (off, pte)
Nat   v76 N '39   pl   p583 (col)

Assyria and Babylonia

BruK   pl 5-6 (1 col)
Dal   v 1   p67-72   pl il (col)
Dav   v 1   p 11 il
HeuO   p74-80 il
Hous2   p 115-16, 140, 146, 154-55 fig 116,
133-34, 141-42, 152
Pot   v 1   pl 5 (col)
TiK   pl 6 fig 11-13,   pl 7 fig 1
Wa   p25-26 fig 35-36
WilF   pl   p9
WilFo   pl   p 13
Wrig   pt3   p20-21   pl   p30

Australia and New Zealand army corps

Nat   v81 Ap '42   il   p410, 412, 418,
pl 427, 429, 453, 456 (4 col)

Austria

See also subdivision Austria-Hungary
under Dragoons; Grenadiers; Hussars;
also Military costume—Hungary

18th century

KnR   p212-46   9 pl
Lez   pl   p222 (col)

19th century

BruK   pl 123 fig 12 (off)
KnR   p212-46   9 pl
Lez   pl   p276-77, 308-11, 345 (col) (off
pte)

20th century

Lez   pl 368, 378 (col) (off, pte)

Aztec

KaAz   pl 6-7 (col)
Nat   v71 Je '37   pl   p735, 740-42 (col)

Belgium

19th century

KnR   p407-11 pl
Lez   pl   p338-39 (col) (off, pte)

20th century

MiI   pl   p 17-18 (off, pte)

Bolivia

20th century

MiI   pl   p21-22 (off, pte)

Borneo

Brad   pl   p39-40

Brazil

20th century

MiI   pl   p26-27 (off, pte)

Cavairy

Nat   v85 Ja '44   pl   p49 (col) (off)

Bulgaria

19th century

KnR   p473-75   pl

20th century

Lez   pl   p369 (col) (off, pte)
MiI   pl   p43

Burgundy

14th century

BruK   pl 38 fig 6,   pl 40 fig 9-12

Byzantine empire

BruK   pl 27-28 (1 col)
Dal   v 1   p225-26 fig 473-76 (col)
Dav   v 1   p81 il
Dot   il   p 121
HousG2   p 129-31, 146 il
TiK   pl 36 fig 13-14, 17-18

Canada

20th century

Lez   pl   p376 (pte)
MiI   pl   p50-51 (off, pte)
Nat   v82 O '42   pl   p454 (col) (pte)

Air Force

Nat   v82 O '42   pl   p455

Women personnel

Nat   v82 O '42   pl   p455 (col)

Chile

20th century

MiI   pl   p 56 (off)

China

18th century

BruK   pl 183 fig 7-10 (col)
TiK   pl 91-93 (col)

19th century

Bis   il p210 (pte)

20th century

MiI   pl   p67-68 (off, pte)
Nat   v71 Ap '37   p491 il

Colombia

20th century

MiI   pl   p72 (off)

Costa Rica

20th century

MiI   pl   p76 (off, pte)

Crete, Ancient

Gor   pl   p8

Cuba

20th century

MiI   pl   p80 (off, pte)

Czechoslovakia

20th century

Lez   pl   p379 (col) (pte)

MILITARY COSTUME—*Continued*

Denmark

18th century

KnR p375-81 2 pl

19th century

BruK pl 123 fig 13 (col) (off)
KnR p375-81 3 pl
Lez pl p314-15 (col)

20th century

Guards and household troops
Nat v77 Ja '40 pl p 17 (col) (pte)

Ecuador

20th century

MiI pl p96-97 (off)

Egypt, Ancient

BruK pl 2 (col)
Dal v 1 p47-52 2 pl il (col)
Dav v 1 p23 il
HeuO p4-32 pl 14 (col)
Hous2 p40-51 5 pl il (off, pte)
VanH pl 1
WilF pl p8
WilFo pl p7
Wrig pt3 p 16-17 pl p28

Eire

MiI pl p 105-06 (off, pte)

England

See also subdivision England under Archers (Military); Dragoons; Hussars; Lancers; Musketeers; Volunteer troops; also names of individual regiments, e.g. Coldstream guards; Gordon Highlanders; Honourable Artillery Company; Life guards; Seaforth Highlanders; Yeomen of the Guard

Ancient to 449

AirB il p6, 18

449-1066

AirS p 11-14 3 pl il
Dav v 1 p 120-22 pl il
Lab p30-32 pl (col)
VanH pl 2
Wa p81 fig 86
Wel pl p3-5
WilFo p57 pl p60
Yar pl p41

11th century (1066-1100)

AirB il p 18
AirS pl p48-49
BruK pl 35-36 (1 col)
Dot il p 123
VanH pl 2

12th century

Nat v95 Ap '49 pl p455 (col)

13th century

AirB il p25
AirM pl p 18
Dav v 1 p 174-75, 177 3 pl
Tru p 127-28 il (off)

14th century

AirB pl p24-25
AirM pl p35
Dav v 1 p 199-200, 208, 211, 213-15 il
Dot p 133-34 il
Tru p 128-29 il (off)

15th century

AirB il p25-26
AirM pl p51
Dav v 1 p349-52, 355, 359 5 pl il
HousM p 199-208 pl il
Law v 1 p3 il (pte)
Tru p 129-30 il (off)

16th century

AirB il p31, 34
AirT il p25
Dav v 1 pl p 164
Gor pl p38
Law v 1 p4-8 il (pte)
Tru p 130-31 il
VanH pl 4

17th century

AirB il p43, 49
AirT il p41-42
BarH p40-51 3 pl (col) (off, pte)
Law v 1 p8-42, 180-84 pl il (off, pte)
Trev v2 fig 29-30
Tru p 131 il (off)

Artillery
BarH p51 pl 4 (col) (off)
Law v 1 p 164-70 il (pte)

Cavalry
BarH p42-43 pl 2 fig 2-3 (col)
Law v 1 p83-99 il (off, pte)

Musicians
Law v 1 p25-28, 113-20 il

18th century

KnR p356-69 5 pl

See also Hanoverian regiments; Honourable artillery company; Horse guards

Irish troops
Law v2 p85-92 7 pl

Scottish troops
Law v2 p77-84 pl il (off, pte)

1702-1714
AirT il p52
BarH p46-49 pl (col) (off, pte)

Artillery
Law v 1 p 173-79 il (off, pte)

Cavalry
Law v 1 p99-105 il

Infantry
Law v 1 p44-53 front (col) il (off, pte)

1714-1760
AirH il p21
BarH p50-53, 72-79 2 pl (col) (off, pte)
Davi v 1 il p97 (off)
LavB p27-28 pl 1-5 (col) (pte)
Law v2 p 198-205 il (off)
Nat v95 Ap '49 pl p494 (col) (off)

MILITARY   COSTUME—England—18th
century—1714-1760—*Continued*

Artillery
BarH   p99, 101-02   pl 5, 7 (col) (off, pte)
Law   v2   p 180-90 (off)

Cavalry
BarH   p52-53   pl 4, 6 (col) (pte)
Law   v2 p 107-55   4 pl   il (off, pte)
Lez   pl   p 198-99 (col)

Engineers
Law   v2   p 190-97   il (off, pte)

Guards and household troops
BarH   p48, 51-52, 100-01   pl 3-4, 7 (col) (pte)

Infantry
AirB   il   p53 (pte)
Law   v2   p 1-21, 25-53   pl   p33, 37, 39, 86-92   il (off, pte)

Musicians
Law   v2   p50-53, 151-52   front (col)   pl (col) il

Scottish troops
Law   v 1   p96-98; v2   p54-76   il (off, pte)
KnR   pl   p393

1760-1820

Ada   v 1   il   p 369, 392 (off, pte)
AirH   il   p21
BarH   p98-106, 116-22, 136-37   pl 5-10 (col) (off, pte)
LavB   p29-31   pl 6-10, 12 (col) (incl pat) (off, pte)
Lee   p 108-09   pl (off, pte)
Lez   pl   p266 (col)
MusM   pl 28 (off, pte)
Nat   v78   Jl '40   pl   p45 (col) (off)
Pric   pl   p 117 (off)
VanH   pl 8
WilFo   pl   p 130 (off)

Artillery
BarH   p 101-02, 117-18, 136-39   pl 7, 9 (col) (off, pte)
KnR   pl   p373 (off, pte)

Engineers
LavB   p30   pl 10 (col)

Guards and household troops
BarH   p 104-05   pl 5, 8-10 (col) (off, pte)
KnR   pl   p365

Infantry
AirB   il   p56 (pte)
Walk   pl 22 (col) (pte)

Sappers and miners
BarH   p 119   pl 9 (col) (pte)

Scottish troops
BarH   p74, 137   pl 5, 11 (col) (off, pte)
KnR   pl   p393

19th century
KnR   p356-69   7 pl

1820-1837
BarH   p 136-56   3 pl (col) (off, pte)
LavB   p31-33   pl 11, 13-14 (col) off, pte)

Artillery
BarH   pl 13 (col) (off)
KnR   pl   p373 (off)

Guards and household troops
BarH   pl 13 (col) (off)

Musicians
BarH   p 141   pl 12 (col)

1837-1899
AirB   il   p61 (pte)
BarH   p 156-58, 174-207   pl 13-17 (col) (off, pte)
Bro20   il   p 17 (pte)
Gern   pl 20 (off)
KnR   pl   p373 (off, pte)
LavB   p33-37   pl 15-24 (col) (off, pte)
QuV   fig85-87, 89, 91-95

Artillery
BarH   p 140-43, 176-77   pl 12, 14 (col)

Camel corps
BarH   pl 24 (col) (pte)

Engineers
LavB   p37   pl 23 (col) (off)

Guards and household troops
BarH   p 143-44   pl 12-13 (col) (off, pte)
KnR   pl   p365
Lez   pl   p267 (col) (off)

Sappers
BarH   pl 13 (col) (pte)

Scottish troops
BarH   pl 14 (col) (pte)
KnR   pl   p393

West India regiment
AirO   il   p 17 (pte)

20th century
1899-1914
BarH   p226-31   2 pl (col) (off, pte)

Cavalry
BarH   pl 23 (col) (off)

Engineers
BarH   pl 19 (col) (off)

Guards and household troops
BarH   pl 18 (col)

Indian troops
Lez   pl   p351 (col) (pte)

Musicians
BarH   pl 18 (col)

Scottish troops
BarH   p202-07   2 pl (col) (off, pte)

Veterinary corps
BarH   pl 19 (col) (off)

Welsh troops
BarH   pl 18 (col) (pte)

1914-1918
AirB   il   p63 (pte)
BarH   p256-61, 268-71   3 pl (col) (off, pte)
Bro20   p38-41   il (off, pte)
Lez   pl   p384 (col) (off, pte)

MILITARY   COSTUME—England—20th
century—1914-1918—*Continued*

Artillery
BarH pl 20, 22, 24 (col) (pte)

Colonial troops
Lez pl p376 (pte)

Guards and household troops
BarH p271 pl 22 (col) (off, pte)

Medical corps
BarH pl 22 (col) (off)

Nurse corps
Bro20 p40-41 il

Sappers and miners
BarH pl 20 (col)

Scottish troops
BarH pl 20 (col) (pte)

Women personnel
Yar il p259 (pte)

1919-1938
BarH p268-75, 294-96 3 pl (col) (off, pte)

Guards and household troops
BarH pl 22 (col) (off, pte)

1939-1945
BarH p294-301 pl (col) (off, pte)
Bro p20 il p78
Lab pl 27 (col)
MiI pl p37-38 (off, pte)

Air-borne troops
BarH p297 pl 24 (col) (pte)

Air force
GrAi pl 7-10 (off)
MiI pl p39-40 (off, pte)

Armoured corps
BarH pl 24 (col) (pte)

Commandos
BarH pl 24 (col) (pte)

Guards and household troops
BarH pl 23 (col) (pte)

Women personnel
Yar il p275 (off)

Etruria
Dav v 1 p53-54 2 pl

Europe
Early to 1100
Dal v2 p48-57, 62-95 2 pl (col)
Dav v 1 pl p 153
Gor pl p36
Lee p82-83 pl
Lis il p28
Wa p97-98 pl

12th century
Dal v2 p48-57 2 pl fig 62-95 (col)
LelD p 12-19 pl, p 177, 212 il
Wa p98-99 fig 93

13th century
BruK pl 37 fig 10-12
Dal v2 p91-97 il
Dav v 1 pl p 153
Gor pl p36

HousM p54-61 2 pl il
LelD p 19, 56 pl p 14 il
WilFo pl p74

14th century
BruK pl 38
Dal v2 p 137-40 fig 224-34 (col)
Dav v 1 pl p 153
Gor p35 pl p36-37
HousM p 122-28 pl il
Lee p88-89 pl p91
LelD p82-83 pl p 14-16 il; pl p 163 fig 1
Wa p 114 fig 110 (incl pat)

15th century
BruK pl 38
Dal v2 p 187-95 pl il (col)
Dav v 1 pl p 153
Gor p35 pl p36-37
HousM p 199-208 pl il
LelD p 19 pl p 14-15, 17; pl p 163 fig 3-7; p212 il
Lis il p41
Wa p 129-30 fig 123, 128, 130A, 130D, 136A

16th century
Dav v 1 pl p 153
Gor pl p38
KelF p49-59 pl p37, 63, 67, 112 (off, pte)
LelD pl p 16-18; p 163 fig 9-10
Lis il p49
Pric p 128-34 2 pl
Wa p 157 fig 141, 144D

17th century
BruK p24-25, 70 pl 97 (col) (off, pte)
Dav v 1 pl p 153
Wa p 199-200 fig 177 (off)

18th century
Wa p223 fig 184, 187, 188C, 196 (incl pat)

Finland
20th century
MiI pl p 108

France
See   also Foreign legion (French army);   Mameluks   (French   army); Swiss guards; also subdivision France under Dragoons; Grenadiers; Lancers; Musketeers

Early to 987
Dal v 1 fig 495 (col)
Wa p68 fig 86
WilFo pl p59

11th century
BruK pl 34
Gor pl p36

14th century
Gor pl p36-37
LelD pl p 16

15th century
BruK pl 41 fig 1-5 (col)
EvjD p45-47 pl 33-36
KerM no3 pl 4
LelD pl p 17

MILITARY COSTUME — France — Continued

16th century

BluE p9, 17-18 pl 1, 5 (off)
BluL p9, 14, 25 pl 4-5, 40, 58, 62 (off, pte)
BruK pl 75 fig 6-8 (col) pl 81
Dav v 1 p 162 il
LelD pl p 16-18; p343 fig 1-3

17th century (to 1715)

BluE p 13, 23 pl 35 (col) (off)
BruK pl 99 fig 2, 5 (off) (col)
Dav v 1 p 164 il
LelD pl p 18 fig 3; p 138 fig 1
WilF pl p88, 90, 95-96 (off)

18th century

BruK pl 119 fig 6-13 (col) (off, pte)
KnR p247-305 12 pl (off, pte)

1715-1774

LelD p 138 fig 2
WilF pl p 112

Guards and household troops

KnR pl p247-53 2 pl
LelD p 193-95 pl fig 2-4
Lez pl p233 (col) (off)

1774-1789

Ada v 1 il p399 (pte)
BruK table 7 fig 21 (pat)
VanH pl 8 (off) (pte)

Cavalry

LelD p98 fig 1

Guards and household troops

LelD p 193-95 pl fig 6-7; p218 fig 4

1789-1799

BluN p 153-56 pl p 169-72 (off, pte)
Lez pl p220, 268 (col)

Artillery

KnR p300-01 pl

Guards and household troops

LelD p 194-95 pl fig 8 (off)

19th century

See also Marshals—France

1799-1815

BluN p 156-64 pl p 173-80 (off, pte)
BruK pl 123 fig 15-21 (col) (off, pte)
KnR p247-305 12 pl (off, pte)
LelD p98, 199, 206-07 il
Lez pl p269-73 (col) (off, pte)

Artillery

Fro pl 7 (col) (off)
KnR p300-01 pl

Camel corps

LelD p 154-55 il
Lez pl p269 (col)

Cavalry

Fro pl 12-13, 16, 20 (col) (off)

Guards and household troops

Fro pl 2-11 (col)
LelD p 194-95 pl fig 9; pl p224 row 1 (col)

Infantry

Fro pl 18 (col) (pte)

Sappers and miners

BruK pl 123 fig 20 (col)

1815-1830

BluN p 164-69 pl p 181-82 (off)

Artillery

Lez pl p275 (col)

Guards and household troops

KnR pl p249
Lez pl p274, 302-03 (col)

1830-1848

BluN pl p 183-84 (off, pte)

Artillery

KnR p300-01 pl

Chasseurs d'Afrique

LelD il p417 fig 2 (off)

Sappers and miners

LelD p373 il (off); pl p374 fig 14-15 (pte)

1852-1870

BluN p 185-89 pl p201-09 (off, pte)
Lez pl p342-43 (col) (off, pte)

Guards and household troops

KnR pl p253
LelD p80-81 pl (col) il; p 194-95 pl fig 13 (pte)
Lez pl p331 (col) (off, pte)

Infantry

LelD p224 pl row 2-4 (col) (pte)

Sappers and miners

LelD p373 il; pl p374 fig 16 (pte)

1870-1900

BluN p 189-91 pl p210
LelD il p67 (pte)

Artillery

KnR p300-01 pl

20th century

LelD p 138 fig 3
Lez pl p374, 378 (col) (pte)
MiI pl p 115-16 (off, pte)

Moroccan regiment

Nat v 101 Je '52 pl p774 (col)

Germany

See also subdivision Germany under Dragoons; Generals; Grenadiers; Hussars; Lancers; Musketeers

13th century

Ni pl 7

14th century

BruK pl 40 fig 1-8

15th century

BruK pl 41 fig 6-15 (col)
LelD pl p 15, 17
Ni pl 14, 25

16th century

Bruh p28-29 pl (col)
BruK p24-25, 62-63 pl 64-65 (col)
Dav v 1 p 162-63 il

MILITARY COSTUME—Germany—16th
century—*Continued*
Gor pl p38, 49
Kle p 179, 241-42 il
LavE pl 24
LelD p241, 343 il
Lez pl p 177-78 (col)
Norr v3 bk 1 p 171-74 2 pl (1 col)
WilFo pl p94

17th century
Bruh p40-41 pl (col)
KnR pl p5
Lez pl p 180-85 (col)
WilF pl p88 (off)
See also Marshals—Germany

18th century
BruK p25, 74 pl 119-20 (1 col) (off,
pte)
KnR pl p79, 103
Lez pl p 186-89 (col)
MusM pl 27 (col) (pte)
WilF pl p 112

Artillery
Lez pl p218 (col) (off, pte)
Guards and household troops
Lez pl p224 (col)
Musicians
Lez pl p208-09 (col)

19th century
KnR p86-88 pl p31, 55, 89, 109, 125,
139, 159, 181, 193, 199, 207

Guards and household troops
KnR pl p21 (off, pte)
Lez pl p240-47 (col) (off, pte)

20th century
1900-1939
Lez pl p367, 371-73, 380-83 (col) (off,
pte)
1939-1945
Erl front, pl 16, 32, 64, 112, 128 (col)
(off, pte)
MiI pl p 124-26 (off, pte)
Nat v76 N '39 pl p685 (pte)

BY STATE
Anhalt
19th century
KnR p 165-68 pl

Baden
18th-19th centuries
KnR p 129-36 pl
Les pl p248-49 (col)

Bavaria
18th-19th centuries
KnR p68-92 4 pl
Lez pl p227, 248-49 (col)

Brandenburg
17th-18th centuries
Lez pl p 182-85, 187-89 (col)

19th century
Lez pl p335, 360 (col) (pte)

Bremen
19th century
Lez pl p322 (col) (off)

Brunswick
18th century
MusM pl 27 (pte)
19th century
KnR p 157-61 pl

Frankfurt-am-Main
19th century
KnR p201 pl p203

Hamburg
19th century
Lez pl p318-19, 322 (col) (off, pte)

Hanover
19th century
Lez pl p326 (col) (pte)

Hesse
18th-19th centuries
Lez pl p226, 229, 353 (col)

Hesse-Cassel
18th century
MusM pl 27 (pte)
19th century
KnR p190-97 pl

Hesse-Darmstadt
18th-19th centuries
KnR p 136-44 pl

Lippe-Detmold
19th century
KnR p 162-64 pl

Lubeck
19th century
Lez pl p322 (col) (off)

Mecklenburg
18th-19th centuries
KnR p 145-49 pl
Lez pl p321, 323 (col) (pte)

Nassau
19th century
KnR p 197-200 pl

Oldenburg
18th-19th centuries
KnR p 149-53 pl

Pomerania
19th century
Lez pl p362 (col) (pte)

Prussia
17th century
KnR p 1-7 pl
18th century
KnR p8-11 3 pl
Lez p56-99 pl p 193-97, 200-17, 224,
236-37 (col) (off, pte)
19th century
BruK pl 123 fig 1-7 (col) (off, pte)
KnR p 18-68 9 pl
Lez pl p225, 228, 238-47, 292-301, 325,
328-29, 336, 354-55, 360 (col) (off,
pte)

MILITARY COSTUME—Germany—*Cont.*

Saxony
18th-19th centuries
KnR   p92-110   5 pl
Lez   pl   218-19,   261-65,   317, 333, 341
(col) (off, pte)

Schaumburg-Lippe
18th-19th centuries
KnR   p   163-65   pl
Lez   pl   p320, 324   (col) (off, pte)

Silesia
19th century
Lez   pl   p363   (col) (pte)

Westphalia
19th century
KnR   p205-10   pl

Württemberg
19th century
KnR   p   111-29   3 pl
Lez   pl   p327, 335, 340   (col) (off, pte)

Wurzburg
19th century
KnR   p203-04   pl

Greece, Ancient
BartC   p95 fig 30
Bra   pl 6
Dal   v 1   p 141-46   2 pl   il (col)
Dav   v 1   pl   p59, 61, 68
Eth   p 13-15   il (incl pat)
Gor   pl   p 12
HousG2   p71-75   il
KerM   no 1   pl 6
Lee   p78-80   pl
LelD   p217   il
Loud   pl 4   (col)
Pot   v 1   pl 10   (col)
Tru   p 127   il
UnW   pl 12   (col)
VanH   pl 1
Wa   p40-41 fig 49
WilFo   p 18-19   pl   p22-23

Greece, Modern
At   pl 1   (col) (off)
Cros   p 18   pl 4   (col)
KnR   p476-79   pl
MiI   pl   p 132   (pte)
Nat   v77 Mr '40   pl   p297;   v79 Ja '41
pl   p98;   v96 D '49   pl   p730 (col);
v 100 D '51   p730 (col)

Guatemala
20th century
MiI   pl   p 136-37   (off, pte)

Haiti
20th century
MiI   pl   p 143   (off, pte)

Hittites
HeuO   p92   pl 54   il
Hous2   p70-71   fig 76

Hungary
See also subdivision Austria-Hungary
under Dragoons; Grenadiers; Hussars;
also Military costume—Austria

16th century
LelD   pl   p 16

18th century
KnR   pl   p229
LelD   p215   il

19th century
BruK   pl 123 fig 12   (off)
KnR   p212-46   9 pl
Lez   pl   276-77, 308-11, 345   (col) (off,
pte)

20th century
Lez   pl   p368, 379   (col) (off, pte)
Nat   v73 Ja '38   il   p3   (pte)

India
16th-18th centuries
Dal   v 1   p400-05   fig 726-38   (col)

Mysore
Nat   v89 Ap   pl   p460-61   (col)

Patiala
Nat   v78 D '40   pl   p735   (off) (col)

Indians of North America
Nat   v72 N '37   pl   p588-90   (col)

Ireland
16th century
Mccl   p39-40, 45-46   pl 23, 28

Italy
Ancient to A.D. 476
Dav   v 1   p52-53   pl   il
See also Military costume Etruria;
Military costume—Rome

14th century
BruK   pl 38 fig 11-17

15th century
BruK   pl 54 fig 11-15   (col)
Dav   v 1   p 160-61   2 pl
Gor   pl   p36

16th century
Dav   v 1   p 164   il; v2   p494   il

17th century
Dav   v 1   p 164   il
Gor   pl   p38

19th century
KnR   p328-35   pl

20th century
Lez   pl   p377-78   (col) (off, pte)
MiI   pl   p 172-73   (off, pte)

Guards and household troops
Nat   v71 Mr '37   pl   p288   (col)

Japan
Ancient and early
RueO   pl 9

MILITARY COSTUME—Japan—*Continued*

14th-16th centuries
LelD pl p 16 fig 6
Pot v2 pl 6 (col)

17th-18th centuries
BruK pl 186 fig 11-13 (col)

20th century
Lez pl p379 (col) (pte)
MiI pl p 182 (off, pte)

Korea
19th century
Keit p70 pl p68D
TiK pl 96 fig 1-11 (col) (off)

Laos
17th century
Pot v2 pl 13 (col)

Lombardy (Republic)
19th century
Lez pl p305 (col)

Mexico
Ancient
Alv p293-96 pl p284C-D, 288-89, 292B-C, 296-97 (col)
DuS p43-45, 49-54 pl 9-16 (col) il
TiK pl 107 fig 2-3 (col)

16th century
BruK pl 195 (col)

20th century
But pl p348 (off)
CovM il p233 (off)
MiI pl p 190 (off)

Morocco
Guards and household troops
Rous pl 17-18 (1 col)

Naples (Kingdom)
19th century
KnR p318-22 pl
Lez pl p307 (col)

Netherlands
17th century
Ada v 1 il p 139
Law v 1 p39-40 il (pte)
WilF pl p90 (pte)

18th century
KnR p397-407 pl
Lez pl p234 (col)

19th century
KnR p397-407 pl
Lez pl p306 (col)

20th century
MiI pl p 195-96 (pte)

Norway
19th century
KnR p393-96 pl

Pakistan
Nat v 102 N '52 pl p643-44

Palestine, Ancient
Wrig pt3 p 11-12 pl p25

Papal state
19th century
KnR p316-18 pl

Paraguay
20th century
MiI pl p214 (off)

Persia, Ancient
BartC p76-78, 80 fig 27
BruK pl 9
Dal v 1 p81-92 5 pl il (col)
Hous2 p 166 fig 159-60
TiK pl 9 fig 5, 7
Wrig pt3 p23 pl p31

Peru
20th century
MiI pl p218 (off)

Philistines
Hous2 p50-51 fig 56

Phoenicia
AirP il p 18

Phrygia
WilFo pl p 14

Poland
To 1700
BruK pl 89 fig 8 (col)
Dz p 1-7 7 pl (col)
WilF pl p98 (pte)

18th century
Dz p8-12 4 pl (col) (off, pte)
KnR p452-60 pl

19th century
Dz p 13-19 7 pl (col)
KnR p452-60 pl
Lez pl p312-13 (col)

20th century
Dz p22-30 9 pl (col) (off, pte)
Lez pl p379 (col)
MiI pl p222-23, 228-29 (off, pte)

Portugal
16th century
LelD pl p 18 fig 2

19th century
KnR p351-55 pl

20th century
MiI pl p228-29 (off, pte)

Rome
AirP p40-41 il
BartC p 107 fig 38
Bra pl 9
BruK pl 17 (col)
Dal v 1 p 196-98 fig 374, 378-87, 393, 400 (col)

MILITARY COSTUME—Rome—*Continued*
 Dav v 1 p87, 90 il
 Dot p 115 il
 Gor pl p 14
 HousG2 p 100-07 pl il
 Lee p80-81 pl
 LelD p82, 137, 243 il
 Lis il p23
 Pot v 1 pl 13 (col)
 RueG pl 2-4
 TiK pl 35 fig 2-3, 5
 VanH pl 1
 Wa p59 pl p62 fig 61
 Wel pl p3
 WilF pl p 12
 WilFo pl p 36, 38
 Wrig pt2 p 10-12 pl p 19
  See also Generals—Rome

Rumania
19th century
 KnR p467-72 pl

Russia
  See also Cossacks; Dragoons—Russia;
Hussars—Russia; Uhlans—Russia
16th century
 BruK pl 88 fig 1, 5 (col)
 Lez pl p 190 (col) (off)
17th century
 KnR p417-18 pl
 Lez pl p 191 (col) (off, pte)
 WilF pl p98 (off)
18th century
 KnR p517-52 9 pl
 Lez pl p 192, 221, 223 (col) (off, pte)
Artillery
 KnR p449-51 pl
19th century
 BruK pl 123 fig 9-11 (col) (off, pte)
 KnR p424-52 7 pl
 Lez pl p279-88, 346-47 (col) (off, pte)
Artillery
 KnR p449-51 pl
20th century
 Lez pl p378 (col) (pte)
 MiI pl p268-69 (off)

Samoa
 TiK pl 101 fig 10

Sardinia (Kingdom)
18th-19th centuries
 KnR p305-16 2 pl

Scotland
  See also Argyll and Sutherland High-
landers (Regiment); Black Watch (Reg-
iment); Cameron Highlanders (Regi-
ment); Gordon Higlanders (Regiment);
Military costume — England — Scottish
troops
To 1700
 Law v 1 p57-73 il (off, pte)
 Lez pl p 179 (col)

18th century
 AirB il p55
 Log p261, 274, 302 pl 259, 270, 299
  (col) (off, pte)
 Mccl front (col)

Scythia
 WilFo pl p59

Serbia
19th century
 KnR p473 pl p475

Somaliland
 AirO il p21 (pte)

Spain
Early to 12th century
 Dal v 1 p271-72 fig 548-50, 552-54
  (col)
 Dav v 1 p 146 pl p 117 il
 Trai p50 il (pte)

16th century
 BruK p24-25 pl 72, 81, 86 (col) (off,
  pte)
 LavR pl p220, 228
 Rea p 18-19 pl 19-20

18th century
 KnR p335-51 3 pl

19th century
 KnR p335-51 5 pl
 Lez pl p290-91 (col) (off, pte)
Cavalry
 Lez pl p316 (col) (pte)
20th century
 MiI pl p241 (off)

Sumeria
 HeuO p55-57 pl 36-38 il
 Hous2 p 109, 112 fig 108, 114

Sweden
18th century
 Berg fig 20-27, 105-07, 144 (off, pte)
 KnR p384-93 2 pl
19th century
 KnR p384-93 2 pl
 Lez pl p289, 348 (col)

Switzerland
18th century
 KnR p412-15 pl
 Lez pl p237 (col) (off)
19th century
 KnR p412-15 pl
 Lez pl p349-50 (col) (pte)

Syria, Ancient
 HeuO p 108-10 il

Turkey
16th century
 BruK pl 90 fig 2, 5 (off)

MILITARY COSTUME — Turkey—*Continued*

17th century
BruK pl 91 fig 6-10 (col)
KnR p461-63 pl

19th century
BruK pl 169 fig 1-9, 12, 15 (col)
KnR p463-67 pl
Nat v75 Ja '39 pl p20 (col)
TiK pl 16 fig 3-5, 25-26 (col)

20th century
Lez pl p369 (col) (off, pte)
MiI pl p257 (pte)

United States
See also Green Mountain Rangers; Mississippi Rifles; Texas Rangers; also subdivision United States under **Admirals; Dragoons; Headdress, Military; Headdress, Naval; Naval costume**

Colonial period
Ada v 1 il p43, 369
Nat v 106 O '54 pl p480-81 (col)

1775-1783
Ada v 1 il p367, 372, 388-89, 392 (off, pte)
Bart p54-55 pl (pat)
But pl p 5 (off)
Davi v 1 pl p 139 (off, pte)
EvnH p 110-16 pl (pat)
Kre front (col) (off)
Kre2 pl 1 (col) (off)
Lez pl p234 (col) (off, pte)
Nat v71 Ap '37 pl p418, 421 (col) (pte); v99 F '51 pl p 181, 183 (off)
Rue pl H (pte)
Trai p 112-13 il (pte)
VanH pl 6-7

Artillery
Kre pl 3 (col) (pte)
Kre2 pl 4 (col)
MusM pl 13, 17, 21 (2 col) (off, pte)
VanH pl 9 fig 3, 6, 11-12

Cavalry
Kre pl 2 (col)
Kre2 pl 3 (col)

Congress' Own regiment
Kre pl 3 (col) (off)
Kre2 pl 4 (col) (off)

Connecticut
MusM pl 5-6 (col) (pte)
VanH pl 9 fig 2

Delaware
MusM pl 7 (col) (pte)
VanH pl 9 fig 14

Georgia
MusM pl 8 (col) (pte)

Maryland
MusM pl 9-11 (col) (off, pte)
VanH pl 9 fig 4, 15

Massachusetts
MusM pl 12-13 (1 col) (off, pte)

VanH pl 9 fig 11-12

New Hampshire
MusM pl 14 (col) (pte)

New Jersey
MusM pl 15 (col) (pte)
VanH pl 9 fig 13

New York
MusM pl 16-17 (col) (pte)
VanH pl 9 fig 3, 6

North Carolina
MusM pl 18 (col) (pte)

Pennsylvania
Kre pl 1 (col) (pte)
Kre2 pl 2 (col) (pte)
MusM pl 19-20 (col) (pte)
VanH pl 9 fig 1, 10

Rhode Island
MusM pl 21-22 (col) (off, pte)
VanH pl 9 fig 7

Sherburne's continental regiment
MusM pl 2 (col) (pte)

South Carolina
MusM pl 23 (col) (pte)
VanH pl 9 fig 8

Vermont
MusM pl 24-25 (col) (off, pte)
VanH pl 9 fig 16

Virginia
MusM pl 26 (col) (pte)

1783-1812
Infantry of the legion
Kre pl 4 (col) (off, pte)
Kre2 pl 5 (col) (off, pte)

1812-1860
Ada pl p 150 (pte)
BruK pl 197 fig 10 (off)
But pl p64, 123 (off)
Kre2 pl 6-7, 9-15 (col) (off, pte)
VanH pl 13 fig 1-9

Artillery
Ada v2 pl p 150 (off)
Kre pl 5 (col) (pte)
Kre2 pl 6, 13 (col) (pte)

Engineers
Kre pl 12 (col) (off)
Kre2 pl 14 (col) (off, pte)

Infantry
Kre pl 6, 9 (col) (pte)
Kre2 pl 7, 10 (col) (pte)

Musicians
Kre pl 5, 9 (col)
Kre2 pl 6-7, 10, 15 (col)

Spy company
Kre pl 12 (col) (pte)
Kre2 pl 14 (col) (pte)

1860-1865
But pl p 177 (off)
EvnH p 153-57 pl il (pat)
Kou pl 54, 65
Kre2 pl 16, 18-22 (col) (off, pte)

MILITARY COSTUME—United States—
1860-1865—*Continued*
Lee p 115-16 pl
Mer fig 68-69, 73-74, 90, 98, 120; pl 21-
26, 40, 73, 80-82, 92, 94, 102, 105,
118-19, 124

Cavalry
Mer fig 126-27

Confederate army
Kre pl 15-16 (col) (off, pte)
Kre2 pl 17, 19-20 (col) (off, pte)
Mer fig 114-15 (off)
VanH pl 13 fig 10-11 (off, pte)

Corps d'Afrique
Kre pl 17 (col) (pte)
Kre2 pl 22 (col) (pte)

Iron brigade of the west
Kre2 pl 18 (col) (pte)

Musicians
Kre2 pl 22 (col)

New York
Kre pl 14 (col) (pte)
Kre2 pl 16, 21 (col) (pte)
Mer pl 57-61

Pennsylvania
Mer fig 80

Vermont
Kre2 pl 18 (col) (pte)

1865-1898
Davi v 1 il p274 (off)
VanH pl 13 fig 14-15

Cavalry
Kre pl 18 (col) (pte)
Kre2 pl 23 (col) (pte)

1898-1917
Kre pl 19-20 (col) (off, pte)
Kre2 pl 25-26 (col)
Lez pl p352, 377 (col) (off, pte)
VanH pl 13 fig 16-19 (off, pte)

Rough Riders
Kre pl 19 (col) (pte)
Kre2 pl 25 (col)

1917-1940
Kre pl 21 (col) (off, pte)
Kre2 pl 27 (col) (off, pte)
MiI pl p280-81 (off, pte)
SmU pl p7-9 (col) (off, pte)
Wa pl p391 (pte)

Nurse corps
Kre pl 22 (col)

Telephone operators
Kre pl 22 (col) (f)

1940—date
Lab pl 27 (col)
Nat v82 Ag '42 pl p261 (off)
RogW p85 il
Wa pl p391 (pte)

Air Corps
Kre pl 23 (col) (off)
Wa pl p391

Armored corps
Kre pl 24 (col) (pte)

Cavalry
Kre2 pl 30 (col)

Military police
Kre2 pl 29-30 (col) (off, pte)

Musicians
Kre2 pl 32 (col)

Nurse corps
Ross p56-57 il (col)
SmU pl p 11 (col)

Parachute troops
Kre pl 23 (col)
Kre2 pl 28 (col)

Rangers
Kre2 pl 28 (col)

Women personnel
Kre2 pl 31 (col) (off, pte)
RogW p85 il
Ross p60-61 il (col)
SmU pl p 11 (col) (off)
Wa p387-88, 390 pl p391
WisF pl 29

Uruguay
20th century
MiI pl p292-93 (off, pte)

Venezuela
20th century
MiI pl p298 (off)
Nat v77 Ap '40 pl p505 (col)

Yemen
Nat v 101 F '52 pl p239 (col)

Yugoslavia
20th century
MiI pl p301 (off)
Nat v75 Je '39 p692-93 il

Zulu
AirO il p37

MILITARY FOOTWEAR. See Footwear,
Military

MILITARY HEADDRESS. See Headdress, Military

MILITARY RELIGIOUS ORDERS. See
Malta, Knights of; Templars

MILITIA. See Volunteer troops

MILK VENDERS
Buenos Aires
Bac pt2 pl 2-3 (col)

England
19th century
Walk pl 14 (col)

France
19th century
BluN pl p58 (f)
GiR pl 40, 74 (col) (f)

MILKMAIDS
England
17th century
Trev v2 p96 il
France
17th century
LavR pl p378
Portugal
BruK pl 156 fig 14 (col)

MILKMEN. See Milk venders

MINERS AND PROSPECTORS
United States
19th century
But pl p 130-31
Gor pl p208-09, 212, 218, 225
Trai p308-10

MINGRELIAN MONKS
Doy pl 10 (col)

MINIATURE CASES
EvnJ p 137-40 pl 7, 93-96, 107-08, 116-
17, 122-23 (1 col) fig 19, 25, 30

MINIM SISTERS OF ST FRANCES OF
ROME
Doy pl 140 (col)

MINIMS
Doy pl p75 (col)

MINORCA. See Balearic Islands

MINSTER LOVELL JEWEL
Jes p89 pl B (col)

MINSTRELS
England
15th century
HousM p 189 fig 318
18th century
Dav v2 p773 il
SitN pl 6
Japan
Haa pl 36

MIRRORS (ACCESSORIES)
LesA p463-67 il
Egypt, Ancient
Dal v 1 fig 66-70 (col)
Greece, Ancient
Dal v 1 fig 257, 259 (col)

MISS LIBERTY. See Fancy dress and
stage costume—Miss Liberty

MISS UNITED STATES. See Fancy dress
and stage costume—Miss United States

MISSISSIPPI RIFLES
19th century
Kre pl 11 (col) (pte)
Kre2 pl 12 (col)

MISTRESS OF THE ROBES
England
20th century
Nat v 104 S '53 pl p316 (col)

MITERS
AirM il p4
HousM p33-35 fig 43-46
LelD p276-77 il
McC p 121-26 pl
NorC p95-107 2 pl (1 col) il (incl pat)
Pic il p21
WilH p26-27 pl p30-31

MITTS AND MITTENS
Dav v2 p634-35 pl
LelD p276, 280 il
Norr v3 bk 2 p552-53 il

MOB CAPS
Bra pl 32
WilH pl p 180, 182

MOCCASINS. See Footwear—Indians of
North America

MOGULS (GREAT MOGULS)
BruK pl 177 fig 6 (col)

MOHAMMEDAN OFFICIALS
BruK pl 91 (col)
MusE pl 37 (col)
See also Imans; Marabouts; Muftis;
Mullahs

MOHAMMEDANS
India
GaU pl 33 (col) (f)
Lee p35-37 pl (m)
Yugoslavia
Brad pl p 165 (f)

MOHAWK INDIANS. See Indians of
North America—Mohawk Indians

MOHEGAN INDIANS. See Indians of
North America—Mohegan Indians

MOLISE. See Italy—Abruzzi e Molise

MONGOLIA
Brad pl p 120-21 (1 col)
Dal v 1 fig 763-64 (col) (f)
Nat v99 Mr '51 pl p399, 406 (col)
Pot v2 p21-22 pl (col)
TiK p37 pl 78, 94 (col)
See also Headdress—Mongolia

MONKS
Armenian church
Doy pl 5 (col)
Buddhist
See Buddhist monks
Catholic church
Hea p50-51 pl
See also names of individual monastic
orders, e.g. Carthusians, Dominicans;
Franciscans

MONKS—Catholic church—*Continued*

To 1200

Lee p85, pl p87

13th-16th centuries

Ab p70-71 pl p53
AirM il p 12
NorC pl p47

Coptic church

Doy pl 6 (col)

Ethiopic church

Doy pl 7 (col)

Greek church

BruK pl 167 fig 3 (col)
Doy pl 10 (col)
Nat v79 Ap '41 pl p469; v85 Ap '44 il
p494; v94 D '48 pl p809

Syrian church

Doy pl 6 (col)

MONTEHERMOSO. See Spain—Estremadura

MONTENEGRO. See Yugoslavia—Montenegro

MOORS

Morocco

OrT pl 259-60, 264, 266, 268, 271

Spain

To 10th century

Dot p 120-21 il

14th century

Dav v 1 pl p238 (m)

15th century

BruK pl 72 (col) (m)

17th century

LavR pl 40-41
Rea p21 pl 40-41

THE MOORS AND CHRISTIANS. See Dancers — Mexico — The Moors and Christians

MORA. See Sweden—Mora

MORAVIA. See Czechoslavakia—Moravia

MORAVIAN BRETHREN
Davi v 1 il p78
Nat v80 Jl '41 pl p59 (col) (f)

MORBIHAN. See France—Brittany

MOROCCO
Brad pl p 123
BruK p 39-40, 91 pl 187 (col)
GaU pl 15-17 (col) (f)
OrT p31 pl 257-72
Rous pl 1-18 (9 col)
TiK pl 28-29 (incl pat) (col)
See also Algeria; also subdivision Morocco under Arabs; Berbers; Festival costume; Footwear; Headdress; Military costume

MORRIS DANCE. See Dancers—England—Morris dance

MOTORING COSTUME

19th century

RogW p24-25 il

20th century

Ada v4 il p 179 (f)
WisF pl 24C (f)

MOURNING COSTUME
Kle p389-90 il (f)

19th century

Bin pl p53 (f)
CunE il p268, 322 (f)
Flow fig 1 (f)
LelD p 148 pl p 149 fig 13-14 (f)

20th century

Bin pl p53 (f)
RogW p 144 (f)

Basque provinces

OrT pl 1, 10-11, 13

Denmark

AndD p22 pl p24 (f)
AndF p 15 pl 4 (f)
WilF pl p60 (f)

England

15th century

Bin pl p 163 (f)

16th century

CunS pl 24 (f)
Norr v3 bk 2 p519, 641-42, 714-15 il
(f)

17th century

Dav v2 fig 1532, 1556 (f)

18th century

SitC pl 22 (f)

Europe

13th century

LelD pl p 149 fig 1 (f)

16th century

Gor pl p62 (f)
WilF pl p60-61 (f)

17th century

Gor pl p80 (f)
LelD p 148 pl p 149 fig 2-11

18th century

LelD p 148 pl p 149 fig 12 (f)

France

15th century

EvjD p37 pl 30-31 (m)

16th century

Dav v2 p476-77 il (f)
Norr v3 bk 2 p455, 752-53 il (f)
WilC pl p 100 (f)

MOURNING COSTUME — France—*Continued*

17th century
BluE p22 pl 29 (f)
Dav v2 p510, 516 il (f)
LavR pl p360 (f)
Lib il p24 (f)
WilC pl p 166 (f)

18th century
Dav v2 fig 1966 (f)
WilF pl p 111 (f)

Germany
16th century
Dav v 1 fig 1003 (f)

17th century
Bin il p83 (f)

Korea
Keit p40 pl (col) (f)

Netherlands
Hij pl 15, 20, 28, 55 (f)

16th century
Rud pl p20
WilF pl p61 (f)

Spain
16th century
Norr v3 bk 2 p455-56 il (f)

19th century
OrT pl 108 (f)

MOURNING JEWELRY. See Jewelry, Memorial

MOZETTA
McC p90-93 il
NorC p 179 pl p 178

MUFFS
16th century
LesA p455-56 il
Norr v3 bk 2 p612-13 il
WilC pl p76

17th century
BroH fig 92 (m)
BroW v2 fig 30 (m)
Dal v2 fig 457-58, 526 (col)
LelD p261 fig 1-5; p304 il
LesA p456-58 il
WilC pl p 181, 190 (m)
WilF p81-82 pl p87, 91-94, 96-97, 99

18th century
Dav v2 p742 il
Dot p 160 il (m)
Lel v 11 p74-75 fig 80; v 12 fig 23, 75
LelD p261 fig 6-7, 10
LesA p458-60 il (m)
WilC pl p215 (m)
WilF pl p 114-18
WisF pl 16

19th century
Ada v4 il p53
CunE il p 155

Gor pl p 146 (f)
LavF pl 1, 4 (col)
LelD p261 fig 8-9 (f)
LesA p460-62, 548-49, pl 47-48 il (f)
ViN fig 5-6, 26
WilC pl p269, 279 (f)

20th century
LelD p261 fig 12-14 (f)
WilF pl p 165-69, 171-72, 175, 177, 180, 209, 215

MUFTIS
Nat v80 Ag '41 il p 147

MULETEERS
France
19th century
GiR pl 27 (col)

MULLAHS
MusE pl 37 (col)

MUMMERS
England
Ken p65 pl 9

MUNICH. See Germany—Bavaria

MUNICIPAL OFFICIALS. See Aldermen; Mayors

MURCIA. See Spain—Murcia

MUSCADINS
LelD p283 il

MUSES
BiE pl 34

MUSICIANS
See also Bagpipers; Drummers; Harpists; Marimba players; Rhumba players; Trumpeters; also subdivision Musicians under Military costume—England; Military costume—Germany; Military costume—United States

African tribes
Nat v79 My '41 pl p642 (col) (m); v81 Mr '42 pl p402; v99 Mr '51 il p264 (m)

Arabia, Ancient
Dal v 1 fig 630, 633-34 (col)

Argentine republic
Spi pl p 16 (col)

Assyria and Babylonia
Hous2 p 140-41, 152 fig 135, 149

Balearic islands
D'Iv pl 39 (col)

Bali
Nat v75 Mr '39 pl p317 (m); v99 Ja '51 pl p 12 (col) (m)

Barbados
Nat v 101 Mr '52 pl p387 (col)

MUSICIANS—*Continued*

Basque provinces
Nat   v 105 F '54   pl   p 161 (m)
OrT   pl 20

Bolivia
Nat   v83 Mr '43   pl   p317 (col)

Ecuador
Hal   pl 27 (col) (m)

Egypt, Ancient
BruK   pl 3 (col)
Dav   v 1   p25 il
Hous2   p56 fig 61 (f)

Egypt, Modern
BruK   pl 189 fig 7-8 (col)

England
To 1066
AirB   il   p6

14th century
Ab   pl   p238, 240, 242
Dav   v 1 fig 577

16th century
Norr   v3 bk 1   p299-300 il

18th century
Dav   v2 fig 2174

Europe
13th-15th centuries
Gor   pl   p27
HousM   p 159 fig 159, 161, 172-73
KerM   no3   pl 8 (m)

France
18th century
Dav   v2 fig 1770, 1780, 1977

Germany
12th-13th centuries
BruK   pl 32 fig 13-17

15th century
Dav   v 1   p373 il

Greece, Ancient
BruK   pl 14
Dav   v 1 fig 204

India
Am   p26-29   2 pl il
Ind   pl   p63, 89 (col)

Italy
14th-15th centuries
Dav   v 1   p233, 249 il

Java
BruK   pl 181 fig 12-13 (col)

Korea
Keit   pl   p68B

Mexico
Too   p299-309 fig 3, 11, 23, 27, 141, 150 (m)

Micronesia
Nat   v69 Ap '36   pl   p493

Morocco
Rous   pl 5

Netherlands
15th-16th centuries
Dav   v 1   p346-47   pl; v2   p481   pl

Peru
TooP   pl 30, 35-36, 53, 60, 66-67, 71-72

Spain
Agu   pl 12, 17, 20-21, 57, 67, 82, 102
Dav   v 1   pl   p 147
Int   v2   pl 15 (m)
OrT   pl 99 (m)

Sweden
Int   v 2   pl 100 (m)

Tibet
Nat   v95 My '49   pl   p673-74, 678 (col)

MUSKETEERS

England
16th-17th centuries
AirB   il   p46
BarH   pl 3 (col)
Law   v 1   p 14-15 fig 7

Europe
17th century
BruK   pl 97 fig 1-2 (col)
Gor   pl   p38

France
16th century
BluL   p25   pl 58
LavR   pl   p 119
LelD   p280-81 il

18th century
LelD   p70-71 il;   p280-81 il

Germany
17th century
BruK   pl 119 fig 1, 5 (col)
KnR   pl   p5

18th century
KnR   pl   p 11 (off, pte)
Lez   pl   p 189, 195 (col)

19th century
KnR   pl   p23
Lez   pl   p238 (col)

Netherlands
17th century
Dav   v2   p604 il

MUSTACHES
LelD   p281-82 il

N

NAGAS
  Nat v99 N '47 pl p616-17 (col) (m)

NANCY. See Lorraine

NANTICOKE INDIANS. See Indians of North America—Nanticoke Indians

NÄRKE. See Sweden—Närke

NATAL
  Brad pl p20 (f)

NATIONAL WOMEN'S COUNCIL OF THE NAVY LEAGUE
  Ross p 16-17 il (col)

NATIONAL SECURITY WOMEN'S CORPS
  Ross p40 il (col)

NAUTCH GIRLS
  Am p79 il
  Kin pl p226
  Nat v82 O '42 pl p481 (col)

NAVAHO INDIANS. See Indians of North America—Navaho Indians

NAVAL AVIATION CADETS
  United States
  UnN pl 7—1 to 7—5

NAVAL CADETS
  England
  Cla p40 pl
  United States
  Nat v79 Ap '41 pl p426; v81 Ja '42 pl p57 (col)
  UnN pl 4—1 to 4—5, 14—1

NAVAL COSTUME
  England
  See also Admirals—England; Headdress, Naval—England; Marine corps—England; Sailors—England
    17th century
  Carm p5-8 pl (off)
    18th century
  AirH il p92
  Carm p9-19 5 pl (col) (off, s)
  Dav v2 p765 il (off)
  Nat v78 Jl '40 pl p44 (off) (col)
    19th century
  Carm p 18-25 2 pl (col) (off, s)
  Pric pl p 124 (off)
    20th century
  Carm p24-27 2 pl (col) (off, s)
  GrA pl 3-8, 16-17 (off)
  Nat v 104 S '53 pl p311 (col) (off)
  Yar p275 il (off)
    Women personnel
  Carm p27-29 pl (off, s)

  France
  LelD p269-70 il
  See also Admirals—France; Headdress, Naval—France

  Germany
  See also Admirals—Germany; Headdress, Naval—Germany
    19th century
  Lez pl p296 (col)
    20th century
  Erl pl p72 (col) (off)

  Netherlands
    17th century
  Nat v78 Jl '40 pl p35 (off) (col)

  Poland
    20th century
  Dz p27, 29 2 pl (col) (s)

  Turkey
    19th century
  TiK pl 16 fig 22 (col)

  United States
  See also subdivision United States under Admirals; Coast Guard; Headdress, Naval; Marine Corps
    1775-1783
  Ada v 1 il p400 (off)
  Rue pl J (pte)
  VanH pl 9 fig 9, pl 14 fig 1 (off)
    1783-1812
  Nat v94 S '48 pl p302, 310 (col) (off)
    1812-1860
  Ada v2 il p 131, 134 (off)
  But pl p65, 139 (off)
  VanH pl 14 fig 7, 9 (off)
    1860-1898
  But pl p283 (off)
  Kou pl 246 (off)
  Mer pl 13-14, 125-26
  VanH pl 14 fig 15, 19 (off)
    20th century
  Mil pl p282-83 (off, pte)
  Nat v69 Je '36 pl p793, 799 (col) (off)
  SmU pl p39-42 (col) (off, s)
  UnN pl 2—1 to 2—7, 10—1 to 10—5, 11—1 to 11—3 (off, s)
  VanH pl 14 fig 24 (off)
    Musicians
  UnN pl 14—1
    Naval reserve
  UnN pl 5—1 to 5—2, 8—1
    Nurse corps
  Ross p52 il (col)
  SmU pl p43 (col)
  UnN pl 3-4 to 3-6

NAVAL COSTUME—United States—20th century—*Continued*
Women personnel
Cra pl p59
RogW p83-85, 87 il
Ross p63-64 il (col)
UnN pl 3—1 to 3—5, 9—1, 13—1 to 13—5 (off, s)

NECKLACES AND PENDANTS
See also Crosses (Jewelry); Brethren pendant; Hope diamond necklace; Tor abbey jewel
Ancient
AirB il p5
AirS il p 15
Dal v 1 fig 508-09 (col)
CovM pl 23
Jes p57-59, 119-22 pl 27-29
LelD p57 il
LesA p 178-83 il
Nat v80 O '41 pl p472
WlsC pl 18

10th century—date
BraF p34 pl p35-39, 57-58, 60, 94, 116, 125, 143-44, 164, 174, 176, 205
Dal v2 fig 766-67 (col)
EvnJ pl III-VI, (col) 33-35, 37, 46, 49-55, 57-83, 87, 89, 100, 102-04, 114-15, 117-19, 121, 125-28, 130, 139, 141-43, 145, 162-64, 171, 173-76
Flow pl 4-10 (col) fig 6-14, 19, 21-22, 25, 52-53, 56, 60-61, 69-80, 98, 103-08
LelD p311 il
LesA p 183-92 2 pl il
NeM pl 19
NeN p3-4 pl 8, 10, 12-16, 18-19
NeR p2-4 pl 2, 4-19, 21-23
Norr v3 bk 1 p 123-24, 360-65 2 pl il; bk 2 p459-62, 766-76 2 pl il
RogF pl p234, 266
Yar il p99, 124, 136, 144, 153, 166

African tribes
Leb pl 7-8, 10-11 (col)
Nat v86 S '44 il p306; v99 Mr '51 pl p253; v 106 O '54 il p492-95, 511 (1 col)

Black Forest
Pet p62-63 pl

Byzantine empire
Dal v 1 fig 492-93 (col)
NeM pl 2, 4, 6

Carpathian Ruthenia
Mak pl 19, 69, 100, II (1 col)

Egypt, Ancient
NeE p 1-4 pl 1-4, 6, 9, 14-15, 17, 20
NeP pl 11-13
Pot v 1 pl 3 (col)
WilC pl p6

Greece, Ancient
NeG pl 5, 10-12, 18

Indians of North America
MasB p66-68 pl il

Mexico, Ancient
DuS fig 29
Norway
Stew p 131-32 il
Rome
Dal v 1 fig 431 (col)
Spain
AnS p90-91, 109-10, 150-52, 218 fig 106, 127-28, 261
NeR pl 9-18
OrT pl 128-30, 141-42, 150, 162, 248-52
Syria
NeN p2 pl 7

NECKWEAR
See also Collars; Fichus; Jabots; Ruffs; Wimples and gorgets
19th century
Bart p72-73 pl (pat) (m)
LelD p 132 pl p 133 fig 13-20
LesA p207-12 il (m)

1800-1810
LelD pl p 116 fig 7 (m) pl p 117 fig 10-11 (f)
LesA p216-17 il (m)

1810-1820
But pl p66-68 (m)
LelD pl p 116 fig 10, 16 (m) pl p 117 fig 13-14 (f) pl p 119 fig 12-13 (f)
LesA p217-18 fig 270, 272 (m)

1820-1830
LesA p217-18 fig 270, 272 (m)

1830-1840
LelD pl p 116 fig 14-15 (m)
LesA p219 fig 271, 272 (m)

1840-1850
CunE pl p 147 (f)
LesA fig 272 (m)
WilC pl p306 (m)

1850-1860
Gor pl p 150 (f)
LelD pl p 116 fig 11-12 (m)
LesA p219-220 fig 273, 275 (m)
WilC pl p293, 306 (m)

1860-1870
Wa p284, 287 fig 235, 237

1870-1880
CunE il p267 (f)
LesA fig 278-79 (m)

1880-1890
LesA fig 279 (m)
WilC pl p306 (m)

1890-1900
LesA p221-22 il (m)

20th century
Bra p343-44 pl 48, 50 (m)
LelD pl p 133 fig 21-27

NECKWEAR—*Continued*

Europe

LelD   p 114-19 4 pl
Pric   p 160-64 pl (m)

16th century

Bra   pl 24
CunS   p90, 110-14, 152, 165, 167-69 pl 35, 38-49, 51-54, 57-68, 71
CunU   p37-39 fig 12 (m)
DeB   p 174-75, 194-95 pl p 176-77, 196-97
KelF   p29-31, 43 pl p73, 75, 77
LelD   pl p 115 fig 2-10 (m) pl p 117 fig 2-3 (m) pl p 119 fig 1-3, 5-6 (f)
LesA   p 194-200 pl il (f)
Pic   p31-32 il
Rey   p 11-12, 23 pl 17, 23, 25, 41, 43-44, 47-48, 50, 52

17th century

BluE   pl 6, 14-18, 28, 38-42, 44-45, 51, 61, 63 (4 col)
Dal   v2 fig 490-505 (col)
Dav   v2 p617-18, 636 il (f)
LelD   p 132 pl p 115 fig 11-19 (m) pl p 117 fig 4-9 (f) pl p 119 fig 4, 7 (f) pl p 133 fig 1-6
LesA   p205, 213-15 pl 31-33 fig 246-47, 249, 263-64, 600, 603
Lint   p 160-70 pl
Pic   il p33, 67 (m)
Rey   p 12 pl 29-38, 51, 55-56 (3 col)
WilC   p 142, 152-53 pl p 140, 148, 157, 173, 183
WisF   pl 12-13 (f)

18th century

Gor   pl p 124 (m)
Kle   p 120, 235-37 il
Lel   v 11 p33 fig 31 (m)
LelD   p 132 pl p 115 fig 1, 22-25 (m) pl p 116 fig 1-6 (m) pl p 119 fig 9-11 (f) pl p 133 fig 7-12
LesA   p215-16 fig 265, 267-68
Wa   p210, 222 fig 183D, 198

19th century

See Neckwear—19th century

20th century

See Neckwear—20th century

Indians of Mexico

CorA   p42-48 pl il

United States

17th century

LesA   fig 261-62, 266 (m)

18th century

But   pl p 16-17 (m)

NECKWEAR, ECCLESIASTICAL

Catholic church

McC   p73-75 il

Protestant churches

Kle   p43 il

NECKWEAR, FUR

16th century

LesA   fig 632-33

20th century

LesA   p553-54 pl il

NEGLIGEES

CrH   p56-57, 62-67, 72-81 9 pl
CrO   pl 43

18th century

Dav   v2 p709-710 il (f)
Lel   v 11 p 15-16 fig 10, 65
LesA   p95 pl 22 (m)

19th century

Mo   p90 pl 39 (f)

20th century

CunPr   pl p 109 (f)
Mo   p 142 pl 79 (f)

NEGROES

Egypt

Ancient

Dav   v 1 pl p30

Greece, Ancient

Dav   v 1 p64 il (m)

Netherlands

17th century

Dav   v2 fig 1625

NEPAL

Brad   pl p86, 89
Nat   v97 Ja '50 pl p33, 38-39 (col) (f)

NETHERLANDS

See also Belgium; Fancy dress and stage costume—Dutch; also subdivision Netherlands under Capes and cloaks; Ceremonial costume; Children; Coats and jackets; Footwear; Headdress; Mayors; Military costume; Mourning costume; Noblemen; Noblewomen

12th-13th centuries

WilC   p62-67 2 pl

14th century

TiK   pl 120 fig 12 (col) (f)
WilC   p63-67 2 pl
WilF   pl p27

15th century

BosF   pl 3 (f)
BroW   v 1 pl p86 (col) fig 47-48, 53
Dav   v 1 p304-11, 314-16, 324, 326-29 6 pl (1 col) il
Dot   p 143 il
Gor   p46 pl p32 il
HousM   p 175-76 fig 303 (f)
SocC   front (f)
Vert   pl p48 (f)
WilC   p63-67 2 pl
WilF   p34, 36 il

NETHERLANDS—*Continued*

16th century
Dav v2 p481 il
Gor pl p46-47, 49-50, 71
KelF pl p 10, 67
KerM no5 pl 7
KerR pl 7
Kle p 176-77 il (f)
LavR p257-62, 281-84 4 pl
Norr v3 bk 1 p296, 307 il
ThiG p 14-15 pl 1-4 (f)

17th century
BroW v2 p31-35 fig 1-3, 5-6, 11, 13-17,
  21-22, 25-26, 37 pl p28, 44 (col)
Bruh pl p45 (col)
BruK pl 92-93
Dav v2 p603-32 fig 1591-95, 1597-1627,
  1638-53, 1656-79, 1682-86 pl p510, 638
  (col)
Gor pl 71-72, 74, 76-77, 80-81, 84, 87-88,
  90
KelF front (col) (f)
Kle p 176-77 il (f)
LavR p262-266, 284-320 35 pl (8 col)
LelD pl p352 fig 4, 6, 9 (f)
LesA pl 30, 33
Nat v78 Jl '40 pl p34 (col) (f)
ThiG p5-13, 15-27 pl 5-60 (8 col)
Vert pl p 104-05 (1 col)

18th century
Gor pl p 106 (m)
Lel v 11 pl 29 (col)

BY REGION OR PROVINCE

Drente
Hij p 10 pl 7-8 (f)
Nat v98 D '50 pl p765 (col) (f)

Friesland
BruK pl 145 fig 4 (col) (f)
Hij p 10 pl 3-6
Sit p67-69, 74-79, 91-93 pl p4, 49, 73
  (1 col)
Ven p20 pl 2 (col)

Groningen
Hij p 10 pl 1 (f)

Guelders
Hij p 13 pl 18-20 (f)
Ven pl 3-4 (col)

Limburg
Hij p23-24 pl 61-64 (f)

Marken
BruK pl 145 fig 5-11 (col)
Hij p 14-16 pl p8 (col) pl 23-28 (f)
Int v2 p 18-22 pl 45, 47-49, 52
Lee p30-32 pl
Sit p44-50 3 pl (f)

North Brabant
Hij p22-23 pl 58-60

North Holland
Hij p 14-18 pl 35-39 (f)
Sit p63 pl p4, 104 (1 col) (f)
  See also Netherlands—Marken; Neth-
  erlands—Volendam

Overysel
Hij pl 9-17
Nat v 106 S '54 pl p411 (f)
Sit p 112-13 pl (f)

Schokland
Sit pl p73

South Holland
Hij p 18-19 pl 40-44 (f)

Urk
Hij p 11-12 pl 15-16 (f)

Utrecht
Hij p 13-14 pl 21-22
Sit p 115-18 pl p 113 (f)

Volendam
Brad pl p80 (f)
BruK pl 145 fig 2, 12-16 (col)
Hij p 16 pl 29-34 (f)
Lee p30-32 pl
Nat v 106 S '54 pl p396, 412 (col) (f)
Sit p43-44 pl p46-47 (f)
Ven p 18 pl 1 (col)

Walcheren
BruK pl 145 fig 1 (col) (m)
Nat v77 F '40 pl p271 (f)
Sit p 155-56 pl p 153 (f)

Zeeland
Brad pl p81-82
Hij p 19-22 pl p 16 (col) pl 45-57
Sit p 155-62 pl (col) (f)

NEUCHÂTEL. See Switzerland—Neuchâtel

NEW CALEDONIA
GaU pl 43-44 (col)

NEW CASTILE. See Spain—New Castile

NEW GUINEA
Nat v96 D '49 pl p835, 838; v 100 N
  '51 pl p671 (col); v 103 Ap '53
  pl p423, 435, 469, 481
  See also Headdress—New Guinea

NEW ZEALAND. See Maoris

NEWHAVEN FISHWIVES
Gern pl 8
MilJ pl 2 (col)

NEWS VENDERS
England
19th century
QuV fig 30

NEZ PERCÉS INDIANS. See Indians of
  North America—Nez Percés Indians

NICARAGUA
Nat v86 Ag '44 pl p 185 (col) (f)
Spi p59-60 il

NICE. See France—Nice

NIGERIA
Brad pl p 19
Nat v85 My '44 pl p545 (col) (m)

NIGHTCAPS
CunU fig 59, 70

16th century
Norr v3 bk 1 p262 il (m)

17th century
ViP v 1 pl 16 (m)

18th century
Kle p28 il (f)
LelD pl p39 fig 16 (m)

NIGHTCLOTHES
See also Pajamas

16th century
CrH p28-29 pl (f)
EvjD pl 69
Norr v3 bk 2 p616-17 il (f)

17th-18th centuries
CunU p61, 66-67, 94, 119 fig 24, 44, 53

19th century
Bart p68-69 (m)
CrH p30-31 pl (f)
CunU p 134, 181, 192, 194 fig 55, 80, 85-86
Gern pl 45 (f)
HaC pl p 195 (f)

20th century
Coh p470-71 il (m)
CunU p224, 233 fig 100 (f)
Kle p267-68 il (f)
WisF pl 25 (f)

NIMBUS. See Halos

NINETEENTH CENTURY
Amer pl 1-12 (col) (f)
Burr p40-41, 44-47, 50-55, 95-101, 135-42, 154-56, 158-65, 177-78, 222-27, 232-37 6 pl
Dal v2 p415-99 pl il (col) (incl pat)
Lab p78-101 front (col) 6 pl (col)
Pic il p 132 (f)
Rud pl p 152, 154 (m)
Set p37-42 2 pl (col) il
UnW pl 86-114 (col)
WisF pl 19-23 (f)
Yar p211-48 20 pl (1 col)
See also subdivision 19th century under Capes and cloaks; Coats and jackets; Evening dress; Riding costume; Wedding costume, etc.

1800-1810
Ada v2 il p 109 (m)
BelQ pl p84 (col) (f)
BluC pl p98, 103
BluN p 13-15, 102-05 pl p29-32, 34, 116-18
Brk pl 13-14 (f)

BroF fig 40
BroW v2 p 130-34 2 pl il
BruK p30-31, 75 pl 121 fig 1-6 (col)
But pl p40, 44, 50
CunE p26-44 11 pl (f)
CunF p42-44, 46-50 front
Dal v2 fig 785, 821-38, 867-75 (col) (incl pat)
Dav v2 p794, 797-99, 803-18 5 pl il
Dot p 164-66 il
EvnH p 118-29 pl il (incl pat)
EvnJ pl 160 (f)
Gor pl p 134-36
Kle p 125 il (m)
LavF p24 pl 1 (col)
LavT p26-29 pl p 18, 22, 28
LavT2 p23-25 front, pl p32
Lee p 112-14 pl
Lib pl p66, 172T (f)
Loud pl 17 (col)
Mo p35-39 3 pl (f)
Pann v2 pl 11-22 (col)
SitC pl 118-19
TiK pl 127 fig 15-19 (incl pat) (col) (f)
Tru p87-92 il
ViN fig 1-12
Wa p244-55, 272 2 pl il (incl pat)
WilC p236-45 4 pl
WilF pl p 124-28
YoR p67-70 il (f)
See also England—George III, 1760-1820

1810-1820
Ada v2 il p 153 (f)
AlF pl p4, 6-8
Bart p60-61 pl (pat) (m)
BluN p 15-20 pl p33-34
BrH pl 125 fig 3-9 (col) (f)
Brk pl 15, 16 (f)
BroW v2 fig 75 pl p 134 (col)
Bruh p70-73 pl (col)
BruK pl 121 fig 7-18 pl 122 fig 1-6 (1 col)
BruM pl p46 (col) (m)
But pl p 71 (m)
CunE p44-69 6 pl il (f)
CunP p9-15 pl (col) (f)
Dal v2 fig 784, 786-93, 876-82 (col) (incl pat) (m)
Dav v2 p794, 798-800, 804-06, 816-31 8 pl il
Gor pl p 128, 136-38 (1 col)
Kle p307-08 il
LavF p24 pl 2 (col) (f)
LavT p30-35 pl p26, 28, 30
LavT2 pl p32, 38
Lecl pl 13 (col)
LelD pl p358 (f)
McP p 18 pl p 17 (col)
Mo p40-44 2 pl (f)
Pann v2 pl 23-28; v3 pl 1-4 (col)
Pic il p52 (f)
Tru p87-92 il
True p 16-17 pl il (f)
ViN fig 13-22
Wa p255-59 pl p244 il (incl pat)
WilC p236-55 8 pl
WilF pl p 127-32

NINETEENTH CENTURY—1810-1820—
Continued
WilFo pl p 147, 163
YoR p70-73 il (f)
See also England—George III, 1760-1820

1820-1830
BluN p 19-22, 105-08 pl p35-38, 119-20
BoeB p587-615 pl p72, 112, 144, 176, 200 (col)
Bra p257-72 2 pl
BrH p 126-29 2 pl (col)
Brk pl 17-18 (f)
BroF fig 39, 41-42
BroH p 173-81 fig 117-20
BroW v2 fig 76-79
BruK p32 pl 121-22 (col)
CrO pl 52
CunA 24b, 26-27
CunE p74-104 10 pl il (1 col) (f)
CunF p56-60 pl p52
CunP p 14-17 pl (col) (f)
Dal v2 fig 794, 799, 883-93 (col)
Dav v2 p794-95, 800-01, 831-40 3 pl il
Dot p 165, 167 il
Gor pl p 139-41
Gre p 136-40 pl
Hea p34-35 il (f)
LavCl pl p80-81, 144 (1 col)
LavF p24-25 pl 3-4 (col) (f)
LavT p33-35 pl p34 (f)
Lecl pl 14 (col)
LelD pl p336 (col), pl p359 fig 1
Lib pl p 172U-172V (1 col) (f)
Mo p45-49 front (col) 3 pl (f)
Pann v3 pl 5-14 (col)
Trev v4 fig 30, 37-38
True p 18-21 2 pl il (f)
ViN fig 23-31 (f)
Wa p259-63 pl p244, 272, 306 il
WilC p247-55 4 pl
WilF pl p 132-34
Yar pl p 201, 205, 207, 210 (1 col)
YoR p74-77 il (f)

1830-1840
Ada v2 il p251, 308
Bart p64-67 pl (pat) fig 25
BluC p 115-22 2 pl
BluN p22-24, 108-10 pl p38, 40, 121-22
BoeB p587-615 pl p232, 264, 328, 400, 432, 464, 480, 496, 528, 568 (col)
Bra p257-86 5 pl
BrH p 130-33 2 pl (col)
Brk pl 20-21 (f)
BroW v2 p 140-42 pl (col) il
Bruh p74-77 2 pl (col)
BruK p32 pl 122, 124 (1 col)
BruM p50-53 pl p47 (col)
CunE p 105-30 10 pl (1 col) (f)
CunP p 18-27 pl p 15 (col) (f)
Dal v2 fig 803, 894-909 (col)
Dav v2 p794-95, 800-01, 843-44, 849-57 il
EvnH p 130-38 pl il (incl pat)
Flow fig 1-3 (f)
Gor pl p 142-43
LavCl pl p224 (col) (f)
LavF p26-27 pl 5-6 (col) (f)

LavT2 p30-51 pl p43, 46 pl 4 (col)
Lecl pl 15 (col) (f)
LelD pl p359 fig 2-6 (f)
Lis p77-80 il
Loud pl 18 (col)
McP p 19 pl p20 (col)
Mo p50-56 4 pl il (f)
NeV pl 1-2 (f)
Ni pl 49-50
Pann v3 pl 15-24 (col)
QuV fig 125-26 (f)
Rue fig L1-L2, M1-M2
True p22-27 3 pl il (f)
Vert pl p 108 (f)
ViN fig 32-39
Wa p263-67 pl p272, 306, 322 il
WilC p271-79 4 pl
WilF pl p 134-36
WilFo pl p 148
YoR p78-83 il (f)

1840-1850
BluN p 111-12 pl p82, 124
BoeB p587-615 pl (col) (f)
Bra p273-86 3 pl
BrH p 134-37 2 pl (col)
Brk pl 22-23 (f)
BroF fig 44 (m)
Chr p 180 fig 353, 358 (col)
CrO pl 53
CunA pl 28 (m)
CunE p 131-69 15 pl (1 col) il (f)
CunF p 113-14, 125-28, 130-34 pl p 116 (f)
CunP p23-27 pl (col) (f)
Dal v2 fig 804-07, 910-22 (col) (incl pat)
Dav v2 p795-96, 801-02, 859-66, 868-74 pl il
Dot p 165-66 il (m)
EvnH p 139-45 pl il (incl pat)
Gern pl 1-3, 6-13
Gor p 130 pl p 147-50, 184
LavF p26-27 pl 7-8 (col)
LavS p43 pl 21-22 (f)
LelD pl p304 (col) (f); pl p359 fig 7 (f)
Mo p59-62 3 pl il (f)
NeV pl 3-7 (f)
Pann v3 pl 25-28 (f) (col); v4 pl 1-3 (col)
QuV fig 127-131
SitC pl 10-11
TiK pl 128 (col) (f)
True p28-35 4 pl il (f)
ViN fig 40-49
Wa p267-72 pl p272, 306, 322 il
WilC p271-305 14 pl
WilF pl p 137-39
Yar pl p212, 214, 218
YoR p84-88 il (f)

1850-1860
BluN pl p83-84, 93, 126
Bra p287-305 4 pl
BrH p 136-37 pl (col) (f)
Brk pl 24-25 (f)
BroH p 193-200 fig 128-29
Bruh p78-81 2 pl (col)
BruK p32-33 pl 125
BruM p53-54 pl p51 (col) (f)

NINETEENTH CENTURY—1850-1860—
Continued

CunE p 169-205 13 pl (1 col) il (f)
CunP p29-35 pl p25 (col) (f)
Dal v2 fig 808-09, 812-13, 923-38 (col)
Dav v2 p796-97, 801-03, 875-95 4 pl il
Davi v 1 pl p515
Gern pl 21, 25
Gor pl p 147-51, 185
KerA p6-11 3 pl (f)
Kle p425 il (m)
Kou pl 13
LavCl pl p 160 (col)
LavF p27-28 pl 9-11 (col)
LavT pl p60, 68
LavT2 pl p50-51
LelD pl p304 (col) (m) pl p359 fig 8
    (f)
McP p22-23 pl p21, 24 (col)
Mer fig 12, 22, 24, 26-28, 57, 60-70, 106
Mo p65-66 2 pl il (f)
Nat v 100 N '51 pl p583 (col) (f)
NeV pl 8-16 (f)
Ni pl 51-52
Pann v4 pl 4-10 (col) (f)
QuV fig 42, 58, 133-34
SitN pl 22, 101, 114
Tru p93-97 il
True p36-39 2 pl (f)
ViN fig 50-58 (f)
Wa p276-82 pl p273, 276, 306, 322 il
WilC p281-92 5 pl
WilF pl p 140-41 (f)
WilFo pl p 149 (m)
Yar pl p216, 218, 220, 227 (col)
YoR p89-93 il (f)

1860-1870

Ada v3 il p 114, 222 (f)
Bart p70-71 pl (pat) (f) fig 27
BluC p 123-30 2 pl
BluN p65-68 pl p81, 84-87, 89, 122,
    125
Bra p287-322 6 pl
BrH p 138-39 pl (col) (f)
Brk pl 26-31 (f)
BroF fig 45 (f)
BroH p 197-204 fig 130-32
But pl p 184, 204-05 (m)
CunA pl 29-30a, 32, 36
CunE p206-253 10 pl (1 col) il (f)
CunP p35-41 pl (col) (f)
Dal v2 fig 810-11, 939-52 (col)
Dav v2 p797-98, 802-03, 898-934 17 pl
    il
Eld pl p6-7, 12-15, 26 (f)
Eth pl p48 (f)
EvnH p 146-52 pl il (pat)
Flow fig 47-48 (f)
Gern pl 36, 38-41, 46
Gor p 130 pl p 156-60, 166, 186-90
HaC p34-51 front 7 pl (f)
Jen pl p 10
KerA p 12-17 3 pl (f)
Kou pl 91 (m)
LavF p28 pl 12 (col) (m)
LavT p59-71 2 pl (f)
LavT2 p49-58 pl p50-51
Lee p 114-16 pl
LelD pl p360 fig 1-2 (f)

Lib pl p98 (f)
Lis p81-86 il
Loud pl 19 (col)
Mer fig 42-43, 47-53, 55, 83, 117, 122
Mo p70-82 7 pl il (f)
NeV p3-4 pl 17-24 (f)
Pann v4 pl 11-19 (col)
Pic il p 126 (f)
QuV fig 59, 124, 135-36, 142, 144
Rue fig R (f)
Trai p326 il (f)
True p40-43 pl il (f)
ViN fig 59-68
Wa p282-95 pl p304, 306, 322 il
WilF pl p 141-45
WilFo pl p 149 (f)
Yar pl p224, 226, 228
YoR p 94-100 il (f)

1870-1880

Bart p74-77, 80-81 3 pl (pat) (f) 29-30,
    32
BluN p68-69 pl p88-89
Bra p307-22 2 pl
BrH p 138-39 pl (col) (f)
Brk pl 32-36 (f)
Bruh p82-84 pl (col)
BruK p33-34 pl 126
BruM p54-57 pl (col) (f)
CrO pl 54 (f)
CrP pl 6 (f)
CunA pl 30b, 33-34
CunE p254-308 front 9 pl (2 col) il (f)
CunF p216-22 pl p212 (f)
CunP p41-48 2 pl (col) (f)
Dal v2 fig 953-64 (col) (f)
Davi v2 il p55
Dot p 168 il
Flow fig 49-50 (f)
Gor pl p 161-63, 191-92
KerA p 18-22 3 pl (f)
Lang p 130 pl (col) (f)
LavF p29 pl 13-14 (col) (f)
LavT p72-83 3 pl
LavT2 pl 8, 10 (col) (f)
Lecl pl 17 (col) (f)
LelD p360 fig 3-4 (f)
Lew fig 2 (f)
Loud pl 20 (col) (f)
McP p26 pl p25, 34 (1 col)
Mer fig 128-36, 144-45
Mo p83-102 11 pl il (f)
NeV pl 25-29 (f)
Pann v4 pl 20-28 (col)
Part p85, 92, 93, 141, 142 il
Pic il p 162 (f)
Pric p95-101 3 pl (m)
QuV fig 43, 146
Rud pl p 160 (f)
Rue fig S1-S2 (f)
SitN pl 129-31
TiK pl 128 (col) (f)
Tru p98-102 il
True p46-49 2 pl il (f)
Vert pl p60-61, 111
ViN fig 69-78
Wa p294-308 pl p304, 306 fig 242
    (incl pat) il
WilC p294-311 8 pl
WilF pl p 144-45

NINETEENTH CENTURY—1870-1880—
Continued
Yar   pl   p226, 228, 230, 232
YoR   p 101-05 il (f)

1880-1890

BluN   pl   p88, 90, 127
Bra   p307-22   2 pl
BrH   p 139-41   2 pl (col) (f)
Brk   pl 37-40 (f)
BroF   fig 46 (f)
BroH   p211-15 fig 137-38
Bruh   p84-85   pl (col)
But   pl   p246-47
CunA   pl 31a, 46b
CunE   p309-66   11 pl (1 col) il (f)
CunF   p250-54, 265-71   pl   p244
CunP   p49-57   pl (col) (f)
Dal   v2 fig 965-77   (col) (f)
Flow   fig 51 (f)
Gern   pl 59 (f)
Gor   p 193-94   pl   p 158, 165-66, **174,**
   195-97
HaC   p52-80   12 pl (f)
Jen   pl   p46-47 (f)
KerA   p 23-33   4 pl il (f)
Kle   p 153-54, 193 il
LavF   p29-30   pl 15 (col) (f)
LavT2   p 189-90   pl (m)
LelD   pl   p360 fig 5-6 (f)
Lib   pl   p 104 (f)
Lis   p87-94 il
Loud   pl 20 (col) (f)
McP   p27   pl   p28 (col)
Mo   p 105-20   9 pl il (f)
NeV   pl 30-40 (f)
Ni   pl 54 (f)
Part   p 136, 137, 147, 170   2 pl il
QuV   fig 32, 60, 149
Rue   fig T1-T2
Tru   p 103-06 il
True   p50-53, 58-59   3 pl il (f)
UnW   pl 109-14 (col)
VanH   pl 11
ViN   fig 79-89
Wa   p308-15   pl p306, 322 il
Wel   pl   p34-35
WilC   p312-17   2 pl (f)
WilF   pl   p 146-48
WilFo   pl   p 151 (m)
Yar   pl   p236, 238
YoR   p 106-09 il (f)

1890-1900

Ada   v4 il p 15, 52, 69
BelQ   pl   p 100 (col) (f)
BluN   pl   p92, 128
Bra   p323-38   4 pl
BrH   pl   p 135 fig 10, 14 (col) (m)
Brk   pl 41-44 (f)
BroH   p216-24 fig 139-42
Burr   p54, 100-01, 310   pl   p55
But   pl   p275 (m)
Chr   p 183-84 fig 365
CunA   pl 40 (f)
CunE   p367-426   15 pl (1 col) il (f)
CunF   p286-92, 304-06   pl   p276
CunP   p57-64   pl (col) (f)
Dal   v2 fig 978-87   (col) (f)
Dot   il   p 169 (f)

Gor   p 169-70   pl   p 198-202
HaC   p81-90   4 pl
Jen   pl   p 14
KerA   p34-43   5 pl (f)
Kle   p87, 192-93, 387 il
Lab   p98-101   pl (col) (m)
LavF   p30   pl 16 (col) (f)
LavS   p54   pl 27 (f)
LavT   p84-95   pl (f)
Lecl   pl 18 (col) (f)
LelD   pl   p360 fig 7 (f)
McP   p30-31   pl   p29, 32
Mo   p 123-41   9 pl il (f)
NeV   p4-5   pl 41-52 (f)
QuV   fig 31, 33, 123, 148
RogW   p4-6, 92 il (f)
Rue   fig U1-U3 (f)
Tru   p 107-11 il
True   p54-57, 60-61   3 pl il (f)
VanH   pl 11
ViN   fig 90-100
Wa   p315-29   pl   p306, 322 fig 253 il
Wel   pl   p35
WilC   p319-27   4 pl (f)
WilF   pl   p 149-51 (f)
WisF   pl 22-23 (f)
Yar   pl   p240, 242, 244, 246
YoR   p 109-14 il (f)

NISKA INDIANS. See Indians of North
   America—Niska Indians

NIVERNAIS. See France—Nivernais

NOBLEMEN

         Arabia, Modern
Nat   v91 Je '47 il p729

         Assyria and Babylonia
BartC   p68-70 fig 24-25
Gor   pl   p8

         Byzantine empire
Gor   pl   p 16

         China
Camm   pl 8, 11, 18

         Chios
Arg   p 129-34 front   pl 37 (2 col) il
   (incl pat)

         Egypt, Ancient
BartC   fig 15
Hous2   p6-7 fig 3, 7, 31
Lee   p74-76   pl
VanH   pl 1

         England
         449-1066
AirB   il   p 13
Tru   p 12 il
Yar   pl   p41

         11th-12th centuries
AirB   il   p20
AirS   il   p46
Lab   p34-36   pl (col)
NorC   pl   p35
Tru   p 16-19 il
VanH   pl 2
Wel   pl   p7
Yar   pl   p45, 47

NOBLEMEN—England—*Continued*

13th-14th centuries
CunA pl 1
Gor pl p24
KerM no3 pl 9
Wel pl p8-9
WilF pl p25

15th century
Norr v3 bk 1 p 17-32 il (incl pat)
Set il p 14
Wel pl p 10
Yar pl p 101

16th century
AirB il p38, 40
BosE pl 27, 29-30, 40
Dav v 1 p435-36, 440-42, 450-52 il
Davi v 1 pl p43
DeB pl p 190
Gor pl p57, 59, 61-62
KelF pl p65
Lab p42-48 2 pl (col)
LavE pl 15, 46 (1 col)
LavR pl p 151-52 157, 160, 166 (2 col)
LesA pl 49
Lint pl 10, 12-13
Norr v3 bk 1 p 190-91, 234-36 pl
  p 166 (col) fig 232 il; bk 2 p393-95,
  399, 524-40, 642-54 3 pl il
Pric pl p32
Rey p 14-16, 18-20 pl 2-4, 9, 12, 19, 24,
  33 (1 col)
Trev v2 pl p20 (col)
VanH pl 4
Yar pl p 108, 114, 126, 129, 131 (1 col)

17th century
AirB il p46, 50
BruK pl 92 fig 3
CunA pl 12
Dav v 1 front (col); v2 p566-67, 574-75
  pl il
Gor pl p74-75
LavR pl p 178, 180, 183 (1 col)
Lee p98-99 pl
Lint pl 16
Loud pl 13 (col)
Pric pl p35, 49
Rey p20 pl 33, 36 (1 col)
Set pl p22
Wel pl p 14-16
Yar p 146 pl p 136, 142 and pl VII
  (col)

18th century
Ada v 1 il p5
AirB il p50
Dav v2 p740-41, 766, 768 il
Lab p62-68 2 pl (col)
Wel pl p 17

France
Early to 987
Loud pl 7 (col)

14th century
WilF pl p24-25, 27-28

15th century
Gor pl p28
Norr v3 bk 1 p 17-33 il
WilF pl p34-36, 40

16th century
BluL p20 pl 16, 20, 32-33
BruK pl 73, 76 (col)
Norr v3 bk 1 p 191 fig 233; bk 2 p558-
  61, 656-59 il
WilFo pl p96

17th century
BluE p22-23, 25 pl 32, 37, 48-49, **51**
  (1 col)
BruK pl 99-100 (1 col)
Dav v2 p538-39, 555-56 il
Gor pl p91, 93
LavR pl p357, 374 (1 col)
Lecl pl 8 (col)
LesA pl 41

18th century
Dav v2 p679, 683 il

Germany
13th-14th centuries
WilF pl p24

16th century
Dav v 1 p407, 412 il
LavE pl 4 (col)
Ni pl 30

17th century
Ni pl 34

18th century
BruK pl 105

Greece, Ancient
VanH pl 1

Hungary
19th century
WilF pl p 152

India
BruK pl 777 (col)
KerM no2 pl 5
Nat v78 D '40 pl p765 (col)
WilFo pl p43

Italy
14th century
WilF pl p24

15th century
Norr v3 bk 1 fig 13
WilF pl p35

16th century
Bruh p26-27 pl (col)
BruK pl 66 fig 2-3
Norr v3 bk 2 p569-70 fig 662-64

17th century
Pric pl p46

Korea
Keit front (col) pl p64

Lorraine
17th century
BluE p21 pl 20-22

NOBLEMEN—*Continued*

Netherlands
15th century

Norr   v3 bk 1   p21-25   pl   p27 il

16th century

Gor   pl p46

17th century

Dav   v2 p627-28, 643 pl   p638 (col) il

Persia, Ancient

Gor   pl p8

Poland
16th century

BruK   pl 89 (col)
WilF   pl p73

17th century

BruK   pl 89 (col)
Nat   v78 Jl '40   pl   p38 (col)

Rumania

SitR   pl   p38B, 40A

Russia
15th century

WilF   pl   p38-39

16th century

BruK   pl 88 fig 6, 8-9 (col)
WilFo   pl   p97

17th century

BruK   pl 88 fig 10, 14-15 (col)
WilF   pl p 100

Scotland
16th century

Norr   v3 bk 2   p528-29 il

Siam

Pot   v2 pl 15 (col)

Spain
16th century

Dav   v 1   p462-63, 467 il (incl pat)
LavR   pl   p224 (col)
Nat   v70 O '36   pl   p442 (col)
Norr   v3 bk 2   p573-74 il
Rea   p 18   pl 15 (col)
WilFo   pl   p97

17th century

LavR   pl   p244-45, 254 (1 col)
Rea   p23, 25-26   pl 50-51, 57, 62 (1 col)

18th century

Gor   pl p 126

Sweden

Berg   pl 1-2 (col) fig 18

Venice
18th century

Mora   pl 12-17, 19-20, 76

NOBLEWOMEN

Austria
16th-17th centuries

LesA   pl 29 fig 243

Burgundy
15th century

BruK   pl 48 (col)

Byzantine empire

Dal   v 1 fig 453 (col)
Gor   pl p 16
HousG2   p 149-50, pl p 144 (col)
WilC   pl p35

China

Camm   pl 11-14, 18
Dal   v 1 fig 749-50 (col)
KerM   no 2 pl 3
Pot   v2 pl 1 (col)

Chios

Arg   p 153-64 front 10 pl (4 col)

Egypt, Ancient

BartC   p62-66 fig 20-21
Eli   p 100-04 il
Gen   v 1 fig 114
Hous2   p6-7, 36 fig 2, 6, 40
KerM   no 1 pl 3
Lee   p74-76 pl
VanH   pl 1

England
449-1066

AirB   il p 13
AirS   il p11-12
Tru   p 11-13 il
Yar   pl p41

11th-12th centuries

AirS   il p46, 48
Tru   p 17 il p 16
Wel   pl p7
Yar   pl p45, 47

13th century

Wel   pl p8

14th century

CunA   pl 1
Dav   v 1 p 198-99, 209, 211, 214-15
   3 pl il
HousM   p 110-12 fig 205
Wel   pl p9

15th century

CunA   pl 2-4, 6, 8a
Dav   v 1 p350-55 6 pl
HousM   p 168 fig 293
Wel   pl p 10

16th century

CunA   pl 10, 24a
Dav   v 1 p439 il
KelF   pl   p63
LavE   pl 49, 51 (1 col)
LavR   pl   p 158, 162, 168, 173, 176
   (1 col)
Norr   v3 bk 1 p207-13, 215-17, 267-
   271, 283-89 pl   p208, 268, 271, 283,
   302 (2 col); bk 2 p425-30, 444, 507-
   11, 517-23, 631-34, 636-41 5 pl (1 col)
   il (incl pat)
Rey   p 14, 16-19 pl 2, 10, 14-15, 26, 28
Trev   v 1 pl 168
Wel   pl p 11-12
WilFo   pl   p96
Yar   pl p 108, 110, 112, 114, 119, 121,
   126, 134

NOBLEWOMEN—England—*Continued*

17th century

AirB il p49
BosE pl 31
CunA pl 13, 15 (col)
Dav v2 p564, 573, 578-79, 591, 597-98 il
DeB pl p 190A
EvnJ pl 112
LavR pl p 175, 181-82, 184
Lee p99-100 pl
LesA pl 51-52
Lint pl 3
Rey p20-21 pl 34-35, 37
Wel pl p 13-15

18th century

AirB il p52, 54
Dav v2 p775-80 il
LavCl pl p209 (col)
Wel pl p 17

19th century

Gern pl 66-67

Europe

14th century

Lee p90-91 pl

15th century

Norr v3 bk 1 p58-62 pl (col) il

France

Early to 987

Loud pl 7 (col)

13th century

Loud pl 8 (col)
WilF pl p22, 25

14th century

Kle p379 il

15th century

Gor pl p28
WilF pl p27, 31

16th century

BluE p 18 pl 4
BluL pl 3, 6, 13-14, 18, 22, 25, 29-30, 34-36, 39, 47, 49, 53, 65 (3 col)
BraF pl p 18
BruK pl 73 (col)
LavCl pl p 17
Loud pl 12 (col)
Norr v3 bk 1 p218-23, 272-78 pl il (incl pat); bk 2 p431-32, 663-65 il

17th century

BluC pl p62
BluE p18, 20-24 pl 6, 14, 17, 25-27, 29-30, 34, 40-41, 45 (2 col)
BruK pl 100
Dav v2 p526-28, 536-37, 544-49, 554 il
EvnJ pl 113, 119
Gor pl p91, 93
LavR pl p350 (col)
LesA pl 26 fig 630

18th century

BluC pl p69
BoeR front (col) pl p 114, 178 (col)

BruK pl 105
Dav v2 p662, 665, 679-82, 685 il
LesA pl 59

19th century

LesA fig 614

Germany

15th century

Gor pl p30
WilF pl p33, 35

16th century

Ni pl 31
WilF pl p60

17th century

LavR pl p238 (col)
Ni pl 35
Rea p21 pl 43 (col)

18th century

BruK pl 105

Greece, Ancient

VanH pl 1

Hungary

19th century

WilF pl p 152

India

16th century

WilFo il p43

Ireland

16th century

Mccl front (col) pl 21

Italy

16th century

Arg pl 49
Bruh p26-27 pl (col)
Dav v2 fig 1316, 1330, 1339, 1343, 1347-48
Norr v3 bk 2 p571-72, 670-73 il
WilF pl p61

17th century

Dav v2 front (col)
EvnJ p 143 pl 105

Korea

Keit p65 pl p64F, 64H

Lorraine

16th century

Dav v2 p486-87 pl (f)

17th century

BluE p21 pl 23

Mexico, Ancient

DuS p79 pl 25-26 (col)

Netherlands

15th century

WilF pl p33-34, 36

16th century

Gor pl p46
Norr v3 bk 1 p 198-99 il

Persia, Ancient

BartC p82-84 fig 29

NOBLEWOMEN—*Continued*

Portugal
16th century
Rea p 16 pl 8

Russia
16th century
BruK pl 88 (col)

Spain
16th century
EvnJ pl 69
LavR pl 226, 231, 234-35 (1 col)
LesA pl 44
Norr v3 bk 1 p204-07 il; bk 2 p581-82, 678-83 2 pl il
Rea p 16, 18, 20 pl 8, 17, 27, 33 (1 col)

17th century
EvnJ pl 92
LavR pl p251
LesA pl 28
Rea p21, 24-25 pl 35, 55, 59-60 (1 col)
Vert pl p40 (f)

18th century
Dav v2 p732 il
Dot il p 164
Gor pl p 126
Nat v78 Jl '40 pl p41 (col)

Sweden
18th century
Berg pl 1, 4 (col)

Venice
16th century
Arg pl 49 (f)
LavE pl 6

NOOTKA INDIANS. See Indians of North America—Nootka Indians

NORMANDY. See France-Normandy

NORTH BRABANT. See Netherlands—North Brabant

NORWAY
BruK pl 127 (col)
Nat v75 Ap '39 pl p504-05, 518 (col)
Prim p34-54 17 pl (2 col)
See also Fancy dress and stage costume—Norwegian; also subdivision Norway under Ceremonial costume; Children; Headdress; Military costume; Wedding costume

18th century—date
Sem p 14-15 4 pl (col)
Stew p203-28 pl il

BY REGION OR PROVINCE

Aal
Prim pl p43

Agder
Stew p224-28 il (f)

Bergenhus, South
Sem pl 2 (col) (f)
UnW pl 3A (col)

Gudbrandsdal
Stew p218-19 il (f)

Hallingdal
Prim p36-37 pl p40-41
Stew p222-25 pl il

Hardanger
Brad pl p 124
BruK pl 127 fig 8 (col) (f)
Lee p50-52 pl
Prim p37-39 pl p46 (col) (f)
Stew p208-10 il (f)

Jölster
Prim pl p47 (f)

Numedal
BruK pl 127 fig 11 (col) (f)
Sem front (col)

Romsdal
Stew p215-16 il (f)

Setesdal
Nat v 106 Ag '54 pl p 176 (col)
Sem pl 3 (col)
Stew p220-22 il

Sogn
Stew p212-14 il (f)

Stjordal
Prim pl p44 (f)

Sunnmöre
Sem pl 3 (col) (f)
Stew p215 il (f)

Telemark
BruK pl 127 fig 10, 15-16 (col)
Prim p37 pl p51-53
Sem pl 4 (col)
Stew p223-24 il (f)

Valdres
Prim pl p46, 48

Voss
Stew p210-12 il

NOSE ORNAMENTS

African tribes
Leb pl 12 (col)

Armenia
Nat v89 Mr '46 il p388 (f)

Guiana, French
Nat v79 My '41 pl p641 (col) (m)

India
Nat v 102 Ag '52 pl p207 (col) il p217

New Britain
Nat v84 S '43 il p306 (m)

New Guinea
Nat v88 D '45 pl p670, 678 (m); v 100 N '51 pl p669, 671, 684-85, 688 (col); v 103 Ap '53 pl p423, 425, 434-35, 438, 442-43, 445, 469-71, 475-76, 488

NUMEDAL. See Norway—Numedal

NUNS

Armenian church
Doy pl 77 (col)

Catholic church
See also names of individual orders,
e.g. Cistercian nuns; Dominican nuns;
Franciscan sisters; Hospital sisters;
Sisters of the Good Shepherd

11th-12th centuries
EvjD pl 74
Lee p85 pl p87

13th-14th centuries
NorC pl p 14

15th century
Dav v 1 p255-56 pl

Coptic church
Doy pl 78 (col)

Ethiopic church
Doy pl 78 (col)

Greek church
SitR pl p 16B

NUREMBERG. See Germany—Bavaria

NURSEMAIDS

14th century
LelD il p286

15th century
HousM p 161-62 fig 277-78

19th century
LelD il p286

NURSEMAIDS, ROYAL

France
17th century
Dav v2 p540 il

NURSES
See also subdivision Nurse corps under Military costume—England; Military costume—United States

13th century
Tru il p20

19th century
RogW p41-42, 82 il

O

OAXACA. See Mexico—Oaxaca

OBIS
Kaw p39-55 10 pl
Lee p42-45 pl
Pic il p 104

ODD FELLOWS
Davi v2 il p419

ODENSE. See Denmark—Fyn

OFFERDAL. See Sweden—Jämtland

OFFICE WORKERS

United States
19th century
Davi v 1 il p547 (f)
Gor pl p202 (f)
Jen pl p80 (f)
Part p58-59, 117 il (f)
RogW p49-50 il (f)

OFFICERS, MILITARY. See Military
costume

OFFICIALS
See also Ambassadors; Ceremonial
costume; Kings and rulers; Mace bearers; Senators

Assyria and Babylonia
Dal v 1 fig 110-13, 124 (col)
Pot v 1 pl 5 (col)
TiK pl 6 fig 1
WilC pl 9

Byzantine empire
TiK pl 36 fig 15
See also Consuls—Byzantine Empire

Ceylon
Nat v94 Jl '48 il p 122

China
Camm pl 8
Pot v2 pl 1 (col)
See also Mandarins

Egypt, Ancient
Dav v 1 p20-21, 25, 33 il
HeuO pl 7

England
See also Lords Chamberlains—England; Lords Chancellors—England; Parliamentary robes—England

13th century
Gor pl p24

14th century
AirB il p33

16th century
BosE pl 28
Trev v 1 pl 146, 169

17th century
AirT il p45
Trev v2 fig 81

France
See also Parliamentary robes—France

15th century
BosF pl 15

17th century
BluE p23 pl 36

OFFICIALS—France—*Continued*
18th century
BluN p 192-200 pl p211-12
BoeR pl p238
LelD pl p265 fig 4
19th century
BluN p 192-200 pl p213-16
Germany
16th century
Dav v 1 fig 1029
18th century
Ni pl 40
Greece, Modern
At pl 5 (col)
India
BruK pl 176 fig 9, 12 (col)
Punjab
Nat v90 D '46 il p771
Italy
15th century
WilF pl p36
Japan
Pot v2 pl 6 (col)
Korea
Keit p47 pl (col)
Rome
BartC p 104-08 fig 36
Lis il p23
Scotland
Nat v 102 Jl '52 il p89
Sweden
18th century
Berg fig 134-35
Tibet
Nat v95 My '49 pl p687
Turkey
BruK pl 91, 169 (col)
Venice
16th century
WilF pl p63

OFFICIALS, MOHAMMEDAN. See Mohammedan officials

OFFICIALS, MUNICIPAL. See Aldermen; Mayors, etc.

OJIBWA INDIANS. See Indians of North America—Chippewa Indians

ÖLAND. See Sweden—Öland

OLD CASTILE. See Spain—Old Castile

OLIVETANS
Doy pl 66 (col)

ONDÁRROA. See Basque provinces

ONEIDA COMMUNITY
Gor pl p 187 (f)

ONEIDA INDIANS. See Indians of North America—Oneida Indians

OPERA CLOAKS. See Evening cloaks

OPTICIANS
England
18th century
SitN pl 5

ORANGE SCHOOL STUDENTS, NORTHAMPTON, ENGLAND
Cla p35-36 pl

ORBS (REGALIA)
England
Nat v 104 S '53 pl p325 (col)

ORDERS, MILITARY RELIGIOUS. See Malta, Knights of; Templars

ORDERS, RELIGIOUS. See Monks; Nuns

ORENSE. See Spain—Galicia

ORIENTAL COSTUME. See China, India, Japan, Persia, etc.

ORLÉANAIS. See France—Orléanais

ORNAMENTS. See Accessories and ornaments; Jewelry

ORONTES VALLEY. See Syria

ORTHODOX GREEK CHURCH. See Ecclesiastical costume—Greek church

ORVELTE. See Netherlands—Drente

ÖSTERGÖTLAND. See Sweden—Östergötland

ÖSTERVALLSKOG. See Sweden—Värmland

ÖSTRA. See Sweden—Småland

OULED NAÏLS
GaU pl 14 (col)
LelD p379 il

OUR LADY OF GRACE, ORDER OF
Doy pl 47, 152 (col)

OUR LADY OF THE ROSARY, KNIGHTS OF
Doy pl 153 (col)

OVERCOATS. See Coats (Overcoats)

OVERSHOES
17th century
LelD p 190 il
WilFo pl p 170-71

OVERYSEL. See Netherlands—Overysel

OVEZANDE. See Netherlands—Zealand

P

PACHOMIAN NUNS
Doy   pl 79 (col)

PACHOMIANS
Doy   pl 7 (col)

PAENULA. See Capes and cloaks—Rome

PAGES
England
16th century
LavR   pl p 169
Norr   v3 bk 1   p298-99 il
Rey   p 18   pl 22

Europe
17th century
Gor   pl p74

France
15th century
Loud   pl 10 (col)

16th century
WilC   pl   p91
WilF   pl   p59

17th century
Dav   v2   p531 il
WilC   pl   p 166, 182

United States
18th century
Dav   v2 fig 2148

PAGEANTS
England
16th century
Hat   p215-34, 277-301 il

Virginia
20th century
Nat   v80 Ag '41   pl p216 (col)

PAJAMAS
CrH   p44-53   5 pl
CunU   p208, 241, 254-56 fig 93, 106, 109, 118
Kle   p293 il (m)

PALATINATE. See Germany—Palatinate

PALESTINE
Ancient
BruK   pl 7 (col)
TiK   pl 12-14 (col)
See also Jewish priests; Jews; Kings and rulers—Palestine, Ancient

Modern
BruK   pl 191 fig 8-14 (col)
Nat   v89 Mr '46   pl p318, 322 (col)
Wrig   pt 1   p7-32   8 pl
See also Children—Palestine, Modern; Wedding costume—Palestine, Modern

PALLA. See Rome

PALLIUM. See Capes and cloaks—Rome

PALLIUM (ECCLESIASTICAL COSTUME)
HousM   p32-33 fig 21, 47
LelD   p294 il
Wa   p62 fig 62

PALMERS. See Pilgrims

PALUDAMENTUM. See Capes and cloaks—Rome

PANAMA
Hal   pl 29 (col) (f)
Nat   v95 Mr '49   pl p387, 391-92 (col)
Spi   p61 pl   p63 (col) (f)
See also Dancers—Panama; Indians of Central America—Panama

PANIERS. See Hoop skirts—18th century

PANTALETS
CunU   p 114-15, 130 fig 57
Dot   p 167 il
LelD   pl   p299 fig 5, 8
Loud   pl 18 (col)
Pic   il p 107
ViN   pl 13
WilC   p263 pl   p271

PANTALOONS. See Trousers—18th century

PAPAL CROWNS. See Papal tiara

PAPAL FOOTWEAR
WilFo   p62-63   pl p73

PAPAL GUARDS
Dav   v2 p605 il
KnR   pl   p317
LelD   p 196, 422-23 pl   p213 fig 7 il
Nat   v71 Mr '37   pl   p309 (col); v75 Mr '39 il p408; v77 Mr '40 il p392

PAPAL ORNAMENTS
16th century
BraF   p33 pl   p35

PAPAL TIARA
HousM   p 146-47 fig 262
LelD   p404 il
NorC   p 108-15 pl   il
TiK   pl 37 fig 24
Wa   fig 102, 120
WilH   pl   p30-31

PAPOOSES. See Children—Indians of North America

PAPUA. See New Guinea

PARAGUAY
Spi   p66-67 pl   il (f)
See also Military costume—Paraguay

PARASOLS. See Umbrellas and parasols

PARIS. See France—Île de France

PARLIAMENTARY ROBES
England
14th-15th centuries
Ab   front
AirM   il p52

PARLIAMENTARY ROBES—England—
Continued

16th century
BosE pl 9

18th century
AirB il p50

France
15th century
BosF pl 5

16th century
BosF pl 36

18th century
BluN pl p211-12
LelD p 102 il

PARSIS
Dal v 1 p381-82 fig 696-97 (col) (f)

PASHAS
Lee p68-70 pl

PASSIONIST NUNS
Doy pl 159 (col)

PASSIONISTS
MusE pl 29 (col)

PASTORAL STAFF. See Crosiers

PATAGONIA. See Indians of South America—Patagonia

PATCHES (FOR THE FACE)
Bra pl 27, 31
LelD p280 il
LesA p98-100 il
Vert p56 il

PATRIARCHS

Greek church
HousG2 fig 171, 173
MusE pl 11 (col)
Nat v 106 D '54 pl p850 (col)

PATTERNS. See abbreviation (pat) after entries under period divisions of England, France, etc.; also after individual garments such as Skirts, Waists, etc.

PAULANERIN NUNS. See Minim sisters of St Frances of Rome

PAULIST FATHERS
MusE pl 35 (col)

PAULITES (HERMITS OF ST PAUL)
Doy pl 2-3 (col)

PEASANT COSTUME
Peasant costume will generally be found under provincial subdivision of European countries, e.g. France—Brittany; Germany—Black Forest; Italy —Tuscany.

PEASECOD DOUBLETS. See subdivisions 16th century under England, France, etc.

PECTORALS
Bra pl 2
Hous2 p 15-17 fig 19
McC p 136-38 il
NorC p 128-37 il

PEDDLERS. See Street venders and peddlers

PEERS. See Noblemen

PEERS' ROBES—ENGLAND. See Ceremonial costume—England; Court dress —England

LA PELEGRINA (JEWEL)
Norr v3 bk 2 p461-62 il

PELISSE. See Capes and cloaks—18th century; Capes and cloaks—19th century

PENDANTS. See Necklaces and pendants

PENITENTIAL NUNS OF ORVIETO
Doy pl 84 (col)

PENITENTS
BluL p23 pl 44
LelD p311 il
Nat v99 Ap '51 pl p507, 514 (col)
OrM pl 159-60, 162-63, 166-67, 170-72

PENMARCH. See France—Brittany

PENSIONERS

England
16th century
Norr v3 bk 1 p291-92; bk 2 p423-24, 689 pl 45

17th century
Gor il p85

20th century
BarH pl 23 (col)
Nat v79 Ja '41 pl p83

PERFUME CONTAINERS
CunS pl 64
LesA p 151-62 il
Norr v3 bk 1 p43-45, 271-72 il; bk 2 p553-54 il
RogF p80-81 il
Yar p 106, 117, 144, 173 il

PERIWIGS. See subdivisions 17th century and 18th century under Hair, wigs, etc. (e.g. Hair, wigs, etc.—France—17th century)

PERPETUAL ADORATION OF THE BLESSED SACRAMENT NUNS
Doy pl 118 (col)

PERSIA

Ancient to A.D. 640
BartC p74-84 fig 27-29
Bra p40-41 pl 5
BruK p6-7, 9-10 pl 9, 25 table 1 (pat)
CrP pl 5 (f)
Dal v 1 p79-92 6 pl il (col)
Dav v 1 p 13-14 il
Dot p 108 il
Gor p8 il (m)
HeuO p83-86 pl 45, 51-53 il
Hous2 p 160-87 9 pl il (incl pat)
Lis p 17-19 il
Loud pl 2 (col) (m)

PERSIA—Ancient to A.D. 640—*Continued*
  Pot v 1 p 19 pl 6 (col)
  RueG pl 14, 16 (m)
  TiK pl 5, 9 (incl pat)
  UnW pl 6 (col)
  Wa p27-29 fig 33, 38-40 (incl pat)
  WilC p24-28 2 pl
  Wrig pt3 p22-24 pl p31 (incl pat)
  Yar p 11-14 pl

  See also subdivision Persia, Ancient under Footwear; Hair, wigs, etc.; Headdress; Kings and rulers; Military costume; Noblemen; Noblewomen; Servants

                    640-1405
  Burr p6, 113, 186, pl p7

                 16th century
  Vert pl p68 (f)

                 1736—date
  Brad pl p 125
  BruK p37 pl 174 fig 7-17 (col)
  Nat v 100 O '51 pl p435 (col) (f)
  Pic il p 110 (f)
  TiK pl 73-75 (col) (incl pat)

PERU
  See also Incas; also subdivision Peru under Bags, purses, etc.; Capes and cloaks; Ceremonial costume; Dancers; Festival costume; Headdress; Indians of South America; Masks; Military costume

                   Ancient
  Zim p5 pl (f)

                   Modern
  BruK pl 194 (col)
  Hal pl 31-39 (col)
  Nat v82 Ag '42 pl p 176-77, 179 (col)
  Spi p68-75 4 pl (2 col)

PERUKES. See Hair, wigs, etc.—Europe —18th century

PETASUS. See Headdress—Greece, Ancient

PETTICOAT BREECHES. See Breeches Europe—17th century

PETTICOATS AND SLIPS

                 18th century
  Bra pl 32
  CrH p4-5 pl
  CunU p92-94 fig 36, 43

                 19th century
  CrH p6-7, 10-13 2 pl
  CunU p 128-30 fig 55; p 145-47 fig 65; p 166-68 fig 74; p 176-77 fig 77, 80
  HaC pl p49
  Pic il p 110
  WilC p313 pl p319

                 20th century
  AlF pl p 162-63
  CrH p 14-19 3 pl

  CunU p212-14 fig 95, 98; p227-29, 246- 50 fig 103, 106
  LelD il p 121

PHARAOH (BIBLICAL CHARACTER). See Biblical costume—Pharaoh

PHARISEES. See Biblical costume— Pharisees

PHARMACISTS. See Apothecaries

PHILADELPHIA CITY CAVALRY
  Kre2 pl 24 (col)

PHILIP, KING. See subdivisions under Kings and rulers—France

PHILIPPINE ISLANDS
  Brad pl p 127
  CroO pl 4
  Nat v78 O '40 pl p432, 443-44 (col); v86 N '44 pl p557 (f)
  See also subdivision Philippine Islands under Dancers; Footwear; Headdress

PHOENICIA
  Gen v 1 fig 196-97 (m)
  WilFo pl p 14 (m)

PHRYGIA
  Bra p35 pl 5
  BruK p45 pl 10
  See also Headdress—Phrygia; Military costume—Phrygia

PHRYGIAN BONNET. See Headdress— Phrygia

PHYSICIANS
  See also Barber surgeons
                   England
              12th-13th centuries
  AirM il p9
  HousM p46 fig 76
  Tru il p20

              14th century
  Ab pl p 196

              15th-16th centuries
  Norr v3 bk 1 p74-75, 293-95 il; bk 2 p691-92 il

              18th century
  Nat v95 Ap '49 pl p503 (col)
  SitN pl 27

                   France
              16th-17th centuries
  LelD p273 pl p362 fig 1
  WilF pl p63

                   Germany
              12th century
  Dav v 1 fig 413

              Greece, Ancient
  Dav v 1 fig 205

PIARISTS
  Doy pl 56 (col)

PICARDY. See France—Picardy

PIERRETTE. See Fancy dress and stage costume—Pierrette

PIERROT. See Fancy dress and stage costume—Pierrot

PIKEMEN
England
16th-17th centuries
AirB il p44
BarH pl 3 (col)
Gor pl p40 (col)
Germany
17th century
KnR pl p5

PILEUS. See Headdress—Greece, Ancient

PILGRIM FATHERS. See Puritans

PILGRIMS
England
14th century
Dav v 1 fig 569
Estonia
Nat v76 N '39 il p831
India
Ind pl p61 (col) (m)
Tibet
Nat v99 My '51 pl p609

PILGRIMS' SIGNS AND BADGES
EvnJ p83-85 pl 39

PILGRIMS' STAFFS
LesA p390-91 fig 480

PINS
Ancient
AirB il p5, 13
Yar pl p39
14th century
Dal v2 fig 168 (col)

PIONEERS AND SCOUTS
BruK pl 197 fig 1-4 (col)
But pl p38, 41
Davi v 1 pl p200
Gor p205-06 pl p204, 207-12 (1 col)
Lee p 109-11 pl
Rue fig F1-F2
Trai p71, 73, 236 il
VanH pl 5
See also Fancy dress and stage costume—Pioneer

PIPE DANCE. See Dancers—Indians of North America—Pipe dance

PIPES AND SMOKING UTENSILS
Rud pl p 100
African tribes
Leb pl 26 (col)

England
16th century
Norr v3 bk 2 p705-06 il
Trev v2 p58 il
Indians of North America
MasB p92-99 pl il (incl pat)
Korea
Keit p67 pl p64C, 64L
Turkey
Nat v75 Ja '39 pl p20 (col)

PIRATES
Ada v 1 il p214
Dav v2 p741 il
See also Fancy dress and stage costume—Pirate

PLANETA
NorC p62-63 (pat)

PLOUGASTEL. See France—Brittany

THE PLUMES. See Dancers—Mexico—The plumes

PLUS FOURS
WilC pl p340
Yar p262 pl p265

POCKETS
Kle p381-84 il
Spain
AnS p 145-47 fig 176, 184, 341

POITOU. See France—Poitou

POLAND
Bene p 115-18, 120-23, 128, 134, 136 pl p 108, 156-57
Wol p 15-17 pl 1-4 (col)
See also Fancy dress and stage costume—Polish; also subdivision Poland under Capes and cloaks; Coats and jackets; Dancers; Headdress; Military costume; Naval costume; Noblemen; Noblewomen; Wedding costume
17th century
BruK pl 89 (col)
TiK pl 40 (col)
18th century—date
Brad pl p 128-30 (1 col)
BruK pl 165 (col)
Glin pl 1-20 (col)
Lee p52-54 pl
Lep pl 31-40 (col)
Nat v75 Je '39 p765-67, 769 pl
Stry pl 7, 9-25, 27-28, 30-31, 33, 35-40 (col)
BY REGION OR PROVINCE
Cracow
Glin pl 1, 6 (col)
Lep pl 31, 39 (col)
Stry pl 1-4, 6, 8 (col)

POLAND—*Continued*

Lowicz
Brad pl p 13 (f)
BruK pl 165 fig 8, 17 (col)
Glin pl 9, 14

Warsaw
Stry pl 7, 9-11 (col)

POLE ARMS
Dav v 1 p 157 il

POLICE
Burma
AirO il p33
Canada
Nat v92 N '47 pl p589 (col); v 106
N '54 pl p710-13 (col)
Danzig
Nat v76 N '39 il p685
England
19th century
AirB il p56
Nat v71 Ja '37 p29 il
Fiji Islands
Nat v83 Ap '43 pl p512
France
18th century
Dav v2 p709-10 il

19th century
KnR p298-301 pl
LelD p 197-98 pl

20th century
LelD pl p 198 fig 12
Paris
Nat v 101 Je '52 il p783
Germany
Berlin
Nat v71 F '37 p 158 il
Gibraltar
Nat v78 S '40 pl p379
Italy
Rome
CamC pl p21
Nat v70 S '36 p375 il
Venice
Nat v87 Mr '45 pl p267 (col)
Korea
19th century
Bis il p444
Spain
Nat v97 Ap '50 pl p453 (col)
OrT pl 193
Sudan
AirO il p45, 48

United States
19th century
Davi v2 il p 159
Gor pl p 199
Kou pl 12
Part p99 il
Chicago
19th century
But il p249
New York City
19th century
Ada v3 il p2
Davi v2 pl p 153
Virgin Islands
Nat v78 S '40 il p290

POLICEWOMEN
United States
RogW p 118 il

POLO COSTUME
19th century
Ada v3 il p347
20th century
Dur pl p164

POLONAISE. See period 1750-1790 under
England, France, etc.

POLYNESIA. See Hawaiian Islands;
Tahiti

POMANDERS. See Perfume containers

POMERANIA. See Germany—Pomerania

PONCHOS
Brad pl p61
Kle p290 il
LelD p328 il

PONDICHÉRRY
GaU pl 32 (col) (f)

PONTEVEDRA. See Spain—Galicia

POOR CLARES
Doy pl 133 (col)

**POOR CLARES OF THE REFORM OF
ST PETER OF ALCANTARA.** See
Alcantarine nuns

POPES
MusE pl 15 (col)
See also Papal footwear; Papal orna-
ments; Papal tiara
To 10th century
HousG2 fig 154
10th-12th centuries
Dav v 1 p 140 il
NorC p 100-02 pl p79, 94 (1 col)
13th century
AirM il p7

POPES—*Continued*

14th century

Dav v 1 p216 il

15th century

BruK pl 30 fig 5 (col)
HousM p 146-48 fig 262

16th century

LavR pl p229, 232, 236

17th century

LelD il p299
Nat v78 Jl '40 pl p 19 (col)

18th century

BruK pl 30 fig 7 (col)

20th century

LelD il p299

PORTERS

Lebanon

Cyr pl 1 (col)

PORTUGAL
Arms p 15-18 pl 1-4 (col)
See also subdivision Portugal under Children; Dancers; Headdress; Military costume; Queens

16th century

BroW v 1 fig 109 (f)
BruK pl 72 (col) (m)
Dav v 1 p457 il (f)
Rea p 19-20 pl 21, 28 (m)

17th century

BroW v2 p31-32 fig 20 (f)
Rea p21 pl 38-39

18th century—date

Brad pl p 132-33, 135 (1 col)
BruK pl 156 (col)
Nat v73 F '38 pl p 180 (col)

POSTILIONS
Kou pl 19
LelD p331 il

POSTMEN
See also Messengers and couriers

France
20th century

Nat v77 F '40 il p204

United States
19th century

Ada v4 il p44

POSTWOMEN

England
20th century

Yar p259 il

POTTERS
England
Early to 13th century

AirP il p 13, 45
AirS il p38

16th century

AirT il p30

Mayas

Nat v70 N '36 pl p627 (col) (m)

POTTERY VENDERS
Mexico

Marq pl 40 (m)
Nat v70 O '36 p430 il (m)

PRAETORIAN GUARDS
Dal v 1 fig 380 (col)
Dav v 1 fig 297
HousG2 p 106 fig 118

PREACHING FRIARS. See Dominicans

PREMONSTRANTS
Doy pl 26 (col)

PREMONSTRATENSIAN NUNS
Doy pl 91 (col)

PREMONSTRATENSIANS. See Premonstrants

PRESIDENTS
Confederate States

But pl p 160

United States
18th century

But pl p2-3, 5, 25

19th century

But pl p35, 73-74, 82, 110, 163, **172,**
185, 197, 221, 232, 243, 286

20th century

AlF pl p 122-23
But pl p317

PRIESTESSES
See also Buddhist priestesses
Assyria and Babylonia

Dav v 1 p4 fig 4
Gen v 1 fig 188

Crete, Ancient

HousG2 p 15 fig 13

Egypt, Ancient

Dal v 1 fig 35 (col)
Hous2 p53-54 pl 3
RueG pl 18
TiK pl 3 fig 9-11

Greece, Ancient

MusE pl 6 (col)
VanH pl 1
WilFo pl p25

Hittites

Hous2 p72 fig 77c

PRIESTESSES—*Continued*
Mexico, Ancient
DuS p82-85 pl 28-29, 31-32 (col)
Rome
Tru il p8

PRIESTS
See also Buddhist priests; Confucianist priests; Druids; Imams; Jewish priests; Shinto priests; Taoist priests; also Ecclesiastical costume for priests of the Christian religion
Assyria and Babylonia
Dav v 1 p4 fig 8-9, 15, 17
MusE pl 4 (col)
Pot v 1 pl 5 (col)
WilC pl p9
Yar pl p7
Aztec
Nat v71 Je '37 pl p735, 739 (col)
Byzantine empire
Dal v 1 fig 467 (col)
Gor pl p 16
Cyprus
Dav v 1 p58 il
Egypt, Ancient
BartC p58 fig 18
BruK pl 2-4 (col)
Dal v 1 p29-35 pl il (col)
Gen v 1 fig 119
HeuO p25 pl 4, 13, 16 fig 17, 30
Hous2 p53 fig 57-58, 87
MusE pl 3 (col)
RueG pl 19
TiK pl 3 fig 5-6 (col)
VanH pl 1
WilC pl p5
WilF pl p8
WilFo pl p7
Ethiopia, Ancient
TiK pl 25 fig 6 (col)
Greece, Ancient
MusE pl 6-7
VanH pl 1
WilFo pl p23
Hindu
Nat v 105 Ap '54 pl p518 (col)
Incas
Nat v73 F '38 pl p232, 235 (col)
Indians of North America
Nat v89 Ja '46 pl p71 (col)
Mayas
Nat v70 N '36 pl p625 (col)
Mexico, Ancient
Alv pl p296 (col)
BruK pl 195 fig 14-15, 18 (col)
DuS p27-29, 33-39 pl 1-8 (col) il
Rome
Dav v 1 p77 il
Gor pl p 14

TiK pl 11 fig 2-3
VanH pl 1
WilFo pl p37

PRIMITIVE AND EARLY COSTUME
Bra p 1-12 2 pl
UnW pl 1 (col)
See also England—Ancient to 449; Europe to 476; France—Early to 511, etc.

PRINCE CHARMING. See Fancy dress and stage costume—Prince Charming

PRINCES. See Noblemen

PRINCESSES. See Noblewomen

PRINTERS
England
15th century
AirM il p43
17th century
AirT il p60
France
16th century
Dav2 p472 il

PRIORESSES
14th century
Ab pl p40
16th century
Dav v2 p500 il

PROCESSIONS
Assyria and Babylonia
Nat v99 Ja '51 pl p 104 (col)
Germany
17th century
Dav v2 p623 il
Shetland islands
Nat v 106 D '54 pl p855-61

PROCESSIONS, ACADEMIC
Nat v97 My '50 pl p586 (col)

PROCESSIONS, CORONATION
England
12th century
AirM il p5
16th century
Hat p215-18 fig 2
17th century
Dav v2 p587 il
20th century
Nat v 104 S '53 pl p327, 331, 334-38, 340-41 (5 col)

PROCESSIONS, FUNERAL
China
Nat v72 D '37 p721 il

PROCESSIONS, FUNERAL—*Continued*

Egypt, Ancient

Dav   v 1 fig 92
Nat   v80 O '41   pl   p503 (col)

England

16th century

Hat   p229-32 fig 6

19th century

Trev   v4 fig 135

France

14th century

EvjD   pl 20b

17th century

Dav   v2 p510 il

PROCESSIONS, RELIGIOUS

Brazil

Nat   v94 O '48   pl   p497 (col)

Egypt, Ancient

KerM   no 1   pl 5

France

Dav   v2 p488-89 il

Germany

Ret   pl   p 126-27 (f)

Hungary

Karo   pl   p78

Italy

Nat   v 100 S '51   pl   p405 (col)

Poland

Bene   pl   p221

Spain

OrM   pl 219-23, 226-28

PROCESSIONS, ROYAL

England

16th century

AirT   il p 13
BosE   pl 26
Dav   v2   p560 il
Hat   p223-28, 232-33 fig 4, 5, 7
Norr   v3 bk 2   p648-50   pl

France

17th century

Dav   v2 p524 il

Peru

Nat   v73 F '38   pl   p230 (col)

PROCESSIONS, WEDDING

China

Nat   v72 D '37   pl   p719

England

16th century

AirT   il p5
Norr   v3 bk 2   p648-50   pl

India

Nat   v78 D '40   pl   p736, 766-71 (col);
   v94 O '48   pl   p422-25 (col)

PROFESSORS. See Academic costume

PROTESTANT CHURCH. See Ecclesiastical costume—Protestant church

PROVENCE. See France—Provence

PUEBLA. See Mexico—Puebla

PUGILISTS

Dav   v2 p831 il

Japan

CamC   pl   p 10-11
Haa   pl 66-68

United States

19th-20th centuries

Dur   p78, 120, 227, 267   2 pl   il

PUNJAB. See India—Punjab

PUPPET SHOWMEN

Japan

Haa   pl 85

PUPPETS

Go   p 14-19 il
Mil   pl 106-08

Japan

Nat   v 104 N '53   pl   p640 (col)

PURIFICATION OF MARY NUNS

Doy   pl 116 (col)

PURITANS

Ada   il   p72-73 (m)
AirO   il   p3 (m)
AirT   il   p38, 45
Dab   pl 13
Dav   v 1 fig 569
Dot   p 156-57 il
EvnH   p73-81   pl   il (incl pat)
CrO   pl 16
Hea   p20-21, 36-37   2 pl
KerM   no4   pl 11-12
Lab   p50-52   pl (col)
Lee   p 100-02   pl
LesA   fig 484 (m)
Lis   p56   pl   p54
Pic   il   p 117
Roj   pl   p29
Set   p26-29   pl
Trai   p 133-35 il
Tru   p64-67 il
UnW   pl 52 (col)
VanH   pl 4, 6
WilC   p 158-60   pl
   See also Fancy dress and stage costume—Puritan

PURSES. See Bags, purses, etc.

PYRENEES MOUNTAINS

Brad   pl   p67 (f)
CosP   p26-27   pl 8, 26-30
LepF   pl 27-30 (col)
Nat   v72 O '37   pl   p435-36, 439, 441-43, 445, 447-50 (col)

PYRENEES MOUNTAINS—*Continued*
  Ogr pl p368 (col) (f)
  RogD pl 31 (col) (f)
  See also Basque provinces; also the following subdivisions under France: Béarn, Foix, Roussillon

Q

QUAKERS
  Ada v 1 il p236-37
  Dot p 157 il
  EvnH p88-92 pl il (incl pat)
  Pic il p 118 (f)
  Rue fig B1-B2 (f)
  Sit pl p 145

QUEENS AND EMPRESSES
  See also Coronation robes; Kings and rulers
        Assyria and Babylonia
  Dot il p 107
  Hous2 p 152 pl 7
  Yar p 10 il

        Byzantine empire
  Dal v 1 fig 449, 455 (col)
  UnW pl 19 (col)
        6th century
  BruK pl 27 fig 11 (col)
  Dav v 1 p81, 85 il
  Dot p 119-20 il
  HousG2 p 136-37 pl
  Kle p71-73 il
  Loud pl 6 (col)
  TiK pl 36 fig 5, 7
  WilC pl p35
  WilFo p61-62 pl p73
  Yar pl p31
        7th century
  HousG2 pl p 144 (col)
        10th century
  Dot il p 122
        11th century
  Dav v 1 p 114 il
  HousG2 p 150-54 pl il
  LelD pl p263 fig 6
  TiK pl 36 fig 11
  WilF pl p 14
  Yar pl p 14, 31
        China
  Dal v 1 fig 751 (col)
        Denmark
        14th century
  TiK pl 120 fig 6 (pat)
        16th century
  Gor pl p50, 54
        17th century
  LavR pl p 125, 177 (1 col)
  Rey p20-21 pl 30, 38 (1 col)
        Egypt, Ancient
  Dal v 1 fig 75 (col)

  Gen v 1 fig 90, 96, 99, 102-03, 109 and table 9 fig 380 (pat)
  Gor pl p6
  HeuO pl 22-24, 28
  Hous2 pl 1 (col) fig 37-39, 42
  Lee p74-76 pl
  Nat v80 O '41 pl p501, 514 (col)
  Pot v 1 pl 4 (col)
  RueG pl 21
  TiK pl 3 fig 8 (col)
  VanH pl 1
  WilC pl p5
  WilFo pl p6

        England
        449-1066
  VanH pl 2
  Wel pl p5
  Yar p41 il
        1066-1154
  AirS il p46
  VanH pl 2
  Wel pl p6
        12th century
  Dav v 1 p 130 il
  Dot il p 127
  Wel pl p7
  Yar p52, 54 il
        13th century
  HousM p 14-15 fig 20, 63
  Wel pl p8
        14th century
  HousM p 114-15 fig 211
  Yar p71, 75 il
        1422-1461
  Wel pl p 10
        1485-1509
  Dot il p 144
  Norr v3 bk 1 p58-59 pl 1, 4 (col) fig 151
  Yar p 104-05 pl
        16th century
  LavE pl 34-36 (1 col)
        1509-1547
  BruK pl 71
  EvnJ p94 pl 62
  Norr v3 bk 1 p64-65, 196-98, 267, 278-85 2 pl il
  WilF pl p57, 64
        Mary, 1553-1558
  Dav v 1 p437 il
  Gor pl p52
  LavR pl p 59, 149
  Norr v3 bk 2 p438-44, 451 3 pl (1 col) il
  Rey p 14 pl 1
  Yar pl p 121
        Elizabeth, 1558-1603
  Bae. front
  BosE p20-21 pl 4, 26
  BraF p62-63 pl p69
  BruK pl 82
  Dav v 1 p443-47 pl il; v2 p560-61 il
  DeB front pl p 191
  Dot il p 146

QUEENS AND EMPRESSES—England—
Elizabeth, 1558-1603—*Continued*
EvnJ   p 116-19 pl 70
Gor   pl p59, 62
Hat   p286, 289 fig 8-9, 58, 61
KerM   no5 pl 3
KerR   pl 9
LavR   pl   p57, 153, 155, 164, 171-72
   (2 col)
LesA   pl 45, 57
Norr   v3 bk 2 p484-98, 602-13 pl 27-32,
   37-43, 45 (4 col) il
Rey   p7, 15, 17, 19   pl 5, 7, 17, 25
   (1 col)
TiK   pl 128 fig 3 (col)
Vert   pl p26
Wa   p 161, 165-69 fig 151
Yar   pl   p 129-31, 134   4 pl (1 col)

1603-1625
Dav   v2 p561 il

1625-1649
BluE   p24 pl 43
Dav   v2 p 572, 574 il
Gor   pl p75
LavR   pl p369
Tru   pl p58 (col) il p59
Yar   p 139, 151 il

1660-1685
Tru   pl p70 (col)

1689-1702
BraF   pl p80

Anne, 1702-1714
Yar   pl p 142

1727-1760
BraF   pl p92

1760-1820
Dav   v2 p810 il
EvnJ   pl 135
Set   pl p24 (col)
SitC   pl 28, 95 (1 col)

1830-1837
BraF   pl p 115

Victoria, 1837-1901
Nat   v71 Ja '37 pl p41 (col)
SitC   pl 127-28

Elizabeth II, 1953-
Kle   p332 il
Nat   v 104 S '53 pl p311, 314-17, 320,
   322-23 (col)

Europe
12th century
UnW   pl 21 (col)

France
Early to 987
Dot   p 121 il

12th century
Dav   v 1 p 137 il
Dot   il p 128
WilFo   pl p76

13th century
BluC   pl p49
HousM   p 12 pl 2 (col)

1364-1380
HousM   p 115-16 fig 213

1498-1515
Dav   v2 p470-71 il

1515-1547
Dot   il p 148
LesA   fig 631
Loud   pl 11 (col)

1547-1559
BluL   p 19 pl 8
Dav   v2 p474-75 il
LavR   pl p90-91 (1 col)
Norr   v3 bk 2 p433-36, 450-51, 566-68,
   667-68 pl il

1560-1574
BluL   p 11, 22, 25 pl 36, 57 (1 col)
EvnJ   pl 68

1574-1589
BluL   p25 pl 59
Norr   v3 bk 2 p563-64, 662-63 il

1589-1610
BruK   pl 84 fig 6-7 (col)
Dav   v2 p511 il
Dot   il p 148
Norr   v3 bk 2 p564-66, 665-67 il

1610-1643
BluE   p20, 22, 24 pl 15, 28, 44 (2 col)
Dav   v2 p511-12, 516 il
LavR   pl p355, 359, 366-67, 370 (3 col)
Lib   pl p34
WilF   pl p87

1643-1715
Dot   il p 152

1715-1774
BoeR   pl p4 (col)
BruK   pl 104 fig 2 (col)
Dav   v2 p666 il
Lel   v 11 pl 18

1774-1789
BoeR   pl p226-46, 290 (col)
Gor   pl p 123

1804-1814
Dot   il p 164
LelD   pl p358 fig 2

1852-1870
LesA   pl 54

Germany
13th-14th centuries
Dav   v 1 pl p 187

16th century
Norr   v3 bk 1 pl p 40

Greece, Ancient
Pot   v 1 pl 12 (col)

QUEENS AND EMPRESSES—*Continued*

Greece, Modern
Nat v77 Mr '40 il p301

Holy Roman empire
17th century
Rea p24 pl 53

Italy
14th century
WilFo pl p77

20th century
Nat v77 Mr '40 il p392

Naples (Kingdom)
19th century
EvnJ pl 159

Palestine, Ancient
Pot v 1 pl 8 (col)

Persia, Ancient
Pot v 1 pl 6 (col)

Portugal
16th century
Dav v 1 p460 il
LavR pl p217 (col)
LesA fig 215
Norr v3 bk 1 p204-05 pl (col)
Rea p 15 pl 3 (col)

Rome
Loud pl 5 (col)
VanH pl 1
WilFo p33 pl p39

Scotland
15th century
HousM p 192 fig 324

16th century
Dot il p 145
Hat fig 85
KerM no5 pl 6
KerR pl 8
Norr v3 bk 2 p436-38, 453-54, 511-17,
  634-36, 747-48 3 pl (1 col) il
Yar pl p 129

Siam
Pot v2 pl 15 (col)

Spain
13th century
Dal v2 fig 156 (col)

15th century
Dot il p 143
Norr v3 bk 1 p62-63 (1 col)

16th century
BruK pl 74
Dav v 1 p457, 460, 466 il
Gor pl p57
LavR pl p216, 221, 223, 225, 227 (1 col)
Norr v3 bk2 p577-82, 684-85 il
Rea p 17-18 pl 11, 14, 16, 18 (1 col)

17th century
BluE p27 pl 62
Dav v2 p510, 638-39, 643-44 il
LavR pl p245
Rea p22 pl 45

18th century
Dav v2 p734-35 il
EvnJ pl 134
Lel v 11 pl 22

Sweden
18th century
Berg fig 13, 140

Tonga Islands
Nat v83 Ap '43 il p514

QUICHUA INDIANS. See Indians of South America—Kechua Indians

R

RABBIS
LelD p341 il
MusE pl 12 (col)

RAIN DANCE. See Dancers—Indians of North America—Rain dance

RAINCOATS AND RAIN CAPES
Kle p232, 300 il

Eskimos
CrO pl 4

France
18th century
Pann v 1 pl 6 (col) (f)

RAJAS
BruK pl 176 fig 8, 13 (col)
Lee p36-37 pl
Nat v78 D '40 pl p765 (col)

RAJPUTS
TiK pl 88 fig 3a (col)

RANGERS

United States
19th century
Gor pl p218-19, 224, 233, 237

RANIS
Lee p36-37 pl

RÄTTVIK. See Sweden—Dalarne

REBECCA (BIBLICAL CHARACTER). See Biblical costume—Rebecca

REBOZOS
Meri pl 1 (col)
Too p46 fig 61, 105

RECOLLECTS
Doy pl 71 (col)

RED CROSS UNIFORMS
  CrO pl 57 (f)
  LesA p71 fig 90
  Ross p 12-13, 89 il (col)
  WisF pl 29 (f)

REDEMPTORISTS
  Doy pl 76 (col)

REGALIA. See Crowns; Orbs (Regalia); Rings, Coronation; Sceptres

RELIGIOUS COSTUME. See Ecclesiastical costume

RELIGIOUS ORDERS. See Monks; Nuns

RELIGIOUS PROCESSIONS. See Processions, Religious

RELIQUARIES (JEWELRY)
  Bra pl 11
  EvnJ p49-50, 78-81 pl 10, 22, 32-34, 37-38
  NeR pl 20-23
  Norr v3 bk 1 p 123 il; bk 2 p462-63 il

RENAISSANCE COSTUME. See period subdivisions of the 14th to the 16th centuries under various European countries, e.g. Italy—15th century

RESTORATION STYLE, 1814-1830. See Nineteenth century—1810-1820; Nineteenth century—1820-1830

RETICULES. See Bags, purses, etc.—18th century

RHINEGRAVES. See Breeches—Europe—17th century

RHODES, KNIGHTS OF. See Malta, Knights of

RICHARD, KING. See subdivision of the 12th, 14th and 15th centuries under Kings and rulers—England

RICHMOND LIGHT INFANTRY BLUES
  Kre2 pl 24 (col)

RIDING BOOTS
        14th-15th centuries
  LelD p220 fig 1-5 (m)
        17th century
  Jae pl 31 (m)
  LelD pl p42 fig 1-3 (m)
        18th century
  CrO pl 13 fig 9
  WilFo pl p 130 (m)
        19th century
  Jae pl 36-37 (m)
  LelD pl p42 fig 13 (m)
  WilC pl p219
  WilFo pl p 149
        20th century
  WilFo pl p 163, 171 (m)

RIDING COSTUME
  Rud pl p 141 (pat) (m)
    See also Jodhpurs; Riding boots; Riding hats; Spurs

        13th century
  Gor pl p24 (m)
        17th century
  LelD p5-6 pl (col) il (f)
        18th century
  BroW v2 fig 56 (f)
  LelD p5 il p6 (f)
  UnW pl 80 (col)
  VanH pl 8
  WisF pl 15C (f)
  Yar pl p 178 (col) (f)
        19th century
  BruK pl 125 (f)
  HaC pl p 199 (f)
  Kle p20 il
  Walk pl 19 (col) (m)
  WilC pl p255, 278
  WisF pl 21 (f)
        1800-1810
  Dav v2 fig 2283 (f)
  ViN fig 8 (m)
        1810-1820
  KerM no4 pl 7 (m)
  SitC pl 113 (f)
        1820-1830
  Brk pl 19 (f)
  SitC pl 115 (m)
  WilC pl p255 (f)
        1830-1840
  CunE pl p 112 (f)
  Dav v2 p853 fig 2439 (f)
  ViN fig 32
        1840-1850
  CunE pl p 132 (f)
  Pann v3 pl 28 (col) (f)
  WilC pl p278 (f)
        1850-1860
  Dav v2 fig 2439
  LavF p27 pl 10 (col)
  Rue fig Q (f)
  SitC pl 114, 116
  WilC pl p292 (f)
        1860-1870
  Eld pl p 16 (f)
        1880-1890
  LelD p5 il p6 (f)
  WilC pl p317 (f)
        1890-1900
  Ada v3 il p431 (f)
  ViN fig 97 (f)
        20th century
  HaC pl p 199 (f)
  LelD p230 il (f)

RIDING COSTUME—20th century—Continued

1900-1910
CunPr pl p90 (f)
Wom p20 il (f)

1910-1920
Wom p20 il (f)

1920-1930
WilC pl p377 (f)

1930-1940
LelD p5 il p6 (f)
Pic il p 140 (f)
Wom p20 il (f)

1940-1950
Kle p 196, 303 il (f)
LelD p5 il p6 (f)
Wom p20 il (f)

Arabia
BruK pl 192 (m)

England
13th century
Gor pl p24

14th century
Ab pl p4, 8, 40
BrH p46-47 pl (m)

15th century
CunA pl 16a
Norr v3 bk 1 p29-30 il (incl pat)

16th century
Norr v3 bk 2 p491, 603-04, 662 fig 714
2 pl (f)

17th century
BrH pl p97 fig 3 (col) (f)
CunA pl 16b

18th century
Bruh p60-61 pl (col)
Set il p36 (f)
SitC pl 102 (m)
TiK pl 128 fig 10 (f)
Yar p 178 pl VIII (col) (f)

France
15th century
WilF pl p40 (f)

16th century
BluL p21-23 pl 32-33, 43
Dav v2 p476 il (m)
LavR pl p89, 104, 108
Norr v3 bk 1 p244-45 pl (m); bk 2
p397 pl (m)

17th century
Dav v2 p525, 535 il
LavR pl p353 (m)
WilC pl p 166 (f)

18th century
BruK pl 114 fig 6 (col) (m)
Lel v 11 p55-56 fig 53 (f); v 12 p41-42
fig 50-51 (f)

Pann v 1 pl 9 (col) (f); v2 pl 3 (col)
(f)
WilC pl p204 (f)

Germany
16th century
Dav v 1 pl p400 (m)

Hungary
16th century
WilF pl p74 (m)

Italy
14th-16th centuries
Dav v 1 p218, 266-67, fig 609, 735-37

18th century
Dav v2 p724 il (f)

Mexico
Gor pl p237
Meri pl 5 (col) (m)
MeriT pl 2 (col) (m)
Spi pl p 10 (col)

Prussia
16th century
WilF pl p64

Rome
AirP il p48

Scotland
16th century
Norr v3 bk 2 p516 pl (col) (f)

Spain
D'Iv pl 62 (col)
Nie pl p 132 (col)

16th century
Lav pl p233 (m)
Rea p20 pl 31-32 (m)

17th century
BluE p27 pl 62
LavR pl p382 (f)

19th century
Agu pl 65 (m)

20th century
Nat v97 Ap '50 pl p425 (col) (f)

Sweden
17th century
LelD p5 il p6 (f)

RIDING HATS
17th century
WilC pl p 148 (f)

18th century
WilH p 156 pl p 164-65, 173 (f)

19th century
WilH pl p236 (f)

20th century
WilH pl p301, 312 (m)

RIF. See Morocco

RINGS
Bae   p 147-55   pl   il
LelD   p8, 25   il

Ancient
Dal   v 1   fig 505-06, 510-13   (col)
Dot   p 105, 114, 118   il
Jes   p67-69, 129-35   pl 35-36
LesA   p322-33   fig 409-29
NeE   p4   pl 11-12, 19
NeG   p4   pl 17
WlsC   p35   pl 19

10th century—date
BraF   p 130-38   pl   p93, 173-75
Dal   v2   fig 145-49, 216-19   (col)
Dav   v2   p478   il
Flow   pl 9   (col)   fig 45-46, 93-94, 117
LesA   p333-49   il
NeN   p3   pl 11
Norr   v3 bk 1   p 126, 358-59 il; bk 2
p463, 779-81   il
RogF   p84-86, 109-23   il
Yar   p91, 98, 106, 117, 124, 136, 144, 153,
158, 166, 173, 179   il

RINGS, CORONATION
Nat   v 104 S '53   pl   p325

RINGS, CURATIVE
RogF   p 113-14   il

RINGS, ECCLESIASTICAL
Bae   p 152-53   il
LesA   p333-34   fig 426
Mcca   p 117-42   pl
NorC   p 183-85   il
Norr   v3 bk 1   p 126   il
RogF   p 111-12   pl   p99

RINGS, POISON
RogF   p 122-23   il

RINGS, WEDDING
Bae   p 156-69   pl   il
Mcca   p 152-82   pl   p 180, 184

ROBES OF STATE. See Ceremonial costume; Coronation robes

ROBIN HOOD. See Fancy dress and stage
costume—Robin Hood

ROCHET
McC   p83-86   il
NorC   p 172   pl   p 162

RÖDÖN. See Sweden—Jämtland

ROEMOE. See Frisian Islands

ROMAGNA. See Italy—Emilia

ROME
This heading is used for costume of the
pre-Christian period. For modern Roman
costume see Italy
AirB   pl 8-9   (m)
BartC   p98-112   fig 36-39
BiE   p42-44   pl 41-53
Bra   p63-78   3 pl

BruK   p 10-11, 47-48   pl 17-19   (1 col)
and table 3   (pat)
Burr   p 10, 115-16, 190-91, 296   pl   p 11
Dal   v 1   p 147-201   19 pl   il (col)   (incl
pat)
Dav   v 1   p73-77, 86-88, 90   2 pl   il
Dot   p 112-14   il
Eli   p32-33, 43-44, 60   il
Eth   p 16-19   il   (m)
Gor   p9-10   pl   p 14-15
HousG2   p86-119   3 pl   (1 col)   il   (incl
pat)
KerM   no 1   pl 10-12
Kle   p280, 282   il
Lecl   pl 2   (col)   (m)
Lee   p80-81   pl
LesA   pl 16   (f)
Lis   p25-27   il   p23   (f)
Loud   pl 5   (col)
Nat   v90 N '46   p576-628   26 pl   (col)
Pic   il   p 148, 168   (f)
Pot   v 1   p33-38   pl 13-15   (col)   (incl
pat)
RueG   pl 1   (f)
TiK   p 14-15   pl 11, 35
Tru   p7-10   il
UnW   pl 13-17   (col)
VanH   pl 1
Wa   p51-62   pl   il   (incl pat)
WilC   p 18-23   3 pl
WlsC   p55-75, 146-66   9 pl   (incl pat)
WisF   pl 4   (f)
Wrig   pt2   p7-12   pl   p 17-20   (incl pat)
Yar   p21-28   3 pl
    See also Etruria; Gladiators; Togas;
Vestal virgins; also subdivision Rome
under Capes and cloaks; Charioteers;
Children; Hair, wigs, etc.; Headdress;
Military costume; Officials; Priests;
Queens and empresses; Senators; Stand-
ard bearers

1st-5th centuries
Early Christian period
BruK   p50-51   pl 26   (col)   and table 4
(pat)
Dot   p 115-16   il

RONCAL. See Spain—Navarre

ROSARIES
EvnJ   p50, 81-83   pl 34
Int   v 1   pl 20
RogF   pl   p90

ROUGH RIDERS. See Military costume—
United States—1898-1917—Rough Riders

ROUNDHEADS. See England—Charles I,
1625-1649;   England — Commonwealth,
1649-1660

ROUSSILLON. See France—Roussillon

**ROYAL CANADIAN MOUNTED PO-
LICE.** See Police—Canada

**ROYAL NAVAL COLLEGE, DART-
MOUTH.** See Naval cadets—England

RUFFS
Kle p 126 il (f)

16th century
CunS p 110-14, 167-68 pl 44, 52, 54, 60-62, 66-68, 71
DeB p 174-75 pl 176-79
Hat p299 fig 137
KelF p29-31 pl p77
LavR p 129-37, 149-72 24 pl (5 col)
LavS p31 pl 13 (m)
LelD p 184-85 pl
LesA p 193-202 pl 27, 29 il
Norr v3 bk 2 p504-05, 623-26 il (f)
Rea p8 pl 16-18, 27, 33 (2 col) (f)
Rey p 11 pl 4, 6, 9-11, 13-18, 29, 39-40, 42-47 (4 col)
ThiG pl 2-3 (f)
Tru p54-56 il
WilC pl p 101
Yar pl p 136

17th century
Kle p 164 il (f)
LelD p 184-85 pl
Rea pl 35, 43-45, 47, 53 (2 col)
Rey pl 34-35, 37, 49, 51-52, 55-56
ThiG p7-8 pl 10-11, 16, 18-19, 21, 30, 35-38, 43, 45 (2 col)
ViP v 1 pl 18
Yar pl p 144

RÜGEN ISLAND
BruK p34-35 pl 132 fig 1-6 (col)
Er p 13-15 pl (col)

RUMANIA
Brad pl p 136-39
BruK pl 163 (col)
Kle p78 il (f)
Lee p54-56 pl
TiK pl 43-44 (col)
See also subdivision Rumania under Children; Dancers; Headdress; Military costume

BY REGION OR PROVINCE
Bukovina
SitR front (col) pl p78B, 84A, 88B

Transylvania
Gri p 18-19 pl 1-3 (col)
Int v2 pl 53-54
Nat v74 N '38 p558-59, 561, 567-69, 576 il
Ret p 129-41 6 pl il

Wallachia
Gri p 18-19 pl 4 (col)

RUNSTEN. See Sweden—Öland

RUSSIA
BruK table 9 (pat)
CrO pl 33-34
Kle p314, 317 il
TiK pl 45-52, 68-73
See also Bashkirs; Carpathian Ruthenia; Circassians; Cossacks; Fancy dress and stage costume—Russian; Kalmucks; Kirghiz; Latvia; Poland; Samoyeds; Siberia; Tatars; Turkomans;
Yakuts; also subdivision Russia under Ambassadors; Barbers; Capes and cloaks; Coats and jackets; Footwear; Headdress; Military costume; Noblemen; Noblewomen; Waists

16th century
BruK pl 88 (col)
WilF pl p63 (f)

17th century
BruK pl 88 (col)
WilF pl p98, 100
See also Kings and rulers—Russia—17th century

18th-19th centuries
Brad pl p 141-43
BruK p37 pl 167-68 (col)
Dot il p 164
Lee p56-58 pl
See also Kings and rulers—Russia—18th century

BY REGION OR PROVINCE
Armenia
See Armenia

Caucasus
Brad pl p 140
BruK pl 171-73 (col)
Kle p392 il (m)
Nat v82 Jl '42 pl p 119
TiK pl 68-69, 73 (col)
See also Russia—Georgia

Estonia
See Estonia

Georgia
BruK pl 171 fig 7 pl 173 fig 10 (col)

Ukraine
Brad pl p 144
BruK pl 89 fig 15-17 (col) pl 168 fig 6-10 (col)

White Russia
BruK pl 168 fig 5 (col) (m)
TiK pl 46 fig 3-4, 6-8 (col)

RUTHENIA. See Carpathian Ruthenia; Czechoslovakia—Ruthenia

S

SABLES D'OLONNE. See France—Poitou

SABOTS
Kle p 177 il
LelD p 167, 368 il
Pic il p 130

SAC INDIANS. See Indians of North America—Sauk Indians

SACK SISTERS. See Sisters of Penance of Christ

SAILORS
16th century
Dav　v 1　p421 il
Brittany
Lee　p20-21　pl
England
449-1066
Carm　p 1-2　pl
15th-16th centuries
Carm　p3-6　pl
Norr　v3 bk 1　p303-05 il; bk 2　p704-07 il
18th century
AirB　il　p53
Lee　p 109-10　pl
19th century
BruK　pl 123 fig 8 (col)
QuV　fig 61, 90
Spain
16th century
Norr　v3 bk 1　p304 il
United States
18th century
Davi　v 1　il　p315
Lee　p 109-10　pl
VanH　pl 14 fig 2
19th century
VanH　pl 14 fig 8, 10, 16, 20
20th century
VanH　pl 14 fig 23

ST AUGUSTINE, HERMITS OF. See Augustinians

ST BERNARD HOSPICE, MONKS OF. See Augustinian canons

ST CATHERINE OF MOUNT SINAI, KNIGHTS OF
Doy　pl 147 (col)

ST CHARITON MONKS
Doy　pl 1 (col)

ST ESPRIT, ORDRE DU. See Holy Ghost, Order of the

ST GALL. See Switzerland—St Gall

ST HILARY NUNS
Doy　pl 79 (col)

ST JAMES OF THE SWORD, ORDER OF
Doy　pl 150 (col)
Norr　v3 bk 2　p676 fig 769

ST JOHN OF JERUSALEM, KNIGHTS OF THE ORDER OF. See Malta, Knights of

ST PAUL'S CATHEDRAL CHOIR SCHOOL, LONDON
Cla　p31　pl　p30

ST SABAS MONKS
Doy　pl 52 (col)

ST STEPHEN, ORDER OF
Doy　pl 160 (col)

ST VINCENT DE PAUL, ORDER OF
LelD　il　p 124

SAINTONGE. See France—Saintonge and Angoumois

SALAMANCA. See Spain—León

SALERNO. See Italy—Campania

SALESIAN SISTERS. See Visitation nuns

SALISH INDIANS. See Indians of North America—Salish Indians

SALLING. See Denmark—Jutland

SALVADOR
Nat　v86 N '44　pl　p593, 599 (col) (f)
Spi　p45 il (f)

SALZBURG. See Austria—Salzburg

SALZKAMMERGUT. See Austria—Salzkammergut

SAMARKAND. See Turkestan

SAMOA. See Dancers—Samoa; Military costume—Samoa

SAMOYEDS
TiK　pl 106 (col)

SAMURAI
TiK　pl 99 fig 4 (col)

SAN BLAS INDIANS
Nat　v79 F '41　p217　pl 209-16 (6 col); v80 N '41　pl　p618 (col) (f)

SANDWICH ISLANDS. See Hawaiian Islands

SANS-CULOTTES. See France—18th century—Assemblies to Directory, 1789-1795 (m)

SANTANDER. See Spain—Castile, Old

SANTIAGO. See Spain—Galicia

SARAGOSSA. See Spain—Aragon

SARAH (BIBLICAL CHARACTER). See Biblical costume—Sarah

SARDINIA
Ar　p 11-22　pl　p 12, 16, 20, 28, 32, 64, 80, 112 (col); pl I-VII (2 col) il
Brad　pl　p97-98
BruK　pl 158 fig 12-16　pl 159 fig 16-17 (col)
Carta　p5-47　39 pl (3 col) il
Gal　p 16-17　pl 4 (col)
See also Military costume—Sardinia

SARIS
Am p90-94 il
CrP pl 9 (f)
Kle p318 il (f)
Pic il p 124
TiK pl 84 fig 3-9

SARONGS
Pic il p 124

SASHES, ECCLESIASTICAL
McC p76-78 il

SAUK INDIANS. See Indians of North America—Sauk Indians

SAVOIE. See France—Savoie

SAXE-ALTENBURG. See Germany—Saxe-Altenburg

SCALP DANCE. See Dancers—Indians of North America—Scalp dance

SCANDINAVIA. See Denmark; Norway; Sweden

SCARABS
NeE pl 5, 11
RogF p 16-17 il

SCARVES
LelD p 156-57 pl

Chios
Arg pl 22, 30

SCEPTRES
LelD p377 il

Cyprus
RogF pl p26

England
Nat v 104 S '53 pl p325 (col)

Mexico, Ancient
DuS pl 21a (col)

SCHAFFHAUSEN. See Switzerland—Schaffhausen

SCHAUMBURG-LIPPE. See Germany—Schaumburg-Lippe; Headdress—Schaumburg-Lippe; Wedding costume—Schaumburg-Lippe

SCHEVENINGEN. See Netherlands—South Holland

SCHLESWIG-HOLSTEIN. See Germany—Schleswig-Holstein

SCHOKLAND. See Netherlands—Schokland

SCHOOLBOYS—ENGLAND. See names of individual public shcools, e.g. Eton college students, Westminster school students

SCHWALM. See Germany—Hesse

SCHWYZ. See Switzerland—Schwyz

SCOTCH REEL. See Dancers—Scotland—Reel

SCOTLAND
May pl p 16 (m)
See also Fancy dress and stage costume—Scottish; also subdivision Scotland under Bagpipers; Children; Court dress; Dancers; Footwear; Headdress; Military costume; Noblemen; Shepherds

To 1300
Dot p 124-25, 127-28 il
LelD il p235 (m)
VanH pl 2
See also Kings and rulers—Scotland—13th century

14th century
See Kings and rulers—Scotland—14th century

15th-17th centuries
BruK pl 147 fig 1-9 (col) (m)
Mccl p3-25 8 pl (m)
Norr v3 bk 2 p513 il (f)
See also Kings and rulers—Scotland—15th-16th centuries; Queens and empresses—Scotland—15th century; Queens and empresses—Scotland—16th century

18th century—date
AirH il p6 (m)
Brad pl p 148 (f)
BruK pl 147 fig 10-14 (col)
Dav v2 p822 il (m)
Kle p206 il (m)
Lee p59-61 pl
Lel v 11 pl 27 (col); v 12 pl 18 (m)
LelD p235 il; p320 il (m)
Mccl p25-62 pl 5-8, 13-19
Nat v71 My '37 pl p602 (col); v 102 Jl '52 pl p93-95, 97 (col) (m)
Trev v3 fig 128-29

Clans and tartans
Only figures wearing their clan tartans, not the tartans as such, have been indexed
Mccl p63-79 3 pl

Buchanan
Eyr v 1 pl p8 (col) (m)

Cameron
Eyr v 1 pl p 18 (col) (m)
Log p 184-85 pl p 182 (col) (m)
Nat v89 My '46 pl p560 (col) (m)

Cameron of Lochiel
ColH p28 pl 17 (col) (m)

Campbell of Argyle
Eyr v 1 pl p26 (col) (m)
Log p225-26 pl p222 (col) (m)

Campbell of Breadalbane
Eyr v 1 pl p36 (col) (m)
Log p56, 58 pl p54 (col) (m)

Chisholm
Eyr v 1 pl p44 (col) (m)
Log p 121-22 pl p 118 (col) (m)

SCOTLAND—Clans and tartans—*Continued*

Colquhoun

ColH p27 pl 13 (m)
Eyr v 1 pl p52 (col) (m)
Log p 153 pl p 150 (col) (m)

Comyn (Cumming)

Eyr v 1 pl p58 (col) (m)
Log p 189 pl p 187 (col) (m)

Davidson

Eyr v 1 pl p66 (col) (m)
Log p 133-34 pl p 131 (col) (m)

Drummond

Eyr v 1 pl p74 (col) (m)
Log p73 pl p70 (col) (m)

Duncan (Robertson)

Eyr v 1 pl p84 (col) (m)

Farquharson

Eyr v 1 pl p98 (col) (m)
Log p48 pl p46 (col) (m)

Fergus

Eyr v 1 pl p 106 (col) (m)

Ferguson

ColH p31 pl 24 (col) (m)
Log p 135-37 pl p 134 (col) (m)

Forbes

ColH p30 pl 23 (col) (m)
Eyr v 1 pl p 112 (col) (m)
Log p 144-45 pl p 142 (col) (m)

Fraser

Eyr v 1 pl p 112 (col) (m)
Log p77 pl p75 (col) (m)

Gordon

ColH p23 pl 5 (col) (m)
Log p85 pl p83 (col) (m)
Nat v 104 S '53 pl p313 (col)

Graham (Græme)

Eyr v 1 pl p 142 (col) (m)
Log p230 pl 233-34 (col) (m)

Grant

Eyr v 1 pl p 152 (col) (m)
Log p 128-29 pl p 126 (m)

Grant of Glenmoriston

ColH p23 pl 4 (col) (m)
Eyr v 1 pl p 160 (col) (m)
Log p 165 pl p 163 (col) (m)

Gunn

Eyr v 1 pl p 172 (col) (m)
Log p65 pl p62 (col) (m)

Kennedy

Log p261 pl p259 (col) (m)

Lamont

ColH p28 pl 16 (col) (f)
Eyr v 1 pl p 178 (col) (f)
Log p200-01 pl p 198 (col) (f)

Logan

Eyr v 1 pl p200 (col) (m)
Log p329 pl p322 (col) (m)

MacAllaster (MacAlister)

ColH pl 20 (col) (m)
Eyr v 1 pl p204 (col) (m)
Log p 180-81 pl p 179 (col) (m)

MacArthur

Eyr v 1 pl p208 (col) (m)
Log p 172 pl p 171 (col) (m)

MacAulay

Eyr v 1 pl p214 (col) (m)
Log p304 pl p302 (col) (m)

MacBean (MacBain, MacVean)

Eyr v 1 pl p218 (col) (m)
Log p274 pl p270 (col) (m)

MacColl

Log p281 pl p278 (col) (m)

MacCruimin

Eyr v 1 pl p224 (col) (m)
Log p249 pl p246 (col) (m)

MacDonald of Clan Ranald

ColH p22 pl 2 (col) (m)
Eyr v 1 pl p244 (col) (m)
Log p81-82 pl p78 (col) (m)

MacDonald of Glenco

Eyr v2 pl p252 (col) (m)
Log p217-18 pl p214 (col) (m)

MacDonald of Keppoch

Eyr v2 pl p261 (col) (m)
Log p266 pl p262 (col) (m)

MacDonald of the Isles

Eyr v 1 pl p233 (col) (m)
Log p209-10 pl p206 (col) (m)

MacDonell of Glengarry

Eyr v2 pl p268 (col) (m)
Log p40-41 pl p38 (col) (m)

MacDougall

Eyr v2 pl p278 (col) (m)
Log p 117 pl p 115 (col) (m)

MacDuff (Duff)

Eyr v2 pl p284 (col) (m)
Log p61-62 pl p59 (col) (m)

MacFarlane

Eyr v 1 pl p90 (col) (m)
Log p 160-61 pl p 158 (col) (m)

MacGillivray

ColH p23 pl 3 (col) (m)
Eyr v2 pl p290 (col) (m)
Log p37 pl p34 (col) (m)

MacGregor

Eyr v 1 pl p 166 (col) (m)
Log p 193 pl p 190 (col) (m)

MacInnes (MacInnis)

Eyr v2 pl p296 (col) (m)
Log p228 pl p227 (col) (m)

SCOTLAND—Clans and tartans—*Continued*

MacIntosh (Mackintosh)
Eyr v2 pl p334 (col) (m)

MacIntyre (MacIntire)
Eyr v2 pl p298 (col) (m)
Log p285 pl p283 (col) (m)

MacIvor
Eyr v2 pl p302 (col) (m)
Log p245-46 pl p243 (col) (m)

Mackay
ColH p30 pl 21 (col) (m)
Eyr v2 pl p306 (col) (m)
Log p 101-02 pl p99 (col) (m)

Mackenzie
Eyr v2 pl p314 (col) (m)
Log p97-98 pl p94 (col) (m)

Mackinnon
Eyr v2 pl p328 (col) (m)
Log p 178 pl p 174 (col) (m)

MacLachlan
Eyr v2 pl p346 (col) (m)
Log p 141-42 pl p 139 (col) (m)

MacLaren (MacLaurin)
Eyr v2 pl p352 (col) (m)
Log p310-11 pl p305 (col) (m)

MacLean
Eyr v2 pl p358 (col) (m)
Log p92-93 pl p91 (col) (m)

MacLennan
Eyr v2 pl p364 (col) (m)
Log p293 pl p291 (col) (m)

MacLeod
Eyr v2 pl p368 (col) (m)
Log p288, 290 pl p286 (col) (m)

Macmillan
Eyr v2 pl p378 (col) (m)
Log p277-78 pl p275 (col) (m)

MacNab
Eyr v2 pl p382, 384 (1 col) (m)
Log p 149-50 pl p 147 (col) (m)

MacNaughton (MacNachtan)
Eyr v2 pl p388 (col) (m)
Log p45-46 pl p43 (col) (m)

MacNeill of Barra
ColH p26 pl 11 (col) (m)
Log p 109-10 pl p 107 (col) (m)

MacNiel
Eyr v2 pl p398 (col) (m)

MacPhee (Macfie)
Eyr v2 pl p402 (col) (m)
Log p221 pl p219 (col) (m)

Macpherson
ColH p27 pl 14 (col) (m)
Eyr v2 pl p406 (col) (m)
Log p319-20 pl p312 (col) (m)

MacQuarie
Eyr v2 pl p414 (col) (m)
Log p 156-57 pl p 155 (col) (m)

MacRae
Eyr v2 pl p420 (col) (m)
Log p253 pl p251 (col) (m)

Matheson
ColH p25 pl 10 (col) (f)
Eyr v2 pl p426 (col) (f)
Log p 125-26 pl p 123 (f)

Menzie
ColH p29 pl 19 (col) (m)
Eyr v2 pl p432 (col) (m)
Log p53-54 pl p51 (col) (m)

Munro
Eyr v2 pl p438 (col) (m)
Log p269-70 pl p267 (col) (m)

Murray
Eyr v2 pl p444 (col) (m)
Log p 168, 170 pl p 166 (col) (m)

Nicolson (Macnicol)
Eyr v2 pl p394 (col) (f)
Log p 197-98 pl p 195 (col) (f)

Ogilvie
ColH p27 pl 15 (col) (m)
Eyr v2 pl p454 (col) (m)
Log p213 pl p211 (col) (m)

Robertson
ColH p30 pl 22 (col) (m)
Log p69 pl p67 (col) (m)

Rose
ColH p24-25 pl 8 (col) (m)
Eyr v2 pl p460 (col) (m)
Log p240-41 (col) (m)

Ross
Eyr v2 pl p466 (col) (m)
Log p 105 pl p 102 (col) (m)

Shaw
Eyr v2 pl p472 (col) (m)
Log p301-02 pl p299 (col) (m)

Sinclair
ColH p26 pl 12 (col) (f)
Eyr v2 pl p478, 484 (1 col)
Log p88-89 pl p86 (col) (f)

Skene
ColH p24 pl 7 (col) (m)
Eyr v2 pl p488 (col) (m)
Log p237-38 pl p235 (col) (m)

Stewart (Royal)
ColH p22 pl 1 (col) (m)
Eyr v2 pl p492 (col) (m)
Log p337-39 pl p331 (col) (m)

Sutherland
Eyr v2 pl p498 (col) (m)
Log p258 pl p254 (col) (m)

Urquhart
Eyr v2 pl p508 (col) (f)
Log p205 pl p203 (col) (f)

SCOUTS. See Pioneers and scouts

SCRIBES
Egypt, Ancient
Hous2 pl 1 (col) fig 11
Nat v80 O '41 pl p451 (col)
Wrig pt3 p 14 pl p27

SCYTHIA
Bra p41 pl 5
BruK p6-7, 45 pl 10
Burr p6, 112, 186 pl p7
Dav v 1 pl p71

SEAFORTH HIGHLANDERS (REGI-MENT)
BarH pl 14, 18 (col) (pte)

SEAMEN. See Sailors

SECRETARIES. See Office workers

SEDAN CHAIR BEARERS. See Chair bearers

SEGOVIA. See Spain—Castile, Old

SEMINARIANS. See Theological students

SEMINOLE INDIANS. See Indians of North America—Seminole Indians

SENATORS
France
19th century
BluN pl p214
Rome
Wa pl p62
WilC pl p21
WilFo p32 pl p37
Venice
16th century
LelD p380 il

SENEGAL
BruK pl 190 fig 1, 5 (col)
GaU pl 6-7, 11 (col) (m)

SEPOYS
AirB il p53
AirO il p25 (pte)

SERAPES
Brad pl p 117, 119 (1 col)
KaM pl 2, 4 (col)
Meri pl 1 (col)
MeriT pl 2 (col)
See also Mexico

SERBIA. See Yugoslavia—Serbia; Dancers —Serbia; Military costume—Serbia

SERVANTS
See also Coachmen; Footmen; Grooms; Livery; Nursemaids; Pages; Porters; Slaves
18th century
Wa p237 fig 190D (m)

19th century
Jen p20 il pl p29 (f)
Egypt, Ancient
Dav v 1 p26 pl
Gen v 1 fig 94
Hous2 p58 fig 64 (f)
England
14th century
Ab pl p 134 (m)
HousM p 120-21 fig 217, 224 (m)
16th-17th centuries
AirT il p58
Norr v3 bk 1 p309-10 il (f)
18th century
SitC pl 26 (f)
19th century
QuV fig 41, 54-56
Trev v4 fig 103, 122
France
17th-18th centuries
Dav v2 p545, 671 il (f)
Persia, Ancient
TiK pl 9 fig 16 (f)
United States
18th century
McP pl p8 (col) (m)
VanH pl 7
Venice
18th century
Mora pl 99-101 (m)

SERVANTS OF MARY, ORDER OF. See Servite nuns

SERVIA. See Yugoslavia—Serbia

SERVITE NUNS
Doy pl 102 (col)

SERVITES
Doy pl 47-48 (col)
HousM p39 fig 51

SETESDAL. See Norway—Setesdal

SEVENUM. See Netherlands—Limburg

SEVILLE. See Spain—Andalusia

SHAKERS
But pl p 125
Chr p20 pl (col)

SHAKESPEARIAN COSTUMES
Bianca
Wel pl p29
Celia
Wel pl p30
Desdemona
Wel pl p30
Gratiano
Wel pl p30

SHAKESPEARIAN COSTUMES—*Con-*
tinued

Hamlet
KerM no5 pl 5
KerR pl 10
QuV fig 111
Wel pl p31

Jessica
Wel pl p29

Juliet
KerM no5 pl 5
KerR pl 10
Wel pl p30

Justice Shallow
DeB pl p 127

Katharina
Wel pl p29

Lady Macbeth
KerM no5 pl 5
KerR pl 10
Lee p83-84 pl

Macbeth
Wel pl p31

Malvolio
Wel pl p30

Othello
Wel pl p30

Pease Blossom
Wel pl p30

Petruchio
DeB pl p 126
Wel pl p29

Portia
Wel pl p29

Puck
Dab pl 7
Wel pl p31

Romeo
KerM no5 pl 5
KerR pl 10
Ving pl 36
Wel pl p30

Shylock
Wel pl p29

Titania
Wel pl p31

Viola
Wel pl p31

SHAMANS
BruK pl 175 fig 17 (col)
Too fig 3-4
See also Medicine men

SHAWL PINS
Peru, Ancient
Zim p22 pl

SHAWLS
Kle p204-05 il
LelD p83 il
LesA p224-36 3 pl il

Assyria and Babylonia
WisF pl 2

Netherlands
Hij pl 58

Peru, Ancient
Zim p 12 pl (m)

Spain
Agu pl D, 44-45 (1 col)
AnS p228-31 fig 276-82
Sub fig 363
Traj pl 9 (col)

SHAWNEE INDIANS. See Indians of
North America—Shawnee Indians

SHEIKS
KerM no2 pl 11
Nat v69 Ja '36 pl p23 (col); v71 Ja
'37 p71, 79 il; v82 S '42 pl p384

SHEPHERDESSES
England
17th century
Trev v2 p97 il

France
15th century
HousM p 183 fig 317

India
Ind pl p81 (col)

Peru
TooP pl 21

Spain
Int v2 pl 9
OrT pl 32, 37

SHEPHERDS
Bulgaria
Vel pl 51

Byzantine empire
HousG2 p 128-29 il

England
Ancient
AirP il p 13

13th century
HousM fig 86-87

France
12th-13th centuries
Dav v 1 p 169 il
EvjD p8-9 pl 8

15th century
HousM p 170-71 fig 296

19th century
GiR pl 35, 43 (col)

SHEPHERDS—*Continued*

Greece, Ancient

WilF pl p 10

Hungary

Lep pl 12 (col)
Palo pl 1, 5 (col) (m)

Madagascar

Nat v81 Je '42 pl p809

Palestine, Ancient

KerM no2 pl 9

Palestine, Modern

Wrig pt 1 pl p26 (incl pat)

Poland

Stry pl 16 (col)

Russia

WilF pl p 154

Scotland

Log p46 pl p43 (col)

Spain

AnS p22-30 fig 22-32
Int v2 p28-29 pl 8

SHERIF. See Mohammedan officials

SHINTO PRIESTS
BruK pl 186 fig 1 (col)
Haa pl 63-64, 78
MusE pl 39 (col)
Nat v96 Jl '49 pl p59

SHIRTS
Pic p 128-29 il (m)

15th century

CunU p23-25 fig 1 (m)
Norr v3 bk 1 p21-22 il (m)

16th century

CunU p36-41 fig 11-13 (m)
Lint p213 pl 14 (m)

17th century

CunU p56-60 fig 21-23, 26 (m)
ViP v 1 pl 20 (m)
Wa p 188, 197-98 fig 169 (incl pat) (m)

18th century

CunU p73-78 fig 29-30, 32-34, 45 (m)
Gor pl p 118 (m)
Lel v 11 p31-32 fig 30

19th century
1800-1820

CunU p99-105 fig 45 (m)

1820-1840

CunU p 123-27 fig 54 (m)

1840-1850

Bart p72-73 pl (pat) (m)

1850-1860

CunU p 138-42, 157-61 fig 62-64 (m)

1880-1890

CunU fig 81-83 (m)

20th century

CunU p204-06 fig 90-91 (m)
Kle p275-76 il (m)

Carpathian Ruthenia

Mak pl 53, 83 (m)

Chios

Arg pl 5, 21 (col)

Hungary

Hol p9-10 pl 11 (m)

Indians of Mexico

CorA p26-31 pl il (m)

Indians of North America

MasB p54-55 il (incl pat) (m)

Peru

Zim p 17-18 pl

Spain

AnS p70, 95, 210 fig 77, 110, 210-11 (m)

SHIRTS, CHILDREN'S
Chios

Arg pl 5, 21 (2 col)

SHOE BUCKLES
EvnJ p 179 pl 153
Lel v 11 fig 33; v 12 p 18-19 fig 14
WilFo p 107 pl p 114-15, 128, 130, 147

SHOE ROSETTES
LelD p366 il
WilC pl p 144, 148, 154

SHOEMAKERS
China

Nat v71 Ap '37 p493 il

Egypt, Ancient

LesA fig 252
WilFo p3 pl 6-7

Egypt, Modern

Nat v77 Ap '40 pl p465

England
Early to 1066

AirP il p45

16th century

AirT il p30

18th century

Trev v3 fig 52

19th century

Set pl p39

France
17th century

Dav v2 p558 il

18th century

Dav v2 p672 il

Germany
16th century

Jae pl 18

SHOEMAKERS—*Continued*
  Scandinavia
  Jae pl 35, 44

SHOES. See Footwear

SHOGUNS
  WilFo pl p54

SHONEN. See Sweden—Shonen

SHOOTING COSTUME. See Hunting
  costume

SHOPKEEPERS. See Merchants

SIAM
  Brad pl p 149-50 (f)
  BruK pl 181 fig 4-6 (col)
  Pot v2 p51-53 pl (col)
  RueO pl 10-11
    See also subdivision Siam under Bal-
  let costume; Dancers; Kings and rulers

SIBERIA
  Brad pl p 147
  Nat v86 D '44 pl p655 (col) (f)
  TiK pl 102-06 (col)
    See also Buriats; Kalmucks; Kirghiz;
  Koryaks; Samoyeds; Tatars; Tunguses;
  Yakuts

SICILY
  Brad pl p99 (f)

SIEBENBURG. See Rumania—Transylvania

SIENA. See Italy—Tuscany

SIKHS
  AirO il p28
  Dal v 1 p379-81 fig 692-95 (col)
  Nat v92 N '47 il p608

SIKSIKA INDIANS. See Indians of
  North America—Siksika Indians

SILESIA. See Germany—Silesia

SILVESTRINES See Sylvestrines

SIMAR
  McC p58-60 il
    See also Cassock

SIOUX INDIANS. See Indians of North
  America—Dakota Indians

SISTERS OF DIVINE PROVIDENCE
  MusE pl 30 (col)

SISTERS OF IMMACULATE HEART
  OF MARY
  MusE pl 33 (col)

SISTERS OF MERCY
  MusE pl 31 (col)

SISTERS OF PENANCE OF CHRIST
  Doy pl 97 (col)

SISTERS OF PENANCE OF ST MARY
  MAGDALENA
  Doy pl 103-04 (col)

SISTERS OF ST FRANCIS
  MusE pl 22 (col)

SISTERS OF ST JOSEPH
  MusE pl 27 (col)

SISTERS OF THE CONGREGATION
  OF NOTRE DAME
  Doy pl 96 (col)

SISTERS OF THE GOOD SHEPHERD
  MusE pl 26 (col)

SJAELLAND. See Denmark—Zealand

SKÅNE. See Sweden—Skåne

SKATES
  17th century
  WilFo p 111-12 pl p 116
  19th century
  LelD il p305 fig 6-7

SKATING COSTUME
  19th century
  CunE il p266 (f)
  Davi v2 il p43
  Gor pl p202 (f)
  Kou pl 23
  LavT pl p86
  LavT2 p71 pl p78
  MooC p70 (f)
  Part p 151 il
  WilF pl p 142
  20th century
  AlF pl p79 (f)
  Jen p 124 il (f)
  LavT p229-31 pl (f)
  LavT2 pl p 188 (f)
  Pic il p 140 (f)
  RogW pl p 19
  Rud pl p36 (f)
  Wom p22 il (f)

SKEDEVI. See Sweden—Östergötland

SKIING COSTUME
  Nat v70 N '36 pl p648, 651 (col)
  WilC pl p377 (f)
  WilF pl p 178 (m)
  Wom p21 il (f)

SKIIS
  Lapland
  WilFo p93 pl p98

SKIRTS
  EvnR p66-72 2 pl (incl pat)
  Hea p44-47 2 pl (incl pat)
  Pic p 134-35 il
  15th-16th centuries
  BroH p70 fig 54-55
  Norr v3 bk 1 p33-37, 167-69, 184-85
  pl p34, 166 (1 col) fig 39-40, 218-19;
  bk 2 p429 fig 519 (pat)
  Wa p 132, 149 fig 134, 145, 150 (incl
  pat)

SKIRTS—*Continued*
17th century
Wa p 194, 201 fig 172, 180 (incl pat)
18th century
Dav v2 pl p769
Wa   p214-16, 224-25, 230 fig 190C, 195B
19th century
1860-1870
CunE p234-35 il
Wa p287 fig 233, 239
1870-1880
Bra pl 44
1880-1890
Wa p312 fig 257 il
1890-1900
Bra p330-32 pl 46-47
CunE pl p382
HaC p81 pl p84b
Wa p322 fig 254
WisF pl 22-23
20th century
Rud pl p 163
1900-1910
CunPr p27-28, 33 pl p32, 49
HaC pl p 104-05
Wa p338-41 fig 263, 265
1910-1920
Bra p346 pl 49-50
Wa   p347-48 fig 267, 269, 271-72
WisF pl 24-26
1920-1930
Bra p364-65 pl 41
Wa p353-54 fig 275, 278
Egypt, Ancient
Bra pl 2, 4
Hous2 p84-88 pl il (incl pat)
Indians of Mexico
CorA p48-51 il
Indians of North America
Hun pl p27
Peru, Ancient
Zim p 19 pl (m)
Savage and primitive races
Bra pl 1
Spain
AnS p51, 138-45, 195-200, 202-03, 207-09, 234-36, 241, 279-81, 287-88, 299-300 fig 56, 125, 170-73, 235-38, 242, 250-51, 283, 290, 334-36, 338, 344-47, 365-66

SKIRTS, GRASS
Nat v69 Ap '36 pl p484, 486

SLAVES
Egypt, Ancient
BruK pl 3 (col)
Gor pl p5
RueG pl 20 (m)

Greece, Ancient
Gor pl p5 (f)

SLAVONIA. See Yugoslavia—Croatia and Slavonia

SLAVONIAN MONKS
Doy pl 12 (col)

SLEEVES
EvnR p52-64 4 pl il (incl pat) (f)
Kle p22-23 pl (f)
LelD p250-59 8 pl il
Pic p 135-37 il
9th-10th centuries
CunM p 16-17 pl
12th century
BrH p24-29 3 pl (col)
EvjD p6-7 pl 3, 7, 10
WisF pl 6 (f)
13th century
BrH p30-35 3 pl (col)
EvjD p 15 pl 12-15
14th century
BrH p34-49 8 pl
BroW v 1 p52 fig 18, 20 (f)
LelD pl p251 fig 1-2 (m)
WisF pl 8 (f)
15th century
BrH p50-73 12 pl
BroH p50-53 fig 39-41
Dav v 1 fig 674-78
LelD p248 pl p251 il
Norr v3 bk 1 p21-23, 59-60 (incl pat)
Wa p 132 fig 133 (incl pat) (f)
16th century
BrH p72-85 7 pl
BroH p72 fig 50-51, 54-55
BroW v 1 p 112, 134 fig 64-65, 76, 83
CunS p 19-21, 55, 59, 61, 64, 91-93, 97-101, 152-59, 165 pl 1-8, 17-18, 21-23, 56-65
DeB p 169-70 pl p 171-72, 177
Dot p 146-47 il (f)
Gor pl p58
LelD p248 il; pl p252; p259 il
Lint p 171-76 pl 6 (f)
Norr v3 bk 1 p31, 203-06, 267-68 il (incl pat); bk 2 p580-81, 585, 627-28, 687, 711 il (f)
Wa p 149-50 fig 142, 145-46, 150 (incl pat)
WisF pl 10-11 (f)
Yar p 115 pl p 114
17th century
BrH p86-107 il pl
Dal v2 fig 481-84 (col) (incl pat) (f)
Dav v2 fig 1695 (f)
Gor pl p70, 92, 94
LelD pl p253-54
Lint p 171-76 pl 3 (f)
Roj pl p 12-13, 16, 20-21, 24-25, 30-31, 34-35, 38, 42 (pat)

SLEEVES—*Continued*

18th century
BrH p 106-25 10 pl
Gor pl p 105 (f)
LelD pl p254-56
WisF pl 18 (f)

19th century
1810-1820
LelD pl p256 fig 3 (f)

1820-1830
LelD pl p256 fig 4 (f)

1830-1840
Kle p 150-51 il (m)
LelD pl p256 fig 5-9 (f)

1840-1850
Bra pl 40, 43 (f)
LelD pl p256 fig 10 (f)

1850-1860
Bra pl 41 (f)
CunE il p 183-84, 190 (f)
Gor pl p 150
LelD pl p256 fig 11 (f)

1860-1870
LelD pl p257 fig 1-6 (f)
Wa p286 fig 237, 239 (incl pat) (f)

1870-1880
CunE il p267 (f)
LelD pl p257 fig 7-10 (f)

1880-1890
Bra pl 44 (f)

1890-1900
Bart p88-89 pl (pat) (f)
Bra p330 pl 47 (f)
CunE pl p368 (f)
HaC p82 pl p84b (f)
LelD pl p258 fig 1-5 (f)
Wa p320-22 fig 254, 257
WisF pl 22-23 (f)

20th century
1900-1910
Bra p345 pl 48-50 (f)
CunPr p33 pl p37 (f)
LelD pl p258 fig 6-8 (f)
Rud pl p 140 (f)

SLIPPERS. See Footwear

SLIPS. See Petticoats and slips

SLOVAKIA. See Czechoslovakia—Slovakia

SMÄLAND. See Sweden—Smäland

SMOCKS
EvnR p80-82 pl il (incl pat) (f)
Kle p212 il (m)

SMOKING UTENSILS. See Pipes and smoking utensils

SNOWSHOES
Ada v 1 il p65

Indians of North America
Lyf p42-43 fig 20-21
Trai p28 il
WilFo p 112 pl p 116

Lapland
WilFo p93 pl p98

SNUFF BOXES
Dav v2 pl p702
RogF pl p 170

SOCKS. See Hose

SÖDERMANLAND. See Sweden—Södermanland

SOFIA. See Bulgaria

SOLDIERS. See Military costume

SOLOMON (BIBLICAL CHARACTER). See Biblical costume—Solomon

SOLOMON ISLANDS. See Headdress—Solomon Islands

SOLOTHURN. See Switzerland—Solothurn

SOMALILAND
GaU pl 21 (col) (f)

SOMBREROS
Kle p347 il
Pic il p73
Spi il p60, 77
Trai p50 il

SONORA. See Mexico—Sonora

SORIA. See Spain—Castile, Old

SOROE. See Denmark—Zealand

SORUNDA. See Sweden—Södermanland

SOUTH AMERICA See Argentine Republic; Brazil; Chile; Colombia; Ecuador; Surinam; Venezuela

SOUTH HOLLAND. See Netherlands—South Holland

SPAHIS
BluN pl p207
BruK pl 187 fig 16 (col)
LelD p390 il
TiK pl 34 fig 1-3 (col)

SPAIN
TiK pl 67 (col)
See also Fancy dress and stage costume—Spanish; also subdivision Spain under Bullfighters; Capes and cloaks; Ceremonial costume; Children; Coats and jackets; Court dress; Dancers; Festival costume; Footwear; Gipsies; Hair, wigs, etc.; Headdress; Herdsmen; Mantillas; Military costume; Moors; Musicians; Noblemen; Noblewomen; Police; Riding costume; Shawls; Shepherds

SPAIN—*Continued*

To 1100

Dal   v 1 p257-77   5 pl il (col)
Dav   v 1 p 115-17 il
Dot   p 120-21 il

12th century

Dav   v 1 p 146-50   2 pl il
Dot   p 129 il (f)
   See also Kings and rulers—Spain—
12th century

13th century

BruK   pl 62 fig 1-2 (m)
Dav   v 1   p 179-84   3 pl il
WilC   pl   p 106

14th century

BruK   pl 62 fig 3-15
Dav   v 1 p237-41   3 pl
TiK   pl 120 fig 2-5 (col)

15th century

BroW   v 1   pl   p58 (col)
BruK   pl 62, 72 (col)
Dal   v2   p 165-79 fig 292-300 (col)
Dav   v 1   p360-66   4 pl   il
Dot   p 142-43   il
Gor   pl   p32
TiK   pl 120 fig 7, 10-11 (col) (m)
WilC   pl   p 106 (m)
WilF   pl   p41 (f)
   See also Kings and rulers—Spain—15th
century; Queens and empresses—Spain
—15th century

16th century

Bart   p26-31   3 pl (pat) fig 6-8
BroW   v 1   pl   p 136 (col)
Bruh   p34-36   pl (col)
BruK   p21-23   pl 74, 86 fig 1-10 (col)
CrO   pl 31
Dav   v 1   p455-68   2 pl   il (incl pat);
    v2   p503   il (m)
Dot   p 150   il (f)
Gor   pl   p54, 57
KelF   pl   p 17, 32
KerM   no5   pl 4
KerR   pl 4
Kle   p 179, 347-49   il
LavR   p 191-200, 215-34   19 pl (4 col)
Lecl   pl 6-7 (col)
Norr   v3 bk 1   p202-07   il (f); bk 2
    p402, 404-14, 429-30, 572-83, 673-85
    6 pl (1 col) fig 494, 521, 678 (incl pat)
Rea   p5-20   pl 1-33 (4 col)
TiK   pl 124 fig 9, 13 (incl pat) (col) (f)
WilC   p 108-11   pl   p 106, 112-13
WilF   pl   p54, 61, 63, 66, 68
   See also Kings and rulers—Spain—16th
century; Queens and empresses—Spain
—16th century

17th century

BruK   p21-23   pl 86-87 (1 col)
Dal   v 2   p299-316   il (col)
Dav   v2   p638-39, 643-51   il (incl pat)
Gor   pl   p81 (f)
LavR   pl   p235-54 (4 col)

LelD   p30   pl   p354 fig 4 (f)
Lib   pl   p36 (f)
Nat   v 101 Ja '52   pl   p86 (col) (f)
Pic   il   p 132 (f)
Rea   p21-26   pl 34-62 (4 col)
TiK   pl 128 (col) (f)
Wa   pl 187 (f)
WilC   p 115-17   pl
   See also Kings and rulers—Spain—17th
century; Queens and empresses—Spain
—17th century

18th century—date

Agu   pl A-G (col)   pl 1-124
BruK   pl 152-55 (3 col)
Dav   v2   p732-35, 809, 868   il
Dot   il   p 164
Gor   pl   p 126
Int   v2   p22-41, 55-60   pl 3-17
Kle   p57   il (m)
Lel   v 12   pl 22, 25-28 (2 col)
NeEu   pl 2 (m)
Sub   p 103-15   pl   p439-55
   See also Kings and rulers—Spain—18th
century; Queens and empresses—Spain
18th century

BY REGION OR PROVINCE

Andalusia

Agu   pl 1, 22-23, 26, 35, 43, 45, 65, **114**
Arm   v 1   p 14   pl 1, 3 (col)
Brad   pl   p 152 (f)
BruK   pl 154 (col)
D'Iv   p 17-19   pl 58-72 (col)
GaE   pl 1, 18-20 (col)
Gom   p 105-14   pl   p48, 60, 106 (1 col)
Int   v2   pl 13
LavR   pl   p230 (f)
Nie   pl   p206, 209 (1 col)
OrT   p30   pl 216-38
Rud   pl   p20
Sub   fig 373, 389 (f)
Traj   pl 4, 6-7 (col)

Aragon

Agu   pl 28, 54-55, 57, 59, 61, 77, 101, **117**
Arm   v2   p 15-16   pl 3 (col)
GaE   pl 2-5 (col)
Gom   p 180-84   pl   p24c, 182, 184 (2 col)
Lee   p62-63   pl
Nie   pl   p 172, 179, 181 (1 col)
OrT   p25   pl 44-64
Sub   fig 364-67 (f)
Traj   pl 8 (col)

Asturias

Arm   v 1   pl 2 (col)
D'Iv   p26   pl 103 (col)
Gom   p 147-52   pl (col)
Int   v2   pl 5 (m)
Nie   pl   p78 (col)
OrT   p30   pl 213-15 (m)

Basque provinces
   See Basque provinces

Biscay

LavR   pl   p229, 237

Canary islands
   See Canary islands

SPAIN—*Continued*

Castile, New

Agu pl 47-48, 70-71, 83, 91
BruK pl 153 fig 3-5 (col)
D'Iv p20-21 pl 75-82 (col)
GaE pl 28-31 (col)
Gom p 107-20 pl p24b, 118 (1 col)
Nie pl 148, 171 (1 col)
OrT p26-27, 29 pl 86-113, 178-83
Sub fig 385-88
Traj pl p (col) (f)

Castile, Old

Agu pl 27, 29, 34, 39, 52, 66-69, **76**,
80-81, 86-87, 102-03, 120
BruK pl 153 fig 1-2 (col)
D'Iv p21-25 pl 83-97 (col)
GaE pl 34-40 (col)
Gom p 155-66 pl p66, 101, 148, **156**,
158, 160, 162 (4 col)
Int v2 p31-34 pl 3, 12
Nat v69 Mr '36 pl p425
Nie pl p 111, 115 (1 col)
OrT p25-26 pl 66-85
Sub fig 374, 384
Traj pl 3 (col) (f)

Catalonia

Agu pl 98-100, 110
Arm v2 p 16 pl 4 (col)
BruK pl 153 fig 6 (col) (m)
D'Iv p 10-13 pl 1-30 (col)
GaE pl 8-10 (col)
Gom p70-84 pl (col)
Nie pl p 182, 185 (1 col)
OrT p29 pl 193-205

Estremadura

Agu pl 53, 62, 72-73, 96-97
AnS p24-319 61 pl il
D'Iv p 19-20 pl 73-74 (col)
GaE pl 11-14 (col)
Gom p 123-28 pl (col)
Nie pl p 166 (col)
OrT p28 pl 151-61
Traj pl 10 (col) (f)

Galicia

Agu pl 78-79, 118-19
Arm v 1 p 15 pl 4 (col)
D'Iv p26 pl 98-102 (col)
GaE pl 15-16 (col)
Gom p 139-44 pl p71-72, 142 (col)
LavR pl p232
Nie pl p64, 67 (1 col)
OrT p29 pl 211-12 (m)
Rea p20 pl 29 (m)
Traj pl 2 (col) (f)

Granada

See Andalusia

León

Agu pl 30, 46, 49, 82, 92-93, 112-13,
115
GaE pl 21-25 (col)
Gom p 131-36 pl p24a-b, 56, 69a,
108-09, 132-34, 140, 152 (3 col)
Int v2 p34-37 pl 10-11
Nat v69 Mr '36 pl p415-17, 420, **422**,
425

Nie pl p 132, 143 (1 col)
OrT p27-29 pl 114-50, 162-77
Sub fig 370, 375-83
Traj pl 13 (col)
See also Maragatos

Murcia

Agu pl 31-33, 88, 90
Brad pl p 151 (f)
D'Iv p 17 pl 56-57 (col)
GaE pl 26-27 (col)
Gom p97-102 pl p52, 98 (1 col)
Nie pl p205
OrT p29 pl 184-87

Navarre

D'Iv pl 108-09 (col)
Gom p 179-80 pl p24c, 165, 176
(1 col)
OrT p24-25 pl 30-43
Sub fig 369 (f)

Pyrenees

See Pyrenees mountains

Salamanca

See León

Valencia

Agu pl E, 75, 95, 111, 116 (1 col)
Arm v2 p 16 pl 1-2 (col)
BruK pl 153 fig 8-10, 12 (col)
D'Iv p 16 pl 44-50 (col)
GaE pl 32-33 (col)
Gom p87-94 pl p44-45, 88 (1 col)
Nat v69 Mr '36 pl p414 (f)
Nie pl p 192 (col)
OrT p29 pl 188-92
Sub fig 371-72
Traj pl 11 (col)

SPAKENBURG. See Netherlands—Utrecht

SPARS. See Coast Guard—United States—
20th century—Women's Reserve

SPATS. See Gaiters

SPECTACLES. See Eyeglasses and lorgnettes

SPINNERS

England

Ancient to 449

AirP il p 13

16th century

Norr v3 bk 1 p309 il; bk 2 p717 fig
831 (f)

France

15th century

HousM p 170-71 il (f)

Rumania

Nat v74 N '38 pl p585 (f)

SPORRANS

Lee p59-61 pl
See also Scotland

SPORT COSTUME
See also names of sports, e.g. Baseball; Bowling; Cricket; Croquet; Fencing; Football; Golf; Riding; Skating; Skiing; Yachting

19th century
Jen p 126-29 il (f)

1860-1870
LavF p28 pl 12 (m)

1880-1890
ViN fig 84 (m)
Yar pl p246

1890-1900
Ada v4 il p62, 70
Mo p 134 pl 73 (f)
ViN fig 91, 99 (m)
WisF pl 23H (f)

20th century
Kle p364-65, 389 il (f)
WisF pl 28 (f)

1900-1910
CunPr pl p90 (f)

1920-1930
WilFo pl p 167 (f)
WisF pl 27 (f)
Yar pl p269

1930-1940
Bro20 p70 il
CunPr p218 pl p232-33
Kle p70 il
WilC pl p390 (f)
WilFo pl p 166 (m)
WisF pl 28 (f)

SPUR DANCE. See Dancers—Mexico—Spur dance

SPURS
Dav v 1 pl p 155
Gor pl p73, 82-83, 86, 92, 238
HousM p57 fig 101, 232
LeID p 165, 329, 384 il
Nat v 104 S '53 pl p325 (col)
Trai p303 il
WilFo p 104 pl p59, 74, 97, 104, 113, 129, 148

SQUIRES
England
18th century
AirB il p52
Gor pl p 113

19th century
AirB il p58

STAGE COACH GUARDS
19th century
Gor pl p224

STAGE COSTUME. See Fancy dress and stage costume

STANDARD BEARERS
England
15th century
Dav v 1 fig 916

17th century
Law v 1 p 145-49 il fig 84-86

France
16th century
LavR pl p 122

Germany
16th century
Dav v 1 p387, 422 il

India
Nat v78 D '40 pl p768 (col)

Netherlands
17th century
Dav v2 fig 1676

Rome
AirB il p8
Dal v 1 fig 381 (col)
HousG2 p 105 fig 116
TiK pl 35 fig 4
WilF pl p 12

United States
19th century
Kre2 pl 11 (col)

STAPHORST. See Netherlands—Oversysel

STAR OF AFRICA. See Sceptres—England

STATE ROBES. See Ceremonial costume; Coronation robes

STAYS. See Corsets

STEEPLE HEADDRESS. See Headdress—15th century; Headdress—England—15th century, etc.

STEIERMARK. See Austria—Styria

STEVNS. See Denmark—Zealand

STIRRUPS
Nat v78 O '40 il p511; v80 Jl '41 pl p109

STJØRDAL. See Norway—Stjørdal

STOCKINGS. See Hose

STOLA. See Rome

STOLES, ECCLESIASTICAL
Bra pl 13
HousM p30 fig 24
LeID p 170 il
NorC p68-69, 88-91 pl

STOMACHERS
Bra pl 24
BroW v 1 fig 91
Dav v 1 fig 1188; v2 fig 1440-41
DeB p 165 pl p 167-68
EvnJ pl 129

STOMACHERS—*Continued*
LelD p 169-70 il
Pic il p 148
WilC pl p 157
WilF pl p87

STONECUTTERS. See Masons and stone-cutters

STRASBOURG. See Alsace

STRAW COATS AND CLOAKS
Portugal
Nat v73 F '38 p 167 il

STREET CLEANERS
Lebanon
Cyr pl 4 (col) (f)

United States
19th century
Ada v4 il p44
Part p 105 il

STREET VENDERS AND PEDDLERS
See also Basket venders; Fishmongers; Flower venders; Milk venders; Pottery venders
Austria
BruK pl 113 fig 1-12
Buenos Aires
Bac pt 1 pl 2-6 (col); pt2 pl 2-3 (col)
China
Nat v69 F '36 pl p285 (m)
Egypt, Modern
Nat v77 Ap '40 pl p461, 463 (col) (m)
England
Early to 1066
AirS il p54

16th century
Trev v2 p61 il

17th century
AirT il p58

19th century
QuV fig 20, 24-27

France
17th century
Dav v2 p514-15 fig 1372-75, 1381

18th century
BruK pl 108
Dav v2 p671-72 il
Gor pl p 113
LelD p 106 il (m)

Germany
Pet p40-41 pl (m)

Rome
AirP il p63

Spain
19th century
Agu pl 2, 18-19, 90, 118-19
20th century
AnS fig 202-03
United States
19th century
Gor pl p 199 (m)
Part pl p 102   ,
Venice
18th century
Arg pl 39 (col) (m)
Mora pl 45-46, 92 (f)
Virgin islands
Nat v78 C '40 il p306 (f)

STUDITE NUNS
Doy pl 81 (col)

STYRIA. See Austria—Styria

SUDAN
Brad pl p21 (f)
GauU pl 8 (col) (m)
TiK pl 26-27 (col) (m)

SUDETENLAND
Mal pl 1-38 (col)

SUITS
19th century
1840-1850
WilC pl p288 (m)
1860-1870
Dav v2 fig 2716 (m)
1880-1890
WilC pl p301 (m)
1890-1900
Bra pl 45 (f)
20th century
1900-1910
CunPr p30, 42, 66-67, 81 pl p35, 46, 64c il (f)
WilC pl p337, 350
Wom p7 il (f)
1910-1920
CunPr pl p 101, 119-20, 123, 132, 134, 136, 142, 149 il p 130, 136 (f)
Lis il p93 (f)
WilC pl p341, 360
Wom p7 il (f)
1920-1930
CunPr p 159, 172-73, 176, 187, 192, 196 pl p 161, 165, 192 il (f)
WilC pl p343, 373
Wom p7-8 il (f)
1930-1940
Wom p8 il (f)
1940-1950
Bra pl 54
Kle p250 il (f)
Wom p8-9 il (f)

SUITS—*Continued*
United States
20th century
1930-1940
KerA   pl   p59 (f)

SUMATRA
RueO   pl   22 (f)

SUMERIA ..
HeuO   p47-65   pl   30-39, 42, 44
Hous2   p 108-14 il

SUN DANCE. See Dancers—Indians of North America—Sun dance

SUNBONNETS
Hea   p58-59   pl (incl pat)
Trai   p296 il

SUNNMÖRE. See Norway—Sunnmöre

SUPERHUMERALE. See Amice

SURGEONS. See Barber surgeons; Physicians

SURINAM
Hal   pl 24 (col) (f)
Nat   v83 Ap '43   pl   p465, 470 (col) (f)
Spi   pl   p53 (col) (f)

SURPLICES
LelD   p395 il
McC   p86-89   pl
NorC   p 168-69 (pat)

SURVEYORS
Egypt, Ancient
Hous2   p61 fig 68

United States
19th century
Gor   pl   p217

SUSPENDERS. See Braces

SUSQUEHANNA INDIANS. See Indians of North America—Susquehanna Indians

SUTLERS
England
18th century
Law   v2 p40-41 il

SVINHULT. See Sweden—Östergötland

SWABIA See Germany—Swabia; also Germany—Bavaria

SWADDLING BANDS
LelD   p249 il

SWAGGER STICKS
WilC   pl   p235

SWAHILI
BruK   pl 190 fig 9-10 (col) (m)

SWEDEN
See also Fancy dress and stage costume—Swedish; also subdivision Sweden under Capes and cloaks; Ceremonial costume; Children; Coats and jackets; Coronation robes; Court dress; Dancers; Footwear; Headdress; Military costume; Waistcoats; Wedding costume
16th century
WilF   pl   p71 (f)
17th century
StocM   pl 2-8
18th century—date
Berg   fig 7-9, 31-34,   36-47, 61-75, 98-99, 109, 118, 127-29 (incl pat) pl 1-4 (col)
Brad   front, pl p 154, 155 (2 col)
Dav   v2 p729 il
Lee   p64-66   pl
Lel   v 12   pl 36 (m)
Nat   v77 Je '40   pl   p799, 802, 817, 819 (col) (f)
StocM   pl 9-64
WilF   pl   p 154
BY REGION OR PROVINCE
Ångermanland
Nyl   p90-91   pl (col) (m)
Blekinge
Nyl   p34-35   pl (col)
Prim   p57-58   pl   p56 (col)
Bohuslän
Nyl   p38-39   pl (col)
Dalarne
BruK   pl 128 fig 6-7, 10 (col)
MusS   pl 1-4 (col)
Nat   v98 N '50   pl   p635 (col) (f)
Nyl   p 17-18, 70-77   4 pl (col)
Prim   p59-61   pl
Salv   pl 2 (col)
Delsbo
Prim   pl   p62-63
Gästrikland
Nyl   p78-79   pl (col)
Halland
Nyl   p36-37   pl (col)
Salv   p 15-16   pl 3-4 (col)
Härjedalen
Nyl   p86-87   pl (col)
Helsingland
MusS   pl 9 (col)
Nyl   p80-85   3 pl (col)
Jämtland
Nyl   p88-89   pl (col)
Mora
Prim   pl   p66, 74 (1 col)
Närke
Nyl   p60-61   pl (col)
Stoc   pl 6 (col) (f)

SWEDEN—*Continued*

Öland

Nyl p48-49 pl (col)

Östergötland

Nyl p50-53 2 pl (col)
Stoc pl 2 (col) (f)

Schonen

BruK pl 128 fig 8, 11-12, 15 (col) (f)

Skåne

Brad pl p 153 (f)
MusS pl 5-6 (col)
Nyl p 19, 22-23, 28-33 3 pl (col)
Prim p58 pl p67-68
Sv p9-312 il

Småland

Nyl p44-47 2 pl (col)
Prim pl p73 (f)

Södermanland

MusS pl 7-8 (col)
Nyl p58-59 pl (col)
Prim p58 pl p65
Stoc pl 3-4 (col)

Uppland

Nyl p62-65 2 pl (col)
Salv p 15-16 pl 1 (col)
Stoc pl 5 (col) (m)

Värmland

Nyl p68-69 pl (col)
Prim p59 pl p66
Stoc pl 8 (col)

Västerbotten

Nyl p90-91 pl (col) (f)

Västmanland

Nyl p66-67 pl (col)
Stoc pl 7 (col) (m)

Vestergötland

Nyl p40-43 2 pl (col)
Prim pl p70-71
Stoc pl 1 (col) (f)

Wingåker

BruK pl 128 fig 9, 14 (col) (f)

SWINEHERDS

France

12th century

EvjD pl 21

Spain

20th century

AnS fig 197

SWISS GUARDS

BruK pl 119 fig 9 (col)
LelD p81-82 il; pl p 194 fig 5; pl p347 fig 4

Papal

See Papal guards

SWITZERLAND

See also Fancy dress and stage costume—Swiss; also subdivision Switzerland under Children; Dancers; Festival costume; Headdress; Herdsmen; Military costume

12th century

Dav v 1 p 141 il (f)

16th century

LavE pl 12, 18-19 (f)
LavR pl p29, 32-33 (f)

17th century

Brad pl p 158-59

18th century—date

BruK pl 143-44 (col)
Nat v72 Jl '37 pl p21 (col) (f)
Pic il p 151 (f)
Vert pl p 110 (f)

BY REGION OR PROVINCE

Aargau

BruK pl 143 fig 8-9; pl 144 fig 13 (col)
Her p 1-2 pl (col) (f)

Appenzell

BruK pl 143 fig 16; pl 144 fig 11 (col) (f)
Er p47-48 pl 12 (col)
Her p3-4 pl (col)
Lee p66-67 pl (f)
Nat v98 Ag '50 pl p213 (col) (m)

Basel

BruK pl 68 fig 5-8 (col) (f)
Her p5-6 pl (col)

Bern

BruK pl 143 fig 3-4, 6-7; pl 144 fig 2, 4-5
Her p7-8 pl (col)
Wit p 17 pl 1 (col)

Fribourg

BruK pl 143 fig 10-11; pl 144 fig 8 (col)
Her p 9-10 pl (col)
Wit p 18 pl 4 (col)

Geneva

Her p 11-12 pl (col)

Graubünden

Her p 13-14 pl (col)

Lucerne

BruK pl 144 fig 5 (col) (f)
Her p 15-16 pl (col)

Neuchâtel

Her p 17-18 pl (col)

St Gall

BruK pl 143 fig 14-15 (col) (f)
Her p25-26 pl (col)

Schaffhausen

BruK pl 143 fig 5 (col) (m)
Her p 19-20 pl (col)

SWITZERLAND—*Continued*

Schwyz
BruK pl 144 fig 7 (col) (f)
Her p 21-22 pl (col)

Solothurn
BruK pl 144 fig 1 (col) (f)
Her p23-24 pl (col)

Thurgau
BruK pl 144 fig 12 (col) (f)
Her p29-30 pl (col)

Ticino
BruK pl 144 fig 10 (col) (f)
Her p27-28 pl (col)

Unterwald
BruK pl 144 fig 6 (col) (f)
Her p31-32 pl (col)
Wit p 17-18 pl 2 (col)

Uri
BruK pl 144 fig 15 (col) (f)
Her p33-34 pl (col)

Valais
Her p37-38 pl (col)
Wit p 18 pl 3 (col)

Vaud
Her p35-36 pl (col)

Zug
BruK pl 144 fig 14 (col) (f)
Her p39-40 pl (col) (f)

Zurich
BruK pl 143 fig 12-13 (col) (f)
Her p41-42 pl (col)

SWORD BEARERS

England
16th century
Norr v3 bk 2 p531, 651 fig 621, 739

SWORD BELTS AND BALDRICKS
Bra pl 1
Dot il p 112
Kle p 104 il
LelD p2, 31-32, 330 il
Pic il p5
WilC p 176 pl p 138, 146, 165, 171, 173, 190, 192

SWORD DANCE. See Dancers—England —Sword dance; Dancers—Indians of North America—Sword dance; Dancers —Italy—Sword dance; Dancers—Scotland—Sword dance

SWORDS AND DAGGERS
Dav v 1 pl p 156
Norr v3 bk 2 p393-94, 408-09, 460, 548-49 il
WilC pl p74, 91, 98, 112, 132, 138, 155, 181, 201

SYLT. See Frisian islands

SYLVESTRINE NUNS
Doy pl 125 (col)

SYLVESTRINES
Doy pl 65 (col)

SYMBOLIC FIGURES. See Fame, Wisdom, etc.

SYRIA

Ancient
BruK p43-44 pl 7 (col)
Dav v 1 p78-79 il
HeuO p99-115 pl 55-58 il
TiK pl 8 fig 9-10 (m); pl 12-14, 17 (col)
See also Druses; Headdress—Syria, Ancient; Military costume—Syria, Ancient

Modern
BruK pl 191 (col)
Cyr pl 3-6, 9-11, 14-15, 22 (col)
Nat v 106 D '54 pl p822 (col)
See also Wedding costume—Syria

SYRIAN CHURCH. See Ecclesiastical costume—Syrian church

SZEPES. See Hungary

T

TABASCO. See Mexico—Tabasco

TABIS. See Footwear—Japan

TABLET DANCE. See Dancers—Indians of North America—Tablet dance

TAHITI
Nat v79 Ja '41 pl p 117
See also Dancers—Tahiti

TAILORS
16th century
Dav v 1 fig 908
17th century
Ada v 1 il p 144
AirB il p50
Dav v2 p558 il

TAOIST PRIESTS
MusE pl 9 (col)
Nat v70 D '36 pl p772-73
NeF p 14-15 pl 46-48

TARA BROOCH
RogF p66-67 pl

TARANTELLA. See Dancers—Italy— Tarantella

TARBOOSH. See Headdress—Moslem

TARRAGONA. See Spain—Catalonia

TARTANS. See Scotland—Clans and tartans

TARTARS. See Tatars

TASSELS. See Fringes and tassels

TATARS
Brad pl p 145 (col)
Pot v2 pl 5 (col)
TiK p37 pl 78 (col)

TATTOOING AND SKIN MARKING
Bra p8-9 pl 1 fig 3
Gen v 1 fig 39 (m)
Nat v72 N '37 pl p659 (f); v96 D
'49 pl 772-73; v99 Mr '51 pl p277
(f)
Rud pl p102-10, 112

TEAGOWNS
CrH p68-71 2 pl
CunE pl p381 il p391-92, 405
CunPr pl 64-65, 83, 164

TEHUANTEPEC. See Mexico—Tehuantepec; also Headdress—Tehuantepec

TELEMARK. See Norway—Telemark

TELEPHONE OPERATORS

19th century
Davi v2 il p 172
Jen p 84 il
Nat v72 O '37 p410-11 il
RogW p51 il

TEMPLARS
AirM p6 il
BruK p51 pl 29 (col)
Doy pl 144 (col)
LelD p403 il
Wa pl p 106

TEMPLE GUARDS

Palestine, Ancient
Wrig pt 1 p 16 pl p28

TEN VIRTUES OF MARY NUNS. See
Annunciate nuns

TENERIFFE. See Canary islands

TENNIS COSTUME

16th century
BluL p23 pl 42 (m)
LavR pl p 108 (m)
Norr v3 bk 1 p 194-95 il (m)

19th century
Dur il p70-72
RogW p21 il (f)

1870-1880
CunE p293 il (f)
Jen pl p 124

1880-1890
CunA pl 37 (f)
CunE il p340 (f)
Davi v2 il p68
Gor pl p 197
LavT p222 pl p224 (f)
LavT2 p 176-77 pl p 180 (f)
Trav v4 fig 108

1890-1900
LavT p222-23 pl p224 (f)
LavT2 p 177 pl p 180 (f)
WilC pl p327 (f)
Yar p246 il (f)

20th century
1900-1910
Bruh pl p89 (col) (f)
CunPr pl p72 (f)
RogW p60 il
Wom p 18 il (f)
Yar p252 il

1910-1920
BrH pl p 149 fig 2 (col) (f)
Dur il p 136-37, 148-49
LavT2 p 178 pl p 180 (f)
RogW p 61 il
WilC pl p364 (f)

1920-1930
AlF pl p73-74
CunPr pl p 175 (f)
Dur pl p 189 (f)
Jen p 132 il (f)
LavT p224 pl (f)
LavT2 pl p 178, 180 (f)
RogW p58, 133 il
WilC pl p377 (f)
Wom p 18 il (f)
Yar p269 il

1930-1940
CunPr p218 pl p209, 253 (f)
Dur il p248-50, 253-55
Kle p 384 il (f)
LavT p224-25 pl (f)
LavT2 p 179 pl p 180 (f)
RogW 132-33 il (f)

1940-1950
RogW p 133 il
Wom p 18 il (f)

TERUEL. See Spain—Aragon

TEUTONIC TRIBES. See Europe—To
476

TEXAS RANGERS
Kre pl 11 (col) (pte)
Kre2 pl 12 (col)

TEXTILE WORKERS

England
19th century
Walk pl 2, 6, 28 (col) (m)

THEATINE NUNS
Doy pl 109 (col)

THEATINES
Doy pl 54 (col)

THEATRICAL COSTUME. See Fancy
dress and stage costume

THEOLOGICAL STUDENTS

Catholic church
Agu pl 94
Nat v71 Mr '37 pl p310-12 (col)

THISTED. See Denmark—Jutland

THISTLE, ORDER OF THE
Norr v3 bk 1 p251-53 pl il

THREE BROTHERS (JEWEL)
Norr v3 bk 1 p347-48; bk 2 p773-74 il

THURGAU. See Switzerland—Thurgau

THURINGIA. See Germany—Thuringia

TIARAS. See Coronets; Crowns; Papal tiara

TIBET
Brad pl p 160-61
BruK pl 182 fig 7-12 (col)
Dal v 1 fig 781, 792-95 (col) (m)
Nat v95 My '49 pl p666-68, 670-75, 687-88 (9 col)
TiK pl 79-80 (col)
See also Buddhist monks; Lamas; also subdivision Tibet under Ceremonial costume; Children; Dancers; Hair, wigs, etc.; Headdress

TICINO. See Switzerland—Ticino

TIERRA DEL FUEGO
Nat v72 D '37 pl p751

TINKERS

England

16th century

Hat fig 105

TIROL. See Tyrol

THE TLACOLOLEROS. See Dancers—Mexico—The tlacololeros

TLAXCALA. See Mexico—Tlaxcala

TLINGIT INDIANS. See Indians of North America—Tlingit Indians

TOGAS
BruK pl 18 and table 3 (pat)
Dot p 113 il
Eth p 16-17 il
EvnR p22 pl 3 (f)
Gor p 10 pl p 14
HousG2 p87-96 il
Kle p 386 il
Lecl pl 2 (col)
Lee p80-81 pl
LelD p405-06 il
Pic il p 155
Pot v 1 pl 13 (col) (incl pat)
Tru p7-8 il
Wa p56-57 fig 60 (incl pat)
WilC p 18-19 pl p21
WlsC p36-54 21 pl (incl pat)
Wrig pt2 p7-8 pl p 17
See also Rome

TOLEDO. See Spain—Castile, New

TOLTECS
Nat v70 N '36 pl p624 (col)

TOMAHAWK DANCE. See Dancers—Indians of North America—Tomahawk dance

TONKING
GaU pl 34, 36-37, 39-41 (col) (f)
Pot v2 p35-38 2 pl (col)
TiK pl 87 fig 7-8 (col) (f)

TONSURE
NorC p 180-81 il

TOR ABBEY JEWEL
BraF p74 pl p57

TOREADORS. See Bullfighters

TORNA DISTRICT. See Sweden—Skåne

TORQUES. See Necklaces and pendants—Ancient

TOURAINE. See France—Touraine

TOURNAMENT COSTUME
Ab pl p232
BosE pl 33
BruK pl 44 (col)
Dal v2 fig 23, 334 (col)
Gor pl p37
Hat p 181-83 fig 93, 99
LelD il p47, 124 fig 2; p239 il; il p411
Ni pl 25
See also Military costume, period subdivisions 12th to 16th centuries under England, France, etc.

TOWN CRIERS

England

Nat v 103 Je '53 pl p812 (col)

France

Nat v77 F '40 il p236

TRAIN BANDS. See Volunteer troops—England—16th and 17th centuries

TRANSYLVANIA. See Rumania—Transylvania

TRAPPERS. See Pioneers and scouts

TRAPPISTS
Doy pl 63

TRICORNS AND BICORNS
Bra pl 30, 32
Kle p 102 il (m)
LelD il p35
Pic il p70, 74 (m)
WilH p 146, 156, 188 pl p 129, 161, 163, 170-71, 191, 203
Yar p 191 pl p 183, 187, 192

TRINIDAD. See Dancers—Trinidad; Festival costume—Trinidad

TRINITARIAN NUNS
Doy pl 95 (col)

TRINITARIANS
Doy pl 36-38 (col)

TROUSERS
BruK table 11 (pat)
Hea p 16-21 3 pl (incl pat)
See also Breeches

Albania
TiK pl 61-62 (col)

Armenia
TiK pl 19 fig 2 (col) (f)

China
TiK pl 89 (col) (incl pat) (f)

Europe
Early to 1000
Dav v 1 p89 il
LelD p94-95, 297-99 pl il

15th-17th centuries
Lint p 10-11 pl 13

18th century
Dal v2 fig 580 (pat)
Lel v 11 p21-22 fig 15-16 (incl pat)
Wa p229 fig 188C, 196

19th century
BroH p 169 fig 115-16
Dav v2 p873 il
Eth p46-47 pl (incl pat)
Kle p 178-80 il
LelD p298-99 pl fig 5-11
Wa p248, 256, 278 fig 204, 210, 256, 278 (incl pat)
WilC pl p270

Iraq
TiK pl 19 fig 6 (col) (m)

Japan
Lee p42-45 pl

Lapland
TiK pl 53 fig 16-17 (col)

Mexico
TiK pl 110 fig 5 (col)

Persia
TiK pl 19 fig 3 (col)

Spain
AnS fig 83

Sweden
Berg fig 86
Sv p89-103 il (incl pat)

Tatars
TiK pl 19 fig 5 (col) (f)

Turkey
TiK pl 19 (col)

Yugoslavia
TiK pl 55-56, 59 (col)

TRUMPETERS
Bhután
Nat v 102 D '52 il p733

England
17th century
Law v 1 p115-20 il

18th century
BarH p 99-100 pl 7 (col)

Flanders
HousM p 181 fig 315

India
Nat v78 D '40 pl p756 (col); v94 O '48 pl p443 (col)

Rome
WilF pl p12

TRUNK-HOSE. See Breeches—Europe—16th century and subdivisions France, Italy, etc. of this period

TUAREGS
GaU pl 1-3 (col)
Nat v74 S '38 pl p343-44

TUNGUSES
TiK pl 104 (col)

TUNICA
NorC p 15-16 il

TUNICLE
HousM p28 fig 21
McC p 145-46 il
NorC p 170-71 pl p 140, 172 (1 col)

TUNISIA
BruK p39 pl 188 (col)
GaU pl 18-20 (col)
Nat v71 Mr '37 p360-61 pl; v83 Ja '43 pl p 127, 130 (m)
TiK pl 28, 30-31, 33-34 (incl pat) (col)
See also Bedouins; Berbers; Kabyles

TURBANS
Pic il p74, 158

18th century
Bra pl 33

20th century
Kle p394-95 il (f)

Flanders
WilH pl p52

Germany
WilH pl p52

India
Dal v 1 fig 686, 712, 717 (col)
Nat v94 O '48 pl p450 (col)

Italy
WilH pl p52-53

Moors
WilH p33 pl p35-37

Persia
WilH pl p 12, 36-37

Turkey
WilH pl p35

United States
18th century
LesA p95 pl 22 (m)

TURÉGANO. See Spain—Castile, Old

TURKESTAN
Brad   pl p 163 (col)
BruK   p37, 87 pl 174-75, 182 fig 13-18
(col)
TiK   pl 76-77 (col)
See also Kirghiz

TURKEY
Lee   p68-70 pl
See also Kurds; Pashas; also subdivision Turkey under Footwear; Headdress; Military costume; Naval costume; Officials

15th-16th centuries
BruK   pl 90
Rud   pl p23 (f)
TiK   pl 66 (col)

17th century
BruK   pl 90 fig 11-15; pl 91 (1 col)

18th century—date
BruK   pl 169-70 (col)
CamC   pl p39 (f)
Kle   p 199 il (m)
Nat   v75 Ja '39 pl p 17-20 (col)
Özb   pl 1-22 fig 1-15 (pat) (f)
TiK   pl 16-17, 20 (col)

TURKOMANS
Nat   v69 Ja '36 pl p32 (col) (m);
v77 Mr '40 pl p405 (f)

TUSCANY. See Italy—Tuscany

TUSCARORA INDIANS. See Indians of North America—Tuscarora Indians

TWENTIETH CENTURY
Pic   il p 132 (f)
Set   p42-48 il
Yar   p249-82 19 pl

1900-1910
Ada   v4 il p 178-79
Bart   p94-95 pl (pat) (f) fig 40 (f)
BluN   pl p91-92
Bra   p339-56 pl 48-50, 61
BrH   p 142-45 2 pl (col)
Brk   pl 46-49 (f)
Bro20   p 15-30 front 2 pl il
BroF   pl p96 (col) fig 47-48
Bruh   p86-98 2 pl (col)
Coh   p461-69 il (m)
CrO   pl 55 (f)
CunA   pl 41-42
CunP   p65-69 2 pl (col) (f)
CunPr   p27-95 front 31 pl (2 col) (f)
Dal   v2 fig 988-89 (col)
Dau   pl p45, 47, 49 (f)
Dot   p 170 il (m)
Flow   fig 97 (f)
Gern   pl 72 (f)
Gor   pl p 175, 244
HaC   p87-96 8 pl (f)
Jen   p58, 116 pl il (f)
KerA   p42-48 4 pl (f)
Kle   p 192-95 il (f)
Lab   p 102-05 pl (col) (m)
LavT   p96-108 pl (f)

LavT2   p82-88, 190-91 pl p79, 96
Lecl   pl 19 (col) (f)
Mo   p 142-63 10 pl il (f)
NeV   p5-6 pl 53-60 (f)
Pic   il p48 (f)
RogW   p45, 92 il (f)
Rue   pl V-X
Trai   p353-56 il (f)
Tru   p 112-17 il
True   p62-65 2 pl il (f)
VanH   pl 12
Wa   p334-43 pl p338, 360, 390 il
Wel   pl p36
WilC   p345-49 pl p337-42, 350-52
WilF   pl p 165-67
WilFo   pl p 164 (f)
WisF   pl 24 (f)
Yar   pl p250, 252
YoR   p 115-19 il (f)

1910-1920
Ada   v4 il p332 (m)
Bart   p96-97 pl (pat) (f) fig 40 (f)
BelQ   pl p 105 (f)
Bra   p339-69 pl 47-51, 61
BrH   p 146-48 2 pl (col)
Bro20   p31-46 3 pl il
BroF   pl p97 (col) fig 49-50
Burr   p56-59, 142-49, 238-39 2 pl (f)
But   pl p338-39, 372, 382 (m)
CrO   pl 31, 39, 42, 55, 57
CunA   pl 43 (f)
CunP   p70-71 il (f)
CunPr   p96-158 23 pl il (f)
Dal   v2 fig 990-99 (col) (f)
Dau   pl p51, 53 (f)
Dot   p 172 il (f)
Gor   pl p 176-77, 245-46
HaC   p96-118 16 pl (f)
KerA   p50-53 2 pl il (f)
Kle   p 183, 192-95 il (f)
LavT   p 109-28 pl p 126, 256 (f)
LavT2   p89-101 pl p97, 112 (f)
Lecl   pl 20 (col) (f)
LelD   pl p336 row 3 (col); pl p361
fig 1-3
Mo   p 164-73 5 pl il (f)
RogW   p92, 95, 96 il (f)
True   p66-69 2 pl il (f)
VanH   pl 12
Wa   p343-51 pl p360, 390 il
WilC   p354-65 5 pl (f)
WilF   pl p 168-74
WilFo   pl p 163 (m)
WisF   pl 25-26 (f)
Wom   p 1 il (f)
Yar   pl p254
YoR   p 120-23 il (f)

1920-1930
BelQ   pl p 107, 111 (f)
Bra   p357-84 pl 51-52, 61-62
Bro20   p47-61 2 pl il
BroF   fig 51
Burr   p60, 142-49, 240-41 pl p61 (f)
CrO   pl 15-16, 18, 20, 29-30, 35, 50, 56-58
CunA   pl 44-45 (f)
CunPr   p 158-206 12 pl il (f)
Dau   pl p55, 57, 59 (f)
HaC   p 118-54 10 pl (f)
Jen   p 141 (f)
KerA   p54-57 2 pl il (f)

TWENTIETH CENTURY—1920-1930—
Continued
Kle p 19, 129-30, 142-43, 145, 203-04, 265-67 il (f)
Lab p 106-09 pl (col) (m)
LavS p60 pl 31 (f)
LavT p 124-39 2 pl (f)
LavT2 p 101-12, 191-95 pl p 113, 190 pl 12 (col)
Lecl pl 21 (col) (f)
LelD pl p258 fig 9-11; pl p361 fig 4-7 (f)
Mo p 174 pl 107-08 (f)
RogW p93, 97-98, 100-01, 144, 159 il (f)
True p70-73 2 pl il (f)
Wa p351-55 pl p360 il
Wel pl p36
WilC p366-72 pl p340-41, 343-44, 373-77
WilF pl p 179-187
WilFo pl p 165, 167
WisF pl 27 (f)
Wom p 1-3 il (f)
Yar pl p263, 265, 267, 269
YoR p 123-26 il (f)

1930-1940
AlF pl p 161-65 (f)
BelQ pl p 113 (f)
Bra p371-84 pl 52, 61
BrH p 150-51 pl (col) (f)
Bro20 p63-78 2 pl il
BroF fig 52 (f)
Burr p62, 139-40, 240-41, 304-05, 312 pl p63 (f)
But pl p412, 418-20 (m)
CunA pl p 164 (col) (f)
CunPr p207-63 22 pl il (f)
Dau pl p61, 63, 65, 67 (f)
HaC p 134-64 11 pl (f)
Kle p 132-33, 135, 145-46 il (f)
Lab p 110-13 pl (col) (m)
LavT2 pl p 113, 190-91
LesA fig 282
Nat v76 N '39 pl p609 (col) (f)
RogW p93 il (f)
True p74-75 pl il (f)
Wa p355-87 pl p360, 390
WilC p379-84 pl p339-41, 344, 385-90
WilF pl p 188-99
WilFo pl p 165-66, 168
WisF pl 28 (f)
YoR p 126-29 il (f)

1940-1950
Bra p385-423 pl 53-59, 61
Bro20 p79-90 2 pl il
BroF pl p 112 (col) fig 54
But pl p244-45 (m)
CrO pl 59-60 (f)
CunA pl 47-48 (f)
CunPr p264-93 24 pl il (f)
Jen p 102-03 il
KerA p62-63, 70-76 4 pl il
Kle p 19, 94-97, 130-32, 134-36, 143, 145-46, 189-90, 270-73, 408-12 il
Lab p 114-17 pl (col) (m)
Lecl pl 22 (col)
LelD pl p361 fig 8-10 (f)
RogW p93 il (f)

True p76-80 2 pl il (f)
WilC pl p337-40, 342 (m)
WilF pl p200-20
WilFo pl p 169-71 (f)
WisF pl 29 (f)
Wom p3 il (f)
Yar p275-81 6 pl

1950-1952
Bra p399-423 pl 55-62

TYPISTS. See Office workers

TYROL
Brad pl p33-35 (1 col)
Breu pl 4 (col)
BruK pl 141 (col)
Er p43-46 pl (col)
Ham p 1-46 23 pl (col)
Kle p386-87 il
Lee p 10-12 pl
Lep pl 2, 6, 8-10 (col)
Nat v77 Mr '40 pl p360 (col); v84 D '43 pl p703, 705, 813 (col); v88 Jl '45 pl p76 (f); v99 Je '51 pl p733 (col); v 100 S '51 pl p388, 391, 403 (col) (m)
Ori p 1-60 30 pl (col)
Pes p5-72 29 pl (col)
Pic il p 159 (f)
Ret p 174-84 5 pl il
Vert pl p 100 (f)
See also Fancy dress and stage costume—Tyrolean; also subdivision Tyrol under Children; Coats and jackets; Dancers; Festival costume; Headdress; Waistcoats; Waists

U

UGANDA
Brad pl p22 (f)
Nat v71 Ja '37 pl p 121, 128

UHLANS

Austria-Hungary
19th century
KnR pl p235
Lez pl p311 (col)

Germany
18th century
KnR pl p51 (pte)

19th century
KnR pl p51, 83 (pte)
Lez pl p264, 292, 337, 361 (col)

Russia
19th century
KnR p443-45 pl
Lez pl p347, 375 (col) (off, pte)

UKRAINE. See Russia—Ukraine

UMBRELLAS AND PARASOLS
Bin p 178-87 pl p208 il
Kle p322-24 il

UMBRELLAS AND PARASOLS—*Continued*

449-1066

AirS il p6

17th century

WilC pl p 183
WisF pl 13

18th century

Gor pl p 121
Lel v 11 p75 fig 81; v 12 p56 fig 76
LelD p289 il
LesA p407-09 il
WisF pl 14, 18

19th century

Ada v4 il p53
LelD p270 il
LesA p409-12 il
WilC p264-65 pl p256, 270, 318
WisF pl 21
Yar p203, 205, 209, 214, 216, 221-22, 234, 248 3 pl il

20th century

LesA p413-14 il
WilC pl p378-79
WisF pl 27
Yar p273 il

Assyria and Babylonia

LelD p300-01 il
LesA p402-03 il
WilC pl p 10
WisF pl 2
Yar p 11 pl p 14

Egypt, Ancient

LesA p402 il

Greece, Ancient

Gen v 1 fig 318
LelD p300-01 il
LesA p404-05 fig 493-94
WilC pl p 17
Yar p 19 pl p20

Persia, Ancient

LesA fig 492
Pot v 1 pl 6 (col)
TiK pl 9 fig 1
WilC pl p28

Rome

WisF pl 4

Tyrol

Ori pl p48

UNDERWEAR
Bin p 114-30 il
See also individual articles, e.g. Chemises; Corsets; Petticoats and slips

16th century

Dav v2 pl p633 (f)

19th century

Jen p24, 136 il
KerA p28 il (f)
LavT p 172-74 pl (f)

1810-1820

CunE p70-73 il (f)

1860-1870

CunP pl p33 (col)
Dav v2 pl p906-07

1870-1880

Dal v2 fig 779
Part p86 il (m)

1880-1890

Ada v3 il p364
CunE p361-66 2 pl (f)

1890-1900

Gor pl p 172 (f)
RogW p4-5 il (f)

20th century

Coh p383-90, 474-82 il
HaC p 192-96 6 pl (f)
Kle p397-98 il (f)
LavT p 174-80 pl (f)
RogW p96, 99 il (f)

1900-1910

CunPr p64-65, 74-75, 84, 94 pl p95 il (f)
Dot il p 171 (f)
Wa p337-38 fig 264-65 (f)
WilC pl p353 (f)

1910-1920

AlF pl p9 (f)
CunPr il p 105, 110-11 (f)
LavT2 pl p 140 (f)
WilC pl p365 (f)

1920-1930

CunPr p 186 pl p 163 (f)
LavT2 p 141-42 pl p 140 (f)
Wa p352 fig 274 (f)
WilC pl p378 (f)

1930-1940

CunPr p210, 215, 218, 225-26, 232, 238 pl il (f)
LavT2 pl p 140 (f)

UNDERWEAR, CHILDREN'S

19th century

MooC pl p23

UNIFORMS, MILITARY. See Military costume

UNIFORMS, WOMEN'S. See names of individual organizations, e.g. American Women's Voluntary Services; Citizens Service Corps

UNITED SERVICE ORGANIZATIONS
Ross p36 il (col)

UNITED STATES
See also Indians of North America; Pioneers and scouts; Puritans; Quakers; also subdivision United States under Academic costume; Children; Coast Guard; Festival costume; Hair, wigs, etc.; Headdress; Military costume; Naval costume; also under names of

UNITED STATES—*Continued*

particular classes of people (e.g. Agricultural laborers, Blacksmiths, Cowboys, Miners and prospectors, Police, Sailors) and individual articles of attire (e.g. Footwear, Headdress)

Colonial period (to 1775)

Ada v 1 il p53-54, 87, 267-68, 274, 299, 304-08, 310
Bart p42-43 pl (pat) (f) fig 13
Burr p48, 97-98, 149-53, 228-31 pl p49
Chr p 176-79 pl (col) il (f)
Dav v2 p748, 752, 756, 764-65, 767, 769, 771, 780-81 il
Davi v 1 pl p 115, 120, 126 (m); v2 pl p337 (m)
EvnH front (col) p94-109 pl il (incl pat)
Lee p 105-07 pl
LesA pl 21 (m)
Nat v71 Ap '37 pl p418-19, 421, 423, 435, 439 (col); v78 Jl '40 pl p29; v94 S '48 pl p304-05 (col)
Pic il p33 (f)
Rue fig G (f)
Trai p 190-94 il (f)
VanH pl 5-7

Carolina
EvnH p64-73 pl il (pat)

Dutch
Dot p 157 il
EvnH p82-87 pl il (incl pat)
McP p6 pl p5 (col)
Trai p89-91 il

New England
McP p 14 pl p 13 (col)
Trai p 160-64 il (m)
VanH pl 6

Pennsylvania
Davi v 1 il p76 (m)
Nat v99 F '51 pl p 182, 184 (col) (m)

Southern states
Dot p 158 il

Virginia
Ada v 1 il p26
EvnH p56-63 pl il (pat)
McP p7 pl p4, 8 (col)
Trai p 109-14, 211-13 il
VanH pl 7

1775-1800
Ada v2 il p7
But pl p2-3, 25 (m)
Dav v2 front (col) fig 2180-81, 2190, 2201, 2203, 2218, 2225-29, 2231-32
Dot p 163-64 il
KerM no4 pl 9 (f)
McP p 15-16 pl (col)
Rue fig D1-E1
Trai p235-38 il
True p8-11 2 pl il (f)
VanH pl 6-8

19th century
Part 15 pl il
See also Nineteenth century

1800-1810
But pl p40, 44
EvnH p 119-29 fig 62-67 (incl pat)
True p 14-15 pl il (f)

1810-1820
Dav v2 p831 fig 2337
KerM no4 pl 8 (f)

1820-1830
Burr p60-61 pl (f)
But pl p82, 86 (m)
Dav v2 fig 2337, 2384-85, 2387
EvnH p 131-38 fig 69-70

1830-1840
Dau pl p7 (f)
Dav v2 fig 2400-03, 2413-18, 2431
EvnH p 131-38 fig 68, 71-72
Trai p270-73 il (f)

1840-1850
But pl p 110, 116, 118-19 (m)
Dau pl p9, 11, 13, 15 (f)
Dav v2 fig 2385, 2407, 2454-57, 2497-98
EvnH p 139-45 fig 73-76 (incl pat)
KerM no4 pl 5-6
Gor pl p 184

1850-1860
Ada v3 il p4, 55
But pl p 140-41, 144
Dau pl p 17, 19 (f)
Dav v2 fig 2501-03, 2533, 2536-40, 2575, 2588, 2598
Gor front (col) pl p 185
KerA p7-9 2 pl (f)
KerM no4 pl 3-4 (f)

1860-1870
But pl p 184, 204-05 (m)
Dau pl p21, 23, 25, 27 (f)
Dav v2 fig 2606-09, 2686-2704, 2717-22, 2727, 2743-54, 2759-76
EvnH p 147-52 fig 77-79 (incl pat)
Gor pl p 186-90
KerA p 12-16 3 pl (f)
McP p22-24 pl (col)
Rue fig R (f)

1870-1880
Burr p52-53 pl (f)
But pl p 197, 221 (m)
Dau pl p29, 31, 33, 35 (f)
Gor pl p 191-92
KerA p17-22 3 pl
McP p25-26, 34 2 pl (1 col)

1880-1890
But pl p246-47
Gor p 193-97 3 pl
Jen pl p46-47 (f)
KerA p23-32 4 pl (f)
McP p27-30 2 pl (col)

1890-1900
Burr p54-55 pl (f)
But pl p275 (m)
Dau pl p41, 43 (f)

UNITED STATES—19th century—1890-1900—Continued
> Gor pl p 198-202 5 pl
> KerA p34-40 4 pl (f)
> RogW pl p4, 92

20th century
See Twentieth century

BY REGION OR STATE
Louisiana
> McP p 17-18 pl

New York
> McP p 19-20 pl

Southwest
> VanH pl 5

Virginia
> Davi v 1 il p364

Western states
> Gor p204-26 18 pl (1 col)

UNITED STATES. NAVAL ACADEMY,
See Naval cadets—United States

UNIVERSITIES AND COLLEGES—COSTUMES. See Academic costume

UNTERWALD. See Switzerland—Unterwald

UPPER AUSTRIA. See Austria—Upper Austria

UPPLAND. See Sweden—Uppland

UPPVIDINGE. See Sweden—Småland

URI. See Switzerland—Uri

URK. See Netherlands—Urk

URSULINES
> Doy pl 111-14 (col)
> MusE pl 25 (col)

URUAPAN. See Mexico—Michoacán

URUGUAY
> Spi pl p81 (col) (m)

UTRECHT. See Netherlands—Utrecht

V

VALAIS. See Switzerland—Valais

VALDRES. See Norway—Valdres

VALENCIA. See Spain—Valencia

VALLADOLID. See Spain—Castile, Old

VANDYKE COLLARS. See Neckwear—Europe—17th century

VANGA. See Sweden—Östergötland

VAQUEROS
> Gor pl p236-37

VÄRMLAND. See Sweden—Värmland

VAROLA. See Sweden—Vestergötland

VASCONGADAS. See Basque provinces

VÄSTBO. See Sweden—Småland

VÄSTERBOTTEN. See Sweden—Västerbotten

VÄSTERGÖTLAND. See Sweden—Västergötland

VÄSTMANLAND. See Sweden—Västmanland

VÄSTRA. See Sweden—Småland

VAUD. See Switzerland—Vaud

VEILS
14th century
> BroH p38 fig 28

16th century
> Norr v3 bk 2 p505, 626-27 il

18th century
> LesA p68-69 fig 82 pl 17

19th-20th century
> LesA p67-73 il

Egypt, Modern
> LesA p62 il

Greece, Ancient
> LesA p63-65 il

Rome
> LesA p65 pl il

Turkey
> LesA fig 77

VEJLE. See Denmark—Jutland

VENAISSIN. See France—Venaissin

VENDÉE. See France—Poitou

VENDERS. See Street venders and peddlers

VENETIANS. See Breeches—Europe—16th century (1570-1575)

VENEZUELA
> Hal pl 40 (col) (f)
> Nat v77 Ap '40 pl p501 (col) (f)
> Spi pl p80 (col) (f)
> *See also* Military costume—Venezuela

VENICE. See Italy—Venice; also Doges; Noblemen—Venice; Noblewomen—Venice; Senators—Venice

VERA CRUZ. See Mexico—Vera Cruz

VERDINGALE. See Hoop skirts—16th century

VERONA. See Italy—Verona

VESTAL VIRGINS
BruK pl 19 fig 12-13

VESTERGÖTLAND. See Sweden—Vestergötland

VESTMENTS, ECCLESIASTICAL. See
Ecclesiastical costume

VIENNA. See Austria—Vienna

VIERLANDE DISTRICT. See Germany
—Hamburg

VIKINGS
AirS il p24
Wa p75-76 pl p62 fig 74-75

VINCENTIAN SISTERS OF CHARITY
MusE pl 32 (col)

VINGÅKER. See Sweden—Östergötland

VISITATION NUNS
BruK pl 29 fig 16 (col)

VIZCAYA. See Basque provinces

VOLENDAM. See Netherlands—Volendam

VOLUNTEER TROOPS
Austria
18th century
Lez pl p235 (col)
England
16th century
Law v 1 fig 111
17th century
Law v 1 p 185-92 il
18th century
LavB p29-30 pl 8-9 (col)
Law v2 p210-23 il (off, pte)
19th century
BarH pl 9 (col) (pte)
QuV fig 145
Walk pl 25, 31, 33 (col)
France
18th century
Dav v2 p714 il (off, pte)
Germany
19th century
Lez pl p253-60, 330 (col) (off, pte)
United States
19th century
Kre2 pl 9, 11-12, 16, 24-25 (col) (off,
pte)
Tod pl 8, 10 (col) (off, pte)

VORARLBERG. See Austria—Vorarlberg

VOSS. See Norway—Bergenhus, South

W

WACS (WOMEN'S ARMY CORPS). See
Military costume—United States—20th
century—1940—date—Women personnel

WAISTCOATS
Hea p22-25 2 pl (incl pat)
Kle p406 il
16th century
Norr v3 bk 1 p237 fig 276
17th century
LelD p426-27 pl
18th century
Bart p48-49 pl (pat)
Bra pl 33, 36
Dav v2 p687, 689-99, 741 3 pl (incl
pat)
Lel v 11 p 15 fig 8-9 pl 14; v 12 p 16-
17 fig 12
LelD p201 fig 1-3, p426-27 pl
LesA pl 21, 58
Pic il p 163
ViP v2 pl 6, 18
Wa p210, 221 fig 183, 187, 195 (incl
pat)
19th century
LelD p201 fig 4-7
Wa p263, 274 il
WilC pl p290
20th century
CunPr pl p 142 (f)
Carpathian Ruthenia
Mak pl I (col)
Hungary
Bud pl 122 (col)
Indians of North America
Hun pl p32
MasB p56, 60 il (incl pat)
Italy
Mora pl 83
Rumania
Lee p54-55 pl
Russia
Lee p57-58 pl
Spain
AnS p68-70, 273-74, 291 fig 78-79, 326-
28
Sweden
Berg fig 101-02 (incl pat)
Lee p64-66 pl
Sv p 104-12 il
Tyrol
Ham p 17-18, 35-38, 43-46, 51-54 7 pl
(col)
Ori pl p 18, 36, 44, 50, 52, 54 (col)
Yugoslavia
TiK pl 54 fig 1-4

WAISTS
Hea   p32-43   6 pl (incl pat)

17th century
Gor   pl   p83, 89
Lib   pl   p25
Roj   pl   p4, 12-13, 20-21, 24, 30, 35, 42 (pat)
ViP   v 1   pl 12-13
Wa   p 182, 192-94, 200-01   fig 163-64, 172 (incl pat)

18th century
Dav   v2   fig 2084
Gor   pl   p 118
Wa   p214-16, 224-25, 230   fig 185-86, 189C, 189D, 197 (incl pat)

19th century
1800-1810
CunE   pl   p28, 30

1820-1830
CunE   pl   p78

1830-1840
CunE   pl   p 106, 108

1860-1870
CunE   p222-23 il

1870-1880
Wa   p301   fig 244, 246 (incl pat)

1880-1890
Wa   p311   fig 248

1890-1900
Bart   p86-87   pl (pat) (f) fig 35a
CunE   p390, 395 il
LavT2   pl   p 116
Wa   p321-24   fig 254

20th century
Kle   p54-55   il (f)

1900-1910
Ada   v4 il   p307 (f)
Coh   p292-94   pl
HaC   pl   p89
LavT2   pl   p 116
Pic   il   p9
Wa   p338   fig 264-65

1910-1920
HaC   pl   p101, 105
Wa   p346-47   fig 268

1920-1930
LavT2   pl   p 116
Pic   il   p9

Black Forest
Pet   p58-59, 88-89   2 pl

Carpathian Ruthenia
Mak   pl III, V, IX, 51, 54 (3 col)

Central America
CrO   pl 14

China
CrO   pl 14

Chios
Arg   p 192-93   pl 14-17 (4 col)

England
16th century
Norr   v3 bk 2   p428-29 fig 518 (pat)

Finland
Prim   pl   p90

France
15th century
SocC   pl   p23

17th century
SocC   pl   p 19

18th century
Lel   v 11   pl 23 (col);   v 12 fig 26

India
CrO   pl 14

Indians of North America
CrO   pl 14

Korea
CrO   pl 14

Persia
CrO   pl 14

Peru
Cro   pl 14

Philippine Islands
CrO   pl 14

Russia
CrO   pl 14

San Salvador
CrO   pl 14

Spain
CrO   pl 14

Tyrol
Ham   p3-4, 9-10, 15-16, 21-24, 39-40, 55-56   7 pl (col)
Kle   p256   il (f)
Ori   pl   p4, 8, 10, 16, 18, 22, 24, 40, 42, 56 (col)
Pes   pl 1-29 (col)

WALCHEREN.   See   Netherlands—Wal-cheren

WALES
Brad   pl   p 164 (f)
Kar   p20   pl 4 (col) (f)
Lee   p70-72   pl
See also Dancers—Wales; Headdress —Wales

WALKING STICKS.   See Canes, walking sticks, etc.

WALLACHIA.   See Rumania—Wallachia

WALLETS.   See Bags, purses, etc.

WAMPUM BELTS
Trai   p 14   il

WARRIORS.   See Military costume

WARSAW.   See Poland—Warsaw

WATCH FOBS
Dav v2 pl p702
LelD il p53

WATCHES
Ada v3 il p 10
AirB il p31
Bae p 196-212 pl (col) il
BraF p 102 pl p 113-14, 186-87 (f)
Coh p 182-207 il
Dav v 1 p403-406 2 pl; v2 p701 pl
EvnJ p 117, 140-41, 177-79 pl 98-99,
  109-11, 115, 120, 123, 146-47, 151, 157
Lel v 11 fig 33; v 12 fig 24
LelD p278-79 il
LesA p375-85 il
Norr v3 bk 2 p784-86 il

WATCHMEN
England
16th-17th centuries
AirB il p35, 47
Hat fig 18

18th century
AirH il p 12
AirT il p58

United States
Colonial period
Rue pl A

WATER CARRIERS
Buenos Aires
Bac pt4 pl 2 (col) (m)

Egypt
Brad pl p60 (m)

England
16th-17th centuries
AirB il p35
AirT il p59

Palestine, Modern
Wrig pt 1 p9 pl p25

Spain
AnS pl p 141, 215 (f)
CamC pl p 16-17 (f)
OrT pl 49, 149, 156, 228 (f)

WATTEAU GOWNS
Dal v2 fig 596, 601-02, 605-09 (col)
  (incl pat)
Gor pl p 104-06
Kle p 15 il
Pic il p 113
StocM pl 13
UnW pl 67 (col)
WilF pl p 109
WisF pl 14
See also subdivisions of the 18th century under various European countries e.g. France—1715-1774

WAVES (WOMEN'S NAVAL RE-SERVE). See Naval costume—United States—20th century—Women personnel

WEAVERS
Egypt, Ancient
Hous2 p58 fig 62 (f)

England
1066-1154
AirS il p38

13th century
AirM il p26

15th century
Norr v3 bk 1 p 128-29 il (f)

16th century
AirT il p30

WEDDING COSTUME
See also Processions, Wedding
19th century
1810-1820
Mo p40 pl 5 (f)

1820-1830
Int v 1 pl 32

1830-1840
Dav v2 fig 2399, 2405 (f)
LavT2 pl 5 (col)
Mo p55 pl 15
NeV p2 pl 1-2 (f)

1840-1850
CunE pl p 156 (f)
Dav v2 fig 2603 (f)
NeV p2 pl 3, 6-7 (f)

1850-1860
Dav v2 fig 2604 (f)
LelD il p430 (f)
NeV pl 9, 11, 16 (f)
WilC pl p291 (f)

1860-1870
HaC pl p40 (f)
Mo pl 34 (f)
NeV pl 24, 27 (f)
True p40-41 il (f)

1870-1880
Eld pl p25 (f)
Mo p93, 96, 102 pl 40, 43, 48 (f)

1880-1890
Ada v3 il p383
But pl p242
HaC pl p56b (f)
Jen p34 il
Mo p 109 pl 51 (f)
NeV pl 30-31, 35-37 (f)

1890-1900
Ada v4 il p51
Mo p 127, 139 pl 65, 77 (f)
NeV pl 41, 43-46, 48, 50, 52 (f)

20th century
1900-1910
HaC pl p 104b (f)
Mo p 156, 163 pl 92, 97 il (f)

1920-1930
CunPr pl p 197 (f)

WEDDING COSTUME—20th century—
Continued

1930-1940
CunPr il p219 (f)

1940-1950
CunPr pl p272 (f)
Kle p60, 332 il (f)

Austria
Lep pl 10 (col) (f)
Nat v71 Ap '37 pl p461 (col)

Aztec
KaAz pl 2 (col)

Bedouin
Nat v71 Ja '37 p83 il

Bhután
Nat v 102 D '52 pl p737, 744, 747 (col)

Black Forest
Pet pl 12-13, 72-73, 84-85 (1 col) front (col)
Ret pl p 193, 195-96 il p 191, 197

Brittany
CosP pl 6

Bulgaria
Vel pl 8, 15, 20-21, 32, 34, 55 (f)

China
BruK pl 183 fig 16 (col) (f)
Camm pl 17 (f)
Vu pl 13

Czechoslovakia
Int v2 pl 61

England
16th century
Norr v3 bk 2 p651 fig 740 (m)
18th century
SitC pl 12
Yar pl p 190

Finland
Prim pl p83 (f)

France
16th century
BluE p 17-18 pl 3
Dav v2 fig 1288
Lib pl p 16

18th century
Lel v 11 pl 1 (col)
19th century
Dav v2 fig 2399 (f)

Franconia
Er pl 16 (col)

Germany
16th century
WilF pl p65 (f)

18th century
BruM pl p31 (col) (f)
Lel v 11 pl 25 (col)

Greece, Modern
At pl 13, 41a (col) (f)

Hesse
Ret pl p20, 38, 53 il p33, 44-45
RetS pl 84-85, 87

Hungary
Hol p21-22 pl 24 (f)
Nat v73 Ja '38 pl p21, 24, 46 (col)
Pif p34 pl p24, 62-63 (col)
WilF pl p 152 (f)

India
Brad pl p92 (f)
Nat v94 O '48 pl p424 (col) (m)

Italy
13th century
WilC pl p44 (f)

Japan
SaJ pl p85 (f)

Kirghiz
BruK pl 175 fig 9 (col) (f)

Korea
Keit p24 pl (col) (f)

Lapland
WilF pl p65, 154

Malaya
Nat v80 N '41 pl p665 (col)

Mexico
CovM pl 80-81
Too fig 76

Nepal
Nat v97 Ja '50 pl p9 (col) (f)

Norway
BruK pl 127 fig 9 (col) (f)
Nat v75 Ap '39 pl p503-07 (col)
Prim p35-36 pl p46 (col) (f)
Sem pl 2 (col) (f)
Stew p 126-27 il p223
WilF pl p65 (f)

Palestine
Nat v 106 D '54 il p842

Poland
Stry pl 8, 35 (col)

Prussia
17th century
WilF pl p 100 (f)

Rome
WlsC p 138-45 5 pl (f)

Schaumburg-Lippe
Ret pl p 56, 61 (f)

Silesia
Ret il p 120
WilF pl p71

Spain
OrT pl 56, 104-05, 109-13

WEDDING COSTUME—*Continued*

Spreewald

Er p23-27 pl (col) (f)

Sumatra

Nat v81 Ja '42 p94 il; v99 Ja '51 pl p20

Sudetenland

Mal pl 5, 11, 18, 27, 35 (col) (f)

Swabia

Ret pl p 159 (f)

Sweden

CrO pl 28
MusS pl 1 (col)
StocM pl 14-15, 24, 43, 50, 54

Syria

Cyr pl 15 (col)
Rud pl p 171

Thuringia

Ger pl 1, 4, 6 (col) fig 57, 66, 82

Uganda

Nat v83 Ap '43 il p522

United States
19th century
1830-1840

Dav v2 fig 2405

1850-1860

KerA pl p 10 (f)

1860-1870

Jen pl p 11 (f)
KerM no4 pl 1

1880-1890

KerA front (col) (f)

Wends

Ret pl p80, 94, 100 il p88, 92-93, 95, 97-98, 102-03 (f)

West Point (Military academy)

Nat v 101 My '52 pl p624 (col)

Württemberg

BruK pl 139 fig 10-11 (col)

WEDDING HEADDRESS. See Headdress, Wedding

WEDDING PROCESSIONS. See Processions, Wedding

WENDS

Nat v71 F '37 p 166 il
Ret p78-112 12 pl il (f)

See also Germany—Spreewald; also subdivision Wends under Children; Dancers; Headdress, Wedding; Wedding costume

WENROHRONON INDIANS. See Indians of North America—Wenrohronon Indians

WEST INDIES

Nat v73 Mr '38 pl p282, 286 (col (f)
See also Martinique; also Carnival costume—West Indies

WEST POINT UNIFORMS. See Military cadets—United States

WESTMINSTER SCHOOL STUDENTS, LONDON

Cla p22 pl

WESTPHALIA. See Germany — Westphalia

WHITE DEERSKIN DANCE. See Dancers—Indians of North America—White deerskin dance

WHITE RUSSIA. See Russia—White Russia

WIGMAKERS

Germany
17th century

DeZ pl 89 (m)

United States
18th century

McP p 10 pl p9 (m)

WIGS. See Hair, wigs, etc.

WIMPLES AND GORGETS

Bra pl 18, 21
Brad pl p 179-180
BrH p28-29, 36-37 2 pl
CunM p51-53 2 pl
Dav v 1 fig 553-54, 975
EvjD p22-24, 35-36 pl 12 il
LelD p 203, 207 il
Nap p33-35 il
Rey pl p 157
WilC pl p45, 61-62
WilH pl p50-51, 59-63
Yar p67, 80-81 pl p64, 68

WISDOM (SYMBOLIC FIGURE)

Set il p7

WISE MEN. See Biblical costume—Wise men

WITCH DOCTORS

African tribes

CamC pl p 115

WOMEN'S ARMY CORPS (WACS). See Military costume—U.S.—1940—date—Women personnel

WOMEN'S AUXILIARY FERRYING SQUADRON

Ross p67-68 il (col)

WRENS. See Naval costume—England—20th century; Women personnel

WÜRTTEMBERG. See Germany—Württemberg

Y

YAKIMA INDIANS. See Indians of North America—Yakima Indians

YAKUTS
TiK   pl 103 (col)

YANAM
GaU   pl 30-31, 33 (col) (f)

YAP. See Dancers—Yap

YEMEN
Nat   v 101 F '52 pl p232-33, 237, 241-44 (col)

YEOMEN OF THE GUARD
AirT   il p6
BarH   p41-42 pl 2, 23 (col)
Hat   fig 163
Law   v 1 p3-4 il
Nat   v71 Ja '37 p3, 19 pl (col) il;
   v93 Ap '48 il p434, Je '48 pl p754
   (col); v 104 S '53 il p308 (col)
Norr   v3 bk 1 p50-52, 289-91 pl (col)
   il; bk 2 p420-23, 686-88 2 pl (1 col)
   il

YUCATÁN. See Mexico—Yucatán

YUGOSLAVIA
CrO   pl 29
   See also subdivision Yugoslavia under
   Dancers; Headdress; Military costume

BY REGION OR PROVINCE
Bosnia
BruK   pl 161 fig 10, 12-13, 16 (col)
Lee   p46-47 pl (m)
Nat   v79 Je '41 pl p803 (f)
TiK   pl 55 (col)

Croatia and Slavonia
Jan   p 16 pl 2 (col)
Nat   v75 Je '39   pl   p707, 711, 731
   (col) (f)
WilF   pl p74

Dalmatia
BruK   pl 161 fig 4-8 (col)
Lee   p46-47 pl (f)
Nat   v75 Je '39 pl p713, 723 (1 col)
TiK   pl 54-55 (col)

Herzegovina
BruK   pl 161 fig 1-3 (col)
TiK   pl 54, 56 (col)

Montenegro
BruK   pl 161 fig 11, 17 (col)
Jan   p 16 pl 3 (col)
Nat   v79 Je '41 pl p804 (m)
TiK   pl 56 (col)

Serbia
Jan   p 16 pl 1 (col)
Nat   v71 My '37 pl p559 (f); v79
   Je '41 pl p797-98; v85 Ap '44 pl
   p501, 503, 508; v99 F '51 pl p 154-
   55 (col) (f)
TiK   pl 59-60 (col)

YUMA INDIANS. See Indians of North America—Yuma Indians

YUNNAN. See China—Yunnan

Z

ZAANSTREEK. See Netherlands—North Holland

ZAMORA. See Spain—León

ZANZIBAR
Nat   v 101 F '52 pl p267, 272 (col)

ZARAGOSSA. See Spain—Aragon

ZEALAND. See Denmark—Zealand

ZEELAND. See Netherlands—Zeeland

ZIPS. See Hungary

ZOUAVES
BluN   pl p204, 208, 210
France
KnR   pl p297
LelD   pl p224 row 4 (col); p435 il
United States
Kre   pl 15 (col) (off, pte)
Kre2   pl 17, 21 (col) (off, pte)
Nat   v99 F '51 pl p201 (col)

ZUG. See Switzerland—Zug

ZULUS
Nat   v 104 Ag '53 pl p159, 173 (col)

ZUNI INDIANS. See Indians of North America—Zuni Indians

ZURICH. See Switzerland—Zurich

LIST OF BOOKS INDEXED

LIST OF BOOKS INDEXED

Prices have been omitted in this SUPPLEMENT because of the frequency with which they change. A Union List has not been included since most of the books, being fairly recent publications, are more widely held than the older publications indexed in 1937.

Ab   Abram, Annie
English life and manners in the later middle ages. New York, E. P. Dutton & co. 1913
Illustrations in black and white drawn from contemporary sources. One chapter on dress

Aaa   Adams, James Truslow
Album of American history. New York, Charles Scribner's sons, 1944-1948. 4v
Some costume illustrations are included in this pictorial account of American life from Colonial times to the 20th century

Agu   Aguilera, Emiliano M.
Los trajes populares de España vistos por los pintores españoles, con 7 laminas en color y 125 reproducciones en negro. Barcelona, Ediciones Omega, 1948
Plates show costumes of the various provinces of Spain as depicted by Goya, Bayeu, Sorolla, Chicharro, etc. Explanatory text of 61 pages. Plates only indexed

AirB   Airne, Clement Wallace
Britain's story told in pictures; over 450 illustrations depicting the history of Britain from the earliest times to the present day. Manchester, Sankey, Hudson & co. 1935
This book and those that follow by the same author consist of many small illustrations in black and white on each page with brief identifying text. They show many occupations of English life

AirH   The story of Hanoverian and modern Britain told in pictures. Manchester, Sankey, Hudson & co. [1935]

AirM   The story of mediaeval Britain told in pictures. Manchester, Sankey, Hudson & co. [1935]

AirO   Our Empire's story told in pictures. Manchester, Sankey, Hudson & co. [1935]

AirP   The story of prehistoric and Roman Britain told in pictures. Manchester, Sankey, Hudson & co. [1935]

AirS   The story of Saxon and Norman Britain told in pictures. Manchester, Sankey, Hudson & co. [1935]

AirT   The story of Tudor and Stuart Britain told in pictures. Manchester, Sankey, Hudson & co. [1935]

AlF   Allen, Frederick Lewis
I remember distinctly, a family album of the American people 1918-1941, assembled by Agnes Rogers with running comment by F. L. Allen. New York, Harper & brothers, 1947
Photographs portray scenes from the life of the period

Alv   Alvarez y Alvarez de la Cadena, Luis
México; leyendas y costumbres, trajes y danzas. México, Editorial Layac, 1945
Costumes of the different states and tribes from Montezuma to modern times, and also pictures of dancers and bullfighters with full text. Only color plates indexed

Am   Ambrose, Kay
Classical dances and costumes of India . . . London, A. and C. Black, 1951
Illustrations, photographs and drawings by the author

Amer   American engraving society, New York
Nineteenth century fashion plates. Andres, inc., New York, American distributors. New York, American engraving society, [1941]
Portfolio of 12 colored plates showing women's dress of the period without more definite subdivisions. Plate numbers have been assigned

AndD   Andersen, Ellen Dorothea Johanna (Brodersen)
Danish folk costumes. Copenhagen, Gylendalske Boghandel, 1948
Sixteen plates in black and white showing regional costumes. Descriptive text

AndF   Folk costumes in Denmark, pictures and descriptions of local dresses in the National Museum. Copenhagen, Hassing, 1952
Thirty plates, some in color, show the dress of many sections. Twelve of the color plates are identical with those in her "Danske folkedragten"

AnS   Anderson, Ruth Matilda
Spanish costume: Extremadura. New York, Hispanic society of America, 1951 (Hispanic notes and monographs. Peninsular series)
A book of 319 pages containing plates and illustrations of local costume of the province

Ar Arata, Giulio Ulisse, and Biasi, Giuseppe
Arte sarda . . . Milan, S. a. Fratelli Treves editori [1935]
Sixteen color plates and more than 200 in black and white include Sardinian costume and jewelry

Arg Argenti, Philip Pandely
The costumes of Chios, their development from the XVth to the XXth century. London, B. T. Batsford, 1953
One hundred twenty-one plates, many in color, illustrations and patterns, full text. Only plates indexed

Arm Armstrong, Lucile
Dances of Spain. New York, Chanticleer press; London, Max Parrish and co. 1950 2v (Handbooks of European national dances)
Volume 1: South, centre and northwest; v2: North-East and East. Each has 4 color plates showing dancers in costume with brief text and with directions and music

Bemidji *Mesabi Comm Coll*

Arms Dances of Portugal. New York, Chanticleer press, 1948 (Handbooks of European national dances)
Brief text on costumes with 4 color plates showing dancers in native dress

St. Olaf has 2d ed *St. Cloud* *Mesabi CC*

At Athens. Mouseion Benaké
Hellenic national costumes, ed by A. E. Benaki; text by Mrs Angeliki Hadzimichali; plates by Nicolas Sperling. Athens, 1948
Eighty-six full-length figures on extra large color plates showing costumes of Greece, Euboea island, Epirus, Macedonia. Text in English, French and Greek describes the costumes that belong chiefly to the Benaki museum

Bac Bacle y Compañía, Buenos Aires
Trajes y costumbres de la Provincia de Buenos Aires. Ed. facsimilar con un prólogo de Alejo González Garaño. Buenos Aires, Viau, 1947
Reprint of a book that appeared in 1833. In 6 parts, each of which has 6 color plates

Bae Baerwald, Marcus, and Mahoney, Tom
Gems and jewelry today; an account of the romance and values of gems, jewelry, watches and silverware. New York, Marcel Rodd co. 1949
Several plates, one in color, and many illustrations

NK5525 .B3

BarH Barnes, Robert Money
A history of the regiments & uniforms of the British army. 2d ed. London, Seeley Service & co. 1951
Full descriptive text accompanied by 22 colored plates

Bart Barton, Lucy
Period patterns by Doris Edson, with text by Lucy Barton. A supplement to Historic costume for the stage. Boston, Walter H. Baker co. 1942
Detailed patterns with directions for making garments from those of the 16th century to the 20th. A few figures in costume of the period are shown on 6 plates at end of book

Concord

BartC Costuming the Biblical play. Boston, Walter H. Baker co. 1937
A pamphlet with line drawings illustrating typical costumes that may be used for many Biblical characters

Mankato

BelQ Bell, Quentin
On human finery. New York, A. A. Wyn, 1949
Discussion of the philosophy of clothes. 4 plates in color

GT521.B4 *1976* *(2d ed)*

Bene Benet, Sula
Song, dance and customs of peasant Poland. New York, Roy publishers, n.d.
Several pages of text with 6 plates showing regional dress

Moorhead

Berg Bergman, Eva Angelika Margareta
Nationella dräkten, en studie kring Gustaf III: s dräktreform 1778 with an English summary. Stockholm [P. A. Norstedt & Söner] 1938
Pictures in black and white and 3 in color. Only plates and illustrations indexed

Gustavus *Adolphus*

BiE Bieber, Margarete
Entwicklungsgeschichte der griechischen tracht von der vorgriechischen zeit bis zur römischen kaiserzeit. Berlin, Gebr. Mann, 1934
Fifty-four photographic plates from authoritative sources display Greek dress of pre-Homeric, classic and Greek-Roman period

Bin Binder, Pearl
Muffs and morals. London, George C. Harrap & co. 1953
Black and white plates and illustrations with chapters on hair, underwear, sumptuary laws, etc.

GT515 .B56

Bis Bishop, Isabella Lucy (Bird)
Korea and her neighbors. New York, Fleming H. Revell co. 1898
A travel book containing a few illustrations of costume

DS902.2 .B57 1970

BluC Blum, André
Le costume en France. [Lausanne] Guilde du livre, 1944 (Collection Gai savoir v2)
Costumes from early times to period of the third republic. Small illustrations

BluE Early Bourbon, 1590-1643. London, George C. Harrap and co. 1951 (Costume of the western world)
Costumes of the time of King Henry IV and of Louis XIII. Sixty-six plates, 8 in color, are reproductions of paintings. Descriptive text

Moorhead

BluL MOORHEAD

The last Valois, 1515-1590. London, George C. Harrap and co. 1951 (Costume of the western world)
Costumes of the time of Francis I, Henry II, Charles IX and Henry III. Seventy-one plates, 8 in color, are reproductions of paintings. Descriptive text

BluN

Blum, André, and Chassé, Charles
Histoire du costume, les modes au XIXᵉ siècle. Paris, Libraire Hachette, 1931
More than 200 plates show civil, regional, official and military costume. Comprehensive text

BoeB

Boehn, Max von
Biedermeier, Deutschland von 1815-1947. 2d ed. Berlin, Verlag Bruno Cassirer, n.d.
One chapter on costume with colored plates indexed. Text in German type.

BoeR

Rokoko, Frankreich im XVIII jahrhundert. Berlin, Askanischer verlag, 1919
Contains a chapter on costume of the 18th century with illustrations and 5 plates in color

BosE nohᴀ

Boston. Museum of fine arts
Elizabethan England. Boston, The museum, 1939 (Museum extension publications. Illustrative set no 1)
Portfolio of 41 plates, 14 of which show dress of the period with 2 pages of text in an accompanying pamphlet

BosF nonᴀ Olaf

The French renaissance by C. E. Boyd. Boston, The museum, 1940 (Museum extension publications. Illustrative set no 3)
Portfolio of 42 plates some of which show costumes of the 13th to 16th centuries by means of illustrations from manuscripts and paintings of the period

Bra 510.B69

Bradley, Carolyn G.
Western world costume, an outline history. New York, Appleton-Century-Crofts, 1954
First chapters describe costumes of the ancient world but remainder of the book relates to general European costume. Sixty-two plates of line drawings in red with descriptions of articles of male and female dress. Glossary of terms used in costume

Brad 596.B7

Bradshaw, Angela
World costumes. New York, Macmillan co. 1953
Native costumes of 79 countries shown in 142 pages of black and white sketches and 16 colored plates

BraF Cloud + Olaf

Bradford, Ernle Dusgate Selby
Four centuries of European jewellery. New York, Philosophical library, 1953
Many photographs of outstanding examples of jewelry accompany text on background, processes and materials

Breu Cloud

Breuer, Katharina
Dances of Austria. New York, Chanticleer press [1948] (Handbooks of European national dances)
Four colored plates with brief text on costumes and directions for dances with music

BrH GT730 .B68 1971 (3) ed)

Bradfield, Nancy Margetts
Historical costumes of England from the eleventh to the twentieth century. London, George C. Harrap & co. [1938]
For each reign one page is devoted to full length costume figures with marginal notes describing each article of attire. Sixty-eight plates, partially colored

Brk UofM, Crookston

Brooklyn institute of arts and sciences. Museum
Two centuries of French fashion... Brooklyn, The museum, 1949
Photographs of 49 mannequin dolls portray French fashions from 1715 to 1906 with brief text. Indexed as costume rather than as dolls

Bro20

Brooke, Iris
English costume 1900-1950. London, Methuen & co. 1951
A continuation of the earlier volumes indexed in the COSTUME INDEX of 1937. Text accompanied by line drawings showing dress of each decade

BroF portions of this are in GT2130.B7

A history of English footwear. London, St Giles publishing co. [1949]
Eight color plates and line drawings on footwear from 1066 to 1948. Introductory text and illustrations include footwear of Greece, Rome, etc.

BroH GT730.B7 1949

A history of English costume. London, Methuen & co. [1949]
From Norman times to 1900. More condensed treatment than in her 6 books on English costume indexed in the COSTUME INDEX of 1937. Four color plates and 142 figures in line drawings

BroW GT720.B7

Western European costume and its relation to the theatre. New York, Macmillan co. 1939-1940. 2v
Colored plates and many illustrations with descriptive text relating to French, Dutch, German, Spanish and Italian costume from the 13th to the mid-19th century

Bruh

Bruhn, Wolfgang
Kostüm und mode. Bilder von Helmut Skarbina. Leipzig, L. Staackmann, 1938
European costume from Bronze age in Germany to 1906 shown in 80 color plates and 88 pages of text in German type

BruK neuville und

Bruhn, Wolfgang, and Tilke, Max
Das kostümwerk; eine geschichte des kostüms aller zeiten und völker vom altertum zur neuzeit. Berlin, Ernst Wasmuth, 1941
Two hundred plates, mostly in color, depict and describe costumes of the world. Twelve plates of patterns

BruM St. Olaf

Bruhn, Wolfgang
Die mode in fünf jahrhunderten. Leipzig, Bibliographisches institut [1936]
European costume from 15th to 19th centuries. Several color plates and others in black and white

Bud   Budapest. Magyar nemzeti múzeum
L'Art populaire hongrois. ₁Budapest, 1928?₁
Text by Sigismond Bátky and Étienne Györffy. Plates, mostly colored, show Hungarian costume from 17th century to present

Buda   Buday, Gyory
Dances of Hungary. New York, Chanticleer press, 1950 (Handbooks of European national dances)
One page of text on costume, accompanied by directions and music for dances. Three plates in color

Bemidji
Mesabi
st. cloud

Burr   Burris-Meyer, Elizabeth
This is fashion, illustrated by Eleanor Beckham. New York, Harper & brothers, 1943
Each of the 29 plates of line drawings is accompanied by descriptions and by sections on color, accessories, fabrics, cosmetics and coiffure for each period

GT510 .B8

But   Butterfield, Roger
The American past, a history of the United States from Concord to Hiroshima, 1775-1945. New York, Simon and Schuster, 1947
No text on costume. Of interest because of photographs of men's apparel of the period

folio E-178
.B988

CamC   Campbell, Heyworth
Camera around the world. New York, Robert M. McBride and co. 1937
Some of the photographs show costumes of peoples of Europe and of the Orient

Mesabi

Camm   Cammann, Schuyler
China's dragon robes. New York, Ronald press co. 1952
Evolution of the dragon robe and related robes shown in 20 plates

Carm   Carman, W. Y.
Uniforms of the navy, past & present. London, Forster Groom & co. 1942
Uniforms of the British navy, shown in 15 plates in blue with slight touches of gold, from early times to the second world war

Carta   Carta Raspi, Raimondo
Costumi sardi. Cagliari, Edizioni della Fondazione Il Nuraghe, n.d.
Costumes of many sections of Sardinia shown in 39 plates

Chr   Christensen, Erwin Ottomar
The index of American design. New York, Macmillan co. 1950
Included are 2 color plates and several figures, 5 in color, with brief text on costume

Ref NK1403 .C5

Christopher, Catherine. See Roberts, Catherine Christopher

Cla   Clare, Wallace
The historic dress of the English schoolboy, illus by Geoffrey Bickers (First series) London, Society for the preservation of ancient customs ₁1939₁
Costumes of 12 public schools with descriptions of their uniforms. Twelve plates, 2 in color

Coh   Cohn, David Lewis
The good old days, a history of American morals and manners as seen through the Sears, Roebuck catalogs 1905 to the present. New York, Simon and Schuster, 1940
Small illustrations from catalogs of the early 20th century. Text gives a general picture of the life of the period

Concordia

ColH   Collie, George F.
Highland dress with colour plates from McIan's The clans of the Scottish Highlands. London, Penguin books, 1948
Brief text accompanies 24 color plates of figures in tartans

Coll   Collins, C. Cody
Love of a glove; the romance, legends and fashion history of gloves. rev ed. New York, Fairchild publishing co. 1947
Photographs and descriptions of gloves from ancient times to the present. Royal and ecclesiastical gloves included

Hibbing CC

CorA   Cordry, Donald Bush, and Cordry, Dorothy M.
Costumes and textiles of the Aztec Indians of the Cuetzalán region, Puebla, Mexico. Los Angeles, Southwest museum, 1940 (Southwest museum papers no 14)
Photographs and drawings with text describing details of shirts, cloaks, belts, etc. of Indians of Puebla

Hill Ref Lib

CorZ   Costumes and weaving of the Zoque Indians of Chiapas, Mexico. Los Angeles, Southwest museum, 1941 (Southwest museum papers no 15)
Black and white plates and illustrations with one section devoted to costume

Winona

CosP   Costumes paysans. Paris, Ch. Massin et cie ₁1930₁ (L'Art populaire français)
Forty plates, 8 in color, show full-length figures of the provinces of France

Cov   Covarrubias, Miguel
Island of Bali, with an album of photographs by Rose Covarrubias. New York, Alfred A. Knopf, 1942
Brief account of costume, detailed description of dances. Photographs following page 405 have been assigned numbers

Concordia

CovM   Mexico South, the Isthmus of Tehuantepec. New York, Alfred A. Knopf, 1946
Photographs and drawings, with 5 plates in color show costume of the region with descriptions

F1359.c6

Cra Crane, John de Murinelly Cirne
The United States Marines, a pictorial history of the Marines. Baton Rouge, Army and Navy publishing co. 1952
Photographs and sketches showing activities of the Corps from 1775 to 1918 and incidentally uniforms of different periods. Pages assigned

CrC Crawford, Morris De Camp, and Guernsey, Elizabeth A.
The history of corsets in pictures. New York, Fairchild publications, 1951
Corsets from ancient times to the 1940's shown in 41 pages with a page of line drawings for each period

_2075.C7_

CrH Crawford, Morris De Camp, and Crawford, Elizabeth G.
The history of lingerie in pictures. New York, Fairchild publications, 1952
Full descriptions of women's underwear, particularly of the 19th century, with plates of line drawings for each garment

_2073.C7_

CrO Crawford, Morris De Camp
One world of fashion. New York, Fairchild publishing co. 1946
Large book of 60 plates in black and white with several articles on each plate. Fashions of the ancient Near East from 3500 B.C. to the 20th century

folio T510.C7
_510.C7 1956_
_GT510.C7 1967_

Cros Crosfield, Domini (Elliadi) lady
Dances of Greece. New York, Chanticleer press, 1948 (Handbooks of European national dances)
Four color plates, with paragraphs on costume, accompany directions and music for dances

loud & st olaf
_ve 2d ed_

CrP Crawford, Morris De Camp
Philosophy in clothing. Brooklyn, Brooklyn museum [1940]
Written for a clothing exhibition held by the Brooklyn museum in 1940. Ten plates show a selection of garments from several countries. Plates have been assigned numbers

CunA Cunnington, Cecil Willett
The art of English costume. London, Collins, 1948
Covers costume from 13th century to 1950 with illustrations and plates drawn from brasses, manuscripts, portraits, etc. Chapters on men's and on women's dress and on sleeves, gloves, headdress

CunE English women's clothing in the nineteenth century. London, Faber and Faber, 1937
Illustrations in black and white and numerous plates, 10 in color, with detailed descriptions of garments of each year of the century

Hist Soc
KATO

CunF Feminine attitudes in the nineteenth century. London, William Heinemann, 1935
The effect of social changes in the 19th century as reflected in the attitude of English women towards costume. Eight illustrations

_of St_
nedict

CunM Cunnington, Cecil Willett, and Cunnington, Phillis
Handbook of English mediaeval costume. London, Faber and Faber, 1953
Deals with individual articles of attire from 800 to 1500. Illustrations from manuscripts, brasses and similar sources. Numerous plates, some colored. Full text

_GT732 .C84_
_2d ed (1969)_
at Bemidji

CunP Cunnington, Cecil Willett
The perfect lady. New York, Chanticleer press, 1948
Costumes of women of the 19th and early 20th centuries with 16 plates in color

MANKATO

CunPr Women's clothing in the present century. London, Faber and Faber, 1952
English fashions for each year from 1900 to 1950. Many plates, 3 in color, line drawings and photographs accompanied by full text

_GT738.M36_
_1973_
(reprint)

CunS Cunnington, Cecil Willett, and Cunnington, Phillis
Handbook of English costume in the sixteenth century with illustrations by Barbara Phillipson. London, Faber and Faber [1954]
Seventy-two plates of line drawings, colored frontispiece. Text covers two periods, 1500-1545 and 1545-1600, on dress of men and women with detailed description of each article of attire. Glossary

_GT730.C872_
_1970b_
(rev ed)

CunU The history of underclothes. London, Michael Joseph, 1951
One hundred nineteen illustrations of every article of underwear for European men and women from medieval times to the 20th century.

new ed at
Winona
fergus falls
normandale
rochester
minn hist soc
college of st ben

Cyr Cyr, Georges
Lebanese and Syrian costumes. Beyrouth, Imprimerie Catholique [1939?]
Twenty-five colored plates. No text

minot

Dab Dabney, Edith, and Wise, Claude Merton
Dramatic costume for children, a book of costumes for children's plays, pageants, operettas, and holiday dramatizations. St Louis, Educational publishers, 1949
Brief descriptions of types and of regional dress accompanied by 30 plates of line drawings

mayville

Dal Dalmau, R. and Soler Janer, J. María
Historia del traje. Barcelona, Dalmau, 1946 2v
Divided by centuries. For each period a general survey of masculine and feminine dress is followed by sections on headdress, footwear, jewelry. Both illustrations and plates are in color

Dan Danske folkedragter. Danish folk costumes. Copenhagen, Hassing [194?]
Twelve color plates from costumes exhibited in the National museum, Copenhagen. These plates are identical with the color plates in "Folk costumes in Denmark" by Ellen Andersen. No text

Dau **Daughters of the American Revolution, Texas**
Historic costume and furnishing . . . presented to the Texas state college for women. n.p. 1940
Photographs of inaugural gowns or replicas of them worn by wives of governors of Texas from 1836 to 1938

GT513.D8 **Dav** **Davenport, Millia**
The book of costume. New York, Crown publishers, 1948 2v
More than 2000 illustrations and 8 plates in color show costume from Babylonian times to 19th century. Full descriptive text for each illustration. In this book some illustrations that cover more than half of a page have been called plates

E178.5 .D3 **Davi** **Davidson, Marshall**
Life in America. Boston, Houghton Mifflin co. 1951 2v
Published in association with the Metropolitan museum of art. Examples drawn from contemporary drawings, prints, etc. include types of dress from Colonial time to 20th century

Concordia Moorhead **DeB** **De Banke, Cécile**
Shakespearean stage production, then & now; a manual for the scholar-player. New York, McGraw-Hill book co. 1953
Three chapters on costume with descriptive text and illustrations of garments worn in Shakespearian time. Line drawings of gowns, neckwear, headdress, etc.

DeZ **De Zemler, Charles**
Once over lightly; the story of man and his hair. New York, 1939
History of beards, hair and wigs with illustrations of barbers and barber-surgeons at work. Plates indexed with some references to text

D'Iv **D'Ivori, Juan, pseud of Juan Villa-Puig**
Vestidos típicos de España. Barcelona, Editorial "Orbis" [1936]
Large color plates. Prefatory and explanatory text divided by provinces and cities

MANKATO & Austin cc have 1st ed
Concordia & MSU have 2ded **Dot** **Doten, Hazel R. and Boulard, Constance**
Fashion drawing, how to do it. New York, Harper & brothers, 1939
Includes 70 pages on the history of costume with line drawings on each page. Many details shown, such as footwear, hair, sleeves

St. Olaf St. Mary's **Doy** **Doyé, Franz von Sales**
Die alten trachten der männlichen und weiblichen orden sowie der geistlichen mitglieder der ritterlichen orden. Leipzig, Vier quellen verlag [1930]
One hundred sixty plates in color with 2 figures on each plate show costumes of monks, nuns and members of military religious orders

Dur **Durant, John, and Bettmann, Otto**
GV583.D85 1973 (3ded) Pictorial history of American sports from Colonial times to the present. New York, A.S. Barnes and co. 1952
Hundreds of illustrations in black and white picture tennis, golf, baseball, football apparel

DuS **DuSolier, Wilfrido**
Ancient Mexican costume. México, D.F., Edicione Mexicanas, 1950
Pre-Hispanic costumes of deities, priests, warriors, ambassadors, kings, women shown on 52 plates in color and some illustrations, with 93 pages of descriptive text. Also published in Spanish with different pagination as "Indumentaria antigua mexicana"

Dz **Dziewanowski, Wladyslaw**
Polish armed forces through the ages. London, "Orbis" Polish travel office, 1944
General impressions rather than sharp outlines shown on 32 color plates. Text in Polish and English

Edson, Doris. See Barton, Lucy. Period patterns

Eld **Eldridge, Charlotte**
grand forks public The Godey lady doll. The story of her creation with patterns for dresses and doll furniture. New York, Hastings house, 1953
Pictures and patterns of dolls dressed in the 1860-1880 period with full directions for making and with patterns for each period. A few plates from Godey's *Lady's Book* included to show corresponding styles in women's dress

Eli **Elicker, Virginia Wilk**
MANKATO Gus Adolph Bemidji St Cloud Biblical costumes for church and school. New York, A.S. Barnes and co. 1953
Costumes for Hebrews, Pharisees, children, and characters, as Esther, Sarah, Joseph

Ema **Ema, Tsutomu**
Historical sketch of Japanese customs and costumes. Tokyo, Society for international relations, 1936
Divided into five periods from ancient times to 1858 with text and costumes illustrating each period

Er **Erich, Oswald Adolf**
Concordia Deutsche volkstrachten. 3d rev ed. Leipzig, Bibliographisches institut [1934]
Plates in color, accompanied by text in German type show peasant costumes of 16 regions

Erl **Erlam, Denys**
Ranks and uniforms of the German army, navy and air force, collected from German semi-official sources and largely based upon Uniformen der deutschen wehrmacht by Eberhard Hettler. London, Seeley service & co. [1940]
Line drawings and 11 plates in color accompanied by text on uniforms and insignia of the 20th century. Plates only indexed

Eth   Ethridge, Ken
         Costume for the amateur. Edinburgh, Albyn press, 1947
         A practical book dealing with stage costume in a broad way. Includes Greek, Roman, medieval, Tudor, and 17th to 19th century (1870) dress, with suggestions for adapting the illustrations to stage performances. Line drawings with patterns

EvjD   Evans, Joan
         Dress in medieval France. Oxford, Clarendon press, 1952
         Costume from 1060 to 1515 illustrated from contemporary sources with full descriptive text. Eighty-four plates in black and white and 11 figures in the text

EvnH   Evans, Mary
         How to make historic American costumes, illustrated by Elizabeth Brooks. New York, A.S. Barnes and co. 1942
         Patterns and directions for making dresses from the Colonial period to the 1870's. Indian and Eskimo costume included

EvnJ   Evans, Joan
         A history of jewellery 1100-1870. New York, Pitman publishing corp. 1953
         Full history of jewels of the period with 10 plates in color and 176 in monotone. Because text relating to the plates is scattered throughout the book, the text has been only partly indexed

EvnR   Evans, R. K.
         Dress; the evolution of cut and its effect on modern design. London, Faber and Faber [1939]
         A practical book in which text, plates and illustrations show development of women's dress. Patterns

Eyr   Eyre-Todd, George
         The Highland clans of Scotland; their history and traditions ... with one hundred and twenty-two illustrations including reproductions of M'Ian's celebrated paintings of the costumes of the clans. New York, D. Appleton and co. 1923 2v
         Plates in color showing figures in tartans of the clans

Faw   Fawcett, Clara Hallard
         On making, mending and dressing dolls. New York, H. L. Lindquist publications, 1949
         In addition to period and character dolls, contains chapters on costume of the 19th century and on that of all the ladies of the White House up to 1945. Line drawings. Some patterns

Flow   Flower, Margaret
         Victorian jewellery. New York, Duell, Sloan and Pearce, 1951
         Ten color plates and illustrations show jewelry of the early, middle and late Victorian period. For each period a few plates show figures dressed in costume of the time

Fras   Fraser, Grace Lovat
         Doll making at home. New York, The Studio, 1940
         Illustrations of 17 types of dolls accompanied by patterns and descriptions of materials

Fro   Froger, Pierre
         Panaches et culottes de peau. Angers, Éditions Jacques-Petit, 1946
         Twenty plates in color showing uniforms of the French army of the first Empire. Descriptive text

GaE   Gallois, Émile
         Costumes espagnols. New York, French & European publications [1939]
         Portfolio of 40 color plates showing costumes of different regions of Spain

Gal   Galanti, Bianca M.
         Dances of Italy. New York, Chanticleer press, 1950 (Handbooks of European dances)
         Four color plates show costumes of Italian dances with notes on dress and with music and directions for the dances

GaP   Gallois, Émile
         Provinces françaises. Costumes décoratifs. New York, French & European publications [1936]
         A portfolio of 40 colored plates of regional dress of France worn by women

GaU   Costumes de l'Union française. Paris, Éditions Arc-en-Ciel [1946]
         Twelve color plates in portfolio show costumes of dependencies of France in Africa, America, Asia and Oceania

         Vêtements et parures du Cameroun français. See Lebeuf, Jean Paul

         Galter, Juan Subías. See Subías Galter, Juan

Gen   Genoni, Rosa
         La storia della moda attraverso i secoli. v 1: Prehistoric, Egypt, Assyria, Babylonia, Greece. Bergamo, Istituto italiano d'arti grafiche, n.d.
         Many small illustrations and 8 color plates

Ger   Gerbing, Luise
         Die Thüringer trachten in wort und bild. 2d ed. Berlin, Herbert Stubenrauch, 1936
         Seventeen colored plates and many illustrations show costumes of different regions of Thuringia with full text

Gern   Gernsheim, Helmut
         Masterpieces of Victorian photography with a foreword by C. H. Gibbs-Smith. London, Phaidon press [1951]
         Among the 72 plates are several that show costumes of the 19th century

GiMi   Giafferri, Paul Louis Victor de, marquis
         Millinery in the fashion history of the world from 5300 B.C. to the present era. New York, Illustrated Milliner co. 1927
         Pages assigned to text and plates. Sixteen plates in color from the author's History of the feminine costume of the world. Many illustrations

Giafferi, P. L. V. de—*Continued*

GiR   Costumes régionaux. Paris, Libraire Gründ, n.d. 2v
Portfolio of 74 color plates with accompanying volume of text showing costumes of provinces of France

Glin   **Gliński, Tomasz** arranger
Polskie tańce ludowe. Polish folk dances. London, Maxwell, Love & co [1943]
Twenty large color plates in case show costumes of regions of Poland and attitudes of dancers. With music

Bemidji Minn Hist Soc

Go   **Gordon, Lesley**
A pageant of dolls; with a foreword by Janet Pagter Johl. New York, A. A. Wyn, 1949
Wax, novelty, wooden, rag dolls, etc. shown in 16 color plates and many line drawings. Some in national dress

Gom   **Gómez-Tabanera, José Manuel**
Trajes populares y costumbres tradicionales. Madrid, Editorial Tesoro [1950] (Tesoro del folklore español)
Descriptive text, photographs and 23 color plates of costumes of many provinces of Spain, the Balearic islands, Canary islands, Basque provinces

folio GT 513. G6

Gor   **Gorsline, Douglas Warren**
What people wore, a visual history of dress from ancient times to twentieth-century America. New York, Viking press, 1952
The text traces the general style changes; plates are drawings from source material. Ten plates in color, many in black and white with several figures on each

GrA   **Great Britain. Admiralty**
Uniform regulations for officers of the fleet, 1937. London, H. M. Stationery office, 1937
Uniforms and insignia of the Royal navy, Royal naval reserve and the Royal naval volunteer reserve shown in black and white plates with descriptive text

Recv'd at Hibbing Itasca

GrAi   **Great Britain. Air Ministry**
Dress regulations for officers of the Royal Air Force. 2d abridged ed. December 1939. London, H. M. Stationary office, 1940 (Air publication 1358)
Descriptive text with 10 plates in black and white. Contains also a section on decorations, ribbons and medals of officers

2nd ed at Moorhead

Gre   **Green, Joyce Mary Conyngham**
Period costumes & settings for the small stage. London, George C. Harrap & co. 1936
Line drawings of figures in costume from the period of William I of England to that of George IV

Gri   **Grindea, Miron, and Grindea, Carola**
Dances of Rumania. New York, Crown publishers, 1952 (Handbooks of European national dances)
Colored plates showing 3 costumes of Transylvania and 1 of Wallachia with music and directions for dances. Brief descriptions of costume

Minot

Haa   **Haar, Francis**
DS811.42
The best of old Japan. Rutland, Charles E. Tuttle co. 1951
Photographic studies of the Japanese people that include dress of adults, children, priests, etc.

HaC   **Hall, Carrie A.**
hibbing minn hist soc
From hoopskirts to nudity; photographs by M. E. Everhard. Caldwell, Idaho, Caxton printers, 1938
A review of fashions from 1866 to 1936 shown in 125 photographs

Hal   **Halouze, Édouard**
case folio GT675 .H3
Costumes of South America. Preface by Dorothy Shaver. New York, French & European publications, 1941
Shown in 27 large color plates. No text

Ham   **Hammerstein, Hans von**
Trachten der Alpenländer . . . Vienna, Herbert Reichner, 1937
Brief text in French and English with 60 color plates of full-length figures wearing Tyrolean dress

Hat   **Hatcher, Orie Latham**
PR 2910 .H35
A book for Shakespeare plays and pageants, a treasury of Elizabethan and Shakespearean detail for producers, stage managers, actors, artists and students. New York, E. P. Dutton & co. 1916
Descriptive text with illustrations of characters in pageants and processions accompany 200 pictures and portraits of life and people of the period

Hea   **Healy, Daty**
Dress the show, a basic costume book. Foreword by Winifred Ward. Evanston, Row, Peterson and co. 1948
A practical book for amateur theatricals. Includes patterns with directions for making various garments such as jackets, trousers, hats. Plates show regional and fancy dress. Spiral binding

this— at mankato St cloud St john

Heik   **Heikel, Yngvar, and Collan, Anni**
Dances of Finland. New York, Chanticleer press, 1948 (Handbooks of European national dances)
National costumes shown on 4 brightly colored plates. Directions and music for dances

Her   **Hermann, Walter**
The costumes of old Switzerland. Munich, F. Bruckmann, 1938
Full-length figures shown on 21 plates. Brief explanatory text for each plate in English, French and German. Small, oblong book. Plate numbers have been assigned

HeuO   **Heuzey, Léon Alexandre, and Heuzey, Jacques**
Histoire du costume dans antiquité classique. L'Orient: Égypte-Mésopotamie — Syrie — Phénicie. [Paris] Société d'édition Les Belles lettres, 1935
Detailed description of ancient dress with 58 plates, 3 in color, and many illustrations

Hij Hijlkema, Riet
National costumes in Holland. 2d ed Amsterdam, J. M. Meulenhoff, 1952
Descriptive text accompanies 64 plates in black and white and 3 in color showing dress of various provinces of the Netherlands

Hol Höllrigl, József Aladár
Historic Hungarian costumes. Budapest, Officina [1939] (Officina hungarica)
Full descriptive text accompanies 32 plates of Hungarian costumes from the 15th to the 19th century. Compiled from the material of the 1938 exhibition of Hungarian costumes arranged by the Arts and crafts museum

Hor Horn, Wilhelm
Die volkstrachten in Mähren vor 100 jahren. Prag, Taussig & Taussig, 1938 (Tschechoslowakische trachtenfibeln bd 1)
No text. Twenty-one small color plates showing full-length figures

Hous2 Houston, Mary Galway
510.H65
v. 1
Ancient Egyptian, Mesopotamian & Persian costume and decoration. 2d ed with nine plates and over 250 drawings in the text. London, A. & C. Black, 1954 (Technical history of costume v 1)
An enlarged edition of the author's "Ancient Egyptian, Assyrian, and Persian costumes, and decorations" 1920, indexed in the 1937 Costume Index. The section on Persia has been considerably amplified

HousG2 Houston, Mary Galway
510.H65
v. 2
Ancient Greek, Roman and Byzantine costume and decoration. 2d ed London, A. & C. Black, 1947 (A technical history of costume v II)
Earlier edition indexed in 1937 Costume Index. Contains 8 plates in color and over 200 drawings in the text

HousM Houston, Mary Galway
732.H68
1965
Medieval costume in England and France. The 13th, 14th and 15th centuries. London, Adam & Charles Black, 1939 (A technical history of costume v III)
For each century there is an account of the construction of costumes of the period accompanied by patterns. In addition to civilian dress, illustrations are included of royal and ecclesiastical costume. Eight plates in color and 350 illustrations in black and white

Hun Hunt, Walter Bernard, and Burshears, J. F.
98.C848
1971
American Indian beadwork. Milwaukee, Bruce publishing co. 1951
Instructions for making belts, bags, etc. with plates of costume in black and white and of beadwork in color

Ind India. Ministry of information and broadcasting
Indian art through the ages. Rev and enl ed Calcutta, Sree Saraswaty press, 1951
Some of these pictures of Indian life show costume. Only color plates indexed

Int International congress of popular arts, Prague, 1928
Art populaire, travaux artistiques et scientifiques. Paris, Duchartre, 1931 2 v
At head of title: Institut international de coopération intellectuelle. Two scholarly volumes which include some peasant costumes of Europe and of Japan, mostly in v2. Plates in black and white

Jack Jackson, Margaret
What they wore, a history of children's dress . . . London, George Allen & Unwin [1936]
Except for 3 chapters on children of ancient times, this book shows English children. Line drawings. Descriptive text

Jae Jäfvert, Ernfrid
Skomod och skotillverkning från medeltiden till våra dagar. Stockholm, Kooperativa förbundets bokförlag, 1938
Full text in Swedish on the development of footwear. Photographs followed by descriptions of fabrics, lasts, etc.

Jan Janković, Ljubica S. and Janković, Danica
Dances of Yugoslavia. New York, Crown publishers, 1952 (Handbook of European national dances)
MiNOT
Costumes of Macedonia and Yugoslavia shown on 4 color plates with brief text. Includes directions and music for the dances

Jen Jensen, Oliver Ormerod
The revolt of American women. New York, Harcourt, Brace and co. 1952
Concordia Moorhead
Pictorial chronicle containing photographs many of which show 19th century costume

Jes Jessup, Ronald Frederick
Anglo-Saxon jewellery. New York, Frederick A. Praeger, 1953
StJohns
Full descriptive and historical text with 40 photographic plates, 4 in color

Joh Johl, Janet Pagter
The fascinating story of dolls. New York, H. L. Lindquist, 1941
Consists chiefly of text devoted to history, materials, patents. Small illustrations of period and character dolls

KaAz Kamps, Norman H.
Aztec costumes & customs from the Aztec picture writing-history of records with text by Rupert Adrian. Pasadena, N. H. Kamps, [1940?]
Twelve color plates in portfolio, 1 page of text

KaM Mexican costumes and customs, with text by Rupert Adrian. Pasadena, N. H. Kamps, 1940
Portfolio of 13 color plates. Descriptive letterpress in English and Spanish

Kar

St. olaf (handwritten)

Karpeles, Maud, and Blake, Loïs
Dances of England and Wales. New York, Chanticleer press, 1951 (Handbook of European national dances)
Brief text on costumes accompanies 4 brightly colored plates. Directions and music for the dances

Karo

St. Johns (handwritten)

Károlyi, Alexander F.
Hungarian pageant: life, customs and art of the Hungarian peasantry with 16 illustrations and 7 songs. Budapest, Dr George Vajna & co. [1939?]
Includes 14 photographs of Hungarian costumes without explanatory text

Kat

St. Olaf (handwritten)

Katsarova, Raina
Dances of Bulgaria. New York, Crown publishers, 1951 (Handbooks of European national dances)
Dancers in national costume shown on 4 color plates. Music and directions for the dances

Kaw

GT1560 .K3 1954 (handwritten)

Kawakatsu, Kenichi
Kimono. [Tokyo, Board of Tourist Industry, Japanese Government Railways, 1936] (Tourist library 3)
Small pamphlet on the kimono, the obi and other aspects of Japanese dress. Twenty plates in black and white, illustrations and color frontispiece

Keit

DS916 .K37 1947 (handwritten)

Keith, Elizabeth, and Scott, Elspet Keith Robertson
Old Korea the land of morning calm. New York, Philosophical library, 1947
From sketches made in the early part of the 20th century of Koreans posed in the old style costume. Many types shown in 16 plates in color and 24 in monochrome

KelF

Concordia has 2d ed (1974) (handwritten)

Kelly, Francis Michael
Shakespearian costume for stage and screen. London, A. & C. Black, 1938
Detailed descriptions of various articles of dress for men and women accompany 9 plates and 93 line drawings showing dress of the period

Ken

Kennedy, Douglas
England's dances, folk-dancing to-day and yesterday. London, G. Bell & sons, 1949
History and description with music. Twenty plates in black and white. Only plates indexed

KerA

*mankato   rochester
St cloud   minn hist soc
mesabi* (handwritten)

Kerr, Rose Netzorg
100 years of costumes in America. Worcester, Davis Press, 1951
Feminine dress from 1850 to 1950 shown on plates in black and white

KerM

Miniature costume folios. 5 pts in 1 v. Worcester, Davis press, 1937
Each part contains 12 plates in black and white. Parts 1, 2 and 5 show Oriental and European dress, part 4 shows American dress from 1620 to 1860. No text. Plate numbers assigned

KerR

Moorhead (handwritten)

Interpretive costume design: Renaissance and Elizabethan costumes. Waldwick, N.J. Fairbairn publishers, 1938
European costume from the 15th to the 17th centuries including one of dress for four Shakespearean characters. Plate numbers have been assigned for the 12 plates in black and white

Kin

*st benedict
bemidji
st cloud
hibbing
gust. adolp* (handwritten)

Kinney, Troy, and Kinney, Margaret West
The dance, its place in art and life. New and rev ed New York, Frederick A. Stokes co. 1924
Photographs, line drawings and etchings illustrate the poses and costumes of dances from ancient times to the present. Descriptive text. Plates only indexed

Kle

Klein, Ruth
Lexicon der mode: drei jahrtausende europäischer kostümkunde. Baden-Baden. Woldemar Klein verlag, 1950
Several hundred two-tone illustrations accompany full text in German dealing with European dress and accessories in alphabetical order

KnR

*normandale &
St olaf
have
eng
translation* (handwritten)

Knötel, Richard
Handbuch der uniformkunde... Leipzig, J. J. Weber, 1896
Contains line drawings showing military uniforms from the 17th to the 19th century for all European countries and for Turkey. About 12 figures on each plate show various divisions of armies. Text in German type

Kou

*Concordia
Moorhead* (handwritten)

Kouwenhoven, John Atlee
Adventures of America 1857-1900. New York, Harper & brothers, 1938
A pictorial record from Harper's Weekly

Kre

*minn hist
soc* (handwritten)

Kredel, Fritz
Soldiers of the American army, 1775-1941; drawings by Fritz Kredel, text by Frederick P. Todd ... New York, H. Bittner and co. [1941]
Large colored plates showing uniforms of officers and privates of infantry, artillery, cavalry, militia, Texas rangers, air corps and parachute troops

Kre2

Kredel, Fritz
Soldiers of the American army 1775-1954. Drawings by Fritz Kredel, text by Frederick P. Todd. rev ed Chicago, Henry Regnery co. 1954
Revised to show uniforms worn in the second World war, with additions of several of the older types

Lab

Labovitch, Mark
Clothes through the ages. London, Quality press, 1944
Costumes of Englishmen from earliest times to 1944 shown on 27 color plates with descriptive text

Lang Lange, Ernst von
Frisuren im wandel der jahr-hunderte. Berlin, Robert Klett & co. 1938
Descriptions of Egyptian and of European women's coiffure from ancient times to the end of the 19th century with numerous plates, some colored

LavB Laver, James
British military uniforms. London, Penguin books, 1948
Twenty-four color plates accompanied by brief text show uniforms from 1742 to 1895. Preliminary review of English uniforms in 26 pages

LavC Children's fashions in the nineteenth century. London, B. T. Batsford, 1951
Brief text accompanies each of the 16 color plates

LavCl Clothes. London, Burke, 1952
(Pleasures of life series)
Only the 16 plates, 7 in color, are indexed since the text describes the relation of dress to literature and economics. One chapter on heroines of fiction and what they wore

T510.L28 1953

LavE Early Tudor 1485-1558. London, George C. Harrap and co. 1951
(Costume of the western world)
Fifty-two plates, 8 in color, with notes on each and with general preface on the dress of the period

T510.L286 1969b

LavF Fashions and fashion plates 1800-1900. London, Penguin books, 1943 (King Penguin books)
Brief descriptive text accompanies each of the 16 color plates

737.L32

LavR Laver, James, and others
Fashions of the Renaissance in England, France, Spain and Holland. New York, Harper & brothers, 1951 (Costume of the western world)
Costume from 1485 to 1650 shown in reproductions of famous paintings, in brass rubbings and in drawings. Forty-eight plates in color and others in black and white

stavus adolphus

LavS Laver, James
Style in costume. New York, Oxford university press, 1949
Brief text and 17 plates of costume from Assyrian times to the 20th century relate the dress of a period to some form of architecture or interior decoration

johns

LavT Taste and fashion from the French revolution until today. London, G. Harrap, 1937
Chiefly of interest for the text, which describes the background and tendencies of fashion for 150 years. Fifty-six plates in black and white

LavT2 Taste and fashion from the French revolution to the present day. New and rev ed with a chapter on fashion and the second World war and twelve new illustrations in colour. London, George C. Harrap, 1945
In the 1945 edition the text has been thoroughly revised with addition of new plates and illustrations

80.L3 1945

Law Lawson, Cecil C. P.
A history of the uniforms of the British army . . . London, P. Davies, 1940-1941
Small black and white illustrations and a few color plates with historical and descriptive text

Mankato Kennedy

Leb Lebeuf, Jean Paul
Vêtements et parures du Cameroun français. Préface de René Maran. Planches en couleurs de Émile Gallois. Paris, Éditions Arc-en-Ciel 1946
Fifty color plates in portfolio with 33 pages of text on costume of the French Cameroons

Moorhead

Lecl Leclère, Rosanne
Histoire du costume; la mode au cours des siècles. Lausanne, Payot, 1949 (Orbis pictus v5)
A small book containing 22 plates in color with 6 pages of text. First 2 plates on ancient times, others on France and on 19th century

Lee Leeming, Joseph
The costume book; drawings by Hilda Richman. New York, Frederick A. Stokes co. 1938
Text accompanying plates in black and white describe dress and accessories of national and fanciful costume. One plate of patterns

Moorhead

Lel Leloir, Maurice
Histoire du costume de l'antiquité à 1914. Tome XI-XII. Paris, Ernst & cie, 1938-1949 2v
A continuation of the set indexed in the 1937 Costume Index. Volume 11 covers the period from 1725 to 1774; v 12 from Louis XVI to the Revolution. Each has 40 color plates, many figures and full text

LelD Leloir, Maurice
Dictionnaire du costume et de ses accessoires des armes et des étoffes des origines à nos jours. Paris, Librairie Gründ, 1951
Hundreds of small illustrations accompanied by brief text describing all details of costume. Many colored plates. In alphabetical form

Lep Lepage-Medvey, E.
National costumes. Designed by Lepage-Medvey with a preface by André Varagnac . . . New York, Hyperion press, 1939
Forty large color plates on costumes of Austria, Hungary, Poland, Czechoslovakia. No text except a general introduction

case folio GT810 .L42

LepF French costumes. London, Hyperion press, 1939
Portfolio showing costumes of provinces of France on 40 color plates. No text

LesA

GTZ050 .L4

Lester, Katherine Morris, and Oerke, Bess Viola
An illustrated history of those frills and furbelows of fashion which have come to be known as accessories of dress. Peoria, Manual arts press, 1940
Cover title: Accessories of dress. Line drawings and reproductions of paintings show adornments of head, neck, waist, and arms as well as fans, laces, ribbons, etc. Comprehensive text

Lew

Lewis, Mary Ernestine, and Dignam, Dorothy
The marriage of diamonds and dolls. New York, Lindquist publications, 1947
Dolls in bridal costume with their attendants shown in 35 black and white plates with text. Period 1750-1945

Lez

Lezius, Martin
Das ehrenkleid des soldaten, eine kulturgeschichte der uniform von ihren anfängen bis zur gegenwart. Berlin, Ullstein, 1938
Dress uniforms of European soldiers from earliest times to 20th century. Over 200 color plates and 174 pages of text in German type

LhA

Moorhead)

Lhuer, Victor
Costume auvergnat et bourbonnais. Paris, Éditions Arc-en-Ciel, n.d.
Portfolio of 48 unnumbered colored plates. Text consists of only a few lines under each costume

LhB

Le costume breton de 1900 jusqu'à nos jours. Paris, Au Moulin de Pen-Mur, n.d.
Color plates, unnumbered, showing costumes of Finistère, Morbihan, Côtes-du-Nord, Loire-Inférieure, Ille-et-Vilaine

Lib

Libron, F. and Clouzot, H.
Le corset dans l'art et les mœurs du XIIIe au XXe siècle. Paris, F. Libron, 1933
Detailed account with many plates and illustrations. Plates at end of book have been assigned numbers from 172A-

Lil

Lilley, Agnes
How to make costumes for school plays and pageants, with 32 costume illustrations. [Winnetka, Ill. 1945?]
A practical book with patterns and descriptions for making costumes for plays and masquerades. Line drawings

Lint

Concordia
Moorhead)

Linthicum, Marie Channing
Costume in the drama of Shakespeare and his contemporaries. New York, Oxford university press, 1936
Detailed study of the material, as well as of the costume, of Elizabethan and Jacobean periods with description of each article of attire. Twenty plates

Lis

Mankato

Lister, Margot
Stage costume. London, Herbert Jenkins, 1954 (Practical stage handbooks)
Describes numerous garments from Assyrian times to 1900 suitable for costuming plays. Line drawings for each period and descriptive text

Log

Logan, James
McIan's costumes of the clans of Scotland. Glasgow, David Bryce and son, 1899
Full-length figures in color representing tartans of the clans with historical sketch of each

LorD

GV1467.L6

Lorenzen, Poul, and Jeppesen, Jeppe
Dances of Denmark. New York, Chanticleer press, 1950 (Handbooks of European national dances)
Four color plates and brief text on costume with directions and music for dances

Loud

Louden, Adelaide Bolton, and Louden, Norman P.
Historic costume through the ages, a portfolio of 20 plates in color, representative costumes, historic ornament, annotations. Philadelphia, H. C. Perleberg [1936]
Masculine and feminine figures shown with footnotes on the events of each period

Louis, M. pseud. See Napolitan, Louis

Lub

St. cloud
St. olaf
mesaby

Lubinova, Mila
Dances of Czechoslovakia. New York, Chanticleer press, 1949 (Handbooks of European national dances)
Four plates show costumes as well as give directions and music for dances

Lyf

MSUhas
2d ed)
(1953)

Lyford, Carrie Alberta
The crafts of the Ojibwa (Chippewa) Phoenix, Phoenix Indian school, 1943 (U.S. Office of Indian affairs. Indian handicrafts 5)
Descriptive text with line drawings

Mak

Makovskiĭ, Sergiĕĭ Konstantĭnovich
Peasant art of Subcarpathian Russia. Prague, Plamja edition, n.d.
One hundred ten plates, 10 in color, showing chiefly embroidery, but several with women's costume

Mal

Mally, Fritzi
Deutsche trachten aus den Sudetenländern mit einer einführung von Josef Hanika. Prag, Volk und Reich verlag [1943]
Thirty-eight large color plates many of which show headdress. Prefatory text describes each plate. Only plates indexed

Marce Marcel-Dubois, Claudie, and Andral, Marie Marguerite
Dances of France: Brittany and Bourbonnais. New York, Chanticleer press, 1950 (Handbooks of European national dances)
Four color plates show costume with brief text. Music and directions for the dances. Continued by Dances of France: Provence and Alsace by N. Nicolette and M. Texier

Marq Márquez, Luis
Mexican folklore. Text by Justino Fernández. México, D.F., Eugenio Fischgrund ₁195?₁
Scholarly studies of the arts of Mexico including some costume. Text in French. Plates in black and white

MasB Mason, Bernard Sterling
The book of Indian-crafts and costumes. New York, A. S. Barnes & co. 1946
Full descriptions with patterns of the dress and accessories of Indians of the woodlands and plains of North America. Many plates and illustrations in black and white

May May hosiery mills, inc.
The story of hosiery. Burlington, N.C. 1931
Brief history with illustrations from footwear of many lands

McC McCloud, Henry J.
Clerical dress and insignia of the Roman Catholic church. Milwaukee, Bruce publishing co. 1945
Illustrations in black and white show many details with full descriptive text

Mcca McCarthy, James Remington
Rings through the ages. New York, Harper & brothers, 1945
Detailed history of rings with plates showing many types including ecclesiastical and wedding rings

Mccl McClintock, H. F.
Old Irish and Highland dress and that of the Isle of Man. 2d and enl ed Dundalk, Dundalgan press, 1950
Scholarly discussion with illustrations from original sources. Three color plates, many illustrations

McP McPharlin, Paul
Life and fashion in America 1650-1900. Pictured and annotated by P. McPharlin. New York, Hastings House, 1946 (Hastings House Americana)
Small book with 15 color plates, a few illustrations and brief text

Mer Meredith, Roy
Mr Lincoln's camera man, Mathew B. Brady. New York, Charles Scribner's sons, 1946
Photographs showing life in the United States in the last half of the 19th century, particularly of the Civil war period, include some pictures of dress of men of the period

Meri Mérida, Carlos
Mexican costume . . . Chicago, Pocahontas press, ₁1941₁
Twenty-five color plates in portfolio showing costumes of Indians of many sections of Mexico. Brief text accompanies each plate

MeriC Carnival in Mexico. México, D.F., 1940
Portfolio of 10 plates in color with brief text

MeriF Festival dances of Mexico. Westport, Artext, n.d.
Ten color plates showing dances in costume

MeriT Trajes regionales mexicanos. México, D.F., Editorial Atlante, 1945
Portfolio of 25 color plates showing costumes of different states with brief text

Met Metcalf, Clyde Hill
A history of the United States Marine corps. New York, G. P. Putnam's sons, 1939
Included are pictures showing uniforms of the Corps from 1775 to 1918 with brief descriptions of those worn in different periods

MiI Military service publishing company
Identification; the world's military, naval and air uniforms. Harrisburg, Military service publishing co. 1943
Sketches in black and white

MilJ Milligan, Jean C. and MacLennen, D. G.
Dances of Scotland. New York, Chanticleer press, 1951 (Handbooks of European national dances)
Four color plates show costumes as well as dances. Music and directions for dances

Mls Mills, Winifred Harrington, and Dunn, Louise M.
The story of old dolls and how to make new ones. Illustrated by Corydon Bell. New York, Doubleday, Doran & co. 1940
Text is chiefly on the history of dolls with directions and patterns for making new ones. Photographic illustrations

Mo Moore, Doris (Langley-Levy)
The woman in fashion. Illustrated with costumes from the author's collection. London, B. T. Batsford, 1949
One hundred eight photographs show costumes from 1800 to 1927 including evening, wedding and sport costume. Explanatory text

MooC The child in fashion. London, B. T. Batsford, 1953
Fifty-four plates, 1 in color, show the dress of children from 1760 to 1934. Descriptive text

Mora Morazzoni, Giuseppe
La moda a Venezia nel secolo XVIII. Milan, 1931
One hundred eight plates in black and white

MusE   **Museum extension project. W.P.A. Pennsylvania unit**
Ecclesiastical costumes. n.p., n.d.
Forty-four color plates of eastern and western dress of priests, monks, etc.

MusI   Indian plates. n.p., n.d.
Thirteen color plates show men and women of Algonquin, Iroquois, Sioux and other tribes

MusM   Military uniforms of the revolutionary period. n.p., n.d.
Twenty-eight plates, all but 2 in color. Twenty-six show uniforms of the United States; 1 of England; 1 of Germany

MusS   Sweden. n.p. [1943?]
Nine color plates show traditional costumes of Dalarne, Skåne, Södermanland and Helsingland. No text

Nap   **Napolitan, Louis**
Six thousand years of hair styling by M. Louis, pseud. New York, Polygraphic co. of America [1939]
Comprehensive book on feminine coiffure with plates and illustrations in black and white

Nat   National geographic. v69-106, 1936-1954. Washington, D.C., National geographic soc.
Continues the indexing done in the 1937 Costume index

NeC   **New York. Metropolitan museum of art**
Chinese jewelry. New York, The museum, 1940
Twenty-two plates of jewelry

NeE   Egyptian jewelry. A picture book. New York, The museum, 1940
Short introduction accompanies 20 plates

NeEu   Eighteenth century costume in Europe. A picture book of twenty plates. New York, The museum, 1937
A few pages of introductory text accompany the plates

NeF   Costumes from the Forbidden City by Alan Priest. New York, The museum, 1945
Fifty-five plates in black and white illustrate Chinese costumes from 1644 to 1874. Brief text

NeG   Greek and Etruscan jewelry. A picture book. New York, The museum, 1940
Twenty-three plates with brief introduction

NeM   Mediaeval jewelry. A picture book. New York, The museum, 1940
Twenty plates with brief text

NeN   Near Eastern jewelry. A picture book. New York, The museum, 1940
Twenty-two plates on 10 leaves

NeP   Private life of the ancient Egyptians. A picture book. New York, The museum, 1935
Twenty plates with brief introduction

NeR   Renaissance jewelry. A picture book. New York, The museum, 1940
Twenty-three plates with brief introduction

NeV   Exhibition of Victorian and Edwardian dresses, New York, March 13th to April 23rd, 1939. New York, The museum, 1939
Sixty-five plates showing women's dresses worn by mannikins. Included are carriage dresses, visiting, walking, afternoon, evening and wedding dresses of the period

Ni   **Nienholdt, Eva**
Die deutsche tracht im wandel der jahrhunderte. Berlin, Walter de Grunter & co. 1938
Ten chapters in German type describe German costume from the 2d century B.C. to the 20th century. Fifty-six plates in black and white

Nie   **Nieto Peña, Roque**
España es así, tipos paisajes monumentos. México, D.F., Ediciones internacionales [1949]
Photographic illustrations and many plates in delicate colors of regional dress. Only plates indexed

NorC   **Norris, Herbert**
Church vestments, their origin & development. New York, E. P. Dutton & co. 1950
Eight plates in color and more than 200 illustrations in black and white accompany detailed descriptions of ecclesiastical costume from earliest times to 1400

Norr   Costume & fashion. v3, book 1-2. New York, E. P. Dutton and co. 1938. 2v
These 2 volumes continue those indexed in the 1937 Costume Index. Book 1 covers 1485 to 1547; book 2, 1547 to 1603. Very full text with copious illustrations, many in color

Nyl   **Nylén, Anna-Maja**
Swedish peasant costumes. Stockholm, Nordiska museet, 1949
From actual garments in the Nordiska museet the author portrays 65 costumes in color from 47 districts. Descriptive text

Ogr   **Ogrizek, Doré**
France, Paris and the provinces. Text by Roger Roumagnac . . . New York, Whittlesey house, 1948
A travel book that shows costume of various provinces of France on color plates. No text on costume

Ori   **Original** Tyrolean costumes in ten-colour reproductions of four hundred standard specimens of national costumes from private and public collections, preface by Baron Georg Franckenstein. Vienna, Herbert Reichner, 1937
Thirty plates in color with brief text in English, French and German show dress of regions of the Tyrol. Issued also as Trachten der Alpenländer. Vienna, 1937

OrM   **Ortiz Echagüe, José**
España mística. 2d ed. Madrid, Editorial Mayfe, 1950
Full-page photographic illustrations of religious orders, festival costumes, monasteries, cathedrals, etc. and 280 plates with general introduction

OrT   España, tipos y trajes. Madrid, Editorial Mayfe, 1950
Two hundred seventy-two plates in black and white showing types of costume of several provinces of Spain, with a few of the Balearic and Canary Islands and of Morocco. Explanatory notes on each plate. Octavo size

Özb   **Özbel Kenan**
Anadolu kadin kiliklair. Kalkevleri Buroso, n.d.
Line drawings show costumes of women of Anatolia

Palo   **Palotay, Gertrud**
Hungarian folk costumes. Budapest, Officina printers & publishers, 1938
Plate numbers have been assigned to the 13 color plates showing regional costumes of Hungary

Pann   **Panni, Arturo**
La moda di tutte le epoche. Milan, G. G. Görlich 1945 4v
Full-length color plates of French costumes of the 18th and 19th centuries. No text

Part   **Partridge, Bellamy, and Bettmann, Otto**
As we were: family life in America 1850-1900 in pictures and text. New York, Whittlesey house, 1946
United States in the decades before the Civil war to the turn of the century. Illustrated by contemporary prints some of which show costume

Pes   **Pesendorfer, Gertrud**
Neue deutsche bauerntrachten, Tyrol. Munich, Georg D. W. Callwey, 1938
Twenty-nine color plates showing full-length figures of costumes of men and women in regions of the Tyrol. Descriptions of dress of each region

Pet   **Pettigrew, Dora W.**
Peasant costume of the Black forest. London, A. & C. Black, 1937
Regional costumes of the Black forest. Full page plates of line drawings and 7 color plates each accompanied by a page of text

Pic   **Picken, Mary Brooks**
The language of fashion, a dictionary and digest of fabric, sewing, and dress. New York, Funk & Wagnalls co. 1939
About 600 small illustrations of wearing apparel and accessories from ancient times to the present, in black and white, with definitions, pronunciations, and explanations alphabetically arranged

Pif   **Piffl, Erna**
Deutsche bauern in Ungarn. Berlin, Grenze und Ausland, 1938
Twenty-three plates in color and many illustrations in black and white show full-length figures in costumes of various sections. Descriptive text

Pot   **Potet, L. Robert**
La couleur dans l'histoire du costume. Paris, L'Officiel de la couleur, 1951
Large color plates, some in double spread. Each shows complete figures as well as accessories of Mediterranean countries

Pr   **Pratt, Elma**
Mexico in color. México, D.F., 1947
Portfolio of 10 color plates

Pric   **Price, H. P.**
When men wore muffs, the story of men's clothes. London, J. M. Dent and sons, 1936
General history of masculine costume, chiefly in England. Twenty-three plates in black and white. Text contains some notes on muffs

Prim   **Primmer, Kathleen**
Scandinavian peasant costume, with notes by M. S. Primer. London, A. & C. Black, 1939
Pencil drawings and 8 color plates

Pro   **Prod'homme, Jacques Gabriel**
La toilette féminine à travers les ages. Paris, Nilsson [1933?] 2v
Volume 1 1490-1645; v 2 1645-1720. Color plates of feminine costume preceded by brief introductory text. Plate numbers assigned. Text not indexed

QuV   **Quennell, Peter**
Victorian panorama, a survey of life and fashion from contemporary photographs. New York, Charles Scribner's sons, 1937
English costume of the 19th century with a general chapter on dress. A chapter on the Victorian stage shows many famous actors as they appeared on the stage

Ras   **Rasmussen, Charles**
Danske folkedragter og udvalgte folkesagn. Copenhagen, Axel E. Aamodts, 1942
Sixteen color plates show costumes of regions of Denmark

Rea   **Reade, Brian**
Dominance of Spain, 1550-1660. London, George C. Harrap and co. [1951] (Costume of the western world)
Sixty-two plates, 8 in color, are reproductions of paintings. Introductory sketch of costume in Spain in the 16th and 17th centuries and brief notes on each plate

Ret   **Retzlaff, Hans**

See GT921 .A4 at UND

Deutsche bauerntrachten, beschrieben von Rudolf Helm. Berlin, Atlantis verlag, 1934

Many full-page photographic illustrations accompanied by text in German type show the everyday and Sunday dress of Hesse, Swabia, Bavaria, Black forest, etc. with illustrations of headdress and of wedding costume

RetS   Die Schwalm, kulturbild einer hessischen landschaft. 107 bilder von Hans Retzlaff mit einführendem text von Heinz Metz. Berlin, Bong & co. n.d.

Photographs of life in Hesse, many of which show costume

Rey   **Reynolds, Graham**

Elizabethan and Jacobean, 1558-1625. London, George C. Harrap and co. 1951 (Costume of the western world)

Plates illustrating English costumes are reproductions of paintings. Each is accompanied by brief descriptive text. Some plates in color, others in black and white

RobC   **Roberts, Catherine Christopher**

winona st olaf minn histsoc

The complete book of doll making and collecting. New York, Greystone press, 1949

Only plates on character dolls indexed

Roe   **Roediger, Virginia More**

E99 .P9Rb 1961

Ceremonial costumes of the Pueblo Indians, their evolution, fabrication and significance in the prayer drama. Berkeley, University of California press, 1941

Indians of Arizona and New Mexico shown in dramatic-religious dress. Forty color plates and illustrations with detailed descriptions of parts of dress and their relation to ceremonies

RodD   **Rogers, Dorothy**

French provincial costumes: paper dolls. With a foreword by James Laver. London, Hachette, 1944

Twenty-four full-length figures of women in folk costumes. Illustrations from figures designed for an exhibition circulated in Great Britain 1943-1944

RogF   **Rogers, Frances, and Beard, Alice**

me st6l st cloud

5000 years of gems and jewelry, with drawings by the authors and sixteen illustrations in halftone. New rev ed Philadelphia, J. B. Lippincott co. 1947

Illustrations show many types of jewelry from ancient times to 20th century, with descriptive text. Stories of many famous jewels included

RogW   **Rogers, Agnes**

folio E161 .R75

Women are here to stay; the durable sex in its infinite variety through half a century of American life. New York, Harper & brothers, 1949

Composed largely of photographs showing women of the 19th and 20th centuries engaged in many forms of activities

Roj   **Rojinskii, Lillian**

mankato

Seventeenth century costume. London, Sir Isaac Pitman & sons, 1952

Costume for men and women from the time of James I of England through the reign of William and Mary, with most space given to the period of Charles I. A page of line drawings and several illustrations for each reign with patterns for all the principal costumes

Ross   **Ross, Mary Steele**

st cloud

American women in uniform. Garden City, Garden City publishing co. 1943

A pamphlet showing uniforms and insignia with brief descriptive text

Rous   **Rousseau, Gabriel**

Le costume au Maroc. Fascicule 1. Paris, E. de Boccard, 1938

Eighteen plates, 9 in color, each accompanied by text

Rud   **Rudofsky, Bernard**

GT510 .R75

Are clothes modern? An essay on contemporary apparel. Chicago, Paul Theobald, 1947

Drawings and photographs accompany philosophical discussion of modern dress

Rue   **Rue, Lena**

Early American costumes. Palms, California, Walter T. Foster, n.d.

Line drawings for the use of designers

RueG   Greek and Egyptian costumes. Palms, California, Walter T. Foster, 1931

Line drawings to aid designers in adapting old costumes to modern dress. Twenty-one plates

RueO   Costumes of the Orient. Palms, California, Walter T. Foster, n.d.

Line drawings of Oriental costumes to aid designers in adapting these costumes to modern dress. Plate numbers assigned

SaiT   **St George, Eleanor**

mankato

Dolls of three centuries. New York, Charles Scribner's sons, 1951

Photographs of famous dolls with text relating to their owners, the material of which the dolls are made and the history of individual dolls. Only character dolls indexed

SaiY   The dolls of yesterday. New York, Charles Scribner's sons, 1948

GV1219 .S3

More than 200 illustrations, many of 19th century dolls. Of interest to the collector because of historical and descriptive text. Only character dolls indexed

SaJ   **Saito, R.**

Concordia

Japanese coiffure. Tokyo, Board of Tourist Industry, Japanese Government Railways, 1939 (Tourist library 28)

Descriptions and illustrations of Japanese hair dress from 18th century to present times. Some of the plates show costumes also

Salv   **Salvén, Erik**
Dances of Sweden. New York, Chanticleer press, 1949 (Handbooks of European national dances)
Four color plates show costumes with brief descriptions and with music and directions for dances

Saun   **Saunders, Dorothy Lynne**
Costuming the amateur show. New York, Samuel French, 1938
Line drawings show types that can be adapted by the non-professional for plays, operettas, pageants, etc.

Sem   **Semb, Klara**
Dances of Norway. New York, Crown publishers, 1951 (Handbooks of European national dances)
Four color plates show regional dress with brief text. Music and directions for dances

Set   **Settle, Alison**
English fashion. London, Collins, 1948
Eight color plates and 23 in black and white accompany text arranged by large periods. Many of the illustrations are reproductions of paintings

Seto   **Seton, Julia Moss**
The Indian costume book. Illustrated by Ernest Thompson Seton. Santa Fe, Seton Village press, 1938
Photographs and line drawings with directions to enable the reader to reproduce the costumes

Sit   **Sitwell, Sacheverell**
The Netherlands, a study of some aspects of art, costume and social life. London, B. T. Batsford, n.d.
Detailed description of regional costume of Holland. Two color plates on costume, several in black and white

SitC   A survey of English domestic portraits and their painters. New York, Charles Scribner's sons, 1937
Reproductions of 130 paintings, 4 in color, show costume chiefly of the period of George II and George III

SitN   Narrative pictures, a survey of English genre and its painters. New York, Charles Scribner's sons, 1938
Some of the reproductions show the dress of groups of figures of the 18th and 19th centuries. Costumes are not shown in detail, but paintings display the general feeling of dress of the periods

SitR   Roumanian journey, illustrated from photographs. . . New York, Charles Scribner's sons, 1938
Several of the photographs show dress of Rumanian peasants

SmU   **Smith, Cleveland Henry, and Taylor, Gertrude R.**
United States service symbols. New York, Duell, Sloan and Pearce, 1942
Most of the plates show insignia of the services, but some also portray uniforms for summer and winter, evening dress, mess jackets, etc.

SocC   **Société de l'histoire du costume, Paris**
Costumes d'autrefois XVIᵉ, XVIIᵉ, XVIIIᵉ siècles. Paris [Frazier-Soye, 1938]
Photographs of French costumes exhibited at the Musée Galliera

Spi   **Spicer, Dorothy Gladys**
Latin American costumes, designed by Jolanda Bartas. New York, Hyperion press, 1941
Twenty-one plates, 14 in color, and some illustrations in black and white

Stew   **Stewart, Janice S.**
The folk arts of Norway. Madison, University of Wisconsin press, 1953
One chapter on regional dress with several pages on jewelry

Stoc   **Stockholm. Nordiska Museet**
Folkdräkter från Mellersta Sverige. [Stockholm, Nordisk Rotogravyr, 1934] (Bilderböcker 6)
Eight color plates show costumes of 7 districts

StocM   Modedräkter från 1600-1900. Stockholm, The museum [1952]
Sixty-four photographs from the museum's collection. Brief description under each plate in Swedish and in English. Preface in English

Stry   **Stryjénska, Zofja (Lubánska)**
Polish peasants costumes; with introduction and notes by Thadee Seweryn. Nice, C. Szwedzicki [1939]
Forty color plates of dress of various districts in portfolio

Sub   **Subías Galter, Juan**
El arte popular en España. Barcelona, Editorial Seix Barral, 1948
General book on the arts of Spain in the 18th and 19th centuries. Some sections show photographs of costume, jewelry, fans and dolls. Brief text for each section

Sv   **Svensson, Sigfrid**
Skånes folkdräkter en dräkthistorisk undersökning 1500-1900. Stockholm, C. E. Fritzes Bokförlags Aktiebolag, 1935 (Nordiska Museets handlingar 3)
Detailed descriptions of the costumes of Skåne with more than 200 illustrations in black and white

Ten   **Tennevin, Nicolette, and Texier, Marie**
Dances of France: Provence and Alsace. New York, Crown publishers, 1951 (Handbooks of European national dances)
Four color plates and brief text on costume with music and directions for the dances. Preceded in this series by Dances of France: Brittany and Bourbonnais by C. Marcel-Dubois and M. M. Andral

ThiG Thienen, Frithjof van
The great age of Holland, 1600-60. London, G. Harrap and co. 1951 (Costume of the western world)
Reproductions of paintings shown on 60 plates, 8 in color, accompanied by introductory sketches of dress of the Netherlands and brief notes on each plate

(handwritten: Moorehead)

TiK Tilke, Max
Kostümschnitte und Gewandformen. New York, E. Weyhe, 1945
European, Asian and African costume from the Babylonian period to the middle of the 19th century shown on large plates, 112 in color, 128 in black and white. Brief text

(handwritten: Winona)

Too Toor, Frances
A treasury of Mexican folkways. New York, Crown publishers, 1947
Detailed descriptions of dances of Mexico accompanied by photographs and drawings. Some general information on Indian costumes with illustrations

(handwritten: GR115 .T55)

TooP Three worlds of Peru. New York, Crown publishers, 1949
Photographic plates include about 25 showing costumes of Indians, as well as of dances and festivals

(handwritten: Moorehead)

Tor Toronto. Royal Ontario museum of archaeology
Chinese court costumes by Helen E. Fernald. Toronto, The museum, 1946
Text descriptive of an exhibition held by the Museum. Forty plates, 3 in color

Trai Train, Arthur Kissam
The story of everyday things. New York, Harper & brothers, 1941
Brief text and illustrations on costume are included in the picture of life in the United States from 17th to 19th century

(handwritten: Moorehead)

Traj El traje regional de España. Barcelona, Electra A. G. [1948]
Thirteen color plates to which numbers have been assigned. Costumes have been drawn from paintings. Accompanied by text

Trev Trevelyan, George Macaulay
Illustrated English social history. New York, Longmans, Green and co. 1949 4v
A few plates in color and several in black and white show costume in each volume. Covers the periods from the 14th to the 19th century

(handwritten: DA32 .T74873)

Tru Truman, Nevil
Historic costume. London, Sir Isaac Pitman & sons, 1936
Descriptions and illustrations of details of dress, chiefly English, from earliest times to 20th century. Useful for theatrical costume. Six color plates

(handwritten: Moorehead / mankato and u of mn - crookston have 2d ed)

True Truett, Randle Bond
The first ladies in fashion. New York, Hastings House [1954]
Eighty-six pictures of wives or hostesses of the presidents of the United States from Washington to Eisenhower with descriptions of gowns worn at inaugurations or of costumes of the period

(handwritten: GT605 .T7)

UnA United States. War department
Personnel. Prescribed service uniform—women personnel of the army. Washington, Government printing off. 1945 (Army regulations no 600-37)
A pamphlet of 31 pages containing line drawings of women's uniforms including caps, insignia, bags. Full text. Plates only indexed

UnN United States. Navy
Uniform regulations 1951. Washington, Government printing off. 1951
Loose leaf. Supersedes regulations of 1947. Consists of several hundred pages of text with full descriptions of uniforms and plates in black and white. For the purpose of this index, plates have been separated from text and indexed as plates only

UnW United States. Work projects administration
History of western costumes. n.p., n.d.
Plates in color show costumes from Babylonian times to the close of the 19th century. Accompanied by text

Val Valdiosera, Ramon
Mexican dances. México, D.F. Editorial Fischgrund Appo, n.d.
Plate numbers assigned to the 12 color plates in portfolio. Brief text

ValM Mexican native costumes, introduction and text by Salvador Echeverria. México, D.F. Eugenio Fischgrund, 1949
Portfolio of 12 color plates showing costumes of Indians of the provinces of Mexico accompanied by descriptive pamphlet of 16 pages

VanH Van Horn & Son, Inc. Philadelphia
Dress through the ages, a condensed pictorial history of costume. Philadelphia, n.d.
Fourteen plates of line drawings, 20 to 30 figures on a page, portray kings, priests, gentlefolk, working people, soldiers. Brief text

(handwritten: no. hennepin comm college)

Vel Veleva, Mariya
Bulgarian national attire (costume). Sofia, 1950
Portfolio of 31 plates in color showing dress of districts of Bulgaria. Introduction and brief descriptions in Bulgarian, Russian, French and English

(handwritten: case folio GT1290 .V4)

Ven Ven-ten Bensel, Elsie van der
Dances of the Netherlands. New York, Chanticleer press, 1949 (Handbooks of European national dances)
Four plates in color show costume. Brief text. Directions and music for dances

(handwritten: st olaf bemidji st cloud mesabi)

Vert Vertès, Marcel
Art and fashion. New York, Studio publications, 1944
Development of modern fashion from dress of the past shown chiefly by comparison of reproductions of prints and paintings with photographs of modern dress

(handwritten: bemidji mankato st scholastica)

Villa-Puig, Juan. See D'Ivori, Juan, pseud

ViN   Victoria and Albert museum, South Kensington
Costume illustration, the nineteenth century. Introduction by James Laver. London, The museum, 1947
One hundred plates in black and white show costume for men and women for morning, afternoon and evening. Brief explanations

ViP   A picture book of English costume. London, Published under the authority of the Board of Education, 1937 2v
Pamphlets of 20 plates each showing costumes of 17th and 18th centuries. Photographs from examples in the Museum

Vu   Vuilleumier, Bernard
The art of silk weaving in China: symbolism of Chinese imperial ritual robes. London, 1939
Fourteen plates in black and white

Wa   Walkup, Fairfax Proudfit
Dressing the part; a history of costume for the theatre. New York, F. S. Crofts & co. 1950
European costume divided by centuries, not by nationality, with detailed descriptions and patterns for costumes. Masculine dress given in detail.

Walk   Walker, George
The costume of Yorkshire. Leeds, Richard Jackson, 1885
Forty plates in color, facsimiles of original drawings, show costumes of country people of the county in the 19th century. Text in English and French

WaS   Walters, Helen
The story of caps and gowns. New York, E. R. Moore co. 1939
History and description of academic costumes for various degrees in Europe and in America. Illustrated in black and white with 1 plate in color

Wel   Weldon's costume through the ages, B.C. 600-A.D. 1900. London, Weldon's [193?]
"With supplementary pages illustrating historical fancy dress, Shakespearean and Dickensian costumes, selection of Gilbert and Sullivan characters and a review of fashion from 1880-1930." Subtitle

WilC   Wilcox, Ruth Turner
The mode in costume. New York, Charles Scribner's sons, 1942
From the Egyptian period to 1942, but chiefly on French and English dress. Line drawings for each period with descriptive text. Plates on headdress, hair, footwear and accessories

WilF   The mode in furs: the history of furred costume of the world from the earliest times to the present. New York, Charles Scribner's sons, 1951
Plates in black and white with several figures or garments on each plate. The fur-clad figures also show general costumes of each period

WilFo   The mode in footwear. New York, Charles Scribners' sons, 1948
Seventeen chapters of text describe footwear from Egyptian times to the 1940's. Each chapter has 3 or 4 plates in black and white with several illustrations on each showing footwear of different classes of people and also displaying complete costumes of the period

WilH   The mode in hats and headdress. New York, Charles Scribner's sons, 1945
Development from early times to the 20th century. Many plates of line drawings with several illustrations on each plate. Comprehensive text

WisF   Wilson, Carrie
Fashions since their debut. Scranton, International Textbook co. 1939
Twenty-nine plates in black and white show women's dress from Egyptian times to 1945. Insets picture details of hats, footwear, sleeves, etc

Wit   Witzig, Louise
Dances of Switzerland. New York, Chanticleer press, 1949 (Handbooks of European national dances)
Four color plates show costume with brief text. Directions and music for dances

WlsC   Wilson, Lillian May
The costume of the ancient Romans. Baltimore, Johns Hopkins press, 1938 (Johns Hopkins university studies in archeology no 24)
Scholarly discussion illustrated in black and white

Wol   Wolska, Helen
Dances of Poland. London, Max Parrish & co. 1952 (Handbooks of European national dances)
Four plates in color show costume with brief text. Music and directions for dances

Wom   Women's Wear Daily
Fifty years of fashion, documented sketches and text from the costume library of Women's Wear Daily. New York, Fairchild publications, 1950
Several sketches on each page with brief text show costume of women from 1900 to 1950

Wrig   Wright, Marion Logan
Biblical costume for use in plays. London, S.P.C.K. 1951
Line drawings show costume of Assyria and Babylonia, Rome, Egypt, Persia. Includes patterns and directions for adapting these typical national costumes for the stage, with many details of dress and of objects in daily use

Yar   Yarwood, Doreen
English costume from the second century to 1950. New York, Crown publishers, 1952
Eleven plates in color and many in black and white accompanied by full descriptive text

YoR

GT510 .Y6
1937

Young, Agnes Brooks

Recurring cycles of fashion 1760-1937. 2d ed New York, Harper & brothers, 1937

Analysis of the development of women's fashions showing illustrations of typical dresses. Two pictures in black and white on each page from year to year

Zim

Zimmern, Nathalie H.

Introduction to Peruvian costume. Brooklyn, Brooklyn museum, 1949

Twenty-four plates accompanied by text on each one Costumes are chiefly those of pre-Spanish period